READER'S DIGEST

GUIDE TO

READER'S DIGEST

GUIDE TO

Love & Sex

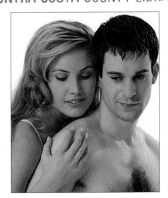
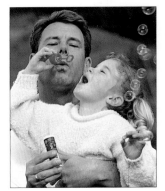

Reader's
Digest

THE READER'S DIGEST ASSOCIATION, INC.
Pleasantville, New York/Montreal

A READER'S DIGEST BOOK

Conceived and produced by **CARROLL & BROWN LIMITED**

Publishing Director Denis Kennedy
Art Director Chrissie Lloyd
Project Editor Kesta Desmond
Art Editors Sally Powell, Brian Rust
Designers Sandra Brooke, Vimit Punater
Production Christine Corton, Wendy Rogers, Karen Kloot
Computer Management John Clifford, Paul Stradling

For Reader's Digest
Project Editor Deborah DeFord
Art Editor Larissa Lawrynenko
Copy Editor Nancy J. Stabile

--------- CONSULTANTS ---------

Dr. Amanda Roberts
MA, MB, BChir

Dr. Barbara Padgett-Yawn
MD

Jacquie Moore
MS, MFCC

Monica Rodriguez
BS Director of Education
(SIECUS)

Dr. Robert D. Visscher
MD, Former exec. dir. ASRM

--------- CONTRIBUTORS ---------

Dr. K. Eia Asen
RDMB, BSLDS, RCS

Stuart J. Baker
BSc Hons, PhD

Dr. Paul Brown
CPsychol, PhD, FBPsS

Susan Conder
BA Hons, MA, Dip. Couple
Counseling

Karen Evennett
BA Hons

Judy Graham
BA Hons

Judy Hildebrand
App. Soc. Studies
CQSW UKCP

Dr. Lynne Low
MB, ChB, DA, DFFP, DipGUM

Dr. Patrick McGhee
MA, D Phil, CPsychol,
AFBPsS

Dr. John Moran
DPsSCMD, MRCPsych.

Dr. Phyllis Mortimer
MB, BS, DRCOG, MFFP

Susan Quilliam
BA Hons, Cert. Ed., Dip. NLP
MNLP

Melissa Roske
BA Hons

Library of Congress Cataloging in Publication Data

Reader's Digest guide to love & sex
        p.   cm.
    Includes index.
    ISBN 0-7621-0043-5
    1. Sex. 2. Sex (Psychology) 3. Love. I. Reader's Digest
Association.
    HQ21.R264   1998
    306.7—dc21   97-40448

Reproduced by Colourscan, Singapore
Printed in Italy by Chromolitho

Foreword

The *Reader's Digest Guide to Love & Sex* deals simply and frankly with the day-to-day questions, problems and mysteries surrounding our sexuality, sexual health and relationships. The idea for this guide evolved from the growing desire in today's society for easily understandable and accurate information about sex and, above all, advice on how to talk to partners and family members about matters relating to sex. Many of the problems we encounter with love and sex in our lives are rooted in misinformation, lack of understanding or lack of communication. We often pick up confusing messages about sex during childhood or adolescence, yet this is something that can be avoided or rectified if parents have a good understanding of their children's needs and provide the information they require at different stages of their development. When partners can communicate with each other clearly and openly about their relational and sexual needs and desires, they are in a better position to feel secure and confident and to answer questions in a way that helps and guides their families.

The *Reader's Digest Guide to Love & Sex* contains a wealth of carefully illustrated, authoritative information, written to be comprehensive and accessible to all. When adolescent girls need help understanding their menstrual cycle and changes in their bodies, a mother, father or friend can show them illustrations and use the information found here to explain the whole process. When men worry about prostate or testicular cancer, or their partner's premenstrual tension, they will find that the *Reader's Digest Guide to Love & Sex* provides an up-to-date, informative discussion about symptoms and signs, as well as available tests and treatments.

Information about every aspect of sex is set in the context of a strong emphasis on love and how to negotiate loving relationships. Why do people fall in love? How long does love last? What practical ways are there to resolve relationship problems? The aim is to encourage open and honest communication and to enhance the relationships that are most important to us.

Contents

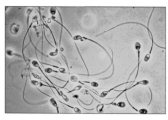

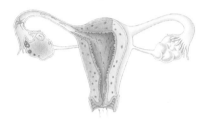

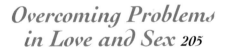

Introduction

Relating to the opposite sex Teens are often preoccupied by their relationships with the opposite sex. The first form of sexual experimentation usually comes in the form of flirting. Chapter 9 (Practical Advice for Parents and Teens) addresses teens' questions directly.

Over the past few decades, great improvements have developed in the way that sexual matters are treated by society as a whole. Gradually, a more open environment has lessened the stigma and secrecy that were once attached to topics of a sexual nature. Issues such as the rise in cases of HIV and teenage pregnancy have highlighted the necessity for a sexually informed public. Although still in its infancy, this openness offers huge and rewarding advances—a greater and more widespread awareness of sexual health issues and the need for safer sexual practices; less guilt, repression and anxiety about sexual feelings; and better communication between sexual partners and between parents and children. A child who feels at ease talking about sex and sexuality with his or her parents is more likely to seek parental guidance when it comes to relationships than a child who feels such discussions are taboo. The *Reader's Digest Guide to Love & Sex* can help to establish such openness within the family and offers both a learning tool for teens and a resource book for parents.

HOW SEXUALITY EVOLVES

Sexuality is how we express ourselves sexually, through dress, flirtation, body language, solitary sexual behavior, fantasies and desires, and ultimately through sex with a partner.

People are born as sexual beings, and we know that babies derive comfort and sensual pleasure from breast-feeding and being kissed and cuddled. The desire to touch and be touched is one of many basic human needs. Studies have shown that touch deprivation can have profound effects on a person's basic sense of well-being. Children growing up starved of touch tend to be withdrawn and unsociable.

Sexual expression can be thwarted if a person believes that she or he is inherently unlovable. This belief can result from feeling neglected in childhood or from a series of failed relationships in adulthood. Someone

Young lovers Young adults are more likely to be sexually responsible if they have grown up in an environment where issues of sex, emotions and relationships could be openly discussed.

Teenage love It is a popular misconception that informing teenagers about sex pushes them into it. Studies have shown that sexually aware teenagers are more likely to want to develop trusting relationships and postpone first sex.

who feels unlovable so fears rejection that they find it difficult to respond positively in a sexual or sensual way. As people go through life, they often absorb negative messages about sex and sensuality. Whether the message is "sex is for people who are young and beautiful," "sexual pleasure is dirty or wrong," or "desiring sex is immoral," the effect can be profound—the freedom and ease they should have in expressing the sensual side of their being is lessened or lost.

The *Reader's Digest Guide to Love & Sex* shows how sexuality and sensuality can be fostered in healthy and positive ways. A child raised by parents who openly demonstrate emotional and physical love will grow into an adult at ease with his or her sexuality. An individual who is comfortable with issues of sex, emotions and relationships will be skilled at giving and receiving love without inhibition.

TALKING ABOUT SEX

Although the taboo inhibiting discussion of sex-related matters within the family has greatly diminished, such discussions can be difficult to initiate. The *Reader's Digest Guide to Love & Sex* aims to facilitate discussion among all members of the family. Suggestions about how to broach sensitive subjects and issues appear throughout the book in special "Can We Talk About It?" features. Chapter 9 (*Practical Advice for Parents and Teens*) is devoted to answering questions on a wide range of sex-related topics, from teenage dating and confusion about sexuality to eating disorders and sexual abuse. The emphasis in this chapter is on practical ways to address these difficult and emotional issues.

DIFFERENT LIFE STAGES

Sexuality changes throughout life. A young man making love for the first time is likely to have ideas about sex that differ from those of a man of 65. The former is apt to be eager and curious about sex, perhaps prone to hyperarousal and premature ejaculation. The latter may desire sex as much as ever but finds that it takes longer to have an erection and to ejaculate. Older men may also place more emphasis on nonsexual factors such as companionship and understanding than younger men. These stereotypes demonstrate that

Sex talk Sex education can start young. When a child asks her pregnant mother about her changing body, Mom can take the opportunity to introduce her child to the facts of life.

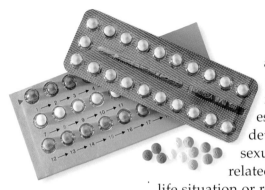

Birth control The pros and cons of different contraceptives, from the pill (shown here) to the condom, are discussed in detail in Chapter 5 (Sex and Reproduction).

age and life situation—such as pregnancy and menopause for women—can have profound effects on sexual needs and responses. Chapter 3 (*Love and Sex Throughout Life*) details the major factors that can influence sexuality at each life stage, whether these are related to an individual's age, physical health, life situation or relationship. Understanding and recognizing changes when they happen, such as a teenage daughter's desire to start dating or a middle-aged man's sudden preoccupation with his appearance, can be the first step toward coping with them.

SEXUAL TROUBLESHOOTING

When individuals or couples become overly anxious about sex, problems can start to emerge. Sexual anxiety can be caused by many factors: inexperience, worries about performance, relationship problems, stress, past sexual trauma or general hangups. Chapter 7 (*Overcoming Problems in Love and Sex*) outlines the different types of sexual difficulties that men and women of all ages can face, including problems that have a physiological origin. The causes and symptoms of different problems are discussed, together with treatment options that enable individuals to overcome inhibitions and express their sexuality in the most enjoyable way for them.

THE SEXUAL BODY

It is important for the sexually active individual to have an awareness of sexual health issues. Chapter 6 (*Maintaining Sexual Health*) informs the reader about sexual hygiene (why obsessive cleanliness can be counterproductive, for example), sexually transmitted diseases, how to recognize symptoms that may need investigating and how to practice safer sex.

From advice on how and where to find a partner to detailed information about sex and reproduction, the *Reader's Digest Guide to Love & Sex* is written and designed to help and inform the entire family. Technical or medical words that may be outside the range of a young person's vocabulary are simply and clearly defined in an extensive glossary at the back of the book. Particularly difficult words and medical terminology are highlighted on the page so that the reader can turn straight to the glossary.

Positive self-image Staying fit, promoting health and maintaining a positive attitude during midlife can counter the negative effects of aging. The physical changes of menopause are described in Chapter 3 (Love and Sex Throughout Life).

ALL ABOUT LOVE

What Is Love?

Love, the most cherished of human emotions, has enthralled men and women since the beginning of history. Although people claim that falling in love is unmistakable when it happens, it is still one of the most difficult emotions to adequately define.

Antony and Cleopatra The story of this tragically fated relationship has endured through the centuries, immortalized in literature and on film. It has come to symbolize the triumph of great passion over political ambition.

The dictionary defines love in diverse ways. *Webster's Dictionary* alone offers seven different meanings for the word "love." These range from "strong affection for another arising out of kinship or personal ties" to "warm attachment, enthusiasm or devotion" to "attraction based on sexual desire" to "unselfish loyal and benevolent concern for the good of another." All of these may be accurate, but none of them accurately portray the subtle nuances of what it feels like to be in love.

Despite being one of the deepest and most powerful of the emotions, love often defies specific definition, and people find other strong emotions, such as anger and sadness, easier to express in words. As a noun, "love" describes an intense feeling of affection or fondness, and/or sexual passion, for another person or a thing. As a verb, "love" means to feel a deep fondness and strong affection for, and/or to greatly cherish, another person or a thing.

Dictionary definitions of love—like most dictionary definitions of psychological concepts—do not help in the identification of where or why a feeling of love arises or of the complex nature of the sensations that accompany it. The definition of love is also very broad—in some contexts it can apply as well to feelings of respect, appreciation and gratitude. Moreover, how encompassing does a feeling have to be to constitute love? How much respect? How much affection? How much attachment? When does someone know for sure that he or she is *in* love?

EXPERT DEFINITIONS

Many artists and writers have made love the central theme of their work, but so too have psychiatrists, psychologists, relationship counselors and therapists from a range of backgrounds. Most psychologists accept the definition of love as an intense feeling of affection or powerful liking for another person or thing, a feeling so strong that it colors all perceptions of, and interaction with, that person or thing. They also include in this definition the resulting desire to be with a person and a concern for that person's well-being. Love does not necessarily imply sexual passion; it can be felt for a parent or child, a pet, a country or a piece of music.

Psychologists approach the issue of love in a number of different ways. First, they acknowledge that different forms of love exist. Second, they look at sexual love in the context of initiating, maintaining and ending adult relationships. Third, they treat love as a human activity much like any other, without attributing to it any magical, mystical or transcendent qualities. This contrasts with the romantic way that love is depicted in the arts: as an all-encompassing transformative power that has the ability to save or destroy people.

In other words, psychologists take the pragmatic view that in order to help people who have suffered in love, they must look at the common sensations and experiences that affect most people.

IS LOVE A CHEMICAL IMBALANCE?

Psychologists also look at love from a physiological perspective—they examine the changes in brain chemicals that occur when a person is in the initial stages of infatuation. Some experts compare the person who has recently fallen in love to someone on a drug high. The limbic system in the brain of the person in love is flooded with stimuli, and a chain of chemical events is set into motion (see page 43). The person feels euphoric, energized, confident and capable of achieving almost anything. Normal everyday activities such as sleeping and eating fade in importance. The person not only feels different, but, to the independent observer, may also behave and look different. This change is what some people describe as the "glow" of being in love.

Just as the person on a drug high suffers if the drug is withdrawn, so too does the rejected lover. The symptoms of unrequited love or betrayal include depression, panic, mood swings, hopelessness and a sense of being lost. The rejected lover may even feel ill, experiencing sensations of listlessness, breathlessness, fatigue and nausea. As Anthony Walsh, author of *The Science of Love,* says, "the more intense the high, the more devastating is the crash."

IS LOVE A MYTH?

Despite the apparent skepticism about lasting love in modern society, idealizations still have a hold on most Western societies,

The Language of Love

The word "love" comes from the Old English word "lufu," which itself comes from Germanic roots. It carries the sense of intense, emotional attachment. Other words, such as "amorous" and "romance" derive from the Latin.

LOVE IN LITERATURE

From angst-ridden love poetry to popular romance novels, love in its many forms and with its many faces is a central theme in literature from all over the world. Whether celebrating its power or despairing of its existence, literary imaginations have been captivated by both the human need for it and the perversity of its nature.

William Shakespeare (1564–1616)
A great playwright and poet, Shakespeare often mocked popular sentimental views of love: "Let me not to the marriage of true minds admit impediments. Love is not love which alters when it alteration finds, Or bends with the remover to remove. O, no! it is an ever fixed mark, That looks on tempests and is never shaken." (Sonnet 116)

Jane Austen (1775–1817)
Although unhappy in love herself, Austen observed and chronicled the loves of the middle classes of her time and was well aware that not all love is either lasting or based on true devotion. She wrote in Pride and Prejudice, *"A lady's imagination is very rapid; it jumps from admiration to love, from love to matrimony in a moment."*

including love at first sight; purity and innocence in youth; sexual abstinence up to a wedding night of private passion; and an enduring, exclusive familial love until death (and beyond).

While many people seem aware of a different reality behind this myth, the sales of romantic fiction, magazines filled with romantic cure-alls and the popularity of soap operas that include portraits of idealistic romantic liaisons indicate an immense appetite for the myth itself. From both a psychological and a historical viewpoint, lifelong monogamous love is more fantasy than a norm to be counted on. Whether or not an individual believes in the monogamy ideal will undoubtedly have a profound effect on his or her emotional life and, in particular, his or her inner feelings of romantic love.

The Nature of Love

Is everyone capable of love? This depends on the way in which love is defined. Most people experience a deep longing for another person at least once in their lives, but some seem unable to feel a deep concern for the welfare of another.

People's varying understandings of what love means grow out of their different life experiences, cultural perceptions and the role models to which they have been exposed. Some people also believe that different perceptions of what love means develop according to gender.

Most people will experience what they perceive as love at some time in their lives, but whether this develops into a successful long-term or even lifelong relationship depends on numerous factors.

BEGINNINGS OF LOVE

Many psychologists agree that the first relationship a baby forms, usually with the mother, sets the pattern for all future relationships in that child's life. The absence of a deep emotional bond, or the presence of an attachment that is inappropriate (see page 89), between mother and baby limits the child's potential to love others later on. In other words, to be able to give love in a healthy way, a person must have received it, particularly in early life, when they were completely dependent and the love of the parent or caregiver offered total security.

While the ability to love does not require high intelligence, it does require a sense of where one person ends and another person

Mother and child
Artists have often attempted to depict the intensity of the maternal bond in paintings. A baby that grows up with an awareness of loving parents is likely to grow into a loving child and adult.

begins. Adult love cannot be given by severely mentally or emotionally impaired people who have no strongly defined sense of self. People suffering from severe depression, with a lack of interest in life and no real sense of self-worth, cannot experience healthy, independent love. Neither can sociopaths—those suffering from a personality disorder involving disturbed social

The Language of Love

In Greek mythology, Narcissus was a handsome man who, incapable of loving any other person, fell in love with his own reflection in a pool and perished there. This is the origin of the psychological term "narcissistic," which describes a person suffering from a personality disorder characterized by excessive self-love.

relationships and antisocial behavior (the term "psychopath" covers similar disorders, but puts less emphasis on the social aspects of the disorders).

For some people, a life without love—in particular without a long-term sexual partner—feels incomplete and unnatural; for others, close relationships with a number of friends and their family offer deep satisfaction. More and more people in the West are choosing to live alone and lead full lives without having permanent intimate relationships. They often derive satisfaction from their careers or such creative outlets as art or music.

The biology of love

Love, beyond its association with a romantic feeling that adults experience toward one another, can be traced to biological causes and effects as well. In order for human beings to survive as a species, they need to reproduce. A long-term loving relationship between two adults frequently results in healthy children who are capable of growing up and themselves reproducing. Attracting and falling in love with a suitable partner or mate typically provides the impetus to reproduce. This loving partnership also ensures that a baby will be protected and nurtured by the two people who are most intimately connected to that child. The biological impulses underlying love apparently came about long before the concept of romantic love evolved.

Looked at in biological terms, the traditional gifts of love, such as engagement rings, indicate the male's ability to invest in and provide for the female and her offspring. The wedding ring originally demonstrated that the woman was the "property" of a particular man. The fact that men are most likely to fall in love with young, healthy women may be linked to the high fertility of young women. Marriage—the most public declaration of love—serves in human society to promote fidelity, sharing of resources, support and protection, confidence in a baby's paternity, and mutual commitment to his or her upbringing.

Parents as role models

An infant experiences his or her first relationship with the mother or mother substitute, and this provides the basis for all future relationships; but children also absorb the relationship patterns that exist among the rest of the family. The way in which other members of a family communicate, respect each other and conduct a shared life will have a profound influence on a child. The same-sex parent—a boy's father or a girl's mother—exerts particular influence in setting a child's future relationship patterns. Later, in adolescence, the opposite-sex parent takes a more significant role as the boy or girl starts to become conscious of his or her own sexuality.

If the relationship between parents is healthy, with good communication, respect, care and a roughly equal balance of responsibility, then their children are more likely to form healthy adult relationships than are those whose parent's relationship is poor, particularly in cases of physical or emotional abuse or a very unequal distribution of responsibility.

A mother who is deeply disappointed in, or abandoned by, her husband may turn to her young son as a substitute partner—the "little man" whose childhood is prematurely ended. A father who is not emotionally happy with his wife may transfer his affections to his daughter, "daddy's little girl," whose innocence is similarly cut short.

In contrast, the constant presence of a nurturing mother and father provides the best environment in which to raise a child. When divorce or death intervenes, resulting in a single-parent family, the effect on the child's eventual long-term adult relationships can range from minor to devastating, depending on such factors as how long the now-absent parent was present; the age of the child when the loss occurred, and how that loss was handled by the remaining parent.

Childhood relationships *The relationship a child experiences with the parent of the opposite sex is important in teaching a child about gender. Happy, interactive relationships often create stable children who are confident about sex roles.*

Competition between brothers
Food shortages meant that siblings had to
fight one another for food. In this case, the
younger brother starved to death.

LOVE AMONG THE IK

The Ik, a small, isolated Ugandan tribe of hunter-gatherers, gained notoriety among psychologists and anthropologists when it was discovered that in the space of just three generations, the tribe's members apparently lost their ability to love.

Once prosperous, the Ik were exiled to a barren mountain terrain, where drought and near starvation forced them to spend every waking moment looking for food. Love seemingly became an unaffordable luxury. Family loyalties withered: three-year-olds were abandoned by families to forage in packs, while babies and old people were left to die of hunger and thirst, their deaths celebrated as one less mouth to feed. Deceit replaced trust and even eye contact disappeared, as each tribal member concentrated only on his or her own survival. Young girls resorted to having sex with cattle herders as a way of getting food. Even when the drought ended and food became available again, the Ik failed to reestablish family ties or bonds of love and friendship.

Experimenting with makeup Girls are socialized to want to be attractive, desirable and lovable. The marketing of beauty products is now targeted at ever younger age groups.

Parents planning to divorce can minimize the damage to their children if they cooperate to make the child's interests a priority.

Socialized to love?

Western society idealizes "falling in love" and presents it as a goal to be pursued. From an early age, girls especially are encouraged to fantasize about falling in love and the rewards it brings—emotional and sexual intimacy, security, status, and children.

The exploitation of love and romance has become a lucrative business in the commercial world. While baby dolls and their paraphernalia have always been presented to young girls as playthings that encourage role-playing and maternal affection, today's children are just as likely to be given teenage dolls with bodies that are sexually mature and outfits that are suggestive. These dolls often come with matching doll boyfriends. In addition, precocious sexual fashions and cosmetics, designed specifically for young girls, and pop videos and love songs that fuel the romantic fantasy promote the idea that attraction and love will be of primary importance in a girl's life.

Media images of love

The media—magazines, television, movies, pop music, novels and especially advertising—have also capitalized on sex and romance. In the process, they perpetuate the myths of idealized romance. Love and romance, for example, are portrayed as the keys to happiness and escape from everyday life. Even if only temporarily, the reader or viewer, like the fictional heroine, is rescued from a mundane existence to become the handsome prince's or tycoon's loved and pampered wife.

The media also suggest, quite unrealistically, that only the young and beautiful enjoy the romantic experience. Images in magazines almost invariably show attractive young men and women. Even advertisements that are aimed at older people are illustrated with youthful-looking, glamorous models.

The myth that successful, rich, powerful or famous people are more likely to find love than are ordinary people also flourishes in the media. Advertisements for luxury items often feature celebrities. Speculation abounds about the love lives of politicians, business figures, pop stars, royalty and athletes. It is ironic that the relationships and romantic affairs that are subject to public scrutiny often fail precisely for that reason.

THE EXPERIENCE OF LOVE

The moods that accompany a new love affair are often extreme and volatile, rapidly changing from good to bad, depending on whether an individual thinks his or her feelings are reciprocated. Emotions range from ecstasy and euphoria to depression and despair, from blind conviction to utter confusion. Such feelings may be exaggerated by sexual desire—especially if it goes unsatisfied.

A person in love typically experiences a desperate sense of need and possessiveness, as well as the impression of being in perfect accord with another person. The beloved takes on the mantle of soulmate—a completion of the incomplete self—the two fusing into a single whole. The new lover often describes his or her feeling for the loved one as seeming as if they have known them all their life. Romantic love, especially if following a period of unhappiness, has often been described as "coming home" after a long, lonely exile.

The love of a more mature person is characterized by less chaotic and dramatic feelings—companionship and commitment rather than addiction and insecurity. The comfort of long-term security and trust replaces volatile uncertainty. Close partnership replaces dependence on and the need to control one another with separateness and interdependence. Respect and concern for the partner replace obsession. The stable framework of mature love can survive the negative effects of diminished sexual attraction and inevitable moments of resentment.

Liking versus loving

Liking implies a less intense, more reasoned evaluation than romantic loving, which, by definition, is a highly subjective state. Liking tends to be a positive assessment

based on someone's stable values, and often reflecting the similarities that exist between two people. Deep warmth, bonding, closeness and perhaps intimacy may be present without passion or long-term commitment.

Just as it is possible to like but not love someone, the reverse is true. In some cases, a person loves someone who is unlikable, even destructive. Blood ties help parents to love but not always like their wayward children, and siblings to love but not always like or respect each other.

Initial liking sometimes evolves into romantic or mature love. For example, in cultures that promote arranged marriages, in which families choose spouses for their children based on social, economic and political factors rather than romantic attraction, many couples grow to love each other.

The power of love

Freud claimed that romantic love is a powerful, irrational force, characterized by a temporary psychosis (a severe mental disorder, with a grossly impaired sense of reality). Jung viewed it as a fatal compulsion.

◀ *Charles and Diana*
The death of Princess Diana in 1997 triggered an international debate on media intrusion into the lives of the famous. When she was alive, Diana's relationship with Prince Charles was under constant media scrutiny by the press. Relationships that are in trouble anyway have little chance of success when subject to the stress of intense public speculation.

Falling in love
Infatuation and new love often inspire rapidly changing and conflicting moods and emotions. Individuals may even fall in love with someone whom they do not actually like very much.

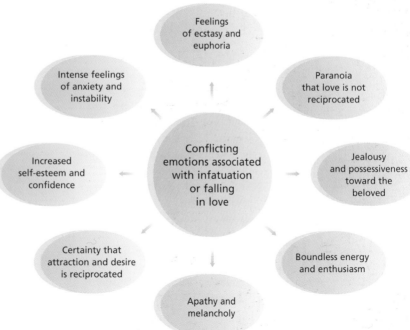

FIRST LOVE

From birth, children have close sensual and emotional ties with parents, but the first experience of sexual love outside the family usually occurs in adolescence, as "puppy love," lovesickness or a crush. The irrational, obsessive quality of such an emotion often contains an element of rebellion against parental restraint in the choice of the beloved. Adolescent love songs tend to describe love's pain more than its joys, the intense loneliness of thwarted love reflecting adolescent isolation from parents, family and society as a whole.

Sometimes an unrequited or unsatisfactory first love sets the pattern for future relationships that repeat the cycle of fantasy, disillusionment and failure.

On the other hand, as an individual matures, he or she can learn to choose more realistic love interests and to develop healthier patterns of relating to members of the opposite sex.

Teenage angst
First love can seem like one of the most intense and daunting experiences of adolescence.

Love in adversity ▶
Romantic love affairs often thrive in traumatic circumstances such as war. When reality returns—in peacetime, for example—individuals may reassess their choice of partners and the intensity of their feelings.

"Love is blind," "falling head over heels in love" and "all's fair in love and war" hint at the immunity of lovers from the usual restraints of everyday life.

Although the strength of human emotions cannot be measured scientifically, the power of romantic and sexual love is often demonstrated in the dramatic actions of individuals who feel driven by the overwhelming force of their emotion. Intense romantic love can lead to extreme acts, ranging from heroism and self-sacrifice to violence and even murder and suicide. For example, British royal Edward VIII chose to give up the throne for the American divorcée Mrs. Wallis Simpson, whom Edward described simply as "the woman I love."

The pathological jealousy associated with extreme romantic love can end in suicide, the murder of the loved person or both. One example of this is Kenneth Halliwell, who beat his partner—the internationally acclaimed British playwright and actor Joe Orton—to death and then committed suicide. Murders fueled by great passion inevitably capture the public imagination—the unsolved murder of the womanizing Lord Errol, in Kenya in 1941, for example, was featured heavily in the press and inspired the book and the subsequent movie *White Mischief*.

The French legal concept of *crime passionnel* makes allowances for crimes resulting from thwarted romantic love. Extreme behavior is not, however, confined to romantic love. The mature love of one partner for the other—or between parent and child—can be expressed in such acts as euthanasia to spare a terminally ill loved one pain, even at the risk of jail. The German author and journalist Arthur Koestler and his wife Cynthia committed joint suicide in 1983 when Arthur reached old age and faced ill health and his wife confronted inevitable loneliness.

Whether extreme romantic feelings will fuel destructive actions depends largely on an individual's outlook and psychological health. A stable individual, leading a fulfilling life, is less liable to behave destructively in the face of thwarted passion than is an emotionally unstable, weak or damaged person, whose life holds little other fulfillment or promise.

Feelings of obsessive romantic love can lead to depression or acts of extreme irrationality. This is especially true during adolescence, a time when uncertain identity, emotional transition and turmoil can engender a type of temporary madness. Shakespeare's characters Romeo and Juliet, who commit suicide rather than live without each other, are the most famous fictional example of adolescent, "star-crossed" lovers. Amy Fisher's attempted murder of Joey Buttafuoco's wife provides a contemporary, real-life example. Extreme acts that are the result of romantic love obviously are not always confined to youth.

The author of the famous Scarsdale diet, Dr. Herman Tarnower, was murdered by his jealous mistress, Jean Harris.

One true love

Part of the myth of romantic love is that for every person there is just one, true love possible in life. This belief is tempting but also unrealistic, simplistic and, ultimately, limiting, especially if it becomes a defense against taking the risks involved in emotional and sexual intimacy.

No relationship is perfect, and the longer any relationship continues, the greater the likelihood that problems will surface. A belief in one true love may prevent an individual from working toward a good relationship, in the naive expectation of finding a so-called perfect one.

If a relationship is tragically cut short, through death or separation, devotion to its idealized memory as the one true love may preclude the possibility of a future, equally rewarding—if inevitably different—relationship. Such an idealized memory may also hide or deny ambivalent, even hostile, feelings toward the former partner.

In fact, there is no single right choice of partner. Rather, many potentially successful choices exist. The long-term success of any one of them depends on both partners' ongoing capacity to nurture the relationship, especially because individuals often develop at different rates and in different directions. This means that, while giving each other room for personal development, both partners give the partnership the same importance as the individuals. Success can also depend on each partner's ability to forgive the other for not being, in reality, the idealized fantasy initially perceived.

Love at first sight

Love at first sight is sometimes the same as infatuation: an intense but transitory obsession with a person, who is appreciated not for what he or she really is but rather for the obsessed's fantasy vision. Infatuation is extreme, irrational, superficial and short-lived; it involves real sexual and emotional arousal but no real intimacy or conscious knowledge upon which to base the relationship or any commitment to work at it.

Infatuation usually dissipates as quickly as it appears, dispelled by the intrusion of reality into the relationship. Unconsum-mated infatuation tends to survive much longer, a prime example being the 14th-century Italian poet Petrarch, who as a young man caught a glimpse of the beautiful but married Laura and responded by writing 366 poems in her honor.

Love at first sight, however, sometimes matures into a long-term, healthy relationship. The sensation of recognition or familiarity that some people claim to have when they first see their future partners may come from the powerful, subconscious attraction that exists between people from families with similar dynamics, histories and problems (see page 36).

Loving more than one person

Starting a new relationship after another has ended is a normal part of life. For people who have been widowed or divorced, it is seen as a positive development after a period of time has elapsed. More controversial in Western culture is being in love with two or more people simultaneously. Strong emotional or sexual attraction to more than one person at the same time is certainly possible; but genuine loving intimacy with two people at once depends on the individual's personal definition of love.

Like waiting for the perfect partner, loving more than one person may be a conscious or unconscious defense against genuine intimacy and the vulnerability that this involves. People with a long history of such behavior may well have had very early experiences of emotionally damaging love. They respond by investing sexual intimacy in one person and emotional intimacy in another, for example, or bits of both in several people. By doing this they instinctively protect themselves from a devastating repetition of their early experiences.

How long does it take to fall in love?

Love is a fluid, complex set of feelings, attitudes and behavior. Sometimes it happens quickly and sometimes it takes years to

Giving birth Support between partners during major life events, such as pregnancy and childbirth, is a sign of mature love.

evolve. The initial sexual and emotional "gut" attraction to someone—the overpowering connection made across a crowded room—may take just moments.

Whether infatuation develops into a caring, committed relationship depends on the maturity of both partners. Infatuation often quickly fades when a person who has been worshiped from afar suddenly becomes attainable. Commitment involves a real relationship, with all its imperfections, challenges and risks.

The time needed for love to "pass the test" depends partly on the tempo of increasing intimacy and trust through direct contact and emotional exchange. A love that is maintained solely through writing letters, for example, could go on for years without either partner developing a true knowledge of the other. Love that blooms in unusual situations, such as during vacations or wartime—and especially in "forbidden" or clandestine situations—can wither in the reality of ordinary life.

Once reality replaces fantasy in a relationship, a transformation into a shared life and a reasonable certainty of stable love takes place. When a couple continue to be mutu-

A monument to love
The Taj Mahal, in Agra, northern India, was built by the Mogul Emperor Shah Jahan as a mausoleum for his favorite wife, Arjumand Banu Begum. It took many years to build and was finally completed in 1648.

ally supportive, when they jointly survive a life crisis—the first year of marriage or the birth of the first child, for example—they have a good indication of the reality and maturing of their love.

Who falls in love first?

Whether men fall in love more quickly than women depends, again, on the way in which love is defined. If strong physical arousal and sexual desire are equated with love, then men may typically be the first to react. If romance and sheer intensity of emotion are indications of being in love, then women are likely to respond first.

For both sexes, age greatly affects the speed of falling in love, as do experience and emotional maturity. Adolescents and people who are emotionally immature tend to fall in love more quickly, more intensely and more frequently than those who have experienced and learned from previous relationships.

Psychological effects of love

Many people lead satisfying, productive lives without being in a committed relationship, but in the West, a secure, loving adult

relationship is traditionally seen as an important aspect of personal well-being. With the increase in geographic and social mobility and the decrease in local extended families, tightly knit communities and job security, a stable relationship can take on huge importance.

A loving relationship removes the tension and uncertainty of attracting and keeping a partner, freeing emotional energy for such other aspects of life as work, parenting, pursuing hobbies or nurturing friendships. In a stable love relationship, an individual not only grows in self-esteem but can also share the burden of any crises.

Unsatisfying relationships, on the other hand, often result in depression, insecurity and lowered self-esteem. These in turn reduce an individual's ability to perform in other areas of life. Ironically, the negative aspects of a new passionate relationship, with its doubts and insecurity, can be as destructive as that of an established unsatisfactory one (the start of a relationship is often marked by feelings of anxiety and nervousness).

Generalizations, however, cannot tell the story of all individuals. People in unhappy relationships may discover important outlets while attempting to escape from the pain of a poor relationship. Many great works of art, music and literature have flowered out of the depths of an artist's dissatisfied emotional life.

Conditions for love to thrive

No single recipe exists for a healthy, loving relationship, but certain qualities are common to all. Most important, say relationship counselors, people need to accept that love evolves. For example, the initial passion and romance of a relationship inevitably wears off to be replaced by something more routine but no less valuable.

Flexibility in defining the roles played by each partner is also important. If two individuals can take turns providing emotional or financial support, parenting, or helping each other through crises, they can build a love that thrives, and each partner can develop a tolerance of the other's shortcomings. When partners openly communicate feelings and needs, they help to minimize misunderstandings and to prevent minor issues from becoming major problems. Sometimes partners have to consciously work on learning to listen to each other's point of view.

Certain religions and cultures, such as Islamic societies, allow polygamous marriages (see page 224). Modern Judaism and Christianity, however, emphasize monogamy: a commitment that requires self-discipline and acceptance of the inherent disappointments and imperfections in any long-term exclusive relationship.

In the West today, most partners in long-term relationships remain committed to the concept at least of serial monogamy. Occasionally, some may decide that the freedom to have other relationships, while maintaining the primary one, mutually benefits both partners. If trust is lost, however—when one partner resorts to secrecy, lying or deceit, for instance—it may never be successfully restored. An ongoing mature love depends on trust and intimacy.

Love can thrive equally well in a marriage or in a less-defined long-term relationship. For some couples, simply living together is enough. For others, the formal, legal and public declaration of marriage is essential and, in practical terms, more difficult to terminate than cohabitation.

Men and women and love

Because love is based partly on personal expectations, abilities and experiences, love can mean different things to different people. To complicate matters further, an individual may profess love without showing any loving behavior, or deny love and yet behave as though totally besotted. Some

fact or fiction?

Women are capable of greater intimacy than men.

Fact. Although this is a generalization, women may find it easier than men to share intimate feelings and tend more often to be encouraged to do so from an early age. As a result, women sometimes have a wider emotional vocabulary than men—men are sometimes labeled "emotionally inarticulate."

DO THE SEXES UNDERSTAND EACH OTHER?

Some people say that loving relationships between the sexes will always be problematic because of the inherent differences between men and women. They say that men and women might as well be from different planets. This view is espoused in John Gray's book *Men Are From Mars, Women Are From Venus*: "But as the magic recedes and daily life takes over, it emerges that men continue to expect women to think and react like men, and women expect men to feel and behave like women. Without a clear awareness of our differences, we do not take the time to understand and respect each other. We become demanding, resentful, judgmental and intolerant."

John Gray claims that happiness in love can only come when men and women make a conscious attempt to recognize and counteract gender differences.

psychologists argue that the greatest differences in concepts and expressions of love are those between men and women.

Women's traditional learned role has been attending to the needs of others. Perhaps as a result of this, an important part of love for women involves emotional communication and nurturing: sharing one's feelings and understanding and responding to another's; and listening sympathetically without judging or offering solutions.

The main role traditionally ascribed to men, on the other hand, has been the pursuit of active achievements and the ability to solve practical problems. Many men find feelings difficult to express and give love instead by providing for their partner's necessities—dealing with the outside world rather than the inner world of the emotions.

Can We Talk About It?

INTIMACY VERSUS INDEPENDENCE

Being in a relationship does not mean that you have to share all the same interests or spend every minute of the day together. Neither does it mean that you have to jealously guard your freedom. Bear in mind that the way people interact in a relationship often reflects past interactions with family and previous sexual partners. Tell your partner what level of intimacy you have had in other relationships and explain the level of intimacy you want in this relationship. Listen to his or her expectations and desires, too.

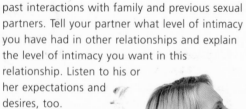

If there is conflict about the level of intimacy you both desire, then use discussion to reach a compromise. Many women prefer to share intimate secrets with female friends rather than with their male partners. Men, on the other hand, may prefer to discuss practical interests with their male friends and avoid talking about emotional subjects altogether. Both of these habits can be either accepted or changed.

These two separate ways of expressing love can lead to misunderstanding and conflict between men and women. Partners mistakenly expect the other to feel, communicate, react and behave in the same way that they do; neither can recognize the form of love offered by the other. Yet for relationships to be successful, it is vital that differences be acknowledged and, if possible, accepted. If these differences can be openly discussed and the needs of each partner stated, the relationship can only benefit.

Ironically, once couples stop criticizing one another for expressing love in the "wrong" way, they create conditions in which rigid gender roles can be relaxed.

Love and sex

The importance of sex in a relationship depends on the needs of the individuals concerned, the stage that the relationship has reached and each partner's strengths and weaknesses. At the beginning of a relationship, sex is often fueled by infatuation, longing and heightened emotional intimacy. Sex acts as one of the main binding forces.

As a relationship becomes well established, a couple's desire for sex can change or diminish for a variety of reasons, among them familiarity, availability, predictable routine, domestic commitments and neurochemistry (see page 43). Couples may find that sex does not always express intense passion anymore but rather enduring love, warmth, gratitude, concern, forgiveness, laziness or even anger.

Sometimes there are other factors in a relationship that diminish the desire for sex, such as pregnancy and childbirth or such major problems as unemployment. Certain drugs and medications can also decrease sex drive (for example, those prescribed for high blood pressure).

Some relationships and marriages, especially long-term ones, can function and thrive with little or no sexual interaction. Others cannot, and the inability or refusal to have sexual intercourse has long been grounds for divorce.

The roles of men and women in modern society are far less rigid than they were in previous centuries or even decades. Yet gender differences remain in people's sexual attitudes and behavior. For example, it is still considered more acceptable for a man to have premarital sex with a number of women, to "sow his wild oats," without any emotional attachment, than it is for a woman.

Sex in the past was sometimes viewed as something unpleasant endured by "nice" women in return for the benefits of marriage and joys of motherhood. This message was passed from mother to daughter for generations. Many a wife saw "not being bothered" by her husband as a mark of respect or as something to be desired to prevent numerous pregnancies. Culturally, a blind eye was turned to men going outside marriage for sex, for example in Victorian England, when prostitution thrived.

Intimacy and independence

Intimacy and independence are mutually compatible in a healthy, loving, adult relationship. Both partners can experience separateness as well as closeness by sharing emotional and sexual intimacy and showing loyalty to one another, while still feeling self-sufficient and confident and leading individual lives. Each partner should be able to form and enjoy strong relationships with colleagues, friends and relatives, without such attachments being seen as a threat.

Intimacy that involves too much dependence is unhealthy. Sometimes—in a crisis, for example—partners do need each other's strong support and reassurance, but the continual dependence of one partner on the other can lead to a suffocating, clinging relationship. This often results in possessiveness, jealousy and even panic when the needed partner is absent.

Overdependence may also prevent one or both partners from forming healthy relationships with others and, more important, from evolving as individuals. Extreme independence that precludes any compromises or sacrifices for the partner or relationship is equally damaging.

Marriage

A loving relationship is not necessarily synonymous with marriage. Love can and does exist without marriage, and marriage can and does exist without love. Research has shown that clear gender differences exist in the way that men and women derive benefits from marriage. Married men are more likely than single men to have successful, high-income, high-status occupations and to lead long, happy, healthy lives. Married

WHY GET MARRIED?

A couple may be motivated to marry for many reasons other than romantic love and passion. They may want children; enjoy each other's company and trust one another; share interests, outlooks and goals; and find it easy to talk and work together. In the past, women commonly sought financial security, improved status and wealth in marriage. Today many women have careers that fulfill their financial and intellectual needs; women do not necessarily view their role as a wife as primary.

People sometimes marry for reasons based on external tension—trying to assert independence from parents, yielding to pressure from their family or peer group, or dealing with an unplanned pregnancy. People may also marry to improve a difficult relationship—unfortunately this rarely has positive results.

Motives for marriage
It is widely believed that love and passion are the only valid reasons for two people to marry. In reality, there may be other criteria in operation. Some people decide to marry because they are afraid of being alone.

women, on the other hand, are more likely to suffer physical illness, depression, stress and anxiety than single women. More wives than husbands become frustrated by marriage relationships and respond by beginning divorce proceedings.

One reason for this difference may be the inferior status afforded the housewife—a role many married women adopt, and a consequence of the "Pygmalion effect" (named after the play by George Bernard Shaw), whereby a woman is traditionally encouraged to redefine both her role and her personality in favor of her husband's needs and wishes.

Like traditional gender roles, the institution of marriage has undergone much scrutiny in modern times. Couples increasingly cohabit before or instead of marriage, postpone marriage and end marriages perceived as unsatisfactory—over one-third of marriages in the West end in divorce. Nonetheless, a strong compulsion endures to marry and to marry a second or even a third time if the previous marriage failed.

Marriage publicly affirms a commitment that has social and legal, as well as private, emotional significance. It creates a contract conferring mutual financial, social and sexual obligations and rights on both parties. Marriage (unless arranged) also declares publicly shared love and a commitment to cherish and comfort one's partner in times of prosperity and adversity alike.

Through marriage, society sanctions the union of two people, binding the couple to a particular system of behavior that ensures a strong family unit. Marriage is traditionally considered the optimum setting in which to raise children, and many religions teach that only within marriage should sexual intercourse occur.

A wedding ceremony is often a big event at which family and friends witness, celebrate and acknowledge the changing family roles. The bride publicly becomes a wife and daughter-in-law as well as a daughter; the bridegroom becomes a husband and son-in-law as well as a son. The ceremony may be civil, religious or both; religious ceremonies may reflect the genuine beliefs of one or both partners or simply add to the formality of the occasion.

Marital satisfaction

No one formula exists for a loving marriage. Some marriages thrive on routine and predictability, others on chaos and drama. It is difficult, if not impossible, to judge another couple's marriage by one's own criteria, since it is the other couple's own perception of the relationship that is most important in determining its longevity. Not all marriages that survive are necessarily based on love; many continue because of such factors as children, finances or fear of loneliness.

A loving marriage is a perpetual balancing act: a negotiation that takes account of the needs of each person and those of the relationship; separateness and togetherness; similarities and differences; independence

THE PROPHET

Kahlil Gibran's famous poem *The Prophet* was written in 1923 and has since been translated into over 20 languages. It describes the balance between dependence and independence in a healthy marriage:

Kahlil Gibran
The Lebanese poet Kahlil Gibran (1883–1931) gained world fame for The Prophet.

"You were born together, and together you shall be forevermore.

You shall be together when the white wings of death scatter your days.

Aye, you shall be together even in the silent memory of God.

But let there be spaces in your togetherness,

And let the winds of the heavens dance between you.

Love one another but make not a bond of love:

Let it rather be a moving sea between the shores of your souls.

Fill each other's cup but drink not from one cup.

Give one another of your bread but eat not from the same loaf.

Sing and dance together and be joyous, but let each one of you be alone,

Even as the strings of a lute are alone though they quiver with the same music.

Give your hearts, but not into each other's keeping.

For only the hand of Life can contain your hearts.

And stand together, yet not too near together:

For the pillars of the temple stand apart,

And the oak tree and the cypress grow not in each other's shadow."

and dependence; safety and risk. Occasional conflict in marriage is healthy. Through conflict, people test their understanding of themselves, their partner and the outside world and often learn from doing so.

Sustaining love

The saying has it that familiarity breeds contempt; in the same way, romantic love almost always fades with the reality of daily life and the passage of time. Fascination with a new partner gradually disappears, and mundane issues such as finances, housekeeping, jobs, children and relatives may intervene and cause friction.

When partners begin to feel that they know each other too well, they may find that the frequency and intensity of their sex life starts to diminish. Mutual boredom is responsible for a huge number of relationship breakups. Forewarned is forearmed, however: if both partners are prepared for a loss of intensity, they may be able to avoid despair and panic when it occurs.

Whether a different but equally rewarding phase of the relationship begins or a change signals the beginning of the end depends on each partner's ability to let go of the myth of eternal romantic love and to accept the value of stable, loving companionship. At this time there may be an overwhelming temptation to seek out new romantic relationships, but it is worth bearing in mind that eventually they too will lose their seductive sparkle.

Ironically, much more is known about alleviating boredom in the workplace than in a marriage. A couple can revive their relationship by building up shared interests—for example, sports, adult education classes, community service, household improvements, vacations or hobbies. They can improve communication, especially about emotional and sexual needs, and make time for being alone on a regular basis. Going away overnight or for the weekend occasionally can also help to strengthen the relationship and keep romance and sexuality alive, even if in a lower key.

Paradoxically, couples can also enrich their marriage by developing separate, individual interests and creating a healthy breathing space between them that makes being together more rewarding. A good example of this is a wife returning to work after a long break.

The changing nature of love

Psychologists define the various types of adult love in many different ways but they broadly agree about love's basic evolution. Initially, a person's passionate love, or infatuation, involves intense sexual arousal with little or no real knowledge of the beloved. In romantic love, which may or may not follow, passion and intimacy combine in a highly idealized form. This may evolve into

Sharing interests
Spending time pursuing joint interests may help to revive a relationship.

The ideal marriage
The factors that make a good marriage are practical rather than romantic.

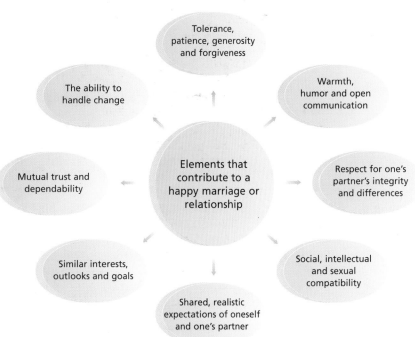

Tolerance, patience, generosity and forgiveness

The ability to handle change

Warmth, humor and open communication

Mutual trust and dependability

Elements that contribute to a happy marriage or relationship

Respect for one's partner's integrity and differences

Similar interests, outlooks and goals

Social, intellectual and sexual compatibility

Shared, realistic expectations of oneself and one's partner

STERNBERG'S THEORY OF LOVE

Psychologist Robert Sternberg has attempted to discover the underlying principles of different forms of love. He argues that there are seven basic categories into which human love can be divided (see below). Each of these types differs according to the strength of three fundamental building blocks of love: intimacy, passion and commitment (these are often presented as three sides of a figure—hence "triangular theory"). According to Sternberg:

- Romantic love involves intimacy and passion (but no commitment).
- Fatuous love involves commitment and passion (but no intimacy).
- Companionate love involves intimacy and commitment (but no passion).
- Infatuation involves passion (but no intimacy or commitment).
- Empty love involves commitment (but no intimacy or passion).
- Liking involves intimacy (but no passion or commitment).
- Consummate love involves intimacy, passion and commitment.

Robert Sternberg
Sternberg's triangular theory (1988) is a comprehensive model that can be used to rate the likely compatibility of partners.

Degrees of compatibility
If one partner places importance on long-term commitment and the other partner values intense passion, their triangles will be mismatched.

Slight mismatch

Complete mismatch

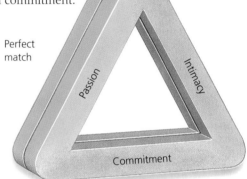

Perfect match

Passion   Intimacy

Commitment

a companionable love, in which passion and romance are largely replaced by shared trust, liking, commitment and intimacy, although passion may recur periodically.

Love styles

Canadian sociologist John Lee argued in 1974 that there are essentially six different "love styles." Individuals usually have a combination of two or more of the following styles—yielding a kind of love profile—rather than being a pure type.

- Storge—love based on companionship rather than passion. Storgic lovers most commonly aspire to marriage and commitment.
- Agape—a form of selfless all-giving love. (Traditionally, agape is a spiritual, religious or altruistic form of love.)
- Mania—an obsessive, dependent love. Manic lovers are often neurotic and suffer from sexual jealousy.
- Pragma—a cool-headed sense of realism in personal attachments. Pragmatic lovers consciously look for the "right" partner with whom to fall in love.
- Ludos—a game-playing approach to love. Ludic lovers are sensation seekers and often move from partner to partner or have several lovers simultaneously.
- Eros—a sentimental, romantic type of love. Eros lovers strongly believe in love at first sight, but once the eroticism of a relationship wears off, they are inclined to move on.

The life span of love

Statistics can accurately chart the duration of marriages, which, in the West, are most vulnerable to divorce within the first two to three years. To chart the life span of love, however, is more difficult. The continuation of a marriage does not necessarily indicate love—some long-standing marriages may lack all intimacy. On the other hand, many divorcing couples say, "We love each other, but we just can't live together."

It is most accurate to describe the life span of love as a series of rises and falls. Couples can be in and out of love many times in a relationship, for weeks, months or years; but their love may be strengthened as a result. One form of love may die, to be replaced by a new form.

THE DEATH OF LOVE

When partners sense that their relationship is in jeopardy, they may experience a wide range of negative feelings, including anger, resentment, betrayal, rejection, hurt, vengeance, disappointment, depression and despair. The causes of discord can also vary greatly: sexual, financial, housing and communication problems; the birth of a child; children leaving home; in-laws; ex-spouses and stepchildren; unemployment or retirement; alcohol and drug abuse; physical or mental illness; and bereavement.

Supposedly joyous occasions such as vacations and even Christmas can serve as a focus for pent-up anger fired by unresolved grievances. For both men and women, mid-life, with its feared loss of youth and sexual attractiveness, can put a relationship under great pressure. Infidelity can also have a profoundly negative impact on a relationship, although the infidelity itself may actually be a reflection of existing problems rather than the prime cause of problems.

Relationships can also be destabilized by changing attitudes toward one's partner. Character attributes that initially attracted each partner can later become a source of friction. A free spirit and sense of adventure that was considered enchanting during the early stages of a romance can later be perceived as immature, irresponsible and impractical in the context of day-to-day life. Similarly, the strong, silent, independent character can come to be seen as inflexible, uncommunicative and domineering.

Paradoxically, strong negative feelings do not necessarily spell the death of love, since they show that there is some emotional energy still invested in the relationship. Indifference and an absence of feelings represent a far more serious threat.

Relationship counselors say that it is not the loss of love—for whatever reason—that determines the survival of a relationship. Instead it is the emotional maturity of the partners, the degree of commitment to resolving problems, and the support avail-able from friends, family or community. If one or both partners are young, they may feel that working at a relationship is not worth the time, energy or emotional commitment. They may have a relatively black-and-white view of relationships: they either work or they fail; love is either present and compelling or completely absent. People who are older or have a mature outlook are more likely to want to make efforts to sustain relationships, particularly if there is a long history of shared experiences with a partner or there are children involved.

In a long-term relationship, the irreversible death of love is usually a slow rather than sudden event. It may take years for a couple to separate. Seeking counseling before a situation becomes irretrievable may help a relationship to survive.

Can We Talk About It?

IS OUR RELATIONSHIP WORTH SAVING?

How can you tell if a relationship is broken beyond repair or if there is still something worth saving? Many people become trapped in dead relationships out of fear of change, an irrational hope that things can improve, or insecurity. Many good relationships come to an end because one or both partners lack the commitment to make it work. You may be helped through these ambivalent feelings by trying to determine the cause of your dissatisfaction. At its best, how good was your relationship? Do you feel that your needs within the relationship are met or ignored? Do you feel your partner genuinely likes you? Do you enjoy physical contact with each other? Do you still do things together that make you feel close? Is your partner able to acknowledge his or her faults? Is he or she willing to change? Do you trust your partner? Are your fundamental outlooks on life incompatible? If one of you has betrayed the other, do you feel the wounds have healed? Assessing the health of your relationship by discussing these kinds of questions may help you to make an objective decision about the future.

Love in Different Cultures

In the West, people assume that romantic love is the basis for every monogamous sexual relationship; but in other parts of the world, people hold very different ideas on how important love is as a basis for marriage, and even whether it exists.

The aboriginal Tahitians and Kalahari Bushmen, among whom sexual constraints are minimal, have no concept of romantic love, perhaps because they neither deny nor postpone sexual gratification. In traditional Eastern cultures, an individual derives identity almost solely from his or her family. A woman perceives herself—and is perceived by others—as a daughter, granddaughter, sister, wife, mother and/or employee; only secondarily is she a person in her own right. Likewise, a man is primarily a son, grandson, brother, husband, father and/or employer. When people define themselves in this context, the idea of romantic love between individuals becomes largely irrelevant. When choosing a spouse, the family's wishes are paramount.

Traditional Hindu and Muslim cultures value family and social obligations over personal emotions in much the same way, as do cultures in which women have grossly inferior status or are seen as possessions. In India and parts of Africa and South America, parents sometimes arrange marriages for their children before they are even born, and child marriages are common. Members of royal families and powerful political or financial families may also take a more business-like approach in the choice of a spouse than do most ordinary members of a community.

Sometimes societies depend on astrology to determine the suitability of a match between two people. In traditional Hindu, Buddhist and Japanese cultures, for example, the compatibility of a couple's birth charts may take precedence over love.

The contemporary Western emphasis on the importance of individual identity and of romantic love has had an impact on other cultures. For example, minority immigrant cultures in the West, such as the Vietnamese in the U.S. and the Indians and Pakistanis in the U.K., experience conflict in their attitudes toward romantic love in marriage. This often results in tension between the older, more traditional members of the family and younger generations, who want to have girlfriends and boyfriends.

FERTILITY RITUALS

Some cultures consider having children the main reason for marriage and therefore focus on the fertility of pairing individuals. There are some Central and East African cultures in which a young woman is not even considered for marriage until she has proven her fertility by becoming pregnant—by whom is unimportant.

Fertility rituals often involve exposing the bride to as many objects connected with reproduction as possible, including babies, grain seeds, phallic-shaped plant roots, ancient magical stones and springs. Handling many-seeded fruits such as apples, figs and pomegranates is a tradi-

Symbols of fertility
In some parts of the world, people believe that a woman's fertility can be increased by handling or eating foods such as nuts, eggs or many-seeded fruits.

tional ritual; fish, with their numerous eggs and young, and cocks, hens, and eggs are also considered to be agents of fertility. Such things are thought to have the power to enhance a woman's fertility simply by association.

From Roman times, nuts, with their obvious similarity to testicles, have been thrown at the bridal couple to ensure fertility. Today a Western equivalent is the distribution of pink and white sugared almonds at Italian weddings. Throwing rice and, formerly, wheat at the bride and groom also hark back to ancient fertility rituals.

ATTRACTING A MATE

Magical potions and philters—drinks intended to arouse sexual desire in the drinker—have long been used to win love and, occasionally, to deny responsibility for having fallen in love. For example, when King Henry VIII grew tired of Anne Boleyn, he let it be known that she had used witchcraft to seduce him. Superstitious people often attributed the necessary magical powers and knowledge of love potions to women; initially witches and later—when the concept of witchcraft dwindled in the eighteenth century—to Gypsies, especially in southern Europe.

Body hair and fluids were often considered powerful aphrodisiacs and controlling agents, magically transferring feelings of love from the donor to the recipient. Through potions, the beloved unknowingly ate, drank or was otherwise exposed to the hair, sweat, blood or saliva of the enamored and, it was believed, would inevitably fall in love with him or her. According to rural Scottish folklore, two candies glued together with a man's sweat gave him power over any woman who ate them.

Other traditional ingredients for love potions include tree sap, symbolic of regeneration; mandrake root, with its likeness to the human form; and ginseng. Eating animal genitals was thought to cause sexual arousal: kangaroos' testicles were used in potions by Australian Aborigines and beavers' testicles by Native Americans. Other ingredients of love potions include rhinoceros horn and snake, with their obvi-

ous phallic symbolism, and, more mundanely, asparagus, artichokes, leeks, truffles, tomatoes, oysters, lettuce, and even partridges. Folklore has it that a male partridge can impregnate his mate by song alone.

Appealing to the relatively primitive sense of smell was, and still is, part of the magic of love potions. In Elizabethan England, women would place peeled apples in their armpits until the fruit absorbed the odor. They then gave these "love apples" to their beloved. In parts of Greece and the Balkans, men still tuck handkerchiefs in their armpits at festivals, then offer them to their female dancing partners.

Charms and spells

According to the concept of magical transference, simple contact with the clothes or the used bath water of a suitor is sufficient to cast a spell. In Indonesia women traditionally conceal their girdles in the clothes of the beloved in order to ensure love in return.

According to voodoo magic, carrying small leather sachets of consecrated feathers, dirt from a grave, dried frog or snakeskin, and powdered human bones imparts the power to win someone's love. In North Africa, the reputed aphrodisiac vervain is planted by the house door to attract a mate.

Individuals often used small figures representing the beloved to cast love spells. A typical Gypsy spell consists of a woman burning and then urinating on a small figurine of the beloved, made from his saliva, hair, blood and nail chippings. This must be done at a crossroads during the moon's first quarter, while she incants her love for him.

◀ *Carved-nut charms* *In New Guinea, nuts or seeds were carved with ancestral faces and worn on necklaces by young men to attract young women during courtship rituals.*

Astrological charts *This Korean astrologer sits near a temple waiting for customers. Some cultures place great emphasis on astrological compatibility between partners.*

Matchmaking and puberty rites

In some cultures in which marriage is not determined solely by others, or by magic or astrology, specially planned festivals or gatherings occur to enable young men and women to meet. In Ireland, for example, an annual matchmaking festival occurs in Lisdoonvarna, and among the Sukuma of Tanzania, communal dances are followed by a traditional game, *chagulaga mayu*, which ends in couples pairing off and having sexual intercourse.

In some cultures the puberty rites that occur when a girl first starts menstruating act as a public statement of her availability, as does a young man's equivalent puberty rites or first successful hunt. This is not always true: men of the Masai tribe of Kenya and Tanzania delay marrying until well into adulthood because they believe that early marriage will diminish their skills as warriors.

WEDDING RITUALS

Many cultures enact a good-humored mock abduction of the bride by the groom and disguise or otherwise protect the bride from the groom, reflecting the time when capturing a bride was acceptable. Anthropologists believe that the archetypal hostility between

a mother-in-law and son-in-law dates from this practice, as does the practice of going on a honeymoon—a month-long period of hiding at a safe, secret destination while parental tempers cooled.

Feasting to celebrate existing or hoped-for wealth and fertility and the joining together of two families occurs across cultures. The bridal couple sharing food and drink is also a common practice.

First-night rituals

Proof of the bride's virginity on her wedding night is important in some societies. Occasionally the marriage contract depends on it, and the woman's first experience of intercourse on the wedding night is followed by a public display of bloody sheets the next morning. Some South American, Hindu and Indonesian cultures, however, endow virginity with destructive magical powers over men, and baby girls have their hymens broken.

Among the Tanzanian Zaramo tribe, two women observe the couple making love. To assess the woman's virginity, they note the ease with which she is penetrated and whether there is any loss of blood. The groom's virility is judged by the amount and consistency of his semen.

Herbal lures In parts of North Africa, vervain, a reputed aphrodisiac, is planted in the doorway of a house in order to attract a lover.

WEDDING RITUALS IN OTHER CULTURES

A Tibetan marriage
The groom's delegates, known as the Nyao, dance in the courtyard of the bride's home. They are encircled by the Khaya, the bride's representatives, who ask questions in song. This is a traditional riddle game.

Hindu decorations
The preparations for a Hindu wedding are lengthy. The bride, for example, is dressed in ornate clothes and has intricate decorations painted on her hands and arms using henna, a natural dye.

A Greek wedding
Guests attending the wedding of a Greek couple traditionally pin money to the bride's dress and veil. This is an alternative to the conventional Western practice of giving gifts to the bride and groom.

Symbols of Love

Society invests certain gifts, such as flowers, chocolates and diamonds with romantic significance. Occasions and rituals, such as weddings and Valentine's Day, also exist as social celebrations and symbols of love and romance.

History is pervaded with symbols that represent love, although their origins and significance are not always obvious.

THE RED ROSE

In Roman mythology, the first red rose appeared when Jupiter saw Venus, the goddess of love, bathing; she blushed, and a nearby white rose turned red in sympathy. In another legend, Cupid, dancing with the gods, spilled nectar over a white rose, staining it red. To early Christians, the red rose symbolized martyrdom. Today it symbolizes perfection and love, especially on Valentine's Day—a custom started when King Louis XVI of France gave Queen Marie Antoinette red roses on that day.

RINGS

Diamond engagement rings, which date mainly from the 19th century replaced earlier, three-part gimmal rings—one ring was worn by the woman, one by the man and one by the witness, and then all three were reunited as the wedding ring. Diamond rings also replaced gold or silver lovers' knots and rings of precious stones.

In the West, the wedding ring symbolizes the everlasting commitment of marriage (a ring has no beginning or end). High-carat, plain gold bands symbolize the union's purity and nobility. In the U.S. and U.K., the ring is worn on the third finger of the left hand; in mainland Europe, the right hand. According to folklore, the third finger has a special vein going directly to the heart.

THE HEART

For thousands of years, the heart was considered the source of intellect and emotions, especially love and courage. This belief has long been medically disproved, but the symmetrical heart motif is still a powerful symbol of love. Heart-shaped chocolate boxes, balloons and cards appear in abundance around Valentine's Day. Some couples draw graffiti hearts bearing their initials in public places; others have hearts tattooed on their skin.

ST. VALENTINE'S DAY

St. Valentine, the patron saint of lovers, was martyred around A.D. 270. To popularize the saint's day, the early Christian church linked it to the older Roman festival of Lupercalia, celebrated around February 15. (According to folklore, February 14 is also when birds begin to seek mates for the breeding season.) During Lupercalia, men drew lots for their women partners. Lot drawing and present giving between single young men and women continued through the centuries on Valentine's Day or eve, although it was frowned upon in Puritan America, where public displays of affection were illegal.

According to some folklores, a girl would marry the first bachelor she saw on Valentine's Day, and so young women took great pains to avoid seeing unsuitable men. The custom of anonymously sending Valentine cards, at first homemade, then commercial, began in the 18th century. Later, giving chocolates, perfumes, cakes and other luxury items became traditional.

◀ *The red rose A symbol of love since ancient Roman times, the red rose continues to have romantic significance to the present day.*

Cupid In Roman mythology, Cupid, depicted as a beautiful young man or a winged, naked boy holding a bow and arrow, was the son of Venus. As the seductive god of love, he caused continual intrigue and chaos. Those shot with his arrows through the heart or eyes (from which came the saying "Love is blind") were smitten with love and lost their reason and willpower.

Platonic Love

Friendships, especially long-standing ones, can involve great intimacy, understanding and trust—qualities that often exist in a long-established marriage. People who meet in childhood and remain lifelong friends typify this kind of relationship.

Friendships that are based on shared interests or shared survival of challenging or even life-threatening experiences may be exceptionally strong. Mutual commitment, including facing and working through difficult issues together, is as important a factor in maintaining a loving friendship as it is in maintaining a loving relationship or marriage.

WHEN FRIENDS BECOME LOVERS

Deep, long-standing friendship can occasionally develop a romantic dimension. People who work closely together or are neighbors or part of the same social group may become romantically attracted, especially if one or both has no close relationship or has a close relationship under stress. A friend who helps in a personal crisis is often idealized—a main ingredient in romantic love.

In arranged marriages romance is typically something that evolves rather than being present from the beginning. However, individuals who voluntarily enter a marriage or close relationship with the hope that passion will develop from companionship and intimacy often find that this fails to happen.

People have long acknowledged that sex can jeopardize friendships between men and women. One reason that relationships between gay men and heterosexual women tend to succeed may be the absence of any sexual tension. Some people believe that platonic friendship between men and women is impossible because affection will always develop into sexual attraction or because the possibility of sexual interaction will inevitably arise. The ability to maintain a nonsexual friendship depends on the strength and depth of the friendship and the level of maturity of those involved.

In some opposite-gender friendships, the issue of sexual attraction never arises. In others, problems occur when one party wants the relationship to become sexual and the other doesn't. Sometimes the timing of sexual attraction is mismatched: one friend is initially attracted to the other but has gotten over it by the time the other responds. Alternatively, both friends may simultaneously desire each other, but one or both are committed to another relationship. Falling in love with a best friend's partner or spouse often leads to this dilemma.

One way that counselors suggest tackling the issue of sex with an opposite-sex friend is to simply acknowledge it, in either a serious or a lighthearted way. Broaching the subject may help to contain, if not resolve, the problem. Mature friends can overcome unfulfilled expectations as surely as mature spouses—friendships do not necessarily have to end because of underlying sexual tension. It is worth bearing in mind that all friendships have their own issues to resolve: for example, a friendship between two heterosexual men or women can be beset with problems of envy or rivalry.

Childhood friendships As young children play together, they form platonic friendships and establish the patterns for adult loving relationships.

WHEN LOVERS BECOME FRIENDS

Intense romantic love may eventually become nonsexual. In marriage, for example, there is often a lessening of the initial sexual attraction. In marriages of many years' duration, the aging process itself may lead to a decline in sexual energy, so that friendship becomes the primary bond.

Lovers cannot always make a smooth transition from a sexual to a nonsexual relationship. They frequently run into difficulties when only one partner makes the decision to end the sexual relationship, when parenting or financial issues are unresolved, or when sex formed the basis of the relationship.

Sometimes friendship with a former lover evolves over time. It can often take a year or more after a separation to resolve animosities and regrets. When both partners have established independent lives, they may well find that friendship becomes possible, especially if this was the basis of their relationship to start with.

PARENTAL LOVE

Most animals instinctively protect newborn babies, in extreme cases at the cost of their own life. Biologists say that this behavior has its origins in the continuation of the species, and that it manifests itself in relationships between human beings as parental love. Parents will unconsciously seek to protect their genes by parenting and promoting their offspring. Parental love can be intense and profound.

The emotional attachment, or bonding, that normally occurs between a mother and her infant shortly after birth reinforces this instinct and sets the basic pattern for that infant's future emotional relationships. Because human infants, unlike those of most other species, are vulnerable for several years, parental love involves long-term nurturing, protection, feeding and guidance —an emotional and financial commitment, often with an element of self-sacrifice. Healthy parental love also involves gradually relinquishing control as the child develops and takes responsibility for his or her own life, an important aspect of parental love.

Parental love involves physical affection—holding, touching, kissing, cuddling, rocking—but also sexual self-control. Well before puberty, girls develop an awareness of the sexual aspects of their relationships with their fathers, and boys with their mothers (see page 91). Parents must then respect their child's emerging sexuality, by reinforcing the child's self-esteem and encouraging a positive sense of masculinity or femininity. In a good, healthy relationship between a parent and a child, the parent makes sure that the sexual potential between them remains unfulfilled. Instead, each parent focuses his or her sexual activity on an adult partner.

Like the love between friends, the love between brothers and sisters can encompass deep emotional intimacy, understanding, tenderness, tolerance and commitment. And like other forms of love, sibling love is often overlaid with other, seemingly contradictory emotions. For example, sibling rivalry in which siblings compete for parental attention and love is a common feature of family life. In fact, relationships with siblings can also set a strong pattern for later relationships in life, both personal and professional.

The Language of Love

Platonic love is named after the ancient Greek philosopher Plato (c. 428–348 B.C.) and describes a close relationship that does not involve any sexual feelings or desires. Plato believed that two parallel worlds existed—the physical, and the mental or spiritual—and that the latter world was superior to and more "real" than the former world. To Plato, friendship, comradeship or love that transcended base physical desires reached a spiritual ideal and was, in his opinion, far superior to a sexual relationship.

Lifelong platonic love Platonic friendships between people of the same or opposite sex may be established during youth and last a lifetime.

THE INCEST TABOO

In the vast majority of cultures, incest—sexual activity between parent and child or other close relative—is forbidden. This helps protect a culture from the genetic problems of inbreeding and the potentially explosive social problems of multiple close sexual relationships within a family. The incest taboo also forbids sexual love between children of the same parents. Studies in Israeli kibbutzim show that children who grow up as brother and sister show remarkably little sexual interest in each other, even if they are not related.

Theories of Attraction

There is a wide range of theories about what attracts one person to another. Some people argue that physical beauty is a primary factor, while others point to similarities or differences between partners as the basis of compatibility.

From childhood onward, attractive people are often given the benefit of the doubt; they tend to be given credit for their positive factors, while their negative factors are attributed to bad luck, other people or circumstances that are "beyond their control." This typically creates a self-fulfilling prophecy, because being consistently seen as good, desirable and successful tends to encourage self-confidence, which in turn encourages success.

Exceptional good looks, however, can be a handicap, distorting others' perception of a person and his or her own sense of self. Popular stereotypes often equate glamorous good looks with shallowness, lack of intellect or arrogance. Some people who are thought of as beautiful may have deep-seated insecurities, feeling that others relate to them on the basis of how they look rather than who they are.

In the West, opinions on ideal physical attractiveness remain surprisingly consistent and are learned from an early age. Young children see book illustrations, television programs and movies featuring images of beautiful princesses and ugly witches, handsome heroes and deformed villains. Most people have a sense of how attractive they appear to others and how they compare to the ideal notion of beauty. This self-rating can be a powerful factor in determining choice of partner. Studies have shown that couples whose attractiveness ratings are similar have longer-lasting relationships than those whose attractiveness ratings are dissimilar.

WHICH FEATURES ARE ATTRACTIVE?

For both sexes, facial features rank high, with the eyes, the "windows of the soul," attracting attention first. Large, bright, receptive eyes are held to be the ideal, and certain types of eye contact are understood to initiate flirting. Western societies find an oval face, prominent cheekbones, a small straight nose, a medium-size mouth and ears that do not stick out attractive. A clear complexion, wrinkle-free skin and even, white teeth are desirable because they are signs of healthiness and youthfulness. The expression "long in the tooth" refers to the natural receding of gums that occurs with age. Any indication of aging, especially in women, is considered to be less attractive, reflecting the relationship between increasing age and the onset of female infertility. Average features tend to be more attractive than extremes: enormous or very small breasts, for example, or excessively muscular or thin bodies are generally not considered to be attractive.

Sexual self-perception Sexual attractiveness is often a self-fulfilling prophecy: if someone believes himself or herself to be attractive, others also find that to be true.

Child is told that he or she is "pretty" or "handsome."

Child comes to perceive himself or herself as attractive.

Child associates being attractive with receiving praise.

Child grows up expecting positive response from people.

Self-confidence is found attractive by person's peer group.

Person is treated positively by others.

Self-esteem is fueled.

Person perceives himself or herself as physically, sexually and socially attractive.

ATTRACTION AND GENDER DIFFERENCES

Men are reputed to respond to a woman's looks more quickly and powerfully than women do to a man's physical attributes. Men admire the particular physical qualities in women that distinguish them from men: fuller lips; thinner eyebrows; softer, smoother skin; and a lack of facial hair. Traditionally, men seek younger women, with their potentially higher fertility.

Men generally consider large, firm breasts, which symbolize fertility and reproduction, to be desirable. The ideal breast is pert rather than pendulous, again reflecting the preference for youth over age (the density of breast tissue declines as a woman grows older, and her breasts become more inclined to sag). Men are also attracted by slim but curvy body shapes with a narrow waistline and long, slim legs. These are all, however, generalizations. Many men have preferences that do not match the stereotypical image of feminine beauty.

Studies suggest that women may be more likely to be attracted by a man's status than his looks. A woman may make a detailed assessment of a partner's personality, dependability and material assets from a very early stage of a relationship. A woman may even reject a potential partner on the basis of his job, wealth and perceived social standing. Traditionally, women also tend to seek slightly older men, with their potentially greater status, wealth and ability to provide for and protect future children. This kind of selection often operates on a subconscious rather than a deliberate level.

The physical characteristics that many women favor include a large, square jaw; a strong chin; a slim, muscular build with a flat stomach; and small, well-formed buttocks. Biologically, these attributes may be symbolic of physical prowess: hunting, fighting and survival skills. In gay and lesbian relationships, considerably less emphasis tends to be placed on both potential fertility and financial resources.

Long and sleek

Long and natural

THE SEXUAL SIGNIFICANCE OF HAIR

For both sexes, thick, healthy hair is considered attractive. In men, plenty of hair symbolizes power and masculinity, as in the Old Testament story of Samson. Shaved heads often connote religious celibacy, old age or pursuit of a particular lifestyle (skinheads, for example). In women, long, thick, shiny hair traditionally symbolizes female sexuality and availability—one of the reasons why strict Orthodox Jewish and Muslim women keep their hair hidden in public. In some cultures, however, long hair can symbolize virginity, which has its own erotic implications. Paradoxically, in the 1920s, women with short, bobbed hair were considered sexually independent. Today short, androgynous haircuts are seen as sexy or fashionable in certain circles because they subvert gender boundaries. Women sometimes perceive balding men as sexually attractive, perhaps because they are reputed to have high levels of the male sex hormone testosterone.

Shaved head

Sexual signals projected by different hairstyles
Some hairstyles have specific sexual connotations.
Cropped or messy hair is androgynous; long,
groomed hair is feminine; stylized hair may be
associated with glamour and vampish sexuality.

Wispy bob

LIKE ATTRACTS LIKE

There is a popular theory that "like attracts like." It could be that a person recognizes sexual compatibility when he or she identifies someone as being similar. Many people are attracted to a partner with a similar background. In such cases couples may share a similar education and religion and similar interests, attitudes and aspirations.

Being attracted to a partner with a similar background may include the subconscious perception of safety and continuity of leaving the childhood home but still remaining connected to it. Paradoxically, this is true even for couples from similar negative backgrounds; people from broken homes, for example, tend to attract one another. Positive similarities, such as wealth, status, religion, political affiliation or education, may be obvious to two people from the start. Negative or more obscure similarities, such as being adopted, the death of a sibling or a family history of depression, may emerge only at a later stage.

Subconscious recognition of similarity

A family's emotional dynamics are in part expressed by its members through body language: posture, facial expression, gesture and way of moving. People from emotionally similar families recognize these nonverbal signals and feel at ease with them, long before any conversation occurs. Individuals from families with secrets or scandals such as illegitimacy or suicide, for example, tend to attract each other, although it may take years for the secrets to be revealed. And people whose emotional development was stopped at a certain stage—so that they struggle with the low self-worth resulting from a lack of parental love or with gaining independence from possessive parents—are commonly drawn to each other.

The more self-confident a person is, the more selective he or she tends to be when choosing a partner. People who are "centered"—self-accepting and nondefensive—tend to choose others with a similar level of stability. No one likes rejection, so someone who lacks self-confidence is likely to choose a partner who is similarly lacking, though one or both of them may have a veneer of self-confidence. Men with low self-esteem tend to choose traditional, dependent and nonthreatening women, while men with a high sense of self-worth feel confident about choosing more assertive and independent women—for example Julius Caesar and Cleopatra.

COMPLEMENTARY PERSONALITIES

Although relationships between matching personalities can be successful, some similar couples lack vitality in their relationship and share a fear of difference. Complementary personalities may function very

Attraction in motion
When two people meet for the first time, they will consciously and subconsciously make assessments of each other. How attractive is this person? Are they like me? In what ways are they different from me? How are we getting along? This couple's body language indicates a growing sense of mutual attraction.

On first meeting, a couple's body language may indicate reserve or even mild hostility. Here, both have their legs crossed away from each other, although mutual interest is signaled by eye contact.

As a conversation evolves, body language becomes less defensive and more open. The couple turn their bodies toward each other, and expressive hand gestures become more frequent.

well together: a dominant character may suit someone who is submissive, a dependent person may deal well with a nurturing person, and an assertive individual can combine well with a passive one.

HOW IMPORTANT IS IQ?

Very different levels of intelligence can be detrimental to a long-term relationship. A highly intelligent person's inclinations to protect, rescue, parent or "improve" a much less intelligent partner, or to make himself or herself feel better by comparison, may later backfire in a relationship. Intelligence and level of education are not synonymous, however. In addition, different, complementary types of intelligence exist: for example, one partner might have the ability to solve practical problems in a direct, logical and rational way, while the other looks at problems from many different angles and seeks creative solutions.

DO OPPOSITES ATTRACT?

Psychologists have long noted the powerful attraction of opposites. Being attracted to someone from a different race, religion or

The Language of Love

The "other half" is used to describe a partner, highlighting the idea of the two halves of the relationship making the whole.

class may reflect the need to express independence from parents and the values they represent, especially around the teenage years and in tightly knit families or communities. Such a choice may also arise from a feeling of isolation from one's family or express a need for constant reassurance of separateness. Someone who has a fragile sense of identity, who has never felt able to have feelings of his or her own, may choose a partner who is as seemingly different as possible, and even move to another culture to reinforce that sense of separateness.

Individuals sometimes create a marriage or partnership of opposites to compensate for the qualities lacking, or perceived to be lacking, in themselves—in short, to gain a sense of completeness. It can also be a way for a person to offload onto the partner the qualities or characteristics that he or she considers unacceptable or dangerous in himself or herself. This type of reasoning is rarely conscious, but it often explains why a shy person selects a socially assertive or dominant partner, why a cautious person selects a risk taker and a repressed person selects an uninhibited one.

WAIST-TO-HIP RATIO

Biologists argue that men find a slim waist and full hips attractive in women for evolutionary reasons. The waist-to-hip "ratio" reflects a high level of estrogen and a low level of testosterone, a combination generally linked to high fertility.

The heavy, Rubenesque female body shape considered beautiful in other periods of history and cultures may also have biological origins. For example, in cultures in which food is scarce, plumpness indicates health, wealth, social status, and the potential to sustain pregnancy and nursing.

Mutual attraction becomes obvious as a couple relax into a conversation. Smiling, eye contact and increasing physical proximity demonstrate a desire for greater intimacy.

Each partner has recognized the other's body language and given tacit permission for things to progress further. The man touches the woman's knee and their postures are roughly symmetrical.

PERCEPTIONS OF BEAUTY

Although beauty is a subjective assessment, biologists say that facial symmetry is commonly found attractive (this may originate in biological impulses that link symmetry to genetic and physical fitness). Babylike features such as big eyes, small noses and ears, and soft unblemished skin are also rated highly—these types of features are thought to inspire a protective response in other people.

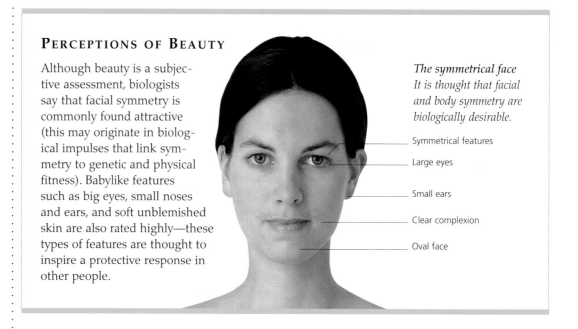

The symmetrical face
It is thought that facial and body symmetry are biologically desirable.

Symmetrical features

Large eyes

Small ears

Clear complexion

Oval face

PARTNERS WHO RESEMBLE PARENTS

According to Freud, part of a young child's normal psychological development is the wish to seduce or even marry the parent of the opposite sex. While in most cultures incest is taboo, this unfulfilled attraction affects the adult's notion of the idealized partner, who tends to resemble childhood memories of the opposite-sex parent.

The conscious search may well be for a partner with the opposite-sex parent's positive qualities. An individual's desire to re-create the dynamics of childhood relationships, however, and to correct any dysfunc-

tions that occurred then, is so strong that the selected partner will almost inevitably have the opposite-sex parent's negative qualities as well.

ATTRACTIVENESS AND CULTURE

What is considered attractive in one culture may be repellent in another. In some non-Western cultures, ritual disfigurations such as an elongated neck, ears, lips, vulva or penis; filed and stained teeth; and scarred face or breasts are considered attractive.

Attractiveness in a multicultural society can be complex. Minority, nonwhite races in predominantly white cultures have, until recently, been presented with white standards of beauty as the only ideal. In countries such as South Africa and India, in which minority whites had political control, the white standards prevailed as well.

In white-dominated cultures, nonwhite skin, hair and body characteristics were often considered inherently inferior to their white correlatives. Attempts to compensate for this sometimes led to mixed messages. For example, black dolls had dark skin but European features. Meanwhile, minority efforts to mimic the "ideal" white appearance ranged from hair straighteners and skin lighteners to cosmetic surgery. Marriage between a member of a nonwhite race and a white spouse symbolized status. Interestingly, the first white settlers and explorers in Africa were considered hideous albinos by the indigenous population.

SIGNS OF COMPATIBILITY

OBVIOUS SIMILARITIES IN	HIDDEN SIMILARITIES IN
Appearance/attractiveness	Emotional dynamics of family
Sense of humor	Experiences of loss in family
Race, religion and social class	Position in family (eldest, only, middle child and so on)
Leisure pursuits and friends	Relationship with opposite-sex parent
Education, intelligence and ambitions	Secrets or scandals in the family
Attitudes toward money, having children and parenting	Sense of self-worth

The Language of Attraction

A person can express sexual attraction in various nonverbal ways, including modifying appearance—particularly dress—flirtatious body language, fragrance and body adornment using jewelry or makeup.

The language in which a person signals his or her initial attraction for another person is usually nonverbal. Some signals are instinctive, probably cross-cultural and made unconsciously. Others are overt and intentional gestures made to increase attractiveness. These tend to be culturally specific—what is considered acceptable and attractive in one culture may be thought repellent or indecent in another.

DRESS

Dress can powerfully express sexuality and give strong clues about sexual interest. What makes clothing attractive, however, is often a matter of taste. Many people find ethnic or exotic clothing erotic, reflecting a common fantasy that foreign cultures are more highly sexed than Western culture. This can be true as well for clothing worn by other social or economic classes in one's own culture, based on a similar fantasy. For some people, sexually ambiguous dress that creates a moment's uncertainty as to the wearer's gender is sexy. Others find uniforms of any sort or cross-dressing—wearing clothes obviously meant for the opposite sex—sexy.

Among some people, loose or disorderly dress suggests that the wearer could easily discard his or her clothes. Similarly, a top that slips off a woman's shoulder or a partly undone garment worn by either sex hints at the possibility of total nudity. Tight, short or otherwise revealing garments that emphasize the breasts, belly, buttocks and/or groin also tend to be erotic—for example, skin-tight jeans, miniskirts or nipple-revealing T-shirts.

The wearing of animal skins in the form of leather, suede or fur has always had strong sexual overtones, although conservation issues have altered the connotations somewhat. In primitive times, someone wearing a fierce animal's skin was thought to absorb its qualities; thus a modern woman wearing fox may be seen as desirable and wily—a "foxy" lady. Black leather, belted, zipped and studded clothing has sadomasochistic overtones. Lizard, crocodile or snakeskin convey wealth and cold-bloodedness.

Sexual dress Certain dress styles send sexual signals. Tight or revealing clothes and spandex or fur all have sexual connotations.

Unbuttoned shirt

Fake animal fur

Tight trunks

Hipster skirt and crop top

Body Language

Although each courtship seems unique to the couple involved, it usually follows a ritualized pattern. In the initial, "attention-getting" phase, territory is established—a space in a room, for example. Exaggerated body movements announce presence and intent. For example, males swagger and laugh heartily and females stretch. As well as announcing desirability and availability, these actions also give the signal that it is safe for a potential partner to approach. Although it may seem as if the male initiates courtship, very often it is the female who actually makes the first move.

During the "recognition" phase, eye contact occurs, followed by "grooming" small talk. What is said is often less important than the intonation.

"Intention cues," such as leaning toward, or moving an arm or leg closer to, the other person, culminate in brief physical contact. Often initiated by the woman, this slight, gentle touch of a non-erogenous zone such as the shoulder is responded to with a smile or return touch that is equally subtle. Eventually, "body synchrony" occurs. The couple moves into a face-to-face position with the shoulders aligned, and their actions—for example, crossing or uncrossing legs, lifting a drink, or laughing—increasingly mirror each other.

Synchrony is a common feature of courtship and a way of expressing sexual intent. Dancing is a form of overt sexual synchrony, or even a prelude to sex itself. Sharing a meal or a drink is another example. Couples may eat in unison and pause to talk simultaneously. Eating is recognized as a sensual activity.

Mistakes or rebuffs during flirtation, such as avoiding eye contact, speaking sharply, saying too much or too little, flinching when touched or responding too hastily or slowly, can hamper the potential courtship.

Female flirtation signals
A woman may send signals of attraction with a range of facial expressions: widening the eyes, raising the eyebrows or drawing attention to her face in general. She may also signal attraction toward someone by smiling and touching her hair.

Signs of intimacy
Close body contact, gazing into the eyes and smiling to expose both top and bottom teeth indicate attraction and the desire to be intimate. Nervous gestures ("displacement activities"), such as rearranging clothes or hair, are unconscious attempts to dispel sexual tension.

Male flirtation signals
Men tend to signal attraction by a change in stance that draws attention to their height or stature. For example, common gestures of flirtation include thrusting the chest outward or pulling the body up to its full height to indicate dominance and physical strength.

FLIRTING AND BODY LANGUAGE

Flirtatious expressions transcend cultural boundaries. A woman smiling at her admirer swiftly lifts her eyebrows, opens her eyes wide, drops her eyelids, tilts her head down and to the side, and then gazes away, possibly touching her face with her hands. Similarly, the "eyebrow flash"—rapidly raising and lowering the eyebrows—is a universal sign of flirtation.

Both sexes employ the so-called copulatory gaze, gazing intently into the eyes of a potential mate. The pupils dilate, then the eyelids drop and the face is turned away. This is often followed by a "displacement activity," a nervous gesture such as touching the hair or straightening clothing, which is an unconscious way of dispelling the sexual tension.

FRAGRANCE

Smells are transmitted, via the olfactory nerve, directly to the brain's limbic system, which is involved in the control of sexual desire and long-term memory. Unlike other senses, the sense of smell is alert even during sleep. Certain smells can evoke intensely erotic feelings, and through smell people often relive events long after they occurred.

The body's own scent is a powerful perfume. Each person's scent is unique; glands in the armpits, around the nipples and in the groin become active at puberty and

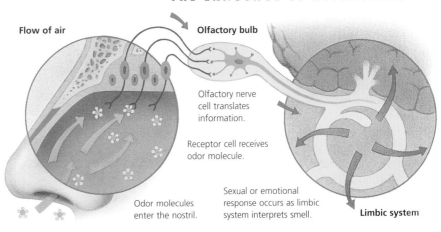

Flow of air
Olfactory bulb
Olfactory nerve cell translates information.
Receptor cell receives odor molecule.
Odor molecules enter the nostril.
Sexual or emotional response occurs as limbic system interprets smell.
Limbic system

release a special scent that is retained by the body hair. This scent contains pheromones, powerful chemical sexual signals that may work on an unconscious level (see page 44).

Some contemporary cultures, such as those of the U.S., Britain and Japan, find sweat and other body odors offensive and, ironically, use manufactured fragrances to conceal the natural ones that originally served as sexual signals. However, some people find the smell of fresh sweat appealing and arousing.

The word "perfume" derives from the Latin for "through smoke" and originally referred to the scents released during burnt offerings. The same perfume smells different on each person. People generally apply scent to the neck, chest or wrist, where body warmth increases the rate of evaporation.

The importance of fragrance Many people underestimate the importance of smell, but specific fragrances can evoke powerful feelings. Smell particles enter the nose and are translated into nervous impulses that travel straight to the limbic system—the part of the brain that controls emotional and sexual responses.

DECORATING THE BODY

Jewelry
Ornamenting the body with jewelry often draws attention to delicate or fragile body parts.

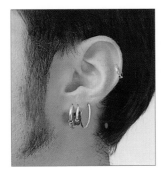

Piercing
Rings and studs that penetrate the skin are often worn on the body's erogenous zones.

Nail painting
Decorated nails symbolize leisure and wealth and may act as a signal of predatory sexuality.

Tattooing
This permanent form of body adornment suggests toughness and machismo.

ADORNING THE BODY

Long fingernails on a woman suggest that she does not do manual work and, by extension, symbolize leisure and affluence. Polished nails, which need frequent attention, reinforce this symbolism. Red nails hint at untamed sexuality, perhaps because they suggest the bloody claws of predatory animals.

In agricultural economies, where most people work outdoors, tanned skin is often considered lower-class and ugly, while pale skin tends to symbolize wealth and leisure. In more industrialized societies, where most people work indoors in office environments, a suntan, especially in winter, is considered alluring. Its desirability may also derive from the Western myth that darker-skinned races are more highly sexed. Current concerns over skin cancer and premature wrinkling, however, have led to a revised attitude toward sunbathing.

In the West, tattoos were traditionally an affectation of working-class men, particularly sailors. Today tattoos, especially small, discreet ones, are fashionable among women as well.

Jewelry

Traditionally, jewelry has carried connotations of social status, wealth and power, even though fake designer and costume jewelry can easily mislead.

People can convey their religious, political or sexual preferences simply by their choice and positioning of jewelry on the body or limbs. A woman's jewelry may also indicate her romantic history and act as a warning (or challenge) to potential admirers.

Jewelry can emphasize parts of the body with sexual connotations: delicate bracelets on slender ankles or wrists, for example; chains, necklaces or pendants against the skin of the chest; and chokers around the throat. For both sexes, earrings call attention to a common erogenous zone—the earlobes. Armlets or "slave bracelets" have connotations of submissiveness.

Pierced body parts hint at pain and sadomasochism, which some people find erotic. Because navel and nose piercing has become much more common than it used to be, it tends to be read as a fashion gesture rather than a serious erotic signal.

Makeup

A woman's style of makeup may indicate conformity to fashion—for example, the bee-stung mouths of the 1920s or the ghostly pale lips of the 1960s. Makeup can also be used as a statement of individual rebellion. However, the goal of most makeup remains to conceal imperfections and signs of aging and to emphasize and enhance attractive facial features.

Many cultures view large eyes as beautiful, and cosmetics are often used to draw attention to them and make them look bigger. Lipstick makes the mouth darker and fuller, possibly mimicking the vaginal lips. Blusher helps create an impression of flushed cheeks and smooth skin.

In the past, makeup was not produced exclusively for women, and today male skin-care products have once again become popular. They are marketed to suggest virility and physical prowess.

Feeding each other
Literally feeding
one's partner is a
courtship ritual that
may precede sex.

COURTSHIP FEEDING

Throughout the animal kingdom, a male animal will feed a female in return for anticipated sexual favors. For example, gorillas offer pieces of fruit to prospective mates. In Western culture, the "dinner date," for which the male traditionally pays, has primitive origins: the male is demonstrating his abilities as a provider to the female. When a man buys a woman an expensive meal as part of a date, there may be an assumption that sex will follow later. The relatively recent custom of sharing expenses reflects the evolving emphasis on equality between the sexes and the rejection of the gender division into provider and receiver.

The Physiology of Attraction

When someone feels strongly attracted to or infatuated with another person, he or she may experience a number of physical symptoms. Anxiety, excitability, sleeplessness, loss of appetite, lack of concentration and mood swings are all common.

The chemistry of the brain plays a key role in both the physical symptoms and the emotions of love. The limbic system (see page 117)—and especially the *HYPOTHALAMUS*, one of the earliest parts of this organ to evolve—is thought to be involved in controlling emotions and the capacity to love. When a person is infatuated, a chemical called phenylethylamine (PEA) floods the brain. For both men and women, this amphetamine-related compound triggers feelings of high energy, pleasure, excitement, giddiness and optimism. PEA also raises the metabolism and curbs the appetite. Levels of another neurotransmitter, dopamine, increase during periods of infatuation, and this results in intensified sexual desire. Levels of oxytocin, the so-called cuddle chemical, also increase.

The decline of infatuation influences brain chemicals as well. Usually within two years of the start of an infatuation, a group of opiate-like chemicals called endorphins are released by the brain to counteract high levels of PEA. Calming and anxiety-reducing, endorphins make a person feel relaxed and secure. Some people respond to this by craving the former levels of PEA to such an extent that they become "love addicts." To ensure that the elation of a PEA high is constantly repeated, love addicts tend to choose consistently unsuitable partners.

With counseling or therapy, the love addict may be able to understand the roots of his or her addiction—frequently traced to dynamics between the family members during childhood—and gradually to form healthier relationships.

PEA is found in certain natural substances, such as cocoa and rose water, which may explain why chocolates are a traditional romantic gift in the West, and Turkish delight, which is made using rose water, has a similar appeal in the East. PEA is also an ingredient of some diet drinks.

THE NERVOUS SYSTEM

The sympathetic nervous system is responsible for the reactions experienced by a person who is afraid or feels threatened: called the "fight or flight" response. This causes the heart and breathing rates to increase, which enables the person to run faster, exercise more muscle power and generally cope better with the threat, either through acts of aggression or by running away.

A similar thing happens when an individual experiences a strong physical attraction toward another. This results in symptoms similar to those associated with fear: a dry mouth, fluttering heart, clammy hands and butterflies in the stomach. The chemicals mostly responsible for these sensations are epinephrine and norepinephrine. These are released from the *ADRENAL GLANDS* and

◀ *Oxytocin This light micrograph shows crystals of oxytocin, a hormone released by the pituitary gland in the brain. Oxytocin levels increase when a person is infatuated.*

Sources of PEA The infatuation chemical — PEA—that floods the brain during the initial stages of a romance is also found in cocoa, rose water and rose petals.

Kissing During a ▶ *kiss, the heart rate increases, saliva is exchanged via the mouth and the first signs of sexual arousal in the genitals occur.*

nervous system and they act on specific body parts.

Lovesickness

At some point in their lives, most people suffer from feelings of deep or lingering sadness as a result of unobtainable, unrequited or terminated relationships. As with initial attraction and infatuation, there is probably a biological basis for this, such as chemical imbalances in the brain.

In some instances, unrequited infatuation can be so severe that doctors treat it as an obsessional disorder. The person cannot accept that his or her feelings are not reciprocated or that a relationship is over. In some such cases, doctors might prescribe an antidepressant drug that causes the levels of 5-hydroxytryptamine—a chemical naturally found in the brain—to increase, and this has been found to be helpful.

PHEROMONES

Before the physical symptoms of love can occur, one or both individuals must become attracted to the other. Sexual and emotional attraction involve a whole barrage of sig-

nals. These are primarily visual (the other person's appearance), auditory (the sound of his or her voice) and tactile (the feel of his or her body). But there are other, subtler forms of communication that are in operation at a primitive level: pheromones, or scent signals.

The role of human pheromones (from the Greek word "phero," meaning "to convey") in courtship has stimulated much debate, but at least some evidence exists for their occurrence in women. It has long been noticed that when females of childbearing age are in close proximity for several months at a time—for example, women soldiers in barracks or nurses living in a dormitory—the timing of their individual menstrual cycles slowly alters until they coincide. This may be due to pheromones.

In bygone eras, the ability to have synchronized menstrual cycles would have been highly advantageous, particularly for nomadic tribes. It would increase the likelihood that pregnancy and childbirth would also occur at the same time, and ensure that the youngest (and most vulnerable) off-

THE BODY'S RESPONSE TO ATTRACTION

Many of the sensations associated with attraction can be attributed to a network of nerve pathways called the sympathetic branch of the autonomic nervous system. This network of nerves is linked to the brain and hormone-releasing glands throughout the body, and is involved in some powerful emotional states. Messages about physical attraction passed via the nervous system cause the adrenal glands to produce epinephrine—this raises the heart and breathing rate, and blood pressure.

The sympathetic autonomic nervous system
This system prepares the body for stress or excitement. A chain of ganglia alongside the spinal cord relays messages to specific organs.

Epinephrine
These are magnified crystals of epinephrine, a hormone that makes people feel excited or "high."

Pupils dilate and mouth becomes dry as salivation is inhibited.

The heart rate speeds up—blood is pumped faster around the body.

The production of gastric juices in the stomach is inhibited.

Arousal occurs—the uterus rises and the vagina expands and lubricates.

spring would be at the same stage of development when it was time to move on. Because women cannot consciously alter their menstrual cycles, a plausible explanation for the change is that they are responding to pheromones. If so, humans may produce other smell signals, perhaps involved in sexual attraction.

Pheromone production in humans

Humans give off a highly individual odor that enables tracker dogs to follow the scent of one person and not be misled by the scent from others (apart from identical twins, who have exactly the same smell). This scent may also contain unique pheromones that people respond to unconsciously.

Human scent is produced by the apocrine glands. These glands are widely distributed in the fetus, but shortly before birth most are lost, with the exception of those found in the armpits, genital and anal areas, and the areolae around the nipples. The apocrine glands do not develop further until puberty, when they start to produce scent.

The secreted scent is milky and viscous and must be diluted before effective dispersal, mainly by sweat. An increase in sweating, which is a common reaction to sexual and emotional arousal, could well have evolved as a way of transmitting pheromones. The male sex hormones (see page 123) androsterone and androsterol have both been found in the underarm scent glands and may act as sexual attractors.

Pheromones may also be transferred by direct physical contact. During kissing, for example, an oily secretion from the mouth and lips called sebum may be exchanged. It is thought that sebum may have pheromonal properties.

Interpreting pheromones

How pheromones could influence the brain and make one person attractive to another is still unknown. Even if research proves that they do, they will almost certainly be only one facet of attraction, with auditory, visual and tactile signals playing a more important role in courtship.

LOVING FEELINGS	
PHYSICAL SENSATION	CAUSES
Dry mouth	Hormonal and nervous stimulation inhibits the salivary glands.
Fluttering heart	The heart is stimulated by the sympathetic nervous system.
Unsettled stomach and loss of appetite	Blood flow is diverted away from the digestive organs, and gut motility is reduced.
Sweating	Epinephrine increases perspiration from the palms, the soles of the feet and the groin.
Trembling	Epinephrine produces a rush of blood to the brain and muscles, causing muscle tremors.

Perhaps a combination of all of these signals is necessary to bring about the physiological response we call sexual attraction, possibly switching on special courtship genes. Each person may respond to a combination of stimuli that is unique to him or her, explaining why one individual appears highly attractive to one person but not necessarily to another.

Artificial pheromones

The role of pheromones has been widely examined in animals and insects. Moths, for example, have the ability to detect pheromone signals from a potential mate from many miles away. For hundreds of years, natural pheromones, extracted from animals' scent glands, have been added to perfumes in the hope that they will act as aphrodisiacs. It is now possible to buy pure, artificial pheromones, which are marketed as "mimicking naturally produced chemicals that make us attractive to the opposite sex." These can be added to commercially produced fragrances, but until more research has established the role of natural pheromones, the use of synthetic versions would seem to be an expensive hit-or-miss experiment.

◀ *Identical twins*
Everyone's pheromone scent is unique, except in the case of identical twins, who share the same smell.

Moths
Moths are able to detect pheromone signals from a mate from many miles away.

Finding a Partner

Much thought, discussion and business focuses on the ways in which individuals may meet compatible sexual partners. Many people meet their partners through peer groups or jobs. Others find partners through dating services or personal ads.

Older people As ▶ *people age, they may find it difficult to meet prospective partners. Specially organized vacations have provided a good way for many older people to meet others.*

Searching for a partner A few people go to dating services to meet a partner, but the majority of people meet others through contact in a social, religious, professional or educational environment.

Searching for a special person with whom to share the emotional side of life can be a compelling impulse, regardless of age or culture. The ways in which people set about finding a suitable partner vary tremendously.

MEETING PEOPLE THROUGH FRIENDS

Relationships often begin with an introduction through friends. Since friends tend to have the same values and interests, their acquaintances are likely to share a common outlook. Friends may also have a good understanding of each other's expectations of a partner and be able to assess possible candidates from among relatives, colleagues, neighbors or friends.

Introductions through friends can happen in a number of ways. Sometimes they occur purely by chance or through a joint invitation to a social event, such as a dinner party or concert. Alternatively, they may occur more formally through a blind date. Each arrangement has its own advantages and disadvantages. Meeting a potential partner in the presence of friends can make both people feel safe or it can make them feel under scrutiny.

A blind date that goes wrong can feel like a failure, but it has the advantage of having no observers.

Introductions by friends or relatives are associated with their own unique problems. The partners may be tempted to use the mutual friend as a source of information about the other's past history and character. This can place stress on the friendship and give rise to a difficult dynamic among all three people. If only one person wants to pursue a relationship, the rejected partner may hold the mutual friend responsible, which also produces tension.

CASUAL MEETINGS

Potential partners may meet for the first time in a highly selective situation. College alumni groups, professional associations, gyms or clubs, for example, bring together people with common interests. Meeting regularly in such an environment opens opportunities for friendships and relationships to develop naturally. In semi-selective situations, such as libraries, bookstores, museums, galleries and religious services, people may also meet through a shared interest.

Potential partners may meet casually on public transportation or in supermarkets, laundromats, bars or nightclubs—places that have little, if any, selective context. Such meetings may seem romantic, but they often develop into short-term sexual liaisons rather than long-lasting relationships. People may also meet on vacation. While such romances can seem appealing, meeting someone in an alluring setting a long way from home, without all the usual

In a work environment

At high school or college

Common ways to meet potential partners

Through friends or family

At an association, club, church or religious activity

Chance meetings at a bar or other public place

constraints, can make the relationship seem more attractive than it actually is and carry it further than good sense would dictate.

With new acquaintances, striking a balance between approachability and personal safety is important. Women may prefer to meet a new date for the first time in a public place, have transportation home already arranged and give a work rather than a home telephone number.

Private party/
social club/gym

Work

School

Elsewhere

Bar/personal
ad/vacation

Church

MEETING AT WORK

The workplace is a well-established venue for meeting potential partners. Long-term, close contact and a common purpose allow friendships to develop gradually. Working with a colleague with whom a good relationship is developing can even enhance professional performance.

Conversely, having to continue working with a colleague when the relationship is stormy or has ended can be embarrassing or depressing and can adversely affect work performance. Because of this, some companies are reluctant to employ two people who are in a sexual relationship, and many companies in the U.S. and Canada have rules against dating coworkers.

A romance between people on different rungs of the professional ladder—for example, boss and secretary, or doctor and nurse—can put the job of the junior employee (often the woman) at risk if the relationship ends. Problems are easier to avoid if the relationship exists between colleagues

from different departments, if one partner works on a part-time basis or if the couple manage to maintain a strictly nonsexual relationship at work.

Some professions, such as construction, are predominantly male, while others, such as elementary school teaching, tend to be female. Although stereotypes are changing and gender biases are called more into question, such imbalances still exist and can reduce the chances of heterosexuals meeting a potential partner.

SINGLES EVENINGS AND EVENTS

Social occasions for single people range from the highly selective, such as those run by an educational organization, to the relatively nonselective—for example, singles evenings in a bar. The less selective the group, the less likely a person is to find potential partners with similar backgrounds, attitudes and goals.

Some singles events, such as sightseeing tours or concerts, are open to all unattached adults; others are intended for particular age groups or for specific religious or ethnic groups. While many events are advertised, others may require an invitation. Events range from intimate gatherings to large crowds. They may last less than an hour or, in the case of vacations, days or weeks. While some events are free, others are very expensive, meaning that the high cost acts as a selective factor.

Where do people meet partners? The most frequent ways for couples to meet in the U.S. and Canada are through school or work or at a social occasion such as a party or a club function. A sizable percentage of people, however, meet outside the categories listed above.

◀ *Lunch dates First dates—whether blind dates, introductions through dating services or meetings with a new acquaintance—are invariably loaded occasions. The rising popularity of lunchtime meetings may be due to the relative informality of this kind of date.*

Graduation day
Graduating from school may mean leaving education behind, but many people sustain the relationships that they form in high school or college. Educational environments are highly selective, meaning that there is a high chance of meeting compatible partners.

Events that simply showcase potential partners can feel artificial or even desperate, especially when the women outnumber the men. In cases like these, attending with a supportive friend or avoiding events that do not have an easy escape route (such as singles vacations) can offset awkwardness. Singles events that have an additional purpose, such as conservation work or gourmet dining, may be more comfortable.

DATING SERVICES
The growth of dating services reflects the increasing tendency of people to move away from their place of origin, to relocate frequently, to spend more time at work and less time at leisure, and to postpone marriage until well into their twenties or later. It also reflects the high proportion of unattached women compared with unattached men—an imbalance that increases with age.

Dating services may be local or nationwide, and some deal only with specific groups. Agencies usually match people based on information provided by detailed questionnaires or in-depth personal interviews. Some also make videos of their clients. Agencies usually guarantee to arrange a specific number of dates.

Lunch-dating services, which organize a set number of business-lunch blind dates, are a relatively new but successful phenomenon. Because such arrangements provide short, daytime contacts, they allow the diners to meet in an informal way and either disengage gracefully or agree to meet again.

The services of marriage brokers, matrimonial specialists or human-relationship specialists cost more. Staffed by trained psychologists or social workers with national or even international contacts, these services help clients improve their social skills, self-confidence and appearance before arranging introductions.

IN THE PAST
In Western cultures today, people have many avenues to meet partners. Until recent decades, however, people tended to settle close to their families and places of birth and to meet and marry those who lived nearby—often people within a mile of home. Limited opportunities for educational and professional advancement meant that people tended to continue in their parents' lifestyles and occupations and to marry partners from similar backgrounds.

Religion played a more important role than it typically does today, and many couples who later married first met at their shared place of worship. Because cultural, ethnic and racial boundaries were more clearly delineated, few people chose a partner beyond these boundaries. The opinion of parents and family carried more weight than personal attraction, and relatives would take an active role in matchmaking, arranged marriages being an extreme example. Placing an advertisement for a partner was almost unheard of.

Internet dating ▶
This couple met and fell in love as a result of communicating on the Internet, a worldwide system of interconnected computers. As more people gain access to the Internet, the number of couples meeting in this way will increase.

Homosexual Love

Homosexuality is sexual attraction between people of the same sex. The word derives from the Greek "homos"—same—and the Latin "sexualis"—sexual. The words "gay" and "lesbian" are more widely used today.

Experimentation with same-sex play is a normal part of the sexual development of most boys and girls both before and during puberty. By the time they reach adulthood, most individuals have developed a clear idea of their sexual orientation, with the majority becoming heterosexual. Sometimes homosexual activity occurs in situations in which otherwise heterosexual individuals are deprived of regular contact with members of the opposite sex, most commonly among long-term prisoners. This form of behavior also occurs, but usually less widely, in institutions such as boys' schools and in the armed forces, where single-sex groups are in close confinement for long periods of time.

GAY SOCIETY

As a result of legal restrictions and the widespread social disapproval that still exists toward public displays of affection between members of the same sex, many homosexuals have formed their own separate social network from which heterosexuals are largely excluded. Information on the gay community travels by word of mouth, through the gay press and on the Internet.

Most cities and large towns have formal or informal places for gay men and women to meet, either for purely social contact or specifically to pursue potential sexual relationships. Gay bars and clubs, parks, beaches, restaurants, public baths, and gyms all serve as gathering spots.

Many homosexuals will readily admit their sexual orientation and the full and open part they play in the gay community. Sometimes they will also express defiance of the heterosexual world. Not everyone is vocal: some people, particularly those in the public eye, present a heterosexual persona in public (some may be married with children) but have homosexual relationships in secret. Their reticence is often due to a fear of social disapproval, job loss and violence.

Gays and their supporters have made a concerted effort in recent years to encourage society to develop a more tolerant attitude toward homosexuality. They have worked to eliminate discriminatory legislation against gay people and also to remove laws that criminalize homosexual activities between two consenting adult men or women.

As part of this process, gay rights activists encourage secretive homosexuals to openly acknowledge their sexual orientation, or "come out of the closet." In a process which is known as "outing," some of the more militant activists have taken to publicizing the

◀ *Homosexuality in the past Ancient artifacts depicting homosexuality suggest that it may have been widely accepted in some cultures.*

San Francisco This city is renowned for its established gay community and liberal attitudes toward homosexuality.

THE GAY GENE

Dean H. Hamer's research into the genetic cause of homosexuality discovered that a small area known as Xq28 at the tip of the X chromosome, inherited from the mother, was shared by 33 out of 40 pairs of gay brothers. A random sample of 314 other pairs of brothers, with about 2 percent assumed to be homosexual, did not show the same link. This would seem to suggest that the chromosomal region Xq28 contains a gene that influences male sexual orientation.

Dean H. Hamer
One of the pioneer researchers into the biological roots of homosexuality, Hamer has also researched the role of genes in complex medical conditions, including the progression of HIV and Kaposi's sarcoma.

The role of the fruit ▶ fly Experiments using this species have resulted in important genetic discoveries, including the isolation of a gene that may affect sexuality.

homosexuality of celebrities and people in the public eye whom they believe to be falsely claiming to be heterosexual. Many homosexual people feel that this highly controversial move only intensifies the social climate of fear and hostility that homosexuals have traditionally had to face. Moderate gays believe that each individual should make their own personal decision about whether or not to live openly as a homosexual.

WHAT MAKES SOMEONE GAY?

Modern society used to take the view that homosexuality is a psychological disorder and that homosexuals cannot lead as satisfactory lives as heterosexuals. As a result, attempts have been made to change or modify homosexual behavior with a range of psychological techniques. Among these techniques are psychoanalysis, aversion therapy, desensitization and group therapy. Even sex therapists Masters and Johnson (see page 257) wrote in the 1970s that, although

they no longer thought homosexuality was a disease, they could "cure" it in a matter of weeks. Attempts to change the sexual orientation of homosexual men in this way have consistently failed to work and have been widely criticized on ethical grounds.

The Canadian Psychiatric Association never listed homosexuality as a disorder, but many professionals were influenced by U.S. attitudes. It was not until 1974 that homosexuality was deleted from the American Psychiatric Association's list of psychiatric conditions, and only in the late 1980s did the World Health Organization follow suit. This perception of homosexuality as a disorder has led to medical research for underlying causes for homosexuality.

Brain differences

In 1994 Dr. Simon LeVay, the American scientist who founded the Institute of Gay and Lesbian Education, published research that claimed to show that there might be a provable biological basis for homosexuality. LeVay studied a group of cells, known as INAH3, that are found near the front of the *HYPOTHALAMUS* in the brain. It has already been established that this group of cells is twice as large in men as in women, but LeVay produced evidence to show that there also may be a size difference in INAH3 between straight and gay men.

LeVay studied the brains of 19 gay men who had died of AIDS and 16 heterosexual men, 6 of whom had also died of AIDS. INAH3 turned out to be between two and three times as large in heterosexual men as it was in gay men, regardless of the cause of death. Statistical analysis of LeVay's results suggests that the probability of this happening by chance was about one in a thousand.

Inheriting sexuality

Other studies, which appear to back up the work of both Dean H. Hamer (see box) and LeVay as to physiological and genetic factors that may influence sexual orientation, have examined the family trees of gay men and lesbians. The combined results of these studies show that 50 percent of the women who were identical twins shared their sister's sexual orientation; among male twins the figure was

57 percent. Among siblings, the percentage of gay people who had a gay brother or sister was 16 percent. The fact that identical twins—who have the same genetic makeup—more often share the same sexual orientation than nonidentical siblings lends some weight to the genetic arguments. It is important to bear in mind, however, that if sexual orientation were determined solely by a person's genes, identical twins would always share the same sexuality—something that has been shown to be untrue.

Can hormones cause homosexuality?

Since the discovery of hormones and their influence on human sexual characteristics, researchers have explored the possibility of a hormonal basis for homosexuality. The first theory proposed by experts was that the level of male and female hormones in adulthood determined sexuality, but this has since been rejected.

More recent theories suggest that fetal exposure to hormones may be important. Exposure to high levels of androgens (male hormones) before birth may lead to heterosexuality in men and homosexuality in women. Conversely, low fetal androgen levels may lead to homosexuality in men and heterosexuality in women. Researchers in this field have drawn the majority of their conclusions from observing the mating behavior of laboratory rats which have been exposed to various levels of sex hormones before birth.

Some studies seem to indicate that the level of hormones present in homosexuals differs from the levels present in heterosexuals. However, while it is well known that physical sexual characteristics such as body hair and fat distribution can be changed by the injection of sex hormones, little evidence shows that sexual orientation can be altered in this way.

Although there are large sections of the scientific community who find the arguments for a biological basis for homosexuality compelling, there remains relatively little consensus about what causes homosexual behavior.

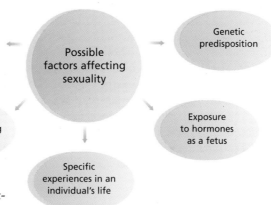

Social conditioning toward a particular sexuality

Possible factors affecting sexuality

Genetic predisposition

Style of parenting

Exposure to hormones as a fetus

Specific experiences in an individual's life

The cause of homosexuality There is little consensus on what factors contribute to sexuality, and many gay and lesbian people feel no need to find a "cause" for their sexual preferences, but the range of possibilities has been the subject of much research.

WHY RESEARCH HOMOSEXUALITY?

Opinions in the lesbian and gay community are sharply divided about the benefits of proving a biological basis for sexual orientation. Early gay activists in the U.S., Canada and the U.K. asked why lesbians and gay men should have the causes of their sexual orientation explored in a way that heterosexuals never would. They argued that if a gene exists for homosexuality, comparable, say, to that for cystic fibrosis, it is theoretically possible to eradicate that gay gene just as scientists believe they will be able to eliminate genes that cause disease.

Another argument against research into biological causes is that parents who discover that their unborn child carries a gene

THE GAY BRAIN

Simon LeVay's research into the anatomy of the brain has revealed that there may be a difference between the brains of heterosexual men and the brains of homosexual men. An area known as INAH3 near the front of the hypothalamus may be significantly smaller in gay men.

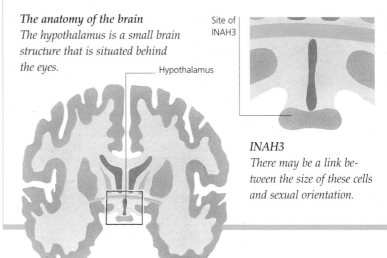

The anatomy of the brain
The hypothalamus is a small brain structure that is situated behind the eyes.

Hypothalamus

Site of INAH3

INAH3
There may be a link between the size of these cells and sexual orientation.

marker that would predispose him or her to homosexuality could, in theory, use this information to justify abortion of the fetus.

The opposing argument suggests that if sexual orientation is inborn, just as are skin color and other physical traits, lesbians and gay men indisputably deserve equal treatment under the law. It also undermines the assumption that homosexuality is a matter of individual choice and therefore can be treated or reversed.

Psychosocial theories

During the early part of the 20th century, sexual orientation was viewed as clear-cut: a person was either heterosexual or homosexual. Sigmund Freud (1856–1939), the Austrian founder of psychoanalysis, theorized that homosexuality is "a variation of the sexual function, produced by a certain arrest of sexual development."

Freud believed that human nature was fundamentally bisexual and that although most people exhibit heterosexual behavior, they repress homosexual desires that exist in their subconscious. Similarly, the "germs of heterosexuality" are present in every homosexual person. He proposed that sexual orientation develops as a result of an individual's life experiences, so that family and social factors ultimately determine whether an individual's "latent homosexuality" becomes evident or remains hidden.

Another theory of homosexuality concentrates on styles of parenting. The "overbearing mother/absent father" theory suggests that boys grow up to be homosexual if their relationship with their mother is too close, if they grow up without a father or if the father does not provide a strong enough heterosexual role model. The highly controversial German psychiatrist Richard von Krafft-Ebing claimed that boys who prefer "girls' games" or dress in "girls' clothing" will grow up to be homosexual. This idea is now almost completely discredited.

Theories such as these assume that certain characteristics and social behaviors are gender-specific and that children must be taught to follow these as rules. These theories also depend on the stereotypes of the effeminate gay man and the masculine or "butch" lesbian, ignoring the wide range of characteristics and identities found within the lesbian and gay community.

LESBIANISM

Derived from the name of the Greek island Lesbos, which was legendary in the ancient world for its female homosexuality, the word "lesbianism" refers to sexual relations between women. This activity has long been one of society's ultimate taboos, more so than male homosexuality, but in recent years social attitudes toward lesbianism have shifted. The so-called lipstick lesbian—young, usually white, fashionably dressed and well groomed—has replaced the masculine-looking gym teacher as the image of female homosexuality in the popular imagination.

Feminism may have allowed more women to explore their sexual options, but, ironically, it is in the era of post-feminism that large numbers of young women have "come out" as lesbians. An examination of the mass media during the 1990s might lead to the conclusion that there are more lesbians than ever before. Some famous actresses and musicians have publicly affirmed that they are lesbians, and glossy magazines now realize that lesbianism sells.

Can We Talk About It?

DISCUSSING SEXUALITY

For parents, accepting that a son or daughter is homosexual may seem like an impossible request. As a result, a gay child may put off telling their parents because they fear a negative reaction or rejection. Many people believe that homosexuality is a psychological problem, possibly brought about by a failure in their parenting. They may feel guilty, have strong moral or religious objections or simply fear for a child living with society's prejudices. They may also resent the fact that their child is less likely to produce grandchildren. A gay child may have to educate parents about what being gay or lesbian means, but attempting to communicate can be fruitful in the end.

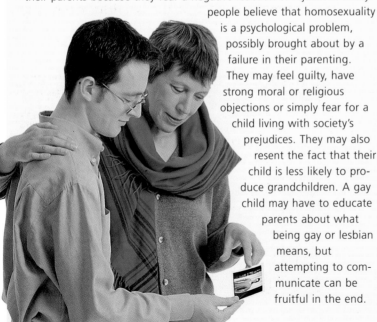

But it remains impossible to obtain an accurate figure for the percentage of women who identify themselves as lesbian. As with male homosexuality, sexual activity and identity are not always the same thing, and not all women who have sex with women are exclusively homosexual.

Theories of lesbianism

In comparison with the burgeoning field of research into male homosexuality, little scientific interest has been shown in the potential causes of lesbianism. Some women are never interested in men as sexual partners, while others experiment with heterosexual sex before settling into a pattern of lesbian relationships. Social expectations can make it difficult for women to resist marriage and motherhood, and some women with lesbian inclinations do not begin to form sexual relationships with other women until their thirties, forties or later.

In the 1970s a commitment to political lesbianism led some women to enter sexual relationships with other women. Rather than being motivated by sexual preference, this may have been an extension of a feminist rejection of men and patriarchal values.

One psychosocial theory of lesbianism states that traumatic experiences with men, such as rape or sexual abuse, can cause women to "turn into lesbians" as a way of avoiding men. Most lesbians would say, however, that men are irrelevant in their choice of sexual partner: they don't hate men; they simply prefer women.

HOW MANY PEOPLE ARE GAY?

No consensus exists about how many adults have had some kind of homosexual experience. Alfred Kinsey's surveys, *Sexual Behavior in the Human Male and Female*, conducted in the 1940s and 1950s in the U.S., revolutionized attitudes toward sexual orientation by suggesting a 7-point scale ranging from 0 (solely heterosexual) to 6 (solely homosexual) with 3—the midpoint—representing bisexuality (sexual relationships with both genders). According to Kinsey, 75 percent of men and 85 percent of women are solely heterosexual; 2 percent of men and 1 percent of women are solely homosexual; and 23 percent of men and 14 percent of women have had a combination of heterosexual and homosexual experiences.

In their study *Evidence for a Biological Influence in Male Homosexuality*, Simon LeVay and Dean H. Hamer state that current estimates for homosexuality range between 1 and 5 percent of the population. They point out, however, that these figures represent only those who are exclusively attracted to members of their own sex.

All these figures can be manipulated for the purposes of those who are quoting them; certainly the number of adults who have had some kind of homosexual experience is greater than the number of adults

Behavior only
Self-identification only
Desire and behavior
Desire and self-identification
Desire, behavior and self-identification
Behavior and self-identification
Desire only

Defining gay feelings
Among those who express gay sexual feelings, the majority desire same-gender sex but do not act on it ('desire'), others act on this desire ('behavior'), and some openly identify themselves as gay ('self-identification'). There is also overlap between these groups.

HOMOSEXUALITY IN OTHER CULTURES

In non-Western societies, particularly Islamic ones, men can have sex with other men without being perceived as gay. Homosexual sex is simply a pleasurable pastime that does not reflect upon an individual's sexuality (in fact, it may have more to do with the inaccessibility of women). The practice of young boys—known as pleasure boys—working as male prostitutes is widespread in countries such as Pakistan.

Homosexuality in Pakistan
Cinemas showing pornography are also popular places for men to pick up other men. These men would be unlikely to define themselves as gay.

Gay festivals ▶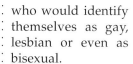
Carnivals, marches, parades and festivals form part of the annual gay calendar in many Western countries. Some of these events are highly politicized; others, such as this one, are fun events that are celebrations of camp exhibitionism.

Gay weddings *Long-term gay lovers may wish to show their commitment formally, although homosexual marriages are still not legally recognized in many countries.*

who would identify themselves as gay, lesbian or even as bisexual.

While not every country openly accepts homosexuality, many do recognize that it exists. For example, some tribes in rural Africa recognize female "husbands"—women who provide other women with the economic support traditionally associated with men. In societies that are intolerant of homosexuality, people may have sex with same-sex partners yet also bow to cultural expectations and marry and have children.

Some bisexuals claim that they are doubly discriminated against: by heterosexual society for having gay relationships, and by lesbian and gay society for being uncommitted, undecided or just too cowardly to come out. Many bisexuals, however, say that their sexual orientation is simply due to a need for greater variety in their sexual relationships.

TRANSVESTISM

A transvestite is someone who takes erotic pleasure in wearing clothes that are associated with the opposite sex (cross-dressing). Because it is more socially acceptable for women to adopt male-style clothing, the term is generally applied to men only. Many transvestites are heterosexual men who enjoy conventional sexual relations with women. Sometimes they are married men whose partners cooperate with their cross-dressing.

For some people, however, cross-dressing is more than just a sexual fetish. Living and dressing as a member of the opposite sex is a fundamental part of their sexual identity and may precede gender reassignment surgery (sex-change operations).

Among gay men, cross-dressing is known as dressing in "drag" and may have nothing to do with transvestism or transsexualism. It has been a popular form of entertainment for centuries. In the U.K., especially, the character of the pantomime "dame," played by a man (not necessarily a homosexual) in a woman's dress and wearing garish makeup, is an enduring part of traditional entertainment.

TRANSSEXUALS

Some people grow up with an overwhelming sensation that they are trapped in a body of the wrong gender and feel that they can live a satisfactory life only if they "change sex." The most radical way to achieve this is to have gender reassignment surgery. In order to qualify for this surgery, an individual must convince a psychiatrist that personal dissatisfaction with the gender they were born with is genuine. The individual is required to dress, live and work assuming the new gender role for a period of two years.

For female-to-male transsexuals, gender reassignment surgery can include removal of the breasts and the female reproductive organs and, in some cases, construction of a penis from vaginal and clitoral skin, and muscle and skin from the forearm. People who have undergone this type of surgery must take male hormones for the rest of their lives in order to maintain muscle bulk, facial and body hair, and deeper voices.

For male-to-female transsexuals, surgery can include CASTRATION, construction of a vagina using tissue from the penis, and breast implants. Female hormones inhibit the growth of facial and body hair and allow the voice to rise in pitch and sound more feminine.

Once gender reassignment surgery has taken place, the individual may receive documents identifying him or her by a chosen new name, although such documents do not include a gender-specific title such as Miss, Ms., Mrs. or Mr.

The Problems of Being in Love

The experience of falling in love can be one of the most exhilarating experiences that life has to offer. Few, if any, relationships flow completely smoothly, though. Negotiations, compromises and communication are always necessary.

Every relationship has its own evolution, and understanding the difficulties that occur at each stage can make them more manageable.

EMOTIONAL DISHONESTY

The ability to distinguish truth from lies is part of a healthy child's psychological development. Once that distinction is understood, children and adults may continue to lie from many conscious or subconscious motives—greed, pride, vengeance, the need to impress or even kindness. Adults are often motivated to lie by the fear that the truth will bring consequences too painful to endure for the liar, the deceived or both. In a relationship this fear can usually be summed up as: "If my partner really understood the truth about me, I would no longer be loved."

This fear may be realistic, it may reflect low self-esteem or it may result from a perception of the world as a dangerous, hostile, unloving place (a view that many carry with them from childhood). Lying as a defense mechanism is often well established by adulthood, and the intense emotions and pressures of a new romantic love may make lying especially tempting.

Conscious lying involves deliberately presenting falsehood as the truth. In specific psychotic conditions, the mind's reality-testing mechanisms are known to be impaired, and the individual may actually believe his or her own lies. Most people, however, are fully aware that they are lying, although for some people it is a deeply ingrained habit and feels like second nature. The subtlest type of lies are those that offer a degree of truth while withholding potentially painful information. These sorts of lies may take a tiny kernel of truth and exaggerate it.

A relationship in which two people hold wildly different perceptions of the same shared experience also presents problems. Each person's perception of the relationship becomes "the truth," but it does not match the other's view of it. When one partner finds out that the other does not exactly reciprocate his or her feelings, accusations of lying may well follow. Although neither person tells explicit lies, the lack of communication makes the partners view their relationship as dishonest.

Reasons for lying
People rarely lie gratuitously. Often lies are told to protect another person. Alternatively, the person telling the lie suffers from low self-esteem and fears negative consequences of self-disclosure.

Lying is a way of concealing horrible aspects of myself.

I am so accustomed to lying that I cannot stop.

The truth is too embarrassing.

I have to lie to avoid hurting my partner.

If I tell the truth, my partner will reject me.

Persistent lying can gradually destroy a relationship and should be perceived as a shared problem, whether both partners lie or one is the perpetrator and the other the "victim." Exploring the reasons why the lied-to partner tolerates dishonesty and remains in the relationship can be helpful.

INFIDELITY

Although not all cultures regard fidelity as important, it is a fundamental requirement of marriage in Christian, Jewish and Islamic religions. In the West, the impact of infidelity varies from minimal to devastating, depending on the circumstances in which it occurs, the length and nature of the relationship with the third party, and the attitudes held by the couple. If infidelity occurs during the romantic, infatuation phase of a relationship, it may well indicate emotional immaturity and an inability to sacrifice sexual freedom for trust and commitment.

Infidelity during the course of a long-established relationship is often a symptom of other problems. It may develop out of emotional or sexual boredom, communication breakdown, gradually diverging lives,

SEXUAL JEALOUSY
Biological impulses for jealousy in both sexes

Male jealousy to ensure that the children he supports are fathered by him

Female jealousy to ensure that her children are supported by a father

Low self-esteem leads to fear of rivals for partner's affection.

He may express possessiveness toward partner aggressively.

She may demand more intimacy and reassurance of affection.

He may abandon relationship to regain self-esteem.

She is more likely to attempt to resolve jealousy but may become obsessive.

sexual problems or a "midlife crisis" in which both men and women face the apparent waning of their own sexuality and seek reaffirmation of their worth. Infidelity can be based purely on physical pleasure, or strong emotional bonds may develop and threaten the primary relationship.

JEALOUSY AND POSSESSIVENESS

Jealousy is a form of anxiety that arises primarily out of insecurity. In relationships, it usually takes the form of suspicion about a partner's affection for a perceived rival. Biologists argue that male jealousy helps to ensure that the offspring he protects and supports were fathered by him. Female jealousy ensures that the man who fathered her children concentrates his energy on supporting and protecting them.

Jealous feelings can range from a slight twinge to an obsession. Jealousy may be appropriate if a genuine rival exists, but sometimes low self-esteem and a sense of inadequacy can make a person imagine rivals where they do not exist. Often the jealous partner needs constant reassurance

Can We Talk About It?

DEALING WITH JEALOUSY

If one partner is jealous, choose an appropriate time to discuss it—not within earshot of children, when you are angry or when time is limited. Find out why your partner feels jealous or explain why you are feeling jealous. If the jealousy centers around a specific person, discuss whether he or she presents a real or imagined threat. If the threat is real, talk about the changes that you and your partner can make to reduce the sense of threat. If the jealousy is irrational—fear of a faithful partner being seduced by a stranger in a bar, for example—it can be helpful to explore both partners' relationship histories, since possessiveness often forms a common theme in previous failed relationships. This tendency to reenact destructive behavior is known as a repetition compulsion. People subconsciously choose a partner who, sooner or later, confirms their fears. Professional counseling may be the best course of action.

from his or her partner and demands ever more commitment and affection. Ironically, these demands may discourage intimacy and eventually lead the other person to seek consolation with another partner, so giving a real cause for jealousy. Jealousy is common among people with dependency problems such as alcoholism—they often display unfounded or paranoid fears that their partner is betraying them.

Jealousy and possessiveness are neither the basis for a healthy relationship nor a measure of love. Just as possessive parents cannot allow their children to gain independence, some people cannot allow their partners to have separate identities, interests and friendships. A partner's colleagues and friends, and any time spent apart, are seen as threatening. Jealousy and possessiveness are usually accompanied by a lack of self-esteem and trust, perhaps reflecting earlier childhood experiences of disappointment and rejection. Both sexes experience jealousy, but women more often try to resolve the problem, while men tend to leave a relationship, often in an attempt to save face and repair self-esteem. Jealous men also tend to resort to violence. In the U.S., male jealousy is the most commonly reported cause of spousal violence and homicide; in Canada, it is one of the most common types of emotional abuse reported by women.

OBSESSIVE LOVE

Obsession is a form of anxiety in which persistent, repetitive thoughts, feelings or ideas dominate a person's consciousness. The person seems possessed or consumed by their obsession, sometimes despite knowing that it is having a destructive effect on their life.

Unlike other obsessions, such as hygiene, money or violence, obsessive love for another person may seem to possess superficially romantic, noble or heroic overtones. Any type of obsession, however, prevents the development of a realistic,

healthy, long-term relationship and can also deplete the time, energy and motivation normally given to such other aspects of life as work or physical health.

Obsession reflects the mental state of the obsessed person more than any inherent worth of the loved one, who is usually idealized. In fact, the object of the obsession, when assessed realistically, may be a totally unsuitable choice of partner. The obsessed person projects his or her needs and fantasies onto the beloved rather than genuinely understanding or being interested in him or her as a person.

Jealousy, possessiveness and obsession are feelings that often go together. Individuals who repeatedly experience these types of extreme emotions may be lonely or emotionally immature and therefore unable to sustain real adult relationships. Obsessive behavior may be treated with counseling or, in some cases, with specific antidepressants prescribed by a medical doctor.

COMMUNICATION BREAKDOWN

Partners in a relationship need to take responsibility for and clearly communicate their feelings, whether positive or negative. Suppressing one's feelings may avoid trouble in the short term, but is likely to exacerbate problems in the long term. Ironically, a nonverbal individual and a very articulate person may actually attract one another, but over a period of time such incompatibility can lead to frustration.

Being emotionally articulate is often harder for men than

Shakespeare's **Othello** *Othello provides a famous literary example of extreme obsession that at first seems to be a manifestation of romance but develops into violence.*

◀ *Edward and Mrs. Simpson Love can inspire extravagant gestures. In 1936 King Edward of the United Kingdom of Great Britain and Ireland gave up the throne to marry Mrs. Wallis Warfield Simpson, an American divorcée.*

How anger builds up
Many people find communicating about painful emotional issues difficult. Poorly expressed feelings can be counterproductive and lead to arguments or even violence.

Individual feels hurt or resentful toward partner.

Individual attempts to express resentment.

Discussion degenerates into angry recriminations, and both partners feel discouraged about being open.

Partner feels that he or she is being attacked or criticized.

Both people feel that they are not being listened to.

Partner responds defensively.

for women. Both sexes, however, find it difficult to communicate feelings that are confusing, ambivalent or only partially understood. An individual who comes from a family where feelings were rarely expressed will almost always have even greater difficulty. For example, saying "I'm sorry" to a partner can be virtually impossible if childhood experience taught that apologizing was dangerous. In addition, some families communicate by shouting and interrupting, a pattern that can be quite hard to break.

Intelligence does not guarantee good communication. A highly intelligent but emotionally troubled person, for example, may expect a partner to understand without having to be told, rather like an infant's expectations of his or her mother. Alternatively, people may constantly talk at cross-purposes, creating a deliberate smoke screen of confusion that serves as a defense against self-disclosure.

Poor communication can be self-perpetuating, as more and more bitter quarrels develop from a cyclical buildup of tension, irritation, anger and resentment. Quarrels about a variety of subjects are often about one underlying theme, such as lack of trust or envy. When a person is consistently frustrated with the apparent ineffectiveness of verbal communication, he or she may ultimately resort to violence.

A number of keys to good communication exist: for example, sticking to the issue at hand rather than bringing in other unresolved issues; setting an appropriate time and place to talk; and allowing each partner to have several minutes of uninterrupted speech. Each partner should acknowledge and value the other's nonverbal communication, such as body language and actions. Many men, for example, find it easier to express affection through practical actions than through words.

ONE-SIDED RELATIONSHIPS

Although the intensity of a couple's feelings varies naturally during the course of any relationship, a healthy long-term relationship has roughly equal input from both partners. The less equally the partners contribute passion, intimacy and commitment, the more unrealistic and vulnerable a relationship becomes.

Obsessive relationships are one-sided from the start. Unrequited love, in which one person deliberately pursues another despite obvious rejection, is another extreme example. Often mistaken for true love, the pursuit of an unrequited love may actually be a defense against the expected or feared disappointments of a real reciprocal relationship. A person pursuing such a relationship experiences extreme preoccupation, panic, despair and eventual detachment—intense feelings resembling those of an infant deprived of his or her mother.

Adolescents frequently choose one-sided relationships again and again, often as a safe means of flirting. In adulthood, such choices may be a sign of emotional immaturity. Adults who prefer to relate in this way typically suffer low self-esteem and a history of unequal or unrequited love. Some theories suggest that a predisposition to pursue doomed attachments is caused by a biochemical imbalance. Although some men form such fruitless relationships, the vast majority are formed by women. Many women's self-help books focus on this potentially damaging phenomenon.

Long-term relationships that were once equally valued by both partners can also become imbalanced. One partner may retain genuine feelings of closeness and commitment, while the other loses them. The partner whose commitment remains strong may feel angry and betrayed by the partner whose commitment has waned. Counseling may help in these situations.

BREAKING UP

A relationship may end suddenly and traumatically, but more often it gradually erodes or simply never achieved emotional health in the first place. Endings that are mutually agreed on tend to be the least painful. Unfortunately, these are a minority.

In many cultures, infidelity is the main reason for the breakup of a marriage. But there are many other common causes for the failure of both marriages and relationships as well: sexual rejection; physical cruelty, particularly by the man; alcohol or drug abuse; frequent arguments; sexual jealousy; irresponsible behavior; nagging; laziness;

the breakdown of communication; and boredom.

A person thinking about breaking up with his or her partner may experience strong feelings of ambivalence and suffer intense anxiety when trying to decide on a course of action. He or she may enter a phase of idealized nostalgia and spend a great deal of time wondering whether the decision to leave is the right one. Unfortunately, this diverts the partner from either trying to make the relationship better or leaving. Some relationships go through several breakups and reconciliations before a couple separate permanently. The final end of a relationship almost always involves a sense of loss or even bereavement, but these feelings may be combined with relief, euphoria, anger and betrayal, especially if the relationship was destructive or lifeless.

How traumatic the end of a relationship is depends on the length and original health of the relationship; whether the decision to end was mutual; the relationship's legal and financial status; the partners' emotional health, ages and religious beliefs; family and peer pressure; whether children are involved; whether other parties are involved; whether the couple live and/or work together; and whether one or both partners experienced previous traumatic relationships, especially in childhood.

Adolescents mutually agreeing to end a noncohabiting relationship of a few months' duration may experience loneliness and depression initially, but the time taken to recover is likely to be far less than that for an older wife, for example, whose husband unexpectedly leaves their long-standing marriage for a younger woman.

Even after a humiliating or painful rejection, a deserted partner tends to continue feeling attached to the one who left. The sequence of feelings that follows resembles that of bereavement: shock; denial that the relationship is over; then a transitional phase that may include panic, lack of confi-

◀ Rejection and grief
This painting by John Everett Millais depicts Ophelia—in Shakespeare's play Hamlet, *she is driven mad with grief and drowns herself after being rejected by her lover.*

dence, regret and depression, or swings between these feelings. People may also be angry with themselves or their ex-partner.

Many people who have been left obsessively review the failed relationship, looking for clues to what went wrong. If the relationship or marriage lasted two or more years before breaking down, this transitional phase may well take a year. It can take even longer if the mourner experiences such additional setbacks as rejection by a new partner, bereavement or job loss.

In the recovery phase that follows grief, a sense of self-esteem and resilience slowly return, and a new identity, separate from the former partner, emerges. The recovering partner may make new friends, pursue new interests and change his or her focus of life away from the past, toward the present and future. Having acknowledged both the good and bad aspects of the lost relationship, the recovering partner can reinvest the intense emotional involvement elsewhere.

Shock

Disbelief

Mourning a relationship The end of a significant relationship often produces emotions similar to those of bereavement.

Acceptance

Depression

Anger

Realization

It can take an individual between two and four years to fully recover from the breakup of a long-term relationship. Specialist counselors and self-help groups can help make the experience seem less isolating. Less effective, and potentially destructive, is seeking consolation in alcohol, drugs or "rebound" relationships.

STARTING AGAIN

Some people react to the failure of a long-term relationship by deciding never again to make a similar commitment. But many more, especially if of childbearing age, decide to try again and "get it right." Fear of being alone, lonely, unlovable, or of facing the unknown, can fuel this determination.

Young people or those in short-lived relationships usually find it easier to start again than do older people emerging from long-term relationships. Single mothers and older people may find starting again especially challenging.

Allowing time to elapse between relationships enables an individual to process and gain insight for the benefit of future relationships. Repeatedly overlapping relationships—each new one dovetailing the old—can be a sign of dependency and a fear of being alone. Just as the capacity to make rational decisions is impaired during times of emotional stress, so rebound relationships may be difficult to sustain.

Counseling A trained and impartial individual such as a therapist or counselor may help resolve problems that cannot be understood by a couple from within their relationship.

Obsession with an ex-partner can pollute new relationships, making them seem as if they consist of three people rather than two. For some people, knowing when to start again comes naturally and feels comfortable; others must take a leap of faith.

RELATIONSHIP COUNSELING

However intelligent and committed two people are, they are likely to have greater success at jointly solving relationship problems with the help of a reputable, trained relationship counselor. He or she (or, in some cases, two counselors) does not judge or blame but creates a safe space for clients to speak openly. The counselor tries to help each partner to understand his or her role in and responsibility for the situation and to enter into a joint exploration of realistic options for change. Counseling is especially important if children are involved; they generally benefit from being raised by both parents, and partners often stand a better chance of reconciling, or at least coparenting amicably, when they enter into a counseling situation together.

Some forms of counseling are short-focus, with a set time limit and a well-defined program: for example, two weeks to explore the problems, two weeks to look at options and two weeks to find a solution. Other types of counseling that are more open-ended may last a year or more. A counselor may focus on the effect of each partner's past—especially their family relationships—on the present relationship. Not all counselors delve into family history, however; many concentrate on the present and future.

Relationship counseling can be noninterventionist, with the counselor mainly observing, reflecting or interpreting what is said, or task-oriented, with the counselor setting "homework" for the couple. Some counselors require both partners to be present; others accept that if one partner cannot, or chooses not to, participate, the other can still benefit. All forms of counseling require commitment, especially because some issues discussed may be painful.

Improving listening and communication skills between a couple is often a key goal, as is readjusting expectations of the self, partner and relationship. If the relationship cannot be saved, counseling can help both parties to move on, ideally with the insight to form healthier future relationships.

THE PHYSICAL EXPRESSION OF LOVE

Sex and Gender

Significant differences exist between male and female sexual behavior and responses. Among other things, men and women often need differing levels of stimulation before they reach orgasm, and they may attach different meanings to sex.

Many differences between male and female sexual behavior can be attributed to social and cultural influences. For example, society has long portrayed the typical male as thinking constantly about sex, being easily aroused and regularly requiring sexual release. Women, on the other hand, have been characterized as sexually more passive and requiring sexual satisfaction less frequently. These kinds of stereotypes can have a direct impact on the way that individual men and women think and feel about their own sexuality.

FEMALE SEXUALITY

Sex researcher Alfred Kinsey (see page 257) highlighted the practical implications of cultural beliefs about sex when he reported that most married women surveyed had never experienced orgasm. Furthermore, a significant number did not even know it was possible for a woman to experience the same degree of sexual satisfaction as her husband. This meant that many women obtained little or no pleasure from sex and even tried to find ways to avoid it. This in turn led to the euphemistic "I've got a headache" response from wives to any sexual overture by their husbands.

Assumptions about female orgasm and sexuality have often originated from social conditioning rather than from knowledge about physiological differences between the sexes. Many women in the past were brought up to believe that they were immoral and unnatural if they enjoyed sex. No one thought it appropriate to teach women about sex, and thus many women entered marriage in a state of total ignorance about intercourse. While society exercised no such scruples about making sexual knowledge available to men, husbands were nonetheless typically as ignorant as their wives about sexual matters. As a result, many women played no active part in sexual intercourse and never discovered how best to achieve sexual stimulation for their own satisfaction.

DO MEN NEED SEX MORE THAN WOMEN DO?

There is a misconception that men have a greater need for sex than women do. In fact, both sexes can survive without sexual intercourse, and many women perceive their "need" or desire for sex as equal to or greater than that of their male partner. Once men and women reach a high level of arousal, both sexes may experience sexual frustration or discomfort if they do not reach orgasm.

Sexual desire and gender
The misconception that men need sex more than women do may have arisen because men ejaculate and women do not. A man does not need to ejaculate through sexual intercourse or masturbation; his sperm can be reabsorbed or released during nocturnal emissions.

Today, society's views about female sexuality and the woman's role in sexual intercourse have changed, and it is widely recognized that a woman has a natural sexual drive that can match or even exceed that of her partner. Now that it is deemed normal—and in fact desirable—for women to take an active role in sex, the differences that exist between male and female sexual behavior have become less marked.

fact or fiction?

Women do not need to masturbate.

Fact. Neither sex needs to masturbate for health reasons, but masturbation is a way of releasing sexual tension and learning about sexual responses. Until recently it was accepted that men masturbated but not that women did. Now masturbation is considered acceptable in both sexes.

IMPORTANCE OF RELATIONSHIPS

While it's clear that everyone responds differently to the experience of sex in a relationship, certain gender-specific differences appear to exist in attitudes toward the need for emotional bonding. In particular, many women consider it much more important for lovemaking to occur as part of a permanent and meaningful relationship than do their male partners.

In *The Hite Report on Love, Passion & Emotional Violence* (1991), the overwhelming majority of women questioned (83 percent) said that they preferred sex in the context of an emotional involvement—in other words "sex with commitment"—to a purely casual sexual encounter.

Although the majority of women surveyed said they had often had sex on a first date (76 percent), most said that they would have much rather waited until the relationship had reached a more established footing, no matter how physically aroused they were. For many men, however, sexual intercourse is seen as a sufficient goal in itself,

REACHING ORGASM

Cultural factors can have a direct bearing on women's experience of sex, but physiological differences also exist between the genders. For example, men experience a stage after orgasm during which they are unable to achieve erection or ejaculation (see page 138). For most women, the equivalent period is very short or nonexistent, giving them the potential to achieve several orgasms in a short period of time (known as multiple or sequential orgasms). While women typically seem able to have more orgasms than men, emotional factors, distractions and anxiety affect their sex drive more easily.

Both sexes may become excited in the presence of someone whom they find attractive, but men are more likely to become aroused by objects or situations that they associate with sex (in extreme cases this is called a fetish).

Men and women reach their sexual peaks at different ages. Many men in their teens report having five orgasms a week—this falls to two or three by their forties. Women experience a much steadier pattern. In a survey by Kinsey (1979), women ranging between ages 20 and 60 who reported masturbating said that they experienced orgasm on average once or twice a week.

Variations and extremes of sexual activity and responses exist in both sexes, so that someone of either sex may become aroused and reach orgasm through intercourse or masturbation several times a day, while another person may remain unexcited and sexually inactive for long periods of time.

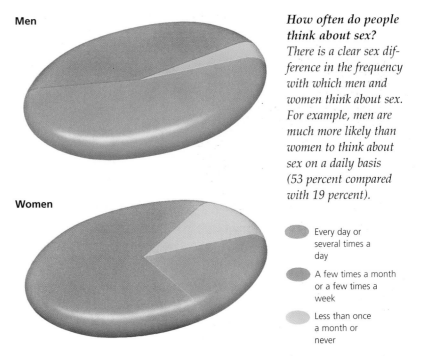

Men

Women

How often do people think about sex?
There is a clear sex difference in the frequency with which men and women think about sex. For example, men are much more likely than women to think about sex on a daily basis (53 percent compared with 19 percent).

- Every day or several times a day
- A few times a month or a few times a week
- Less than once a month or never

and they will commonly find it easy to separate the purely physical aspect of lovemaking from any emotional feelings.

This gender difference is often reflected in sexual encounters occurring outside of a steady relationship. Men are more likely than women to have casual sexual affairs, and more men than women say that such encounters are for sex alone, resulting from a purely physical attraction, and have no emotional significance.

Women who have affairs, on the other hand, more often say that they were attracted to a man for emotional reasons and that sex is a secondary factor. A woman might be attracted to a man because he shows a more considerate or caring attitude than her regular partner or because he shares many of her ideas and interests. Such encounters are frequently an indication that a woman is unhappy with her present partner and lead to her breaking up the relationship, whereas men who have affairs usually return to their existing partner.

According to Shere Hite's report, most women are motivated primarily by the desire to form a permanent bond when seeking a sexual partner. The majority of women in her survey (84 percent) said they believed that having loving relationships is one of the first priorities in life but did not believe men had the same priorities. In fact, 85 percent of women in their teens and twenties, when questioned, said they thought most men "see sex as a sport" and "try to get a girl just to increase their score."

PREMARITAL SEX

Someone who has a greater than average number of sexual partners is often termed promiscuous. What that average number is varies from culture to culture, and even for people of similar backgrounds it is largely a matter of individual perception. Cultures that regard virginity as an important sign of personal morality frown on premarital sex for both sexes, but especially for young women. In the West, however, premarital sexual activity is becoming more prevalent and less stigmatized.

In a U.K. survey conducted in 1994, *Sexual Behaviour in Britain*, men consistently reported greater numbers of partners than did women. In the 16 to 24 age group (this is usually the most sexually active group), 11.2 percent of men, compared with 2.5 per-

The Language of Sex

"Nymphomania" is a word that was invented in the 18th century, combining "nymph" (a beautiful maiden in Greek mythology) and "mania," a word used to describe a mental abnormality or obsession. In the past the term was used to describe any woman with a sexual appetite, since it was considered wrong for a woman to enjoy sex for its own sake. The pressure for women to conform to society's expectations was once so strong that what people would now regard as normal sexual expression was then seen as a disease. Today the term "nymphomania" has become largely obsolete except in cases of sexual obsession, usually arising from mental illness.

cent of women, reported 10 or more partners in the previous five years.

The latest figures in the U.S. and Canada tend to support these findings. Of those currently aged 16 to 24 years, 73 percent of American men and 56 percent of women experienced first intercourse before the age of 18. This compares with only 55 percent of men and 35 percent of women in the early 1970s. A Canadian survey conducted in 1994–95, *The Canadian Health Monitors*, reported 27 percent of 15-year-old men engaging in sexual intercourse compared to only 7 percent of 15-year-old women. In the 15 to 19 age group, 12 percent of men reported 6 or more partners (no women did).

Men and, especially, women are having sex at a younger age, and this may result in their having more sexual partners during their life than previous generations had.

FANTASY AND EROTICA

One area of sexual behavior in which men and women are becoming more alike is in their attitude toward erotic literature and even pornography. Traditionally men have found a greater number of sources to feed their sexual fantasies, particularly in terms of images of women as sexual objects, in newspapers, magazines, advertising, and in erotic films or books.

Today, however, many more women admit that viewing sexually explicit material increases their interest in sex. As a result, publishers are aiming an increasing number of erotic magazines and books primarily at women. The work of Nancy Friday (see page 222) shows that women can be aroused by a wide range of stimuli and that erotic images help them to achieve sexual arousal.

For women, as for men, erotic material can provide the raw material for sexual fantasies. Sex researchers now know that fantasies play as important a part in a woman's sexual behavior as they do in a man's. Just like men, women use fantasies to enhance their sexual arousal and to aid masturbation. But important gender differences exist in the types of sexual fantasies experienced by men and women.

For most women, romance plays a much greater part in their fantasies than for men. Many women fantasize about a man who is well known to them, usually their current sexual partner or a former lover. Women often prepare themselves for a sexual meeting by fantasizing about the evening ahead.

On the other hand, men typically fantasize about a woman other than their current partner, such as a complete stranger, celebrity, friend or neighbor.

As a rule, more men have fantasies in which they are the dominant partner, while more women imagine situations in which they play a submissive role. With fantasies, however, as with most other aspects of sexual behavior, numerous exceptions exist to such rules. In fact, a significant number of women report having fantasies in which they have a male sex slave, while some men fantasize about being forced to have sex by a woman. A woman brought up in an environment in which it was considered wrong to have strong sexual feelings may imagine being forced to have sex as a way to free herself of any feelings of guilt associated with sexual intercourse. In effect, the woman is creating a scenario in which she has no control over the sex act and so cannot be blamed for taking part and enjoying it. For similar reasons, some women experience arousal only during bondage sex—being tied up before sex.

CHANGING SOCIAL ATTITUDES TOWARD FEMALE SEXUALITY

Shere Hite
Social historian Shere Hite produced some of the most pioneering studies of sexuality in the 20th century. Her book The Hite Report is a collection of first-person accounts of female sexual experience.

Strip shows for women ▲
In the past, strip shows were performed by women for the benefit of men. Today shows in which men strip and dance naked or semi-naked for women are common.

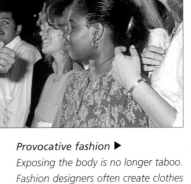

Provocative fashion ▶
Exposing the body is no longer taboo. Fashion designers often create clothes that emphasize the female form—less exaggerated forms of these clothes filter down onto the street.

Masturbation

Taboos surrounding masturbation have lessened in recent decades. Experts have dispelled long-held beliefs that self-stimulation can lead to blindness, weakness, madness or loss of virginity.

It used to be assumed that only boys and men masturbated, but it is now widely acknowledged that women of all ages masturbate too. In a 1966 survey, 46 percent of women admitted to having masturbated by the age of 20. The same survey, when repeated in 1981, indicated that this figure had increased to 73 percent. The work of Nancy Friday (see page 222) offers ample evidence of the rich fantasy and masturbatory lives of women.

Although babies and children gain sensual pleasure from genital touching, true adult masturbation begins around adolescence. Adult masturbation usually involves stimulating oneself to orgasm, often employing fantasies or erotic thoughts.

WHAT HAPPENS DURING MASTURBATION?

People masturbate in different ways. Boys and men usually stroke the penis repeatedly with the hand until they ejaculate. The penis also can be stimulated in other ways, such as being rubbed against a towel or mattress. To reduce friction and increase sensation, men sometimes apply a lubricant such as massage oil or saliva to the penis when they masturbate.

Girls and women usually masturbate by rubbing or stroking the clitoris with one or more fingers, but *The Hite Report* (1976) revealed a great variety of different methods—some women insert their fingers or a dildo into the vagina and rub the clitoris at the same time;

The instinct to masturbate Young children and infants of both sexes handle their genitals for comfort, pleasure and out of curiosity. Childhood masturbation is both normal and natural.

some hold a vibrator or a jet of water from a shower against the clitoris; others move themselves against a soft object such as a pillow or a bed; others cross their legs and squeeze them together rhythmically. Some women stimulate or caress other areas of their bodies, such as the breasts or the anus, while they masturbate.

Both men and women commonly have sexual fantasies during masturbation. Some people look at erotic material—reading a sexy story or watching a film in which people make love—and as they become sexually aroused, stimulation of the genitals tends to increase arousal and erotic thoughts, which results in more genital stimulation and so on, until this cycle of pleasure culminates in orgasm.

The physical changes that accompany masturbation are the same as those that accompany intercourse. A man's penis becomes erect and a clear secretion may appear at the opening. When sexual arousal reaches its peak, he ejaculates semen. A woman's vagina produces lubrication, and the labia and clitoris become engorged with blood. With sufficient clitoral stimulation, the woman reaches orgasm.

In years past, people believed that masturbation could damage an individual's capacity for sexual enjoyment during intercourse. In other words, a man or a woman would become so dependent on masturbation for sexual pleasure that he or she would be unable to enjoy stimulation from a partner. Today most sex therapists agree that masturbation serves an important function in helping people to learn about their own sexual potential. When a person has first explored and come to fully understand his or her own body in private, he or she may find it easier to communicate their sexual needs to a partner and therefore derive greater sexual satisfaction.

MASTURBATION WITH A PARTNER

Couples often engage in masturbation as part of foreplay or as an alternative to sex. One partner stimulates the other's genitals to orgasm, or both partners stimulate each other simultaneously. Mutual masturbation is commonly a feature of heavy petting in couples who, for whatever reason, do not want to have penetrative sex.

Stimulation may be with fingers, vibrators, dildos or other sex aids. Partners can show each other how they like to be touched, or each can learn what the other wants by watching his or her partner masturbate. Many people feel self-conscious and inhibited when discussing masturbation and what they require for sexual satisfaction. Women are embarrassed about showing a partner how to give clitoral stimulation. If reservations and inhibitions can be overcome, many people find masturbation a very useful and enjoyable accompaniment to lovemaking.

Masturbation during intercourse

Apart from mutual masturbation as foreplay or as an alternative to sex, women can masturbate during sex when the penis is inside the vagina. A sex therapist may recommend this for women who do not reach orgasm from penile thrusting alone or for women who wish to reach orgasm more quickly than penile thrusting allows.

Some sexual positions make masturbation during intercourse easier than others. The missionary position gives limited access to the clitoris, whereas woman-on-top or rear-entry positions provide easy access. A man can also use his hand to stimulate his partner's clitoris in any sexual position that allows this.

Masturbation may also enhance a sexual encounter after sexual intercourse, if either partner (more often the woman) did not reach orgasm or wants to have more orgasms. If a man is suffering from premature ejaculation, postcoital masturbation provides a good way for a woman to reach

The glans, or head, is the most sensitive part of the penis.

The frenulum (the fold of skin that joins the foreskin to the glans) responds to friction during masturbation.

The shaft is rhythmically stroked in masturbation.

Some men enjoy having their testicles cupped or stroked during masturbation.

orgasm (although in severe cases of premature ejaculation, the sufferer may require proper treatment—see page 213).

Some people think that masturbation has no place in the context of lovemaking. They feel that it violates the spirit of lovemaking, which is about the giving and receiving of sexual stimulation by a partner—not by oneself. Others enjoy masturbation during lovemaking, and argue that any technique that increases arousal is not a failure.

Stimulating the penis
Everyone has their own masturbation technique. Women can talk to their partners about how they like to be touched and then ask for feedback.

Mutual masturbation
Although couples may feel inhibited about masturbating in front of one another, it is a good way to learn about a partner's sexual responses.

Foreplay

The arousing behavior that a couple enjoy before sexual intercourse is called foreplay. It can include kissing, cuddling, gentle biting, stroking each other's bodies, caressing the breasts and genitals, sensual massage, oral sex, and using sex toys.

Foreplay allows the body to become ready for sexual intercourse. As a couple kiss, cuddle and stroke each other's bodies they become sexually aroused, and their bodies prepare for penetrative sex (although foreplay does not always have to lead to intercourse). The man's penis becomes erect, and the woman's vagina lengthens and produces lubrication that will allow penetration to occur comfortably. The *LABIA* around the vagina swell and open, making the vagina more readily accessible. Since women, in general, reach arousal more slowly, foreplay is usually more important for them than for men, especially if they want to become sufficiently aroused to reach orgasm.

Undressing Foreplay can begin before a couple get into bed. Many couples enjoy a bath together or undressing each other.

Foreplay also helps a couple to relax, enjoy each other's proximity and feel close emotionally as well as physically. Sexual intercourse requires openness, trust and mutual acceptance. Foreplay allows people to reach this necessary level of intimacy.

CREATING AN INTIMATE ATMOSPHERE

The right setting is important for any sexual intimacy. Privacy is essential—both partners should be equally committed to not answering the door, the telephone or the pager. The importance of personal hygiene can vary among couples (and cultures), but the generally accepted standard and unspoken consideration between partners includes clean teeth, hair and skin—especially armpits, feet and genitals. Many couples find that sharing a bath or a shower helps them to unwind together. Aromatherapy oils added to bath water can have relaxing or energizing properties, and washing each other's hair or massaging each other with scented lotions or oils encourages feelings of closeness (see page 72). The bathroom can also be an exciting place in which to make love.

Preparing a room for sexual intimacy can enhance pleasure. The right temperature, soft music, soft lighting (candles) and even seductive scents (heated essential oils, scented candles, incense or fresh flowers) can all be used to set the scene.

The buildup to intercourse

Individuals vary greatly in the amount of foreplay they enjoy. Sometimes couples like to take their time and engage in a variety of activities until they feel unable to postpone penetration any longer. In this case, foreplay ensures a slow buildup to the consuming excitement of intercourse. Other times a couple may become aroused very quickly and may indulge in little or no foreplay before they have intercourse. Some couples have intercourse several times with foreplay that lasts as long as the man's *REFRACTORY PERIODS*; in this case, foreplay may be as important as intercourse itself.

THE POWER OF SUGGESTION

In sexual matters, subtlety can be very arousing—a glimpse is often more erotic than complete exposure. A wide range of moods are possible—ripping each other's clothes off in the height of passion can be very exciting on occasions, but sometimes it may be more seductive to reveal one's body very slowly, bit by bit. Many people find it extremely arousing when their partner concentrates on touching subtler erogenous zones such as the thighs, buttocks or feet rather than immediate stimulation of the breasts or genitals.

Suggestion can be used in many other ways to heighten sexual arousal. Simply creating a mood or an awareness of sexual intimacy is a type of foreplay. A telephone call or a letter hinting at sensations to come can kindle desire even at a distance. A romantic dinner or a country walk may serve as a preamble to sex no matter how long a couple have been together. Devoting plenty of time to kissing, caressing and touching before sexual intercourse may also build excitement. The power of suggestion can even be applied to genital touching: one partner gently circles the other's genitals without directly stimulating them.

EROGENOUS ZONES

Specific areas on the body, known as erogenous zones, often produce a high level of sensual and sexual pleasure when touched. While the breasts and genitals are the two most obvious erogenous zones, there are many other parts of the body that respond to stimulation as well. By exploring these parts, partners can make sex an experience involving the whole body, rather than one concerned just with genital stimulation.

Starting at the top of the body, many people enjoy their hair being stroked, brushed, kissed or even gently pulled. Many also respond to having their ears and earlobes nibbled, caressed with the tongue or gently blown or whispered into. Stroking, licking and kissing the back of the neck, lips and mouth and the area around the breasts, such as the inner arm, chest and armpits, gives great sexual pleasure to many men and women. Men's nipples vary in sensitivity—some men enjoy having them nibbled or sucked; others do not.

The buttocks and the inner thighs are also erogenous zones that respond to caressing, gentle biting and even playful slapping. Lower down the legs, the backs of the knees, calves and ankles are sensitive, as anyone who has ever played "footsie" under a dinner table knows. Finally, the feet and toes are well-known erogenous zones— many people enjoy having them massaged, licked and sucked. Most people have their

ALL-OVER TOUCHING

Kissing, licking, nibbling and stroking the erogenous zones can be highly erotic for both giver and recipient. The toes, backs of the knees, fingers and eyelids are areas that are often neglected during foreplay. Giving this sort of sensual pleasure provides a slow, luxurious buildup to sex, and can be a novel experience for many couples.

Stimulating the erogenous zones
Prolonged caressing of the erogenous zones can set the scene for sex or can be a type of sexual play in its own right—sex need not involve penetration.

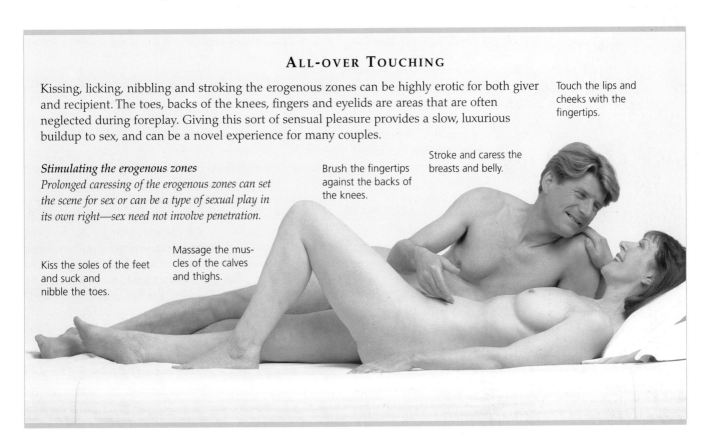

Touch the lips and cheeks with the fingertips.

Stroke and caress the breasts and belly.

Brush the fingertips against the backs of the knees.

Massage the muscles of the calves and thighs.

Kiss the soles of the feet and suck and nibble the toes.

own personal preferences about how and where they like to be touched, and a perceptive lover will discover these and use them to give pleasure during foreplay.

KISSING

The lips, among the most sensitive areas of the body, contain a rich supply of nerve endings. Kissing is a deeply erotic and intimate act. The great number of works of art that depict the kiss in all media— painting, sculpture, literature and film—testify to its erotic power. The meaning of a kiss can range from the urgent passion of a new relationship to the everyday currency of affection in a long-standing one. Kissing often initiates the first intimate physical exchange between people who are going to become lovers. It is also said to be the first activity to stop (even before intercourse) when a relationship is under strain.

As many lovers know, kissing is not the same activity over and over again but a mutual and varied exploration of the lips, tongue and mouth. Some people find deep penetration with the tongue very arousing, but so too subtler kisses, licks and nibbles. In fact, it is the variety that many people enjoy, from light kisses to deep ones and back to light ones again.

CARESSING

Touching and stroking are important parts of foreplay. A caress eloquently expresses love, affection and sensuality. Lovers may begin foreplay by kissing and touching the face, neck and hair and move on slowly to other areas, such as the shoulders, back and belly. Movements can be light strokes in which the flat of the hand barely touches the skin, gentle scratching along the back using the fingernails or massage strokes (see page 72).

Passionate kissing
Kissing can be one of the most intimate and erotic ways for lovers to express their feelings. Passionate kissing is often the sign of a new love, and something that longer-term couples may neglect.

THE KAMA SUTRA ON KISSING

Along with a wealth of other advice on lovemaking, the *Kama Sutra* lists many different types of kissing techniques, among them the straight kiss, the bent kiss, the turned kiss and the pressed kiss. In the straight kiss, the two lovers bring their lips into direct contact; for the bent kiss, lovers bend their heads toward each other; for the turned kiss, one partner "turns up the face of the other by holding the head and the chin"; and for the pressed kiss, the lower lip is pressed with "much force."

The book's author, Vatsyayana, described French kissing as "fighting of the tongue." He considered it to be an extension of the clasping kiss, which is where one partner takes the lips of the other between his or her own. The parts of the body that Vatsyayana recommended for kissing included "the forehead, the eyes, the cheeks, the throat, the bosom, the breasts, the lips and the interior of the mouth."

Caressing often leads to more focused genital stimulation and possibly sexual intercourse, but it can also be very relaxing and rewarding in itself. By definition, caresses are not rushed, painful or ticklish, especially when concentrated around the sensitive genital areas. Partners can show each other how they like to be caressed and take turns massaging each other.

NONPENETRATIVE SEX

Foreplay does not necessarily conclude with sexual intercourse. Many couples enjoy foreplay on its own, and sex therapists say this type of lovemaking, which takes place without the penis entering the vagina, can be as satisfying as penetrative sex: both partners can reach orgasm in their own time, under less performance pressure and with a strong emphasis on the sensual enjoyment of sex.

Many people practice both penetrative sex and nonpenetrative sex, adding variation to their sex life, but there are many reasons why couples may choose nonpenetrative sex, other than the sheer enjoyment of foreplay in its own right.

If one partner has a sexually transmitted disease, foreplay provides a sexual outlet that avoids the danger of infecting the healthy partner. Nonpenetrative sex in this case still requires safer sex practices (see page 178). Some people avoid penetration with a new partner because they do not know enough about that person's sexual history, or because they want to wait until they feel sure that their relationship has a stable basis. Others avoid penetration for personal or religious reasons, usually in the belief that intercourse is appropriate only in the context of marriage. Advanced pregnancy and certain medical conditions or disabilities may preclude full intercourse, and other circumstances such as menstruation may make nonpenetrative sex desirable.

During adolescence many teenagers, especially girls, explore their sexuality through nonpenetrative sex because they do not feel ready to engage in sexual intercourse or fear the risk of pregnancy. Experimenting with kissing and cuddling provides an outlet for sexual feelings without having to make the major emotional decision to have sexual intercourse for the first time. An adolescent should not feel pushed into having sex either by their partner or by peer pressure. Many people who have first sex at a young age later wish that they had waited until a time of greater maturity or until they had found a partner to whom they felt total commitment.

Some adolescents simply have little or no interest in sex, and this is perfectly natural too; there is no obligation for anyone to be sexually active if they do not want to be.

SENSUAL MASSAGE

Whether or not it leads to lovemaking, massage provides a good way for partners to explore each other's bodies and become intimate in a sensual, relaxed setting. The rules for foreplay apply to massage as well. Complete privacy and a warm and comfort-able room create the best atmosphere. Massage oils, which can be bought commercially or mixed at home, increase the pleasure by eliminating friction. Aromatherapists recommend adding specific essential oils that are thought to have relaxant properties to a base oil (see page 72).

Can We Talk About It?

FOREPLAY THAT DOES NOT LEAD TO SEX

Foreplay focuses on fun, affection and becoming aroused. It can lead to sexual intercourse, but it does not have to. Couples may feel just as fulfilled by massage, masturbation and stroking as by penetrative sex. If, however, sexual encounters begin and end with foreplay when you desire intercourse, or if your partner is pressuring you to have intercourse when you do not want to, you should discuss the situation.

If you are frustrated that foreplay does not progress to intercourse, gently and sympathetically question your partner and encourage him or her to talk about their feelings. Is your partner inexperienced sexually? Have you had intercourse with your partner before? If not, would intercourse with this person have traumatic consequences or lead to overwhelming guilt? Have you ever asked your partner what sort of foreplay he or she likes or does not like? Is there tension in your relationship? Is your partner anxious, depressed or fearful of pregnancy? Has your partner ever suffered from a sexual problem such as vaginismus or premature ejaculation? Has your partner had a disastrous or traumatic sexual encounter in the past? Does your partner simply not feel interested in or ready for intercourse?

If, on the other hand, you feel that your partner is pressuring you to go further sexually than you want to go, try to explain your reasons for resisting this. Say what you do and do not feel comfortable doing. If you do not want sexual intercourse, but are happy stimulating your partner to orgasm then say so. It is fine to say that things are moving too fast for you, that you do not feel ready to have sex or that you would like your partner to do different things during foreplay. Open discussion may enable you to work out how your sex life should progress.

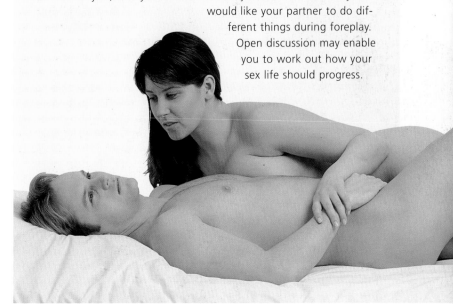

Sensual Massage

No particular skills are needed to give a massage, but knowledge of some simple guidelines and the basic massage strokes can help. The person receiving the massage should lie flat on a firm surface. The person giving the massage can sit astride the buttocks, between the legs or at the head of the partner. The hands should be coated in oil so that they glide smoothly over the skin, and once the hands have made contact with the skin, they should be removed as little as possible for the duration of the massage. Bear in mind that massage oil damages condoms, so make sure to wash before intercourse.

MAKING A SENSUAL OIL

- Choose an essential oil such as jasmine, neroli, lavender, sandalwood or ylang-ylang.
- Add three drops of the oil to every tablespoon of base oil (such as almond or wheat-germ oil).
- Mix the oil and pour into a convenient container.
- Stand the oil bottle in a bowl of hot water or rub it between your hands to warm it before applying.

Giving a massage
The person receiving the massage should communicate about what feels good.

EFFLEURAGE

This is a long gliding or sweeping stroke in which the flat palms travel across a large expanse of skin such as the back. If different parts of the body are being massaged—the buttocks and the shoulders, for example—effleurage strokes can be used to move the hands from one place to another.

PETRISSAGE

This stroke involves kneading movements. The person giving the massage gently squeezes, twists and rolls the flesh between the hands and the fingers and thumbs. Petrissage aims at getting rid of tension spots in muscles that have built up through stress, anxiety or bad posture.

FRICTION

A variation of petrissage, friction involves constant pressure or small circular movements applied to a small area. The pads of the thumbs or the knuckles are used to apply pressure. Like petrissage, friction helps to ease knotted muscles.

HACKING

The person giving the massage forms the hands into loose cup shapes and chops or hacks the skin. As an alternative, hacking can be performed with the hands held straight. Hacking is designed to invigorate and energize rather than relax.

The Role of Erotica

Erotica, in varying degrees, plays an important role in the sex lives of many people. It is used to trigger or increase sexual desire, intensify physical pleasure and make the art of lovemaking more exciting.

Many individuals and couples use books, magazines, pictures or videos describing or depicting sexual activities to stimulate their sexual appetites and imaginations before making love. Couples who enjoy using such material do so because it arouses and entertains them, often reduces their sexual inhibitions, and broadens their knowledge of sexual activities and techniques.

Contrary to popular belief, most women can enjoy erotica as much as men do; but they are less likely to be aroused by material that presents sex from a purely male point of view, and they usually prefer women to be depicted as equal sexual partners rather than providers of male pleasure. Many people—male and female—find the explicit depiction of sex distasteful in any form. No one should be forced to view explicit sexual material.

Sexually arousing material is often divided into two broad groups—erotica and pornography—but these categories are sometimes difficult to distinguish. In general, erotica portrays sexual activity in a subtle and sensitive manner and has, or aspires to, some artistic or literary merit. "Pornography" is a term used to describe material that objectifies and degrades a person (usually a woman) with the sole aim of titillating the audience. Psychologists argue that objectifying potential sexual partners dehumanizes them and robs sex of any emotional intimacy. Highly explicit pornography is referred to as hard-core; less explicit pornography is referred to as soft-core.

Erotic literature and art have a long history, and examples of sexual imagery can be found in the cultures of most of the ancient civilizations, including those of China,

India, Egypt, Greece and Rome. The Chinese "pillow books," for example, were illustrated books of sexual instruction and advice, one of the most famous being the *Su Nue Ching* (*The Classic of the Plain Girl*), which dates back to about 200 B.C.

Today the range of sexually explicit material available is wide. It extends from mainstream books and movies that include erotic scenes of conventional lovemaking, through soft porn magazines and books, to the kind of extremely hard-core pornography, usually cheaply produced and expensive to buy, that most people would find disturbing. Any couple wanting to use erotica to enhance their sex life should have no

Indian erotic paintings There is a wealth of erotic paintings depicting 18th- to 19th-century Indian princes and their lovers engaged in exotic or athletic sex positions.

trouble finding suitable material, but when deciding what to choose, partners should take account of each other's likes and dislikes.

EROTIC CLOTHING

Clothes can exert a powerful erotic influence, and dressing in a way that a partner finds alluring may stimulate his or her sexual desire as a form of foreplay, a prelude to making love. Clothing that draws attention to or emphasizes certain body parts, particularly the breasts or chest and the hips, buttocks and crotch, is overtly sexual, and most people respond to it. Individual preferences can vary greatly, though.

Underwear

Seductive underwear and nightwear are the most common forms of erotic clothing. Most underwear is inherently sexy because it is worn next to the skin, normally hidden from view and revealed and removed when couples undress for lovemaking. The choice

Sexual stereotypes
There are popular stereotypes about what is sexy in men and what is sexy in women. Black garter belts and stockings or white silk or lacy underwear feature heavily in erotic images of women, whereas men are depicted in clothes or states of undress that emphasize their muscularity.

The Language of Sex

The term "erotica" comes from the Greek word "erotikos," itself derived from the Greek word for love, "eros," while "pornography" is derived from "pornographos," which is a Greek word meaning "writing about prostitutes." Usually simpler and more explicit than erotica, pornography often makes little effort to create a credible storyline or context for its graphic depictions of sex.

of underwear and nightwear for men is limited. Women enjoy far more varied and imaginative choices—intimate wear that shapes, conceals and reveals. For example, push-up and peep-hole bras emphasize the sexual nature of the female breasts; corsets make the waist look slimmer, which enhances the rounded shapes of the breasts and buttocks; and stockings and garter belts create a visual framework for the crotch and buttocks.

The visual impact of erotic clothing can be enhanced if it also has a sensual texture, which is why silk and satin are generally preferable to nylon and why some couples prefer more exotic materials such as leather, plastic and rubber. Erotic clothing made from these materials is usually smooth, shiny and tight-fitting, molding itself to the contours of the body like a second skin and hinting at the dark and mysterious aspects of human sexuality.

APHRODISIACS

Any food, drink, drug or other substance that is thought to stimulate sexual desire is termed an "aphrodisiac." Throughout history, countless foods have been associated with aphrodisiac properties. Some can simply be eaten in a suggestive manner. Sometimes a food's shape, texture, taste or smell is suggestive of genitals, semen or vaginal fluids—for example, asparagus, celery, eels, oysters, mussels, caviar, freshly picked tomatoes, fresh figs, bananas, potatoes, and roots such as carrots, ginseng, ginger and eryngo (the testicle-shaped root of sea holly). Whether or not there is any scientific basis for the action of these and other reputed aphrodisiacs, the claims made for them tend to be self-fulfilling—they work for people who believe in them.

Hot spices also have a reputation as aphrodisiacs, partly because they cause an apparent rise in body temperature and a flushing of the skin, both of which are asso-

ciated with sexual arousal. They also mildly irritate the bowels and bladder in a way that can actually encourage sexual arousal, and this is the principle behind one of the most notorious of all the aphrodisiacs: cantharides.

This substance, also called Spanish fly, is made from the dried and crushed bodies of a bright green beetle that produces a secretion that can blister the skin. Cantharides works by irritating the urethra, the tube through which the bladder empties. Although it may be an effective aphrodisiac, Spanish fly is also a dangerous poison, and its use can be fatal.

The only other substance that has been shown to have a definite and repeatable aphrodisiac effect is yohimbine. Obtained from the bark of a central African tree of the same name, it causes erections in men and physical arousal in women by dilating the blood vessels of the genitals. Yohimbine is not widely available as an aphrodisiac because it can cause a potentially fatal drop in blood pressure. The drug amyl nitrate ("poppers") can also have the same effect and may be extremely dangerous.

The placebo effect

Apart from cantharides and yohimbine, almost all of the other aphrodisiacs work only if the user believes that they will; their effects are psychological rather than physical (which is known as the placebo effect). The exceptions, including

certain narcotics, generally cannot be used safely owing to highly dangerous side effects. Food, however, can help to enhance sexual arousal—a meal for two in intimate, softly lit surroundings can be a sensual prelude to lovemaking, especially if it includes foods that can be eaten suggestively, such as asparagus, oysters, ice cream and soft, juicy fruit.

Sex and scent

Animals signal their readiness to mate by secreting substances called pheromones that are related to hormones. The smell of these substances triggers an instinctive sexual response in potential mates. The extent to which pheromones trigger arousal in humans is far less important. Pheromone preparations advertised to make men irresistible to women have no proven effect—

◀ *The Orgy This painting by Cézanne (from the late 1860s) depicts naked figures after a feast. Orgies and bacchanalia were featured frequently in the painting and literature of this time.*

Sensual foods
Although it is rare for a food to have provable aphrodisiac properties, many foods have erotic or sensual associations. Figs, champagne and oysters are just three examples.

Champagne

Figs

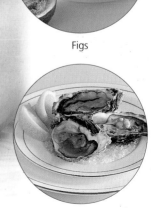

Oysters

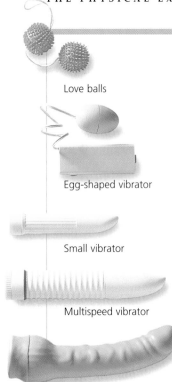

Love balls

Egg-shaped vibrator

Small vibrator

Multispeed vibrator

Penis-shaped dildo

SEXUAL AIDS

Some sex toys are designed to closely resemble a man's penis in texture and shape, while others are designed solely with function and discretion in mind. Love balls differ from vibrators and dildos in that they are intended to be inserted into the vagina for a sustained period of time. Once inserted, the covered metal balls are designed to produce pleasurable sensations by moving against each other. Vibrators are probably the most popular type of sex toy—when such a device is moved against a woman's clitoral area, the high-speed vibrations can provide a reliable way of reaching orgasm for many women.

Using sex toys
Sex toys should not be used on swollen or inflamed body parts or skin eruptions. Shared sex toys, such as vibrators, must be covered with a condom.

not because they have no detectable smell but because human sexuality is far more complicated than that of other animals.

Smell does, of course, play an important role in getting people into the right mood for lovemaking. Some aromatherapy oils, such as rose oil, are said to have an aphrodisiac effect. Two other aromatic substances, musk and civet, have been used since ancient times as the basis of perfumes. Musk is obtained from a gland near the penis of the male Himalayan musk deer and civet from the anal scent glands of male and female civet cats. These two substances play a part in triggering sexual activity in the animals that produce them.

SEX TOYS
Vibrators and dildos are the most popular sex toys, and both provide a very direct and reliable form of sexual enhancement. Sex toys can be used by individuals during masturbation or by couples during lovemaking.

Vibrators
The typical vibrator is a penis-shaped sex toy containing a small, battery- or electricity-powered motor that makes it vibrate. When it is held lightly against a woman's

clitoris, labia, nipples, PERINEUM or anus, or inserted into her vagina, its vibrations arouse her by stimulating the abundant nerve endings in these places. This arousal can be sufficiently intense to trigger orgasm, even in women who do not normally climax during intercourse. This has made the vibrator a popular aid to masturbation, but it can be equally effective in lovemaking.

During foreplay, a woman or her partner can use a vibrator to heighten her enjoyment and arousal, perhaps even bringing her to orgasm before intercourse begins. Vibrators can also be used on a man's penis, scrotum, perineum or anus to increase his excitement, especially when he is trying to regain an erection after orgasm. They can likewise be used to great effect during intercourse, especially in a woman-on-top position, where it is easy for the woman or her partner to apply the vibrator to her nipples or clitoris, or to the shaft of his penis.

Most vibrators are made of plastic or metal and range in length from about 5 to 12 inches (23 to 30 cm). The surface of the body, or "shaft," may be smooth, ribbed or grooved. Some models are covered with a thick layer of soft, fleshy latex molded into a lifelike representation of an erect penis. Some vibrators have a projection at the base that presses against the clitoris when the vibrator is inserted into the vagina.

Dildos
A dildo is similar to a vibrator, but it does not have a vibrating action and is usually used as an artificial penis during masturbation and lovemaking. Some dildos have a rubber or soft plastic bulb at the base that can be filled with warm water, which is then squirted out to simulate ejaculation.

Vibrators and dildos should always be carefully washed and dried before and after use or they will soon become a source of bacterial or fungal infection. For extra safety, they can be covered with a condom before use and the condom disposed of afterward. Sex toys, including vibrators and dildos, should never be shared by partners if one of them has, or may have, a sexually transmitted disease, especially HIV.

Clitoral stimulators
A woman's clitoris is usually the most sensitive part of her genitals, and her enjoyment of lovemaking and her chances of

orgasm are greatly increased if it is stimulated directly during intercourse. It is possible for her or her partner to stroke her clitoris with a finger or a vibrator while making love, or a clitoral stimulator may be attached to the man's penis. This typically takes the form of a ring that fits around the base of the penis and has a small projection that rubs against the clitoris during intercourse. Certain condoms also incorporate projections with similar purposes; these usually have a ribbed or knobby surface texture designed to increase vaginal stimulation as well.

SEXUAL FANTASIES

Most people have sexual fantasies, in which they imagine what it would be like to make love—or indulge in other sexual or romantic activities—in a variety of situations and with various partners. These fantasies may be sexual daydreams, mental aids to masturbation, or scenarios that are played out in the mind before or during lovemaking. Like nonsexual daydreams, they provide a brief escape from reality into a realm of endless possibilities.

Common fantasies

Common fantasies of both men and women include having sex with someone—real or imagined—other than one's partner; making love with more than one person at a time; watching one's partner make love to another person; making love while someone else is watching; being coerced into having intercourse; and homosexual or bisexual lovemaking.

Daydreaming about different ways of making love, and mentally rehearsing them, helps a person to be a more imaginative, confident and fulfilling lover. Fantasies can trigger and help to maintain sexual desire, and so are often useful to people who have difficulty becoming fully aroused.

Some people fantasize only during foreplay. Others begin fantasizing during intercourse. Still others may have sexual day-dreams, especially when with a new partner, but do not fantasize at all when making love. Men and women tend to use fantasy differently. Men may fantasize to help them get more aroused before intercourse, but they tend not to fantasize during it because the extra arousal can make it difficult to control ejaculation. Women, who may not be as readily aroused as men, often fantasize throughout lovemaking to help them achieve orgasm.

Sharing fantasies

While many people prefer to keep their sexual fantasies to themselves, others like to tell them to their partners, and some couples construct joint fantasies that they can enjoy together. This allows them to act out simple fantasy scenarios before and during lovemaking. Acting out sexual fantasies can be an exciting way to liven up a sexual relationship, as long as both partners consent fully.

The power of the imagination is a vital ingredient of an acted-out fantasy, but simple props such as soft cords, blindfolds and clothes can add to the sense of excitement.

◀ *Sex in other settings* *Some people enjoy fantasizing about making love with their partner in an unusual or exotic setting. Popular locations include tropical beaches, waterfalls and airplanes.*

Dominance and submission *Partners who are accustomed to playing equal roles during sex can find experimenting with power games an erotic experience.*

Sexual Intercourse

Different couples make love in different ways. Some people use a wide range of sexual positions and change position several times during intercourse. Others have just one or two favorite positions in which they habitually make love.

Missionaries and ▶ natives *The missionary position is so called because it was allegedly the sexual position recommended by Christian missionaries to their Polynesian converts in the era of European colonialism.*

Each lovemaking position has its own particular advantages. In several face-to-face positions, such as the missionary position, the woman's clitoris gets direct stimulation from the contact with her partner's pubic area, which helps to heighten her arousal. This does not happen in rear-entry positions, but when making love using a rear entry position, the man or the woman can more easily stimulate the clitoris manually. Rear-entry sex positions stimulate the woman's G-spot (see page 126), according to some, as do the woman-on-top positions.

MAN-ON-TOP POSITIONS

The missionary position, the basic man-on-top position, is probably the best known and most widely used of all lovemaking postures. The missionary position allows

sexual partners to kiss, embrace and maintain eye contact to see the pleasure that they are giving each other. Penetration can be shallow or deep, and the pace of lovemaking can vary from slow and sensual to wildly passionate. The main drawback of the missionary position is that it restricts the woman's freedom of movement during sex. This means that her ability to control the rhythm and speed of intercourse and the depth of penetration are fairly limited.

To adopt the missionary position, the woman lies on her back with her legs parted, and the man lies on top of her with his legs between hers and then gently inserts his penis into her vagina. By supporting his weight on his elbows or his hands, he can allow her more freedom to vary the sensations for both of them as he thrusts. The woman can move her pelvis up and down, from side to side or in a circular fashion.

The woman can vary the depth and angle of penetration in this position by lying with a pillow supporting her buttocks, by opening her legs wider or by wrapping one or both around her partner's torso. She can also lie with her buttocks on the edge of the bed and her feet on the floor, so that her partner can make love

The missionary position *Although it is sometimes dismissed as unimaginative and boring, many men and women find the missionary position one of the most enjoyable ways of making love.*

to her from a kneeling position. If the woman is sufficiently supple, she can draw her knees up to her chest so that when her partner enters her, his pelvis is against her buttocks. She can also place one or both of her feet flat against her partner's chest (in the *Kama Sutra*, this is known as the pressed or half-pressed position). This position allows the penis to penetrate the vagina very deeply, so the man should be careful not to thrust too hard.

The Language of Sex

In English-speaking countries, most sexual positions do not have names that are widely or consistently used, the exceptions being the missionary, doggie and spoons positions. This reflects an aversion to the open discussion of sex and means that when people want to mention a sexual position, they usually have to describe rather than name it. Attempts to borrow names from less reticent cultures have so far not met with much success.

WOMAN-ON-TOP POSITIONS

In the various woman-on-top positions, the woman has greater control because she can decide the speed of the movements and the depth of penetration. The man assumes a relatively passive role. Some women find that a woman-on-top position is the easiest one in which to reach coital orgasm.

In the simplest type of woman-on-top position, a straightforward reversal of the missionary position, the man lies on his back and his partner lies on top of him, her legs straddling his, and she inserts his penis into her vagina. Then she moves her pelvis while her partner lies still or responds by thrusting. He has both hands free to stroke and caress her. To vary the sensations, she can bring her legs inside his to tighten the grip of her vagina on his penis.

Alternatively, the woman may sit or kneel astride her partner. She can alter the angle of penetration by leaning forward or back,

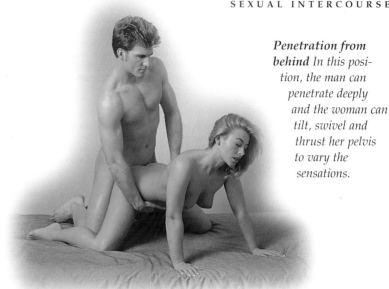

Penetration from behind *In this position, the man can penetrate deeply and the woman can tilt, swivel and thrust her pelvis to vary the sensations.*

Woman-on-top *Kneeling astride her partner allows a woman to move freely and exert control over the angle and depth of penetration.*

and if she is kneeling she can raise or lower her pelvis and so control the depth of penetration. In this position, both partners have their hands free to caress each other, and it is easy for the woman to increase her pleasure by stimulating her clitoris manually or with a vibrator.

The woman can further vary this position by sitting or kneeling with her back to her partner instead of facing him. This posture, which is actually a rear-entry position, makes eye contact difficult and kissing impossible, but many couples find it an erotic variation.

REAR-ENTRY POSITIONS

The best known of the rear-entry positions is the so-called doggie position, which gets its name from its similarity to the way in which dogs mate. The woman kneels on all fours on the bed or on the floor, and her partner kneels behind her, then he or she

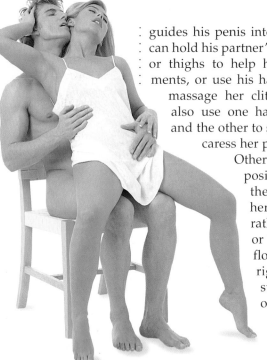

guides his penis into her vagina. The man can hold his partner's shoulders, waist, hips or thighs to help him control his movements, or use his hands to caress her and massage her clitoris. The woman can also use one hand to support herself and the other to stimulate her clitoris or caress her partner's testicles.

Other versions of the doggie position are achieved by the woman supporting herself on her forearms rather than on her hands or by her kneeling on the floor in a virtually upright position, perhaps supported by the edge of the bed. Rear-entry sex is also possible with the woman lying face down.

Sitting positions
Sensations can be enhanced by rhythmically contracting the vaginal muscles.

STANDING POSITIONS

Using a standing position can be an exciting change from making love on a bed, but it can also be awkward, especially if one partner is much taller than the other or if either

partner is infirm. The simplest standing position in which to make love is that in which the partners stand facing each other, in effect creating an upright version of the missionary position.

If the woman is light enough, or if her partner is strong enough, he can lift her up after he has entered her and support her by locking his hands beneath her buttocks or holding her thighs. She can help him by putting her arms around his neck, crossing her ankles behind his back and gripping his body with her thighs. This is easier to achieve when the woman's back is supported by a wall.

In the rear-entry standing position, the woman stands with her legs slightly apart and bends forward from the waist, then her partner enters her from behind. This position is virtually the same as the doggie position but with the partners standing rather than kneeling; it allows the man similar deep penetration and freedom to thrust, and both partners the opportunity to use their hands to provide extra stimulation. As with the face-to-face standing position, however, height differences can be a problem, and if the difference in height is too great, the couple might not be able to use this position at all.

The woman can make penetration much easier and deeper if she bends fully at the waist so that her body is at right angles to her legs. For support, she can reach back and hold onto her partner, put her hands against a wall, or hold onto the bed, a table or any other stable object.

SITTING POSITIONS

Making love in a sitting position does not permit either partner a great deal of movement, but it allows a gentle, unhurried and very intimate form of intercourse, and the face-to-face sitting positions allow the partners to kiss, cuddle and caress each other.

To make love sitting on a bed, the man sits with his legs extended, and his partner sits in his lap, facing him and with her legs behind his back. She carefully slides her vagina onto his penis. When on a chair, the woman sits on the man's lap with her legs straddling his, either facing him or with her back to him.

Can We Talk About It?

ASKING FOR WHAT YOU WANT DURING SEX

When you start a relationship, you may be cautious about expressing some of your sexual wishes. Perhaps you feel embarrassed or anxious that you will shock your partner or make him or her feel like an inadequate lover. Or you may feel you should wait for the "right time." For some couples, though, the time never seems right, and before you know it, sex has become a routine performance, and it feels inappropriate to ask for changes.

First of all, define exactly what it is you want to add or change about your sex life. This will allow you to make positive suggestions to your partner instead of negative statements, such as "our sex life is boring" or "we never do anything different." Talking to your partner should never involve criticism of his or her past performance. Simply say that you are curious or that you think it would be fun to experiment.

Asking for what you want sexually can also be nonverbal. For example, during foreplay gently guide your partner's hand or mouth to the parts of your body where you want to be touched and caressed.

80

SIDE-BY-SIDE POSITIONS

The simplest version of a side-by-side position is the face-to-face style. A couple can reach this position by carefully rolling over onto their sides from a basic man-on-top or woman-on-top position, sustaining penetration as they do so, or they can lie beside each other and then insert his penis into her vagina. To vary this position, one of them can hook his or her uppermost leg over the other's, or the woman can raise her uppermost leg, allowing her partner to slide his legs between hers.

The rear-entry version of this position is known as the spoons position, because its shape can be likened to a pair of spoons nested together, one bowl inside the other. The woman lies on her side and her partner lies behind her, snuggled up against her back. Then she draws her knees up a bit and opens her thighs slightly to allow him to enter her from behind, and he tucks his knees into the back of hers. In this position, the man can kiss and nuzzle his partner's neck and shoulders and

Spoons position
The man lies behind his partner and enters her from the rear.

use his free hand to caress her breasts and gently massage her clitoris. Because of its restful nature the spoons position is a good way to have sexual intercourse during the later months of pregnancy or for older or infirm couples.

Side-by-side sex This type of sex position best serves tender, unhurried lovemaking.

FACILITATING FEMALE ORGASM

Some sexual positions are more likely to facilitate female orgasm than others. Women who find it difficult to reach orgasm from intercourse alone—for instance without manual or oral stimulation—often find that a woman-on-top position is helpful.

The woman can use her hands to push herself backward and forward to create friction on the clitoris.

Maximum contact
Women-on-top positions can maximize the amount of friction between the clitoris and the man's pubic bone.

The woman can move horizontally by pushing against the man's feet.

The male and female pelvises are aligned so that his pubic bone puts pressure on her clitoris.

The man can use his hands to pull his partner close to him and increase the pressure on her clitoris.

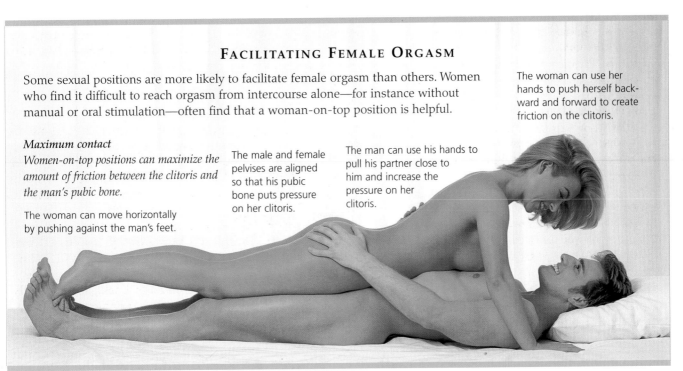

Prolonging Sexual Intercourse

The duration of a couple's lovemaking often depends on the man's ability to control his ejaculation. There are various techniques for sustaining intercourse that can help a couple prolong their sexual pleasure.

After a man ejaculates, he quickly loses his erection, which means that intercourse is over. He can continue to stimulate his partner in a variety of ways—"afterplay" can include all the same activities as foreplay—but some couples enjoy prolonging the act of penetrative sex itself.

There are some simple and enjoyable techniques that prolong sexual pleasure. They include delaying ejaculation and resuming intercourse immediately after ejaculation—many techniques derive from tantric sex.

TANTRIC AND TAOIST SEX

Tantra is an ancient doctrine that evolved in India at least 1,500 years ago. It is based on the idea that the power of sexual energy can be harnessed to unite the male principle or force (Shiva) within each person with its female counterpart (Shakti) to achieve spiritual liberation.

Taoism is an even older doctrine that developed in China and first appeared in written form more than 2,500 years ago. Based on the concept that health, longevity

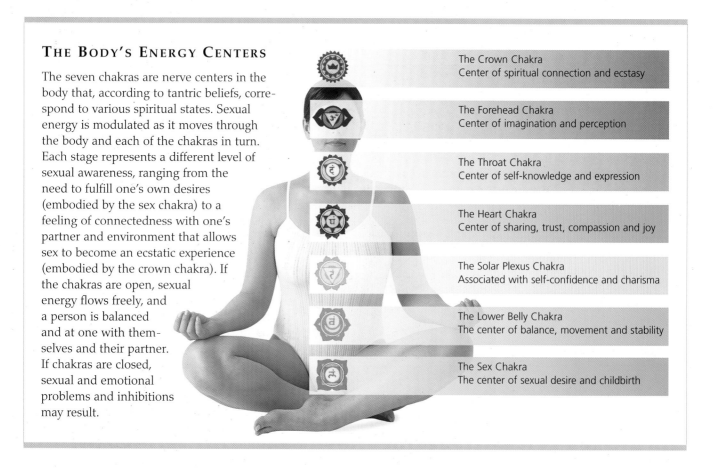

THE BODY'S ENERGY CENTERS

The seven chakras are nerve centers in the body that, according to tantric beliefs, correspond to various spiritual states. Sexual energy is modulated as it moves through the body and each of the chakras in turn. Each stage represents a different level of sexual awareness, ranging from the need to fulfill one's own desires (embodied by the sex chakra) to a feeling of connectedness with one's partner and environment that allows sex to become an ecstatic experience (embodied by the crown chakra). If the chakras are open, sexual energy flows freely, and a person is balanced and at one with themselves and their partner. If chakras are closed, sexual and emotional problems and inhibitions may result.

The Crown Chakra
Center of spiritual connection and ecstasy

The Forehead Chakra
Center of imagination and perception

The Throat Chakra
Center of self-knowledge and expression

The Heart Chakra
Center of sharing, trust, compassion and joy

The Solar Plexus Chakra
Associated with self-confidence and charisma

The Lower Belly Chakra
The center of balance, movement and stability

The Sex Chakra
The center of sexual desire and childbirth

and tranquillity can be achieved by harmonizing the male (yang) and female (yin) within each individual, it teaches that one way to attain this harmony is to use male self-control to ensure female sexual satisfaction. As a means to these ends, both Tantric and Taoist teachings include techniques such as shallow thrusting, muscle control and soft-entry sex, to make intercourse last for as long as the participants wish.

Shallow thrusting

One of the simplest methods a man can use to help him delay ejaculation is the shallow-thrusting technique. As he nears ejaculation during intercourse, he instinctively begins to thrust deeper and faster, but with practice he can prevent himself from ejaculating by resisting this instinct and making his thrusts slow and shallow. This technique becomes even more effective if combined with breath control. Very rapid breathing usually accompanies impending ejaculation. By taking slow, deep breaths, a man can curb the urge to ejaculate.

Other techniques

If shallow thrusting and breath control are unsuccessful, simultaneously contracting the anal sphincter and the *PUBOCOCCYGEAL (PC) MUSCLES* can often help to delay ejaculation. The ring of muscle called the anal sphincter keeps the anus closed; the PC muscles are the same ones that a man can use to stop the flow when he is urinating. Alternatively, he can partly withdraw his penis and grip its base, with his thumb on the underside just above the scrotum and two fingers on the upper side of the penis where it joins the body. By squeezing firmly for about four seconds, he can quell his urge to ejaculate.

A man can also try pulling down on his testicles to delay ejaculation. As ejaculation approaches, a man's scrotum tightens and his testicles are drawn up against his body.

Soft-entry sex

Sometimes a man will partly or completely lose his erection when trying to control his ejaculation and then

have difficulty regaining it. He can continue to have intercourse without a full erection by using the technique known as soft-entry sex. The soft-entry technique can also be used when a couple want to make love again after the man has ejaculated, but masturbation or oral sex fails to bring about erection. It can also be of help if a man cannot achieve a full erection before lovemaking begins. Soft-entry sex does not, however, cure long-lasting impotence.

To perform soft-entry sex, the man uses his fingers to gently guide the end of his penis into his partner's vagina. When it is in, he firmly grips the base of his penis with his forefinger and thumb. This will trap blood in his penis, hopefully making it swell and stiffen enough for the man to be able to thrust gently inside his partner's vagina. This thrusting may be sufficient to produce a full erection. When the man feels that this is happening, he should release his grip on his penis so that lovemaking can continue.

Synchronizing heart rates The couple place their hands on each other's hearts and adjust their breathing rates so that they are synchronized.

◀ *Shiva Nataraja The Hindu Lord of the Dance represents divine harmony between opposing forces and energies. The figure unites the male and female principles of Shiva and Shakti, in a gesture that embodies perfect balance.*

Oral Sex

In 1948, when sex researcher Kinsey produced his report on sexual habits, almost half of all married adults reported having had oral sex. More recent statistics show that roughly three-quarters of men and women have had oral sex.

The pattern of giving and receiving oral sex seems to have changed over the years. It used to be seen as an advanced or an experimental sexual technique that couples moved on to after intercourse as something more daring. Studies, such as *Sexual Behaviour in Britain* (1994), suggest that today oral sex typically happens before intercourse, sometimes instead of it—young women in particular will offer partners oral sex if they are not yet ready to allow penetration.

CUNNILINGUS

Oral sex performed on a woman's genital area is known as cunnilingus. Cunnilingus includes any type of genital kissing, licking, sucking or nibbling. A partner may begin by licking a woman's labia to lubricate her and then move on to her clitoris, licking and sucking with perhaps downward strokes from root to tip or flicks from side to side. The tongue can also be inserted into the vagina, simulating intercourse, but this often is not as arousing as clitoral stimulation. Many women gain pleasure from oral sex because it directly stimulates the clitoris and often arouses women in ways that intercourse does not. In fact, some women may find it difficult to reach orgasm any other way The clitoris is packed with nerve endings and is the erotic center of the female body.

Emotionally, cunnilingus is an intimate act that can make many women feel desired and loved. It also allows them to receive pleasure without feeling any obligation to give. This is important for women who find reaching orgasm difficult because they focus on their partner's pleasure.

The Hite Report (1976) on female attitudes toward sexuality revealed that although many women surveyed gained enormous sexual pleasure from cunnilingus, some women disliked it because they felt it to be dirty or immoral, or that their partners would be repulsed by the smell of the genitals. A minority of men questioned were unwilling to perform cunnilingus, feeling it to be subservient and unmanly. However, many men reported that they enjoyed the experience and felt proud of their ability to give their partner pleasure. In *The Hite Report on Male Sexuality* (1981) one man was quoted as saying, "I feel that the genital kiss given by a man to a woman is one of the most intimate expressions of love there is. I often have dreams involving sex, most of which do not end with my orgasm or ejaculation but do include a protracted period of my kissing the woman's genitals."

FELLATIO

Oral sex performed on a man's penis is called fellatio; the word comes from Latin and means "sucking," although this action by itself may not be particularly arousing. More often, a woman uses one of two techniques: either she licks the man's penis and testicles with her tongue, or she thrusts the penis directly into her mouth and out again, simulating the movements of intercourse. Fellatio can be combined with manual stimulation of the penis.

According to *The Hite Report on Male Sexuality*, the majority of men enjoy fellatio. Some do find it distasteful, degrading for

Cunnilingus
The clitoris and vagina are stimulated with the lips and tongue, as part of foreplay or afterplay.

partners or morally wrong, due in part to their social upbringing or religious beliefs. But most men find fellatio emotionally rewarding. It is an act of intimacy, and the movement of jaw and lips, combined with the warm, moist skin of a partner's mouth, is intensely stimulating. Some men find that intercourse produces more intense sensations than fellatio, simply because it is a more mutual experience, but oral sex allows other men to relax, without the pressure to perform.

Many women say that they enjoy giving fellatio because they like the actual sensation, the intimacy or the pleasure that it gives their partner. But some women are wary of tasting body parts that are so close to those used for urination. Others become nauseous or gag, particularly if their partner's penis thrusts deeply into their mouth. Some women who feel happy to give oral sex to their partner feel unwilling to go as far as ejaculation. No health reason exists for why a man should not ejaculate into his partner's mouth—unless, of course, he has an infection—but many women dislike the texture and the taste of semen, and prefer to pull away just before ejaculation or spit the fluid out. Conversely, other women feel it is the ultimate intimacy to swallow a lover's body secretions. Because of reservations about ejaculation, fellatio quite often happens as part of foreplay, a preliminary to sexual intercourse in which the woman arouses the man, but he then penetrates her before he actually ejaculates.

MUTUAL ORAL SEX

A position that is known as "sixty-nine" ("soixante-neuf" in French) enables a man and woman to give oral sex to each other simultaneously. The two partners—one kneeling on top of the other or the two lying side by side—can be likened to the numerals 6 and 9 in close proximity. Couples who practice this technique say that it is an exciting variation on normal lovemaking. Sixty-nine does have disadvantages. The positions can be uncomfortable, particularly if there is a big height difference between partners. Also, because neither partner can focus fully on giving or receiving pleasure, it can be problematic to continue sixty-nine through to orgasm; the spasms of climax in one partner can cause discomfort if he or she is still orally stimulating the other.

fact or fiction?

A woman can become pregnant by swallowing her partner's semen.

Fiction. Pregnancy from oral sex is impossible unless a woman somehow transfers semen, perhaps on her fingers, to her vagina and cervix. Even semen transferred in this way would be unlikely to cause pregnancy.

ORAL SEX AND LABOR

Some African tribes recommend that women who are due to go into labor drink their husbands' semen. This is based on the fact that prostaglandins (substances found naturally in semen) cause uterine contractions. Whether or not semen taken orally can induce labor is a subject for medical debate. Many doctors argue that the prostaglandins in semen would be destroyed by stomach acid and therefore have no effect on the uterus. Pregnant women are certainly not advised to avoid oral sex at any stage during pregnancy.

HEALTH RISKS OF ORAL SEX

Oral-genital contact should be avoided if either partner has a sexually transmitted disease. Herpes (see page 188) on the mouth, face or genitals can be transmitted through oral sex. Any kind of oral contact with a partner's feces may transfer bacteria that can lead to infection. It is important to wash thoroughly before oral sex if it is going to include the perineum and anal area.

The herpes virus
Genital herpes is caused by the herpes virus hominis, type 2 (magnified at right). It is a chronic condition, characterized by painful sores. There is no absolute cure for herpes.

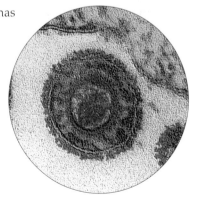

Anal Sex

Anal intercourse, in which a man puts his penis into his partner's anus and rectum, is common among homosexual men. Although some heterosexual couples experiment with anal sex, it is rarely practiced as frequently as vaginal intercourse.

In the past, before reliable contraception became available, anal sex was more common among heterosexual couples because it provided a sure way to avoid pregnancy. Today couples may experiment with anal intercourse because it is a novel technique, providing unique sensations. Many couples never try it, finding the idea unappealing or distasteful.

Some men report that being anally penetrated is intensely exciting because it stimulates the prostate gland, which is situated next to the rectum behind its upper wall (the side nearest the penis). In terms of sexual arousal, the prostate gland can be thought of as the male equivalent of the woman's G-spot (see page 126).

Many women find anal sex painful. One reason for this is that the anus, unlike the vagina, does not produce its own lubrication. Unless the anal sphincter muscle is very relaxed, tearing of the delicate tissues can occur. Deep penetration in particular can cause great pain or discomfort.

Some people experiment with anal stimulation rather than full penetration. This involves stroking the area around the *PERINEUM* and anus. To avoid any risk of infection, the hands must always be thoroughly washed immediately after giving anal stimulation, and a man should never touch his partner's genitals after he has touched her anal area.

HEALTH RISKS

For either sex, anal intercourse carries a high risk of injury and infection because the lining of the anus is not designed to withstand friction, and the blood vessels within it are delicate and easily broken. This causes bleeding, which is why sexually transmitted diseases, such as HIV and hepatitis, are transmitted more readily through anal than vaginal intercourse.

Doctors advise men who have anal intercourse to wear a condom and to make sure that the anus of the receiving partner is lubricated with a water-based lubricant (oil-based lubricants destroy condom rubber). The risk of infection makes using a condom an essential precaution, and it should be one of the extra-strong types designed specifically to withstand the rigors of anal intercourse. However, even extra-strong condoms cannot guarantee complete safety.

Vaginal intercourse must never follow anal intercourse unless the man has safely disposed of the condom and thoroughly washed his genitals and hands with soap and water. Otherwise a high risk exists of transferring bacteria from the woman's anus to her urethra and vagina.

The Kinsey Institute New Report on Sex (1990) recommends that "Anyone—male or female, heterosexual, bisexual or homosexual—who receives anal sex should have regular checkups that include examination of the anus and rectum."

Health considerations
Because of the high levels of bacteria found in and around the rectum, unhygienic anal sex can lead to infections in other parts of the urogenital tract. People practicing anal sex should always use a condom.

Painful tearing of delicate tissues may occur in the anus and rectum.

Rectal bleeding encourages transmission of STDs.

Transfer of bacteria to urethra may result in infection.

Risks associated with anal sex

The anal sphincter may be stretched and weakened.

Transfer of bacteria to vagina may result in infection.

LOVE & SEX
THROUGHOUT
LIFE

Childhood

Even before a baby's eyes are able to focus, he or she has an awareness of a loving presence. A newborn baby taken up in mother's arms or offered the breast quickly understands that mother provides nurture and nourishment.

Mother and baby
There is a unique emotional and physical bond between a mother and her child. Breast-feeding activates hormones that encourage closeness and intimacy.

Childhood is an intense learning period. In the first few years of life, a child learns not only to exert control over his or her body but also to express thoughts, needs, wishes and desires through language. Ideally, learning takes place with the guidance of two loving adults. Love, care, attention and support in the formative years of life are known to be essential for a child's healthy emotional and psychological development.

MOTHER LOVE

From the early stages of pregnancy, a special relationship exists between mother and child. Although cocooned within the mother's body, a baby is affected by her physical and emotional responses. At birth, the child is already intimately aware of his or her mother and often shares her responses. For example, their sleeping patterns may be synchronized.

An interactive relationship between mother and baby may be evident just moments after birth. In response to her baby's cries, a mother lifts the infant to her breast, where the baby instinctively latches on to her nipple and begins to suck. This stimulates production of a hormone known as oxytocin, which causes the uterus to contract and expel the placenta. The uterus remains contracted, helping to slow down bleeding and ensuring the mother's survival.

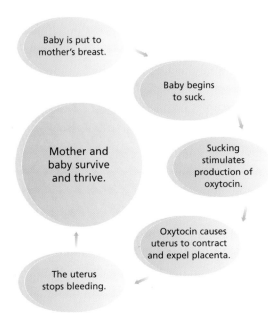

Baby is put to mother's breast.

Baby begins to suck.

Mother and baby survive and thrive.

Sucking stimulates production of oxytocin.

Oxytocin causes uterus to contract and expel placenta.

The uterus stops bleeding.

Hormonal connections
This highly simplified sequence of events indicates the feedback mechanisms involved in breast-feeding. Sucking stimulates not only oxytocin but also prolactin, a hormone involved in milk production.

A mother recognizes her baby's cries from early on and can identify the different sounds of hunger, pain and anger. Even "motherese," the style of speech that mothers (and fathers) adopt—speaking in a higher than usual pitch, using simple or nonsense words and frequent repetition—dovetails with a baby's level of understanding.

Research carried out in Sweden in the late 1970s suggests that however close a father and baby are, the baby still has an inborn preference for the mother. Even babies who are cared for by their fathers in the first month of life tend to prefer their mothers.

LEARNING TO RELATE

Child psychologist John Bowlby has suggested that loving behavior from adults, in the form of touch, eye contact and speech, forms the basis of all future relationships. The mother-child bond is a highly reciprocal, ongoing interaction that starts in babyhood and continues through childhood. With her baby, a mother continually reinforces attempts at communication: baby smiles and mother smiles in response; baby gurgles and mother speaks. Later on in childhood, parents can reinforce their child's emotional growth by being attentive and affectionate.

Emotional development
Psychologists agree that healthy emotional development is a result of love and attention in childhood.

Nonverbal behavior such as smiling indicates trust and intimacy.

Eye contact makes mother and child feel they have each other's undivided attention.

Physical proximity is important when a child needs reassuring or comforting.

Touching and cuddling makes a child feel safe and secure.

While infants will approach either parent when they feel relaxed, they show a definite preference for their mother when afraid.

FATHER LOVE

The love that a father feels for his children is often categorized as being more active and physical than a mother's love. This may lead the mother to be even more protective and attentive toward the baby, resulting in a complicated relationship among the three. Fathers rarely perform as much day-to-day care as mothers, but the bond between them and their offspring can be of similar intensity. Babies may become as upset when their fathers leave them as when their mothers do and, if bottle-fed, will feed as happily with their fathers as their mothers.

BONDING PATTERNS

Attachment grows over time rather than happening instantaneously. Theorists in the 1970s claimed that there is a critical period during which mothers must bond through physical contact with their babies, or irreparable psychological damage will be done to their children. These ideas are now largely discredited.

Psychologists identify four types of bonding patterns that evolve between young babies and their mothers. A secure attachment is one in which a child enjoys contact with his or her mother but can cope with her absence. An avoidant relationship is one in which the child actively rejects the mother. An ambivalent attachment is characterized by the child sometimes seeking and sometimes rejecting the mother. A disoriented relationship involves seeking contact and rejecting at the same time—for example, a child may hold out his or her arms for the mother but look away.

About two-thirds of all mother-child relationships are of the secure type. The remaining third are avoidant, ambivalent or disoriented, usually because mothers are abusive, depressed and/or lack adequate parenting skills. The disoriented mother-child relationship often occurs when the mother has experienced emotional problems in childhood and has never resolved her grief or anxiety.

The secure mother-child relationship creates the most emotionally stable child. Psychologists have also found that securely attached children grow up to enjoy more

LOVE DEPRIVATION

In 1945 Rene Spitz, an American psychologist, compared the fate of children who were brought up in either an orphanage (where little or no affection was shown by the undertrained casual staff) or a prison nursery (where much affection was given to the infants by inmates, wardens and the babies' own mothers). The orphanage children were later found to have more emotional disturbances. The educational dropout, unemployment and arrest rates were all higher for the former orphans.

fulfilling romantic and sexual relationships. Although there is no simple recipe for creating a secure attachment—styles of attachment may, in part, be biologically determined—there is evidence that a parent's love, acceptance and responsiveness are very important. In particular, parents should respond to the child's nonverbal requests for physical contact and social interaction. The emphasis should be on the quality of interaction just as much as on the quantity. This is why mothers of adopted children can bond securely with their children even though they have never experienced the biological bonding that occurs during pregnancy and/or breast-feeding.

GENDER ROLES

Children quickly develop an awareness of what it means to be male and female. Even if parents do not adhere to traditional masculine and feminine roles, children learn about gender from the behavior of their peers, older siblings and teachers and from the portrayal of the sexes in the media.

Often parents unknowingly transmit messages about gender. Where a father is the sole car driver and fixes household appliances, a young boy will unconsciously accept this as male behavior. He may think cooking and caring for the sick are female tasks if he sees them done only by his mother. Most children can identify their gender by age four, and may come to perceive the activities of their same-sex parent as gender-specific and try to emulate that parent.

Sex-specific toys Play is just one way in which children learn about gender roles, but giving action toys to boys and dolls to girls can convey compelling messages to young children.

PRESSURE TO CONFORM

Girls and boys reach an age at which they are expected to behave in gender-appropriate ways.

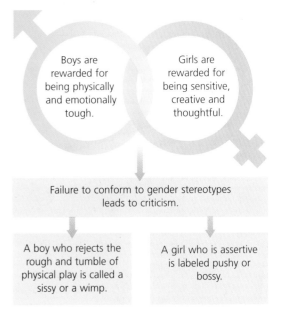

Boys are rewarded for being physically and emotionally tough.

Girls are rewarded for being sensitive, creative and thoughtful.

Failure to conform to gender stereotypes leads to criticism.

A boy who rejects the rough and tumble of physical play is called a sissy or a wimp.

A girl who is assertive is labeled pushy or bossy.

Some psychologists believe that children adopt gender roles because they receive praise or rewards for certain behaviors and not others. This idea is called social learning theory. In practice, it means that girls are encouraged if they display so-called feminine attributes, such as being caring, nurturing, kind, nonaggressive, peaceable, cooperative and concerned with their appearance. Boys will be rewarded if they exhibit independence, competitiveness and resilience. Studies show that a baby dressed in blue and described as a boy receives more attention and physical contact than a baby described as a girl and dressed in pink.

SEXUAL CURIOSITY

Between ages two and five, several developments take place that encourage sexual curiosity. First, a child's muscle control develops, enabling genital exploration and masturbation. Second, language skills increase, enabling the child to pose questions about sexuality. Third, children have more contact with other children of the opposite sex, promoting physical comparison. In parallel with these changes, a child may receive increasingly negative messages about self-touching, whether spoken or unspoken, generated in part by false assumptions about a child's capacity for self-control.

FREUD'S THEORY OF CHILDHOOD SEXUALITY

The Austrian psychoanalyst Sigmund Freud (1856–1939) was one of the first people to suggest that children have a sexual instinct. He used the word "sexual" to mean sensual pleasure or gratification. Freud proposed that the libido (sex drive) develops through three stages—oral, anal and phallic—and then lies dormant until puberty. The phallic stage is the most complex stage. Freud also suggested that how parents deal with the stages can affect a child into adulthood. For example, a stubborn or obsessive adult is said to be anally retentive.

Freud's theory of the phallic stage of infantile sexuality is an account of the way that children learn about gender. He believed that the phallic stage of development begins around the end of the third year when a child becomes aware that boys have a penis and girls do not. Boys become sexually attracted to their mothers (the Oedipus complex). Girls, meanwhile, reject their mothers and fall in love with their fathers. This is known as the Electra complex—Electra was a figure in Greek mythology who plotted to kill her mother to avenge her father's death.

Although Freud's theories were revolutionary, no scientific evidence exists for them. Nevertheless, his concepts have permeated Western thinking and fostered discussions of childhood sexuality.

Sigmund Freud
Freud formulated many of his theories on childhood sexuality from observations he made of the adult patients he treated.

The oral stage
This occurs when the infant breast- or bottle-feeds and derives pleasure from sucking with the mouth and lips. Excessive drinking, eating and smoking characterize the orally fixated adult.

The anal stage
As a child learns to control bowel movements, the area of pleasure shifts to the anus. During this stage the child becomes very concerned with the elimination and retention of feces.

The phallic stage
Boys fall in love with their mothers during this stage. Freud named this the Oedipus complex—Oedipus was a figure in Greek mythology who killed his father and married his mother.

A child's sexual curiosity, combined with parental disapproval, can generate tension that both parents and child find frustrating and sometimes disturbing. The best advice is to be as open and accepting of a child's natural curiosity as possible. When a child asks questions about sexual matters, family therapists advise parents to answer him or her briefly, using age-appropriate language and concepts. Parents should talk to any other caregivers (grandparents, baby-sitters and so on) to ensure that the child does not receive contradictory or confusing messages from different people.

Masturbation may cause parents embarrassment, but touching the genitals provides sensual pleasure and is a habit that children derive comfort from, rather than a response to sexual arousal. Masturbation may continue into puberty or stop and recur in puberty or later in adult life. It is important that childhood masturbation be thought of as genital play and in that way distinguished from adult sexual arousal and masturbation. Genital play appears to be universal across culture and time—it certainly does not cause or indicate physical or psychological illness. Masturbation is a cause for concern only when it is a response to emotional stress or abuse. Some children masturbate frequently when they are bored or lonely or afraid. Parents who feel that their child masturbates excessively or in response to stress should consult a doctor.

Puberty

Sometime between childhood and adulthood, a surge in sex hormones triggers sexual development. The sex organs mature, and associated hormonal activity makes sexual intercourse and reproduction possible.

The physical changes that characterize puberty make male and female bodies both fertile and attractive to the opposite sex. Puberty usually starts between ages 8 and 14 in girls and between 10 and 15 in boys. For girls, the first sign is the beginning of breast development, while boys notice that their genitals start to enlarge. For both sexes, these changes are followed by the appearance of hair in the genital area and armpits.

Puberty is often a time of rapid physical growth. After body hair appears, the hormone somatotropin is released by the pituitary gland in the brain to trigger bone and muscle growth.

Girls normally experience this growth spurt earlier than boys. Around age 12, they are often taller than boys of the same age, but by age 15 boys tend to be taller. Most girls are close to their adult height when they start to menstruate. Body shape also changes: girls gain body fat and their hips become wider; boys gain more lean body tissue, so their overall percentage of body fat drops, and their shoulders and chests become broader than their hips.

MALE SEXUAL DEVELOPMENT

In boys, follicle-stimulating hormone (FSH; see box, right) triggers development and production of sperm, and luteinizing hormone (LH) triggers production of testosterone. Testosterone, which is the most important of all male sex hormones, is responsible, in one form or another, for the development of most of the male *SECONDARY SEXUAL CHARACTERISTICS*.

Ninety-five percent of testosterone is secreted by the testicles and 5 percent by the *ADRENAL GLANDS*. In addition to sexual changes, testosterone causes bone ends to fuse, or close over, terminating growth in both boys and girls. The testicles and scrotum respond to testosterone by increasing in size. The surface of the scrotum becomes

| STAGE 1 | STAGE 2 | STAGE 3 | STAGE 4 | STAGE 5 |

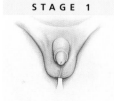    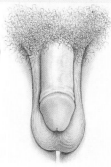

The scrotum is drawn up close to the body.

The testicles enlarge and the scrotum hangs lower.

The testicles continue to enlarge and the penis grows longer.

The penis increases in girth and pubic hair grows. The skin of the penis and scrotum deepens in color.

The penis grows in length and girth to reach its adult state. The testicles are fully functional.

Genital development in a circumcised male
There are roughly five stages in the development of the penis and testicles. Stage one is the immature genitals of babyhood. By stage five the sex organs are sexually mature, making reproduction possible.

ONSET OF PUBERTY

The way in which puberty begins is not fully understood. Scientists believe that an inhibitory mechanism exists in the brain, which at puberty is removed. The part of the brain known as the hypothalamus then releases a surge of hormone that triggers puberty. This is how puberty starts in both girls and boys.

The trigger hormone is known as gonadotropin-releasing hormone (GRH). It travels to the pituitary gland—located beneath the hypothalamus. The pituitary gland then secretes two important hormones known as follicle-stimulating hormone (FSH) and luteinizing hormone (LH). These hormones travel through the bloodstream and trigger the ovaries and testes to become active for the first time.

Before she can begin to menstruate, about a quarter of a girl's total body weight must be composed of fat. This is why the development of wider hips and fuller breasts during puberty is thought to be important in triggering menstruation. When girls have low body fat, the pituitary gland does not release the required amount of FSH and LH for normal menstruation to take place.

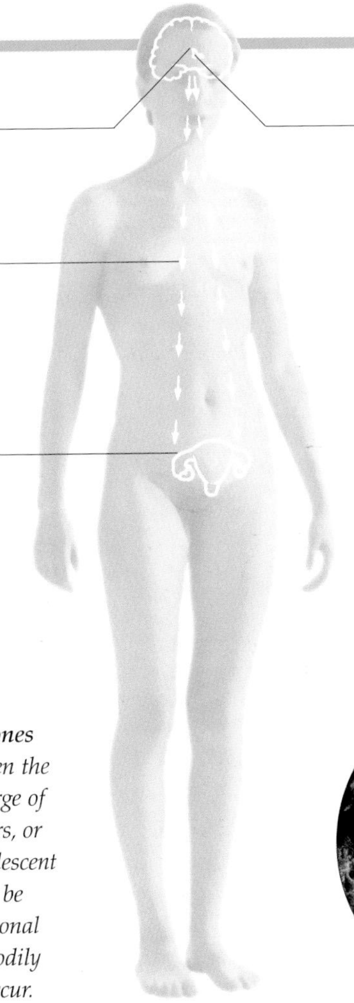

The hypothalamus releases GRH.

The pituitary gland is stimulated to produce FSH and LH.

FSH and LH travel through the bloodstream to the ovaries.

FSH causes the egg follicles in the ovaries to start maturing for the first time.

Ovulation
When the ovaries become active for the first time, an egg, or ovum (shown below), is released from the ovary. This is an event that will continue to happen periodically for the rest of a woman's reproductive life span.

The flow of hormones
Puberty begins when the brain releases a surge of chemical messengers, or hormones. The adolescent girl or boy will not be aware of this hormonal activity until the bodily changes begin to occur.

---

more wrinkled, redder and darker. The penis grows longer and then increases in width. After this, pubic and axillary (armpit) hair grows, followed by facial and chest hair. The testicles, scrotum and penis continue to enlarge.

Testosterone also causes the prostate gland (see page 121) and the voice box, or larynx, to enlarge. The vocal cords become longer and thicker, eventually causing a deepening of the voice. While this is taking place, some boys have an uncomfortable feeling in their throats for a few weeks, but for most, the change is gradual and free of any symptoms.

fact or fiction?

Erections occur even when you're not sexually aroused.

Fact. During puberty boys have high levels of testosterone causing spontaneous erections. This can be embarrassing, but it is not unusual or abnormal. It can also happen in prepubescent boys.

Between 30 and 50 percent of pubescent boys develop a slight increase in size in one or both breasts. Known as gynecomastia, this results from an excess of estrogen in the body and can cause a great deal of anxiety among boys and their families; doubts about masculinity are a common concern. Most cases disappear spontaneously within a year.

Ejaculation

The male equivalent of a girl's first menstrual bleed is a boy's first ejaculation. This is called spermarche and is usually experienced at about age 13. The first ejaculation

CHANGES AT PUBERTY

At puberty, both sexes undergo rapid physical development as their bodies change to become sexually mature.

Changes in girls include the following:

Breasts and nipples enlarge.

Menstruation begins.

Vaginal secretions increase.

The inner and outer lips of the vulva enlarge.

The vagina becomes longer and wider.

Changes in boys and girls include the following:

Height increases.

Sebaceous (oil) glands become active, and acne becomes common.

Body and pubic hair grows.

Sweat glands in the armpits and genitals become active, and adult body odor is produced.

Changes in boys include the following:

The voice becomes deeper.

Muscle mass starts increasing.

The penis and testicles enlarge.

Ejaculation becomes possible.

Facial hair develops.

Hair follicle — Surface of skin

Sebaceous gland — Sweat gland

The cause of acne
Sebum is an oily substance secreted onto the skin by the sebaceous glands. Excess sebum production at puberty can result in oily skin and acne.

often occurs at night during sleep and is known as a nocturnal emission or, more commonly, a "wet dream." Wet dreams are experienced by about 75 percent of pubescent males (but rarely by adult males). They typically occur during the rapid eye movement phase of sleep.

Ejaculation during puberty does not guarantee fertility (see page 152); it simply indicates that seminal-fluid production is beginning and that the testicles and prostate gland (see page 121) are adequately performing their secretory functions.

FEMALE SEXUAL DEVELOPMENT

In girls, the release of FSH and LH tells the ovaries to produce estrogen, which triggers the development of female sexual characteristics. The breasts begin to grow, although rarely evenly. It is common for one breast to be slightly larger than the other until sexual maturity is reached, when they may roughly even out. Pubic hair begins to appear on the pubic mound in a flat-topped triangular shape and on the outer lips (labia majora) surrounding the genitals. In about 45 percent of girls, pubic

hair growth occurs before breast growth. Hair also starts appearing in the armpits, and the fine, downy hair on the legs becomes thicker and longer.

The uterus enlarges and the external genitals become darker and more prominent. The vagina also enlarges and a slight discharge may be noticeable. The surge in estrogen levels that comes with puberty can make the skin oilier and prone to blocked pores, blackheads, spots and acne.

Menarche

The most dramatic development in puberty is the onset of menstruation (see page 140), an event called the menarche. It normally occurs between ages 9 and 17. In Western societies it usually occurs after the age of 11. There are several causes of late menarche, or primary amenorrhea (see page 192). Low body weight caused by *ANOREXIA NERVOSA* or overexercising can inhibit menarche.

After menarche a girl's menstrual periods may be very irregular for a while, since she may ovulate some months but not others. It may take a couple of years for the menstrual cycle to become regular.

Adolescence

Adolescence is fraught with mixed messages. Young people are aware of and excited by their burgeoning sexuality, yet most societies discourage them from acting on their newfound sexual urges. This can cause conflict, insecurity and frustration.

Teenagers are popularly characterized as rebellious, moody and defiant. Adolescence marks a period of transition between childhood and adulthood, in which emotional maturity often lags behind physical maturity. As a result, the typical adolescent desire to break away from parents is frequently accompanied by confusion. The teenager wants to prove that he or she is independent but continues to exhibit a fair amount of childishness.

During adolescence, sexual thoughts and feelings become increasingly prominent. Girls and boys begin to discover their sexuality through fantasies and crushes. During middle and late adolescence, physical contact becomes more important, and holding hands, kissing and heavy petting may lead to a desire for sexual intercourse.

While channeling their sexual and romantic feelings into fantasies and crushes, both girls and boys often relieve emerging desire through masturbation. This is a common and natural outlet that teaches teenagers to know and appreciate their bodies.

Teenagers may experiment sexually with members of the same sex (see page 99), and this may pave the way for a physical relationship with a member of the opposite sex later on, or it may indicate a preference for the same sex. Sexual experimentation is thought to be more common among boys, but this may just be a reflection of the cultural stereotype that assumes boys are more interested and active in sex than are girls.

CRUSHES

As a rule, crushes help teenagers to cope with their sexual feelings and to learn about love and relationships without becoming involved with another person and facing the possibility of pain and rejection. Teenagers may develop crushes on "accessible" people such as their classmates, neighbors or the friends of older, opposite-sex siblings, but they more often focus on unobtainable figures such as famous actors, sports personalities or pop stars. While crushes typically remain fantasy, crushes on accessible people—often teachers—can lead

Teenage styles The image of the rebellious teenager was created in the 1950s with James Dean. Since then teenagers have continued to adopt styles considered alternative or risqué.

Punk, 1970s

Hippy, 1960s

Vamp, 1980s

Grunge, early 1990s

Teenage friendships ▶
Growing independence during adolescence can mean that friendships take on special importance. Close friends take the place of parents as confidants.

Discovering sex
Sexual experimentation can be exciting, but many teenagers feel intense pressure to appear sexually confident or experienced.

to problems for the teenager or the focus of their crush. Some people are acutely embarrassed at becoming the focus of a teenage crush and deal with it badly, while others take advantage of adolescent adulation and abuse their position. Rarely, crushes develop into obsessions and cause a great deal of pain and anguish. Not all adolescents experience crushes, and teenagers develop at different rates, but such feelings are normally a healthy outlet for a developing sexuality and a vital part of coming to terms with it.

PEER PRESSURE

As personal and sexual identity develops, the desire to belong to a peer group and to be popular becomes particularly strong. Teenagers want to be accepted by their peers in order to feel that they are normal. Because of this, they may feel pressured to conform with the ideas and activities of a group. This typically includes wearing the latest clothes and hairstyle and, in terms of sexual development, having a boyfriend or girlfriend. Pressure can push a young person into having sexual intercourse because "everyone else is doing it." Teenagers may find themselves giving in to such pressure before they are emotionally ready, in many cases before the legal age of consent. Some teenagers overcome this by simply talking about "doing it" but in fact abstaining from intercourse until they feel completely ready.

ADOLESCENT SEXUAL BEHAVIOR

Because teenagers are fascinated with their newly emerging powers of sexual attraction, they are curious to test them out. Flirting provides a fun, normally harmless form of sexual teasing that has the added benefit of not requiring any sexual performance. Sexual party games, especially kissing games, serve an important function as well: they allow teens to test the sexual water in a friendly, noncommitted environment. They also teach adolescents how to interact with the opposite sex on a sexual rather than a platonic level. For shy, less adventurous participants, however, such games can be awkward, uncomfortable experiences that lead to feelings of failure and social inadequacy.

Most young people begin their journey toward sexual maturity by forming friendships with members of the opposite sex. In this way they test their powers of attraction without involvement in a full-fledged relationship. Later, after a teenager becomes involved romantically and is formally dating, he or she may try experimenting with kissing, heavy petting and, in some cases, sexual intercourse.

When it comes to forming sexual relationships, important gender differences surface. Boys tend to search for physical gratification because their sex drive at this time is intense. Girls, on the other hand, typically place greater emphasis on the loving and romantic aspects of relationships. Sadly, boys often receive positive attention when they attract, date, kiss and have sex with as many girls as they can, while girls meet with disapproval if they behave in a similar way. In fact, neither gender should have a fear of saying "no" or worry about being called "frigid" or boring because they are deciding for themselves when they are ready to have sex.

Deciding if and when to have sexual intercourse for the first time is one of the most important decisions that a teenager can make, and adolescents often feel rushed. Research shows that the most common source of pressure experienced by young teenage girls is from boyfriends. Boys, on

the other hand, are more likely to feel pressured into having sex by boasts, jibes or claims from other boys, or by cultural expectations of male sexuality.

Adolescents' expectations of sexual intercourse and the reality are often quite

DOUBLE STANDARDS

Increasing sex drive in adolescent boys and girls leads to a desire for sexual expression.

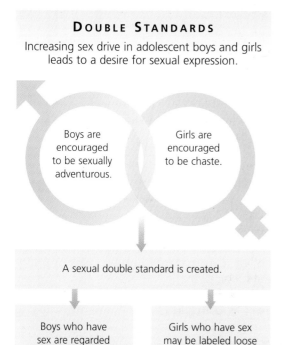

Boys are encouraged to be sexually adventurous.

Girls are encouraged to be chaste.

A sexual double standard is created.

Boys who have sex are regarded as cool or macho.

Girls who have sex may be labeled loose or promiscuous.

different. First-time sex is rarely the mind-blowing experience often portrayed by Hollywood. It is more likely to be messy, awkward and disappointing. Most women do not reach orgasm, and if a woman is unprepared, nervous or still has her hymen (see page 125) intact, it can cause pain, soreness and bleeding.

Adolescents who defer intercourse until adulthood, when they are married or in a stabler relationship, may benefit from increased emotional maturity. Maintaining a solid relationship requires self-confidence, commitment, empathy and trust—characteristics that are more likely to develop as adolescents approach adulthood.

Dating

Courtship in the form of boy-girl outings, or dates, gives teenagers a chance to develop intimate relationships away from the scrutiny of parents. This makes the dating process very inviting and intensely exciting. There

is no prescribed activity that constitutes a date, although going to the movies and eating out are traditional. Many teenagers avoid the awkwardness of one-on-one dating by going out in groups. Around age 14 or 15 for girls and 16 for boys, teenagers may opt for a more private arrangement. Single dating can lead to the more serious, more exclusive romantic involvement of going steady. This arrangement has its drawbacks, including increased pressure to perform sexually before the adolescent is ready to engage in a full sexual relationship.

Parents should not confuse their teenagers' noncommunication about sex with lack of interest in it. Many teenagers are very anxious about sex and often feel too reluctant or inhibited to talk about it with their parents or to seek contraceptive advice. This is regrettable, because first-time intercourse that is unplanned is less likely to be protected. For parents to be helpful and supportive, they need to initiate discussion on sexual matters and ensure that their children's knowledge on sex is sufficient and correct.

UNWANTED PREGNANCIES

A study in *Family Planning Perspectives* in 1988 revealed that out of the approximately 10 percent of American girls aged 15 to 19 who become pregnant every year, five out of six pregnancies are unplanned. More recent statistics indicate that teenage

AGE OF EXPERIENCE

Today the average age for first intercourse is reported to be between ages 14.5 and 16 for both men and women. Since the 1950s, changes in male teenage sexual activity have been minimal, but increases in female sexual activity have been dramatic. When interviewed, 75 percent of adolescents said that they believed sex before marriage was acceptable when both partners loved each other.

In a study of 2,600 American teenagers living in metropolitan areas, 22.5 percent of girls had had sex by age 15 and 69 percent by the age of 19. Fifty percent of boys had had sex by age 17 and 77 percent by age 19.

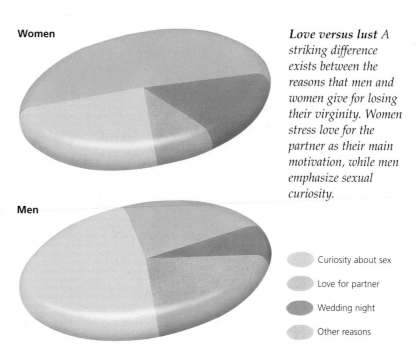

Women

Men

Love versus lust A striking difference exists between the reasons that men and women give for losing their virginity. Women stress love for the partner as their main motivation, while men emphasize sexual curiosity.

Curiosity about sex

Love for partner

Wedding night

Other reasons

Can We Talk About It?

TEENAGE PREGNANCY

The initial shock of finding out that you are pregnant can be overwhelming, so it is very important that you have people to talk to. Telling people who can help you that you are pregnant will make it easier for you to make the best decision about what to do next. When it comes to telling your parents, think carefully about the best time to tell them. When will they be most likely to listen calmly? Is there anyone you would need or like to have present when you talk to them—an older sister, a friend, your boyfriend, a teacher or a relative whom you trust?

Spend some time thinking about what you want and need from your parents. Their first reaction may well be anger, disappointment or grief, but after the initial burst of emotion it can help if you tell them what kind of support you need. This can range from saying that you are frightened and don't know what to do, to saying that you have decided on a course of action and you want them to accept your decision. You can also ask for practical help, such as having someone to accompany you to see a doctor or go to the hospital.

When you tell your boyfriend, try to avoid arguments about whose fault the pregnancy is and instead concentrate on what you are going to do. He may want to influence you, but ultimately the decision on a course of action is yours. Try to think ahead and imagine how you will manage as mother of a baby. Try to get information from people you trust and from agencies that specialize in helping pregnant teenage girls. Above all, don't delay in deciding what to do next.

pregnancy is on the increase throughout the world. In the U.S., 11 in every 100 teenagers become pregnant, which is the highest rate of teenage pregnancy in the West.

A teenage girl who unintentionally becomes pregnant faces enormous emotional upheaval, confusion and sometimes ignorance. Her boyfriend—if he is still her boyfriend—may be unsupportive. She may be terrified of her parents' response and delay telling them as a result. In extreme cases, she may try to hide the pregnancy, attempt a home abortion or consider suicide. Help is available. There are three ways of dealing with an unplanned pregnancy: motherhood, adoption or abortion.

Motherhood

Teenage motherhood is a controversial subject. According to Masters, Johnson and Kolodny, in their book *Heterosexuality* (1994), "early parenthood almost inevitably puts the future of young mothers and their children in jeopardy socially, economically and educationally."

Some teenagers decide that keeping their baby is the right choice. Counselors advise pregnant girls to analyze their motives carefully. Is pregnancy a way of trapping a partner into commitment or marriage? Will having a baby simply provide someone to love? Does bringing up a child seem like a distraction or an escape route from the bad things in life? Is having a baby the only option they have considered? A pregnant teenager needs to think carefully when choosing parenthood. Having said this, some teenagers go on to be excellent parents, fulfilled and happy in their role of mother or father.

Adoption

For young women who do not want or are unable to bring up a baby, adoption provides a strong alternative to either keeping the baby or having an abortion.

Hospitals can usually put a mother-to-be in contact with a public or private adoption agency that will find a suitable adoptive couple. Pregnant teenagers considering adoption need to think carefully about whether they will be able to part with the baby—many people underestimate the emotional impact of the experience of childbirth. Counseling may help teenagers to come to a decision.

Although parting with a baby can be traumatic, research shows that young women who put their babies up for adoption suffer no more negative psychological consequences than do young women who go on to parent their children.

Of American teenagers who carry their babies to term, it is estimated that less than 4 percent enter into an adoption plan.

Abortion

Termination, or abortion, means ending the life of a fetus while it is inside the uterus. Attitudes are intensely divided about the morality of abortion—some people feel that taking the life of an unborn child is murder and should be made illegal; others believe that every woman has the personal right to choose whether or not to go ahead with a pregnancy. The decision to have an abortion needs to be made as quickly as possible. The earlier the abortion, the fewer health risks there are for the woman.

The most common type of abortion is vacuum aspiration, also called suction curettage. This is carried out up to the 12th week of pregnancy under general or local anesthetic. The opening in the cervix (see page 126) is dilated, and a tube connected to a suction pump is passed into the uterus to draw out the fetus and placenta.

Dilatation and curettage (D&C) is a technique that can be used later into a pregnancy. The contents of the uterus are scraped out under general anesthetic using an instrument called a curette.

For late abortions (beyond the 14th week of pregnancy), induction methods are used. An induction abortion is similar to the experience of labor. *PROSTAGLANDINS* are introduced into the uterus to induce laborlike contractions that expel the fetus. Prostaglandins are put into the uterus by injection through the woman's abdomen, by an infusion into the uterus or by placement of a prostaglandin suppository high into the vagina. It usually takes between 12 and 24 hours for the fetus to be expelled.

There are also drugs called "abortifacients" that cause pregnant women to miscarry. One of these, manufactured in France, is nicknamed the "abortion pill." The medical name is mifepristone or RU-486, and it can only be used by women who are under nine weeks pregnant. Mifepristone remains controversial but is available in the U.S.

SEXUAL IDENTITY

During adolescence, young people of both sexes question their sexuality and try to define their sexual feelings. As part of this process, girls may develop crushes on supermodels or actresses, and boys may find themselves excited by male pop stars or sports figures. Girls or boys may take part in same-sex play. Girls sometimes kiss and cuddle, and boys may masturbate together, even holding masturbation competitions. These feelings and experiences are not wrong but are a normal part of discovering sexual identity.

Homosexuality

Same-sex physical experimentation is often nothing more than a passing phase, but some adolescents are consistently attracted to the same sex. Recognizing and discussing homosexuality in adolescence is difficult. Gay teenagers are outnumbered by heterosexuals, but they naturally want to fit in with their peer groups. This pressure may lead to a denial of sexual identity, which can cause much suffering.

Homosexual behavior is not usually established until middle or late adolescence. Genetic and social factors may influence homosexual orientation (see page 50). Social factors for boys are sometimes thought to include lack of male role models, or an emotionally distant father and an overprotective mother. In girls, sexuality may be influenced by a rejecting mother, an over-affectionate father, or parents who favor a male sibling.

Attitudes have changed over the past few decades—parents are more aware that their child may be gay, and young people have learned that not everyone is the same. Yet it is still difficult for gay young men and women to be open about their homosexuality, especially if their parents have religious or moral beliefs that are openly hostile to homosexuality. In this instance, understanding and frank discussion with other sympathetic adults can help alleviate some of the feelings of anxiety, fear and depression young teenage homosexuals may experience. Parents may feel a range of emotions from grief and confusion to guilt and anger when confronted with the news that their child may be gay (see page 280). Counseling or family therapy can help all parties.

Gay relationships
When teenagers are trying to fit in and gain acceptance from their peers, it can be a shocking revelation that their sexual feelings are focused on the same sex. If adolescents do enter into gay relationships, they may decide to keep them secret.

Adulthood

Adulthood is the time when sexuality becomes established. Men and women become aware of their sexual needs, responses and preferences, and usually sex becomes an important part of a marital or other monogamous relationship.

Family life The decision to settle down and have children is a turning point in adult life. Many couples say that creating a family is one of life's most enriching experiences, bringing a sense of permanence, fulfillment and joy.

While sexual intercourse in adolescence takes place in the context of increasing financial, social and domestic freedom, sex in adulthood is commonly defined by growing responsibilities in these areas. Sexual behavior in adulthood typically changes from decade to decade. A couple who are in their twenties generally have sex more often than a couple in their thirties or forties. Couples in their twenties are also likely to be highly fertile.

Adulthood is the time when most people have their children, and the emotional highs and lows that accompany the presence of new family members transform relationships in ways both good and bad.

A WOMAN'S SEXUAL RESPONSES

The patterns of arousal and orgasm that women experience in their twenties will form the basis of their future sexuality. These years are a time for learning about sex and

exploring the body's responses. Many women may be unfamiliar with their bodies and have great anxieties about their sexual performance. They may concentrate on their worries (about not reaching orgasm, for instance) rather than their pleasure. The study *The Social Organization of Sexuality* (1994) by Edward Laumann and others found that women in their twenties are less likely to reach orgasm from sex or to masturbate than older women.

By their thirties, most women have developed a good degree of sexual self-knowledge, and this is reflected in their enjoyment of sex and their ability to achieve orgasm. Laumann's study found that 88.5 percent of women in this age group reached orgasm regularly, compared with 79 percent of women in their twenties. Women in their thirties are often less inhibited about communicating their sexual needs to their partners. One problem that some women in this age group begin to experience is a lack of libido, brought about by stressful working conditions and/or fatigue related to pregnancy and childrearing.

The forties signal a time when hormonal changes may begin to affect a woman's sexuality (see page 107). Nevertheless, according to sex therapist Helen Singer Kaplan, women are more likely to experience multiple orgasm at this stage of life because they have resolved past sexual problems and attained sexual and emotional ease.

A MAN'S SEXUAL RESPONSES

Men in their twenties usually find that sexual arousal happens very easily. They often have short refractory periods, meaning that they can achieve an erection within minutes of their last ejaculation, and can have sex several times in succession. The main sexual problem that young men encounter is premature ejaculation (see page 213), since they may not have learned to exert control over their ejaculatory responses. They may also have little interest in foreplay.

Men in their thirties may notice that their sexual responses have slowed down slightly, and that they have more difficulty sustaining repeated erections. On the positive side, however, men are less likely to suffer from hyperarousal and premature ejaculation at this age, which means that sexual intercourse can last longer. Lack of libido as a result of work- or family-related stress is not uncommon at this time; nevertheless, it need not be a problem if neither partner sees it as such.

Men in their forties may notice that a full erection can take longer to achieve than previously, but only a tiny percentage of men of this age group suffer from impotence.

ROMANTIC LOVE

According to popular culture, adolescents have crushes and infatuations, while adults fall in love. Modern societies consider this feeling of romantic love to be sufficient justification for most, if not all, adult relationships (see page 14).

The initial feeling of being in love with someone may lead to placing the loved person on a pedestal and thinking obsessively about him or her. This state of intensity may be accompanied by physical sensations such as weakness, sleeplessness and loss of appetite. Relationship counselors agree that adult relationships follow a natural evolution in which this state of being in love gradually transforms itself into a state of caring love. If this transformation does not occur, once the state of being in love has run its course, a couple generally splits up.

In a good relationship, being in love will evolve into a state of deep, reciprocal caring in which partners allow each other to express themselves and grow as individuals—this is known in psychological terms as the facilitating role of love. Often, however, couples panic when they realize that their initial feelings of passion and intensity are fading, taking this as a sign that they must be falling out of love and the relationship is losing its meaning. Relationship counselors say that this is the stage at which couples have to start contributing to

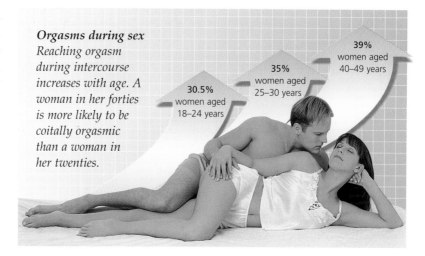

Orgasms during sex
Reaching orgasm during intercourse increases with age. A woman in her forties is more likely to be coitally orgasmic than a woman in her twenties.

30.5% women aged 18–24 years

35% women aged 25–30 years

39% women aged 40–49 years

the relationship in practical ways (see page 25), rather than relying on the sheer force of their emotions.

The ways in which people respond to adult relationships depend strongly on the lessons they learned during childhood. Counselors usually try to help couples articulate their unspoken rules and expectations about love and sex in order to help them

THE COURSE OF LOVE

Adults measure the intensity of a relationship by how romantically attached or "in love" they feel.

Two people meet and fall in love.

A period of romantic infatuation follows.

Growing intimacy and familiarity gives couple the feeling that they are not so in love as they used to be.

Couple separates with the conviction that they have fallen out of love.

Relationship develops in a different way.

Companionable love replaces romantic love.

The wedding day
Weddings are emotion-ally charged, romanti-cized occasions. But if a marriage is to last, companionship rather than romance must be the driving force.

Common pressures on a married couple
Psychologists say that the most common sources of stress in marriage are money, work and children.

work out problems within a relationship. Above all, they encourage people to cultivate good listening skills, whereby one partner is able to listen uncritically to what the other is saying, not what one wants or expects the other to say.

MARRIAGE

Although many societies no longer consider marriage the only way to sanctify sexual relationships, many couples still make this form of commit-ment to each other. About 75 to 80 percent of people who have been through divorce remarry, and in some cases more than once. In its ideal form, marriage represents a loving, nurturing relationship in which two people offer each other ongo-ing emotional support, security and com-mitment. Marriages are rarely perfect, but relationship counselors argue that a good or healthy marriage is one in which couples communicate well, acknowledge their dif-ferences and disagreements and are pre-pared to work at the relationship.

Despite the romantic associations that many people attach to marriage, long-term relationships can be stressful. Once a couple marry, money and children commonly become sources of pressure. Uncertainty

about their future level of income places a well-documented pressure on married cou-ples. Current societal factors, such as unem-ployment and a move toward contracted, part-time, service-based work, mean that permanent employment can no longer be assumed. Another common source of stress comes from disagreements about when or even whether to have children.

Perceptions of the ideal marriage vary from culture to culture. A report in the *Journal of Social and Personal Relationships* (1993) suggests that, in Japan, socioeconom-ic factors such as the husband's income are very important in marital satisfaction. In Western cultures, the quality of spouses' interactions is thought to be a good indica-tion of satisfaction.

Until the 1960s, pressures on marriage tended to result in affairs and marital col-lapse but not divorce. In the past 40 years divorce has become relatively easier, and the pressures on marriage are more clearly indicated by divorce rates. Statistics show that almost one in two marriages in North America end in divorce.

In the West, where love is emphasized as a reason for marriage, marital satisfaction declines with age. In other cultures, where love is seen as a consequence of marriage, this appears not to be the case. Yet even though satisfaction declines over the years, most long-term married couples in the West decide that, on balance, being married is preferable to not being married.

Adultery

Estimates of the incidence of adultery vary enormously. In the American study *The Social Organization of Sexuality* (1994), a dra-matic downward revision occurred from earlier estimates of the number of couples engaging in extramarital sexual activity. The figures were revised from 65 percent of men and 50 percent of women to 26 percent and 21 percent, respectively.

The reasons offered by people who have had extramarital sex are diverse. Some cite revenge on an unfaithful partner or seduc-tion by another person. Others claim they are naturally polygamous. The reasons offered respectively by men and women for indulging in extramarital sex point to clear gender-specific differences between them. Adulterous husbands give the desire for increased sexual excitement as the main rea-

Should we have children? When is the right time?

What if my partner doesn't want me to work?

If I lose my job will my partner respect me?

How many children should we have?

Child- and work-related marital stress

Suppose we can't have children?

What will happen to my partner if I lose my job or die?

Do we earn enough money? Should I work harder?

Will I be a good enough parent?

son for infidelity, while adulterous wives state that emotional dissatisfaction with their husband is the main reason.

A study in the *Journal of Social and Personal Relationships* (1995) found that when wives discover that their partner has been unfaithful, they are most likely to respond with self-doubt and disappointment, even though they feel just as angry and betrayed as husbands of adulterous wives. This is especially true of women who suffer from low self-esteem. The wife's sense of jealousy is reduced when she herself has already been unfaithful.

Although many people believe that adultery is sufficient basis to end a relationship, most marriages do manage to survive infidelity. Relationship counselors say that honest communication is one of the keys to recovery. The reasons for infidelity need to be established so that both partners can avoid a repeat of the circumstances that led to an affair in the first place.

PREGNANCY

Women may experience profound emotional and sexual changes during pregnancy. Some women report feeling fertile, energized and sensual, while others suffer from nausea and simply feel drained. Women's sexual desire may fluctuate during pregnancy, and frequency of intercourse tends to decline as pregnancy progresses, although some women report heightened desire in the middle stages of their pregnancy.

There is no physiological reason for couples to abstain from sex during pregnancy unless intercourse is painful or there is a risk of miscarriage. The fetus, suspended in amniotic fluid, is protected from any bumps or bruising. However, a protruding stomach and sore breasts can make face-to-face intercourse uncomfortable. Alternative positions such as side-by-side, rear entry and sitting may be more suitable during pregnancy.

Having children

The presence of a newborn baby may have dramatic effects on a couple's relationship and sex life, particularly in the first three to six months after birth. Couples often report feelings of intense love and joy alternating with fatigue and, sometimes, mild depression. Although women are able to have regular intercourse as soon as feels comfortable after giving birth, many couples take much

longer than this to resume an active sex life. The reasons for this delay include exhaustion, pain during intercourse (from stitches, for example), breast pain (from enlargement or cracked nipples during nursing), poor body image in women and lack of privacy. Some new fathers find it hard to reconcile the sexuality of their wife with the pain they may have witnessed her experiencing

THE PREGNANT BODY

The two most obvious changes to a woman's body during pregnancy are weight gain and a protruding belly, but many other changes occur as well. For example, the volume of blood in the body increases dramatically to provide an adequate supply to the growing fetus and the woman's vital organs. The pumping power of the heart likewise increases. The blood flow to the skin is greater than before, and many women notice that they feel hotter than normal. They may also find that their skin looks healthier, giving rise to the radiant glow often associated with pregnancy.

Hair may grow faster and become more luxuriant during pregnancy.

The breasts swell and become sensitive and tender, and the skin around the nipples may darken.

Skin rashes and stretch marks are not uncommon.

The uterus expands, and the fundus (the top of the uterus) may push out the navel.

Blood flow to the genitals increases during pregnancy, leading to heightened sexual arousal and more intense orgasms.

The glow of pregnancy
Some women find the symptoms associated with pregnancy debilitating, but after the first trimester has passed many women feel positively energized.

The feet may swell and cramps may affect the legs.

during childbirth. Nonpenetrative sex is ideal for regaining intimacy and can be just as satisfying as penetrative sex.

Children can cement and affirm a relationship between two people; an intense three-way bonding process can take place between mother, father and child. Although early parenthood can be hard work, many parents compare their feelings for a child to the sensations experienced when falling in love. To some extent, these loving feelings can be caused by hormones, because levels of a hormone called oxytocin are higher than normal in mothers with very young children. Nicknamed the "cuddle chemical," oxytocin encourages nurturing behavior. Levels of the hormone also rise, although to a lesser extent, in fathers.

In the first five years of marriage, children can sometimes undermine overall marital satisfaction. This may be due to the stress and demands inherent in childcare or to the shift in focus of a relationship from the emotional needs of the couple to the needs of a child. Men and women also experience stress over the new roles they adopt when they become parents. Are they "good" parents bringing up the child in the right way? How should they divide up the tasks involved in childcare? Who takes primary responsibility for the baby? What happens if the division of work leaves the man feeling excluded or the woman feeling overburdened? What happens if the woman wants to return to work? Some or all of these questions are likely to arise between partners who have become parents. Although some couples are lucky

New parenthood
Getting to know a new baby can be an exhilarating experience, but it can also be a tiring one. Combining work and parenthood is an acquired skill.

Sensual touch
Intercourse may be uncomfortable during pregnancy or after childbirth. Sensual massage is a good way to stay intimate with a partner.

enough to fall into a pattern that immediately suits both of them, others may need to work hard to negotiate solutions.

NONMARITAL RELATIONSHIPS

Although many adults choose to make the lifelong commitment of marriage, others retain their single status throughout adulthood. Some people decide that marriage will not provide the right context for their relationship—they may be unwilling to make a serious commitment or they may feel that a relationship does not need to be sealed with a public announcement and a ceremony. Alternatively, relationships may not evolve to the point where marriage becomes a possibility. Some people have experienced failed marriages and become disillusioned with intimate, long-term relationships. Other people find that their sexuality makes marriage impossible.

Cohabitation

An increasing number of adults are turning to cohabitation as an alternative to getting married. Often, however, this arrangement is a deferral rather than an actual rejection of marriage; most couples who cohabit do eventually marry

one another. Some couples perceive living together before marriage as advantageous. It lets them assess how they relate to each other before they actually commit themselves. When such couples marry, they have already developed common routines, habits and expectations.

A study in the *Journal of Social and Personal Relationships* (1994) reported a number of unexpected differences between cohabiting and married couples. Cohabiting couples reported having more sex than married couples, fewer affairs, a greater frequency of women initiating sex and a higher level of sexual satisfaction than in married women. Cohabitants typically either get married or break up within two years.

If cohabitants do get married, they are more likely to divorce than couples who did not cohabit before marriage. This may be because people with strong religious views tend neither to cohabit nor divorce.

Couples who cohabited before marriage seem to have a different set of values to those who did not. The former have wider sexual experience, employ more equal division of domestic chores and spend a greater amount of their leisure time together.

Celibacy

Since adulthood is the time when many people engage in long-term relationships, those who opt out of sexual relationships are often considered to be unusual.

People may give a number of reasons for being celibate. These include spiritual growth, waiting for the right partner, work pressure and mental adjustment after the breakup of an important relationship, fear of contracting a sexually transmitted disease or of becoming pregnant, a lack of interest in sex, sexual-identity questions, long-term physical separation from a partner, or being widowed or divorced in later life.

Celibacy has different significance for different individuals: some find it liberating and empowering; some accept it as the best available option; others find that celibacy is forced upon them when they do not want it.

People who cohabit

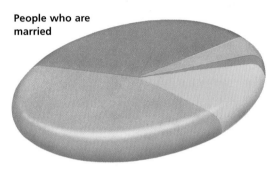

People who are married

- Not at all
- A few times a year
- A few times a month
- Two/three times a week
- Four + times a week

By definition, people who are celibate do not have sexual intercourse but they can relieve sexual tension through masturbation and they can give and receive physical affection by touching and embracing.

Long-term homosexual relationships

Although some societies allow homosexual couples to marry (Norway and Denmark are two countries that have introduced legislation for this), this is not the most common way to express love and commitment in the homosexual community. Monogamy varies with gender in gay relationships: it is estimated that 18 percent of gay men and 72 percent of lesbians are monogamous in their relationships.

Sexually nonexclusive or "open" relationships are more common in long-term relationships between homosexual men, especially if a significant age difference exists between the partners. Research suggests that unlike partners in heterosexual open relationships (which are comparatively rare), gay men in open relationships are more likely to negotiate their own rules on safe sex with their partners.

The Language of Sex

Many people use the word "celibacy" to refer to a lack of sexual activity through choice. In fact, the original meaning of the word "celibacy" was "unmarried."

How often do most people make love? Differences exist between the lovemaking habits of people who are married and people who cohabit. For example, people who cohabit are more likely to have sex four or more times a week.

SERIAL MONOGAMY

It has been suggested that people in Western societies, where monogamy is respected as the ideal, are effectively polygamous, because a significant number of people have long-term partners in succession. This behavior is referred to as serial monogamy.

In the U.S. the majority of young adults between the ages of 18 and 24 engage in serial monogamy. They have relationships that may be relatively short, but they remain sexually faithful to their partner for the duration of the relationship. This pattern can also apply to married relationships. People can marry and divorce several times during a lifetime.

Middle Age

Middle age can be a time when couples become closer, since lifestyle changes enable them to spend more time together. A marriage or relationship that has endured over years can confer a sense of great emotional security and sexual intimacy.

Entering midlife
Middle age may allow a more careful selection of priorities and activities than previously. It can mean focusing on relationships and spending more time on leisure.

Middle age can be a turning point for many people. Children grow up and leave home, and careers can become stabler and demand less primary attention than previously. People may choose this time to reassess the various elements in their lives, such as their relationships, their work and their long-term goals. Middle age is also a time when physical changes take place. For women, one of the biggest challenges of middle age is the natural decline in female sex hormones that occurs around the time of menopause.

MENOPAUSE

A wide range of physical and emotional symptoms accompanies falling estrogen levels during menopause, and these can have an effect on relationships. Some women see menopause as defeminizing, as an end not just to fertility but also to sexual attractiveness. They can experience anxiety and low self-esteem. Other women see menopause as freedom from reproductive concerns; a liberating experience.

Although hormonal decline in men (see page 109) does not follow such a clear pattern as female menopause, men may experience a "midlife crisis," in which they start to doubt their looks, virility and achievements.

The last menstrual period in a woman's reproductive life cycle is referred to as the menopause, and it marks the end of her fertility. All women will have experienced the menopause by the time they reach 60.

The years and months leading up to and following a woman's last menstrual period are referred to as perimenopause ("peri" means "around"). For most women, perimenopause is between ages 45 and 58. During this time, the ovaries produce fluctuating amounts of estrogen (the main female sex hormone) before stopping production altogether.

As menopause approaches, ovulation becomes less and less likely in each menstrual cycle (see page 140). Menstruation becomes increasingly unpredictable: a woman may menstruate some months and not others, and the flow of blood may be heavy one month and light the next.

At the end of the perimenopause, when estrogen is no longer produced by the ovaries, postmenopausal symptoms may start to appear (see page 111).

A WOMAN'S SEXUAL RESPONSES

Women's sexuality in midlife may be characterized by increased sexual confidence and experience. Women in their forties and fifties have generally learned what sort of stimulation they require in order to become aroused and to reach orgasm. They also may feel more relaxed about expressing their needs and desires. While many women are able to use this self-knowledge to maximize their sexual pleasure, others find that the changes of menopause eclipse the positive aspects of growing older.

Physical and emotional changes during perimenopause sometimes combine to cause a loss of or decrease in sex drive. For example, night sweats may lead to insomnia, chronic fatigue and depression, all of which result in loss of libido. A woman may experience symptoms that directly affect the UROGENITAL TRACT, such as vaginal dryness, stress incontinence (see page 196) or genital itch, any of which can make intercourse uncomfortable. Lack of vaginal lubrication during sexual arousal is common during and after perimenopause.

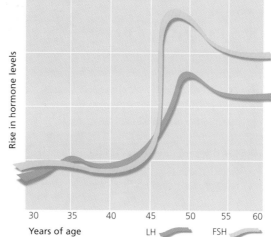

Years of age — LH — FSH

Rising hormone levels When menopause is about to happen, there is a dramatic increase in the amounts of luteinizing and follicle-stimulating hormones circulating in a woman's bloodstream. The average age at which menopause occurs is 51 years.

By contrast, some women notice that their sex drive increases at menopause. One reason for this is that during their fertile years women produce both male and female hormones. When estrogen levels fall at menopause, there is a comparative excess of the male hormone testosterone, which is largely responsible for sex drive in both sexes. This phenomenon does not occur in women who are on hormone replacement therapy (HRT), because their estrogen levels remain high. Occasionally, gynecologists use testosterone pills or implants to treat a decrease in a woman's sex drive.

SYMPTOMS OF THE FEMALE MENOPAUSE

PSYCHOLOGICAL	PHYSICAL
Depressed mood	Hot flashes and night sweats
Feeling nervous or anxious	Muscles that are easily fatigued and sore
Memory changes, particularly a tendency to be forgetful or distracted	Less vaginal lubrication, resulting in soreness and dryness around the vagina and vulva
Inability to concentrate	Bloated abdomen
Feelings of pessimism	Frequent urination
Irritability	An unusual taste in the mouth
Sudden changes in mood for no apparent reason	Increased tendency to stress incontinence and prolapse of pelvic organs
Inability to make decisions	Breasts prone to sagging
Tearfulness	Increase in breast pain

Tackling menopause Menopause should not be seen as a time of illness or sexual decline. A positive attitude will go a long way toward helping a woman cope with her symptoms.

HORMONE REPLACEMENT THERAPY

The main treatment for menopausal symptoms is hormone replacement therapy (HRT). This treats menopause as a hormone deficiency condition and serves to restore hormone levels to normal. HRT usually involves taking, in the form of pills, skin patches or creams, a combination of estrogen and progestogen (the synthetic version of progesterone—see page 129). The estrogen alleviates menopausal symptoms and offers long-term bone and heart health. The progestogen causes the uterine lining to be shed, as in a menstrual period, which is important in the prevention of endometrial cancer.

HRT protects the body from the long-term dangers of an estrogen deficit, which include osteoporosis and heart disease. Because estrogen contributes to the health of many organs, the body remains in its premenopausal state. The waist-to-hip ratio remains the same (whereas the waist would normally fill out after menopause), hair remains thick, muscles keep their strength and tone, and the skin retains its elasticity. HRT also maintains sex drive and the health of the sex organs.

HRT must be prescribed by a doctor. Not all women respond well to HRT—some experience a worsening of symptoms such as mood swings, while others are advised against taking HRT because it is thought to be linked with a very slight increased risk of breast cancer. Women with a previous history of breast, uterine or ovarian cancer are usually not offered HRT by doctors.

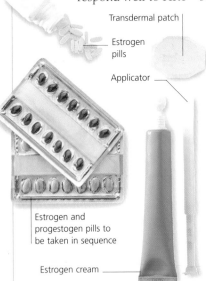

Transdermal patch

Estrogen pills

Applicator

Estrogen and progestogen pills to be taken in sequence

Estrogen cream

Types of HRT
The hormones found in HRT can be administered in a variety of ways: through the skin in the form of adhesive patches, via the vagina in the form of creams and suppositories or orally in the form of pills.

Low self-esteem during perimenopause can also create sexual problems. Some middle-aged women describe themselves as "out of the running" or "out of the mating game." They feel that menopause represents a loss of youth and beauty as well as fertility. As a result, they become self-conscious about sex. If a woman worries about how her body looks to her partner during lovemaking, she may find it difficult to become aroused or to reach orgasm. These

problems are compounded if the man is also experiencing low self-esteem associated with midlife changes.

Although fertility declines in midlife, a woman should continue to use contraception until she knows that she is no longer fertile. Most doctors say that this point is reached one year after the last menstrual period. Perimenopausal women need to pay attention to the type of contraceptive they use. The birth control pill (see page 164) carries a slightly higher risk of thrombosis in older women, especially if they smoke. Also, by maintaining an artificially high level of hormones, the pill may disguise the onset of menopause. Doctors may prescribe the progestogen-only pill or the intrauterine device (IUD; see page 167) for older women. Natural or rhythm methods of family planning are not effective in the perimenopausal period. The erratic nature of the menstrual cycle at this time makes predicting ovulation impossible.

A MAN'S SEXUAL RESPONSES

Men in their forties and fifties may notice a few minor changes in their sexual responses, but none of these have a serious impact on their ability to make love. For example, men may notice that the angle and hardness of their erections diminish, or they may feel that their orgasms are less intense. Having intercourse more than once a day may present more of a challenge at 50 than at 20, especially if a man is feeling tired or stressed. Also, middle-aged men often find that the quickest route to erection is direct stimulation of the penis, rather than fantasy. Middle-aged men also tend to ejaculate with much less force, which may in part explain why orgasms feel less intense.

Many of the men interviewed in Shere Hite's *The Hite Report on Male Sexuality* (1981) said that sexual enjoyment reached a peak in middle age, because they had gained an intimate knowledge of both their own and their partner's sexual responses. This gave them sexual confidence, enabling them to shed their inhibitions, to talk more openly about sex and to experiment more than they had in the past. Some men also said that the connection between love and sex had become more important to them. They appreciated and enjoyed the emotional intimacy of lovemaking. From a woman's perspective, the sexual changes that men

Performance anxiety
Feeling that they have to try especially hard to
prove themselves in the work environment is an
anxiety that many middle-aged men face.

experience in midlife may be advantageous: sex becomes more loving; there is more emphasis on foreplay; and men take longer to ejaculate, which means that intercourse can be slower and more sensual.

Male insecurity

For men who feel that their roles as worker, husband and father are slowly eroding, midlife can be a difficult time. During these years problems often converge, creating intense insecurity. Minor or major health difficulties—including those caused by poor diet and bad habits such as smoking—make men aware of their own mortality. They may compare themselves with younger, fitter men and feel that they are no longer sexually attractive. At work they may experience rivalry with younger colleagues. At home a wife or partner may be suffering from menopausal symptoms that affect not just the couple's sex life but their entire relationship. A man's role as father may also diminish as his children grow up and leave home.

Common questions arise for men in midlife: "Have I fulfilled my ambitions?" "Am I still attractive?" "Do I still command respect?" "What does the future hold?" "Can I still perform sexually?" Negative answers to such questions can lead to stress, depression and even sexual difficulties, including the inability to achieve and maintain an erection. A deterioration in midlife marital relationships sometimes causes men

to seek sex outside marriage. One frequently cited explanation for affairs—particularly those with younger women—is that they provide a way of recapturing feelings of youth. Affairs can reassure men of their virility and potency and provide the energy and sexual tension lacking in relationships with a wife or partner. Unfortunately, insecurity rarely provides a basis for a stable relationship; sooner or later most men are compelled to confront their real fears.

If emotional or psychosexual problems run deep, professional help from a relationship counselor or a sex therapist may be the best hope for resolution. Some couples find that honesty, frankness and mutual recognition that middle age is a time of transition helps to guide them through the changes.

Does male menopause exist?

Male menopause is a much more controversial subject than female menopause, which doctors acknowledge can have a profound effect on women's sense of well-being.

Men experience a gradual decline in testosterone levels from about age 45 to 70, followed by a marked decline after 70. Whether this causes menopause-like symptoms is debatable. Many doctors attribute male midlife symptoms (see below) to stress and declining health rather than hormones.

HRT FOR MEN

Men who are given replacement testosterone generally experience a sense of greater well-being and higher energy levels and sex drive.

In the U.S., testosterone can be administered as pills, injections, implants or skin patches; in Canada, it is available only in the form of pills and injections. Before HRT is prescribed, men need a thorough health check, including blood tests to give a hormone profile and screening for any liver abnormalities. An ultrasound study of the prostate gland should also be carried out to check for the presence of cancer.

SYMPTOMS OF THE MALE MENOPAUSE

PSYCHOLOGICAL	PHYSICAL
Depressed mood	Noise sensitivity
Inexplicable mood changes	Fatigue and decreased energy
Hyperanxiety (feelings of intense worry or panic)	Loss of strength and stamina
Reduction in alertness	Decreased facial hair growth
Failing memory	Dry skin
A sense of aging	Increased perspiration
Irritability and feelings of impatience and intolerance	Hot flushes
Reduced concentration span	Aches and pains in joints
A decline in libido: in sexual interest and sex drive	Erectile problems

Advanced Age

A misconception has long existed that older people cease to be interested in sex. Growing evidence suggests that many older people maintain the sexual desire of their youth, and although lovemaking may be less vigorous, it remains satisfying.

Jay and Fran Landesman Married since 1950, this prominent couple from the beatnik generation said in 1996 that their marriage was better than ever. "It's as though the relationship has started over again."

In *The Hite Report on Male Sexuality* (1981), 57 percent of men between ages 61 and 75 said that their desire for sex either increased with age or remained the same. When asked how age affected their enjoyment of sex, only 11 percent of men between 61 and 75 reported a decline. In Shere Hite's 1976 study of women's sexuality, the results were similar.

For many people, sexual desire and enjoyment seem to remain constant throughout life, though the frequency with which people have intercourse may decrease. In a survey conducted in 1994, titled *The Social Organization of Sexuality*, it was found that only 20 percent of American men and 12 percent of women in their fifties had sex at least once a week, compared with 35 percent of both men and women in their twenties and thirties.

A report in 1992 in the *Harvard Health Letter* suggests that although frequency of intercourse does decline with age, the best prediction of an active sex life after age 60 is high levels of desire and activity when young. Conversely, a couple who have never had an active sex life may be content with celibacy in their old age.

Some researchers have questioned the validity of statistics on the links between sexual activity and old age. They point out that elderly people were brought up in less permissive times and may be reluctant to provide accurate and honest information about their sex lives. In addition, they say, the meaning of celibacy in older people is easily misinterpreted. Not having sexual intercourse may indicate diminished desire, but it may also result from the death of a partner or failing health.

SOCIAL ATTITUDES

In the majority of cultures, sexual attractiveness is strongly identified with youth, health and beauty. Society does not consider aging to be beautiful or sexy, and many older people feel they are not expected to be sexual beings. In fact, they may feel pressured to deny their sexuality.

Leading feminist writer Germaine Greer argues that this is particularly true for women: "The older woman is simply not perceived as a sexual entity, unless she

makes an unsubtle display of herself, which amounts to a statement of availability, which is a turnoff to all but the least desirable partners."

Some cultures actively discourage older people from engaging in sexual activity. For example, the Meru of Kenya expect a woman's sex life to end on the marriage of her daughter, and the Hokkien in Taiwan insist that both men and women stop having sex when they become grandparents.

In Western society, an increasing number of older people are expecting and demanding a more active old age. They are rediscovering sex as a pastime, and workshops encourage them to relearn dating skills and brush up on sexual techniques.

PHYSICAL CHANGES

Three physical factors affect sexual activity in older people: the hormonal changes that affect desire and cause the aging of the *UROGENITAL TRACT*; muscle weakness and lower energy levels associated with advanced age; and the increased probability of chronic medical conditions such as *DIABETES* and heart disease. All of these pressures can take their toll on an individual's sex life. In addition, some of the medications used to treat conditions such as high blood pressure have an adverse effect on the libido or male erectile function.

A woman's sexual responses

Hormonal changes have the most direct impact on female sexual behavior. After menopause women stop producing estrogen in their ovaries, and this can give rise to a range of postmenopausal symptoms, including atrophy (the shrinking, thinning and drying) of the vagina, vulva and clitoris. Postmenopausal women produce a great deal less vaginal lubrication when they are sexually aroused— this can result in painful intercourse. The muscles that surround the sex organs can also weaken, leading to prolapse (see page 195) of organs such as the uterus and bladder into the vagina. The likelihood of vaginal and urinary infections also increases. If women continue to take hormone replacement therapy in the postmenopausal period, they should not suffer from these symptoms.

A man's sexual responses

In men, lower production of testosterone decreases sexual desire. Genital sensitivity declines, and as a result the penis needs more direct stimulation to become erect. Many men find that whereas they once had an erection within seconds of being physically or mentally stimulated, this now takes much longer. They may notice that their ability to ejaculate diminishes, and less semen is expelled with less force. Also, the refractory period (see page 138) usually becomes longer.

The physical changes associated with advanced age may be exacerbated by a couple's reaction to them. For example, the man who finds erection difficult becomes anxious, and this hinders arousal. Similarly, the woman who is slow to lubricate finds intercourse painful and may become reluctant to have sex as a result. In extreme cases, couples may even stop all sexual activity.

- Desire increases.
- Desire is unchanged.
- Desire decreases.

Age and desire Shere Hite interviewed men between the ages of 61 and 75. Although some men said that libido declined with age, the majority thought that it stayed the same or increased.

fact or fiction?

Older men no longer become aroused by visual stimuli.

There is a small amount of truth in this. A young man can become sexually aroused very quickly when looking at something provocative, whether it is his partner undressing or a sexually explicit photograph. In contrast, an older man may find these things psychologically erotic, but he is less likely to respond by having an erection. Erections in older men are more often a response to direct physical stimulation.

Adapting sexual behavior

People in their later years are able to take advantage of their slower sexual responses by spending more time on both foreplay and lovemaking, so that sex becomes a more sensual experience. Sex does not always have to be penetrative—couples can try to be inventive and increase their repertoire of activities (see page 70).

Vaginal lubricants
Using a lubricant before sex can eliminate the problem of vaginal dryness. Lubricants are available as jellies or creams. Suppositories are available only in the U.S.

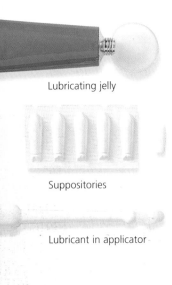

Lubricating jelly

Suppositories

Lubricant in applicator

The benefits of sex
There is a positive relationship between sexual activity in advanced age and a sense of well-being.

Older women may need different kinds of sexual stimulation than they previously required. For instance, the tissue covering the clitoris may shrink and thin, leaving the clitoris exposed and extremely sensitive. This can make direct stimulation painful, in which case cunnilingus (see page 84) and gentle touching using plenty of lubrication are alternatives. If a woman feels anxious because sex is sometimes uncomfortable, she may want to try sexual positions in which she is on top, which will allow her to control the depth and angle of penetration as well as the pace of lovemaking.

Although advanced age may cause physical impediments to sex, it also brings many sexual benefits. Birth control ceases to be an issue, and age and experience often give people the confidence to express their desires openly. Older couples have more time and privacy to devote to sex, with fewer distractions and worries. Sexual activity into old age also has positive implications for the health of the sex organs. For women in particular, regular intercourse or masturbation, combined with contracting the *PUBOCOCCYGEAL (PC) MUSCLES*, helps maintain vaginal muscle tone and the ability to produce lubrication.

Some long-term couples come to realize that they have made love the same way for years without experimenting or talking about sex; others have unresolved emotional problems within the relationship that have affected their sex life; still others find that sex has become routine and takes sec-

ond place in their relationship. Older couples can visit sex therapists for help with and advice about these issues.

Masturbation

Self-stimulation can be very important in old age. Masturbation enables women and men without partners or with infirm partners to release sexual tension (with the benefit of maintaining the health of the vulva and vagina). For men, masturbation can also help allay fears about impotence—if a man can achieve erection through masturbation, intercourse remains possible. In addition, since sexual activity aids the production of testosterone, masturbation can help to maintain sex drive.

Loving touch

If a long-term couple have always been physically and emotionally close, sexual touching and intimacy will probably carry on into old age. In her autobiography, *A Quest for Love* (1980), Jacquetta Hawkes described her early relationship with her husband, the English novelist J. B. Priestley, as "magnetic." They continued to make love until he was 85 years old.

Couples who have been able to express affection only in a sexual context find that as the frequency of lovemaking decreases, so too do all forms of affectionate expression. Most gerontologists believe that intimate, but not necessarily sexual, touching promotes a sense of happiness and well-being. Lack of touch can result in feelings of isolation and loneliness.

Loving physical gestures, such as holding hands, linking arms, hugging and kissing, become much more important during old age. A person who has lived a long time often craves something deeper than a sexually fulfilling relationship, and close friends or relatives can provide this. Loving gestures convey a sense of caring, acknowledgment and support, especially at an age when many elderly people may feel that their worth to society is limited.

Elderly people who have lost their spouse or who live a socially secluded life often focus their love and affection on their pets. Stroking, cuddling and caring for domestic animals may be as emotionally satisfying as the exchange of physical attention with a human being. Owning pets has also been shown to lower blood pressure and to

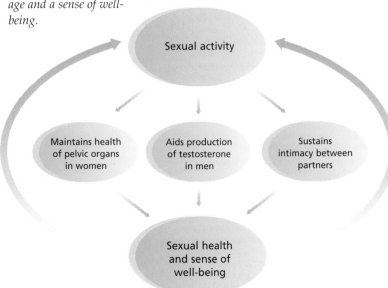

release endorphins (these are chemical substances that are found in the brain; their release provides a sense of well-being).

NEW AND RENEWED RELATIONSHIPS

Older people can often look forward to the prospect of grandparenthood (it is estimated that three-quarters of North Americans over age 65 are grandparents). Relationships with grandchildren can be among the most fulfilling. Grandparents enjoy the luxury of giving their love freely without the burdens and stresses of domesticity, work and childcare. Because grandparents usually have more time than parents to talk and listen, they can act as valuable confidants. They can also provide a positive role model for aging and a link to the past. By relating stories of life several decades past, they can give their grandchildren an understanding of how society and attitudes change.

The birth of grandchildren often provides a sense of purpose to older people. A couple who have drifted apart over the years can be brought together by the mutual interest they have in their grandchildren. The presence of grandchildren may also help to heal any family discord between grandparents and their own sons or daughters, or sons- or daughters-in-law.

SEX IN SPECIAL CIRCUMSTANCES

Many people have continuing good health throughout their life. Some are not so fortunate, and their difficulties become more pronounced the older they get. It is estimated that three in five people over 85 suffer from a longstanding illness. Ailments that commonly afflict elderly people include heart disease, arthritis and diabetes. Fortunately, with a little imagination and some simple techniques, satisfying sex can be achieved no matter what degree of health impairment a person experiences.

Heart disease

Heart-disease patients may worry that an active sex life could be detrimental to their health, but the American Heart Association reports that a heart patient can resume usual sexual activity as soon as he or she feels ready to do so. Because many heart-disease patients suffer from fatigue and may be too tired in the evening, the best time for sex may be late morning or early afternoon. Sufferers should also wait at

LOVE IN ADVANCED AGE

Contrary to the myth that older people do not fall in love, new romantic relationships can and do happen. Advanced age can bring a sense of freedom to some people: they no longer feel accountable to their parents or their children, and, having spent a lifetime living up to society's expectations, they may feel that it is time to act self-indulgently, especially if they have been single for a number of years.

Romantic relationships can arise in the most unexpected ways: between people who have been friendly for years (perhaps all their lives); in retirement communities, when people are brought together for the first time; or through new activities such as bridge or exercise classes. Some older people may decide to vigorously pursue a new lifestyle in order to find a partner, others may join a specialized dating agency.

Some older couples entering new relationships want to marry or remarry, although this is a trend that is more likely for men than for women. Research has shown that a number of women reject marriage in later life because, having been on their own for a long time, their independence has become important and they do not want to resume the role of wife and caregiver.

Many gerontologists say that love promotes longevity because it gives

Reviving relationships
Romance can come in the form of a new relationship, or it can be revived in a current one. Taking up a hobby such as hiking can create a common interest and a new sense of intimacy.

meaning to life and prevents isolation and loneliness. Although any relationship involves a certain amount of stress, couples who meet in later life tend to express more tolerance toward each other than younger couples. There is also the benefit of being free from worries about pregnancy, settling down, childrearing, careers and social mobility—all factors that commonly threaten the relationships of younger couples.

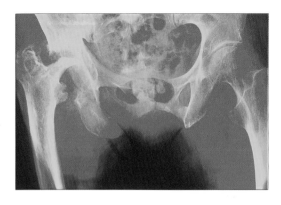

Arthritic joints A common affliction in older people, arthritis causes the slow destruction of the joints. The hip joints are commonly affected —in severe cases hip replacement surgery may be necessary.

Preparing for sex If joints are stiff, a shared hot bath can ease discomfort and improve flexibility.

least two hours after eating before making love to ensure that their bodies have properly digested the meal.

Arthritis

Stiff joints can make sexual intercourse painful. To ease the pain, the partner suffering from arthritis should sit or lie down to avoid bearing any weight on affected joints. If both partners suffer from arthritis, the side-by-side spoons sexual position (see page 81) is ideal. Heat makes the joints more mobile, so having sex in a well-heated room could be helpful. A gentle massage using warm oil can increase flexibility and relaxation. A warm bath can also help.

Diabetes

Noninsulin-dependent, or Type II, diabetes develops mainly in people over 40. In men the illness can cause damage to nerve fibers that affect erection, and in uncircumcised men and in women, it can cause genital yeast infections (see page 193).

Appropriate dietary and weight-control measures can decrease the fatigue of diabetes and help prevent nerve and heart damage. A doctor should be consulted to make sure that medications prescribed for diabetes do not affect libido. Individuals suffering from diabetes also have an increased risk of developing hypertension and cardiovascular disorders, in which case they should follow the recommendations for heart-disorder patients (see above).

Postoperative sex

Any abdominal or pelvic surgery involves the formation and healing of scar tissue. This can take up to eight weeks, during which time sexual intercourse should be avoided. Serious surgery, such as heart surgery or hip replacement, can require a recovery period of up to three months. Individuals vary greatly, so it is essential to follow the advice of a doctor. Unless otherwise advised, a patient who is recovering well and feeling relaxed should be able to partake in gentle sexual activity within a few weeks. A chair offers better support than a bed, and pillows can be used to cushion sensitive areas. Side-by-side positions, with the affected partner doing the least work, may be best.

Hysterectomy

After an *EPISIOTOMY*, a hysterectomy is the second most common surgery for women in the Western world. It has been estimated that approximately one woman in three undergoes hysterectomy by the age of 60. Hysterectomy consists of the removal of the uterus—and sometimes also the fallopian tubes and cervix—to remedy a number of female gynecological problems. These include cancers, endometriosis, fibroids, painful and heavy periods, prolapse, and pelvic inflammatory disease (see pages 190 to 198). If the ovaries are also removed, the surgery is known as a hysterectomy and oophorectomy.

After a hysterectomy, loss of libido is common. Sex should resume only after scar tissue and any internal bruising have healed and the woman feels relaxed and ready. When the cervix is removed, some women complain that they lose the ability to reach orgasm. This may be due to the loss of sensitive nerve endings in the cervix. Strengthening the *PUBOCOCCYGEAL (PC) MUSCLES* by repeatedly contracting them and massaging the G-spot (see page 126) can help revive orgasmic response.

Although some women experience long-term sexual problems after hysterectomy, most recover very quickly and feel more sexually confident after the operation. *The Maine Women's Health Study* (1989 to 1991) of 798 women found that hysterectomy left 71 percent of the women feeling better mentally, physically and sexually than they had before the operation.

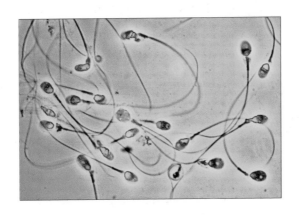

SEXUAL
ANATOMY &
PHYSIOLOGY

The Sexual Body

Some parts of the body function solely for sex and reproduction, but other body parts make vital contributions to successful sexual activity. Without hormones released by the brain, for example, sexual maturation would never even start.

The sensual body
The most intense site of erotic pleasure is the genitals, but many other parts of the body play important parts in arousal and sensual enjoyment.

The genitals are the focal point of sexual pleasure. During masturbation or intercourse, with the right stimulation, muscles around the genitals contract rhythmically, producing the pleasurable sensations of orgasm. Although the male genitals and the female genitals and breasts receive the most attention as sexual areas, the whole body, in one way or another, enhances sexual attraction and response.

Parts of the body far from the genitals, such as the lips, have their own responses to sexual arousal. The skin all over the body contains millions of nerve endings that make it highly responsive to touch, with skin-to-skin contact often triggering sexual arousal. Although orgasm is felt most strongly in the genitals, sexual pleasure radiates throughout the entire body. When a woman climaxes she may arch her feet and back and curl her toes. She may have involuntary muscular contractions all over her body, and her chest and neck may become covered in a fine rash (see page 132).

Other parts of the body act as sexual attractors. Pubic hair is a sign of sexual maturity, and the lips, buttocks and belly are full of erotic significance. Some anthropologists argue that they are examples of sexual self-mimicry: the lips mimic the labia; the breasts mimic the buttocks; and the navel mimics the vagina (self-mimicry is significant because human ancestors used to mate using rear-entry positions).

INSIDE THE BODY

A complex interplay of hormones is necessary to promote sexual desire and fertility. Hormones also maintain masculinity and femininity. Testosterone is responsible for a man's characteristic muscle strength, facial hair and deep voice, while estrogen and progesterone stimulate breast growth and regulate a woman's cycle of fertility.

The cardiovascular system also plays a vital role in sexual arousal and function. During arousal, the heart pumps

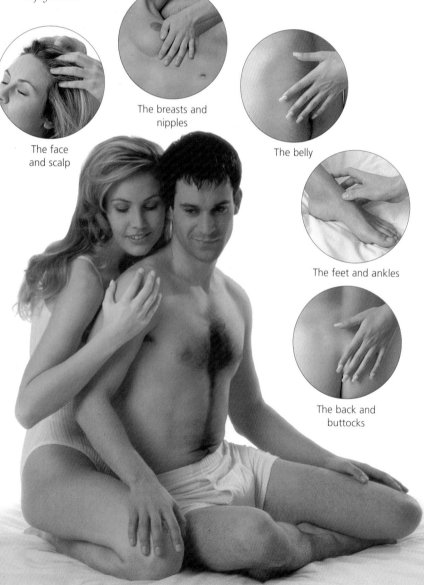

The face and scalp

The breasts and nipples

The belly

The feet and ankles

The back and buttocks

faster, sending an increased blood flow to the genitals and causing them to become engorged. This makes the penis erect and causes physical changes in the vagina and clitoris that enable orgasm and may even aid conception (see page 135).

THE BRAIN

The brain plays both a conscious and subconscious role in the process of sexual arousal. Before arousal takes place, a person usually perceives something as sexy—a photograph, a smell or the proximity of another person. This perception initiates sexual desire and is followed by physical changes in the genitals or the rest of the body.

An area in the brain known as the limbic system processes information received from the senses of sight, smell, taste, hearing and touch, as well as emotional stimuli such as thoughts, desires and fantasies. If the signals sent to the brain are positive ones, then the person experiences feelings of pleasure. If the information relayed to the limbic system has a positive sexual component, messages will be sent from the brain to increase blood flow (vasocongestion) to the genitals. This sort of arousal is termed psychogenic, because it originates in the mind.

Sexual arousal also can occur without any perception of pleasure to start the process and without involving the limbic system. A direct touch or pressure on the genitals can cause the blood flow to increase to this area, a phenomenon known as reflex arousal. While it is a much simpler response than psychogenic response, it is just as important. During sexual intercourse, psychogenic and reflex responses work together. A man's reflex response tends to override his psychogenic response during sex, and continuous stimulation of his genitals will almost certainly lead to ejaculation and orgasm. A woman, however, can be distracted by the sound of a telephone ringing or a child crying, which can block her progression to orgasm despite continuous physical stimulation of the genitals.

At the moment of orgasm, both men and women suddenly release substances called beta-enkephalins (a type of endorphin). These chemical messengers resemble opiates such as morphine. Beta-enkephalins

latch on to receptors in the brain, known as opiate receptors, and cause the diffuse rush of pleasure and euphoria felt during orgasm.

FETAL SEXUAL DEVELOPMENT

Most people associate sexual development with the changes that take place at puberty, but the real beginning of sexuality occurs inside the fallopian tubes at conception and

◄ *Homunculus*
Some parts of the body are more responsive to touch than others. The proportions of this body reflect the amount of space devoted to them by the cerebral cortex in the brain. One of the functions of the cerebral cortex is to respond to touch.

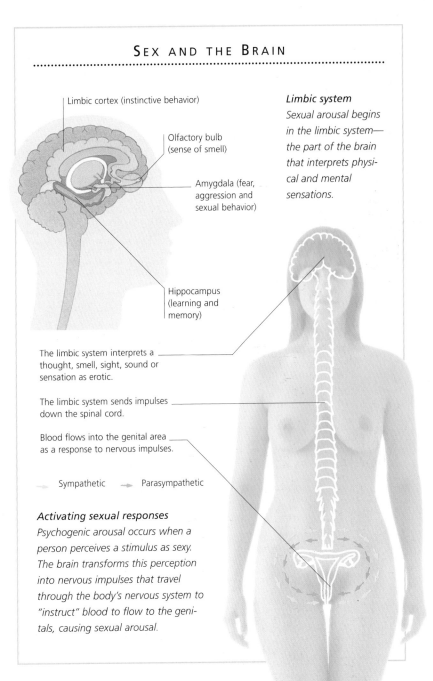

SEX AND THE BRAIN

Limbic cortex (instinctive behavior)

Olfactory bulb (sense of smell)

Amygdala (fear, aggression and sexual behavior)

Hippocampus (learning and memory)

The limbic system interprets a thought, smell, sight, sound or sensation as erotic.

The limbic system sends impulses down the spinal cord.

Blood flows into the genital area as a response to nervous impulses.

→ Sympathetic   ⇒ Parasympathetic

Limbic system
Sexual arousal begins in the limbic system— the part of the brain that interprets physical and mental sensations.

Activating sexual responses
Psychogenic arousal occurs when a person perceives a stimulus as sexy. The brain transforms this perception into nervous impulses that travel through the body's nervous system to "instruct" blood to flow to the genitals, causing sexual arousal.

SEXUAL DEVELOPMENT IN THE UTERUS

During the first six weeks after conception the genitals of boys and girls are identical. They will not start to change or "differentiate" until they receive special instructions from the fetus's genetic material. Depending on the child's sex, a structure called the genital tubercle

will go on to develop into the glans (the tip of the penis) or the clitoris. The urogenital folds will join up and fuse together in boys and stay partially separated in girls. The labioscrotal swelling goes on to form the scrotum in boys and the labia majora (outer lips) in girls.

Genital tubercle

Labioscrotal swelling

Urogenital fold

GIRLS AT	BOYS AT
WEEKS 6—8	WEEKS 6—8

The genitals develop along female lines—the genital tubercle elongates to form the clitoris and the urogenital folds and the labioscrotal swelling develop into the labia minora and labia majora, respectively. The anus also starts to form.

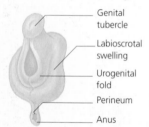

Genital tubercle

Labioscrotal swelling

Urogenital fold

Perineum

Anus

The genitals start to differentiate—the genital tubercle starts to enlarge to resemble the tip of a penis, and the urogenital folds move closer together. The labioscrotal swelling begins to form the scrotum.

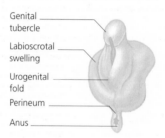

Genital tubercle

Labioscrotal swelling

Urogenital fold

Perineum

Anus

WEEK 12

The fetal genitals consist of a clitoris and labia rather than a penis and scrotum. The urethral folds have moved together, but in contrast to male fetal genitals, they have not become fully sealed—an opening in the folds marks the entrance to the vagina.

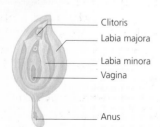

Clitoris

Labia majora

Labia minora

Vagina

Anus

WEEK 12

There is a distinct line or ridge where the urethral folds have joined—this is called the raphe. The urethral folds enclose the urethra and the shaft of the penis has formed. The scrotum has also formed—the testicles drop into the scrotum shortly before birth.

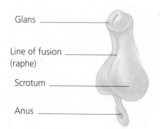

Glans

Line of fusion (raphe)

Scrotum

Anus

inside the uterus over subsequent weeks. An individual's gender is determined at fertilization, when a single sperm from the father enters the mother's ovum and the parental chromosomes join to make a combination of XX (female) or XY (male) sex chromosomes (see page 146).

Testicles or ovaries?

Until the sixth week of development, male and female fetuses are identical. Both sexes have a pair of identical gonads that will develop into either testicles or ovaries. Their development appears to be controlled by a single gene on the Y chromosome that produces an enzyme called testis determining factor, which causes the gonads to become testicles. If the gene is not present, the gonads develop as ovaries.

In addition to gonads, all embryos contain precursors for male and female sex organs. During the third month of development one of these precursors develops and the other withers away. The direction of organ development (male or female) is controlled by the presence or absence of hormones secreted from the testicles. Without these hormones, development takes place along female lines. In fact, even the ovaries are unnecessary for the development of the female sex organs. For example, Turner's syndrome sufferers (see page 204) develop female sex organs without functioning ovaries.

The testicles produce two hormones—one to prevent development of the female system of ducts and tubes (Mullerian duct) and the other to stimulate development of the male system (Wolffian duct). In the presence of these hormones the Wolffian system develops into the epididymis, vas deferens, seminal vesicles and prostate (see page 121). In their absence, the Mullerian system develops into the fimbriae, fallopian tubes, uterus and inner two-thirds of the vagina.

Penis or clitoris?

The development of the external genitalia—the penis or clitoris and scrotum or labia—is also determined by the presence or absence of male hormones. Research has shown that during the early weeks of development the fetus is very sensitive to male hormones, and female fetuses exposed to male hormones during the first three months of development have shown evidence of masculinization.

Male Sex Organs

Unlike the female sex organs, the male genitals are clearly visible. Because of this, most men have a good knowledge of their external sexual anatomy. What both sexes may be less aware of is the function of the structures inside the male body.

The most obvious male sexual organ is the penis. It has two functions: transporting urine out of the body and carrying sperm-containing semen for fertilization of the ovum. Most of the time the penis rests in its relaxed, or flaccid, state and hangs down in front of the testicles. While a flaccid penis is convenient for passing urine, it cannot penetrate the vagina to deposit sperm during sexual intercourse. For intercourse to be possible, the penis must become at least partially erect.

THE ANATOMY OF THE PENIS

Externally, the penis consists of a body, called the shaft, and a head, called the glans. The shaft is covered in loose skin that wrinkles up when the penis is flaccid. In uncircumcised men this skin forms a hood, or foreskin, over the glans.

The shaft

The tube that carries urine and semen along the length of the penis is called the urethra. It begins at the bladder and ends at the opening in the glans. Three columns of spongy tissue in the shaft of the penis are responsible for its great erectile ability. The smallest column is the corpus spongiosum, which surrounds and protects the urethra and expands at the tip of the penis to form the glans. It also thickens at the base of the penis, where it is encircled by a muscle that contracts rhythmically during ejaculation to force semen out of the penis.

On top of the corpus spongiosum lie two other columns, called the corpus cavernosa, that run parallel along the length of the penis. They are attached to muscles that are connected to a bone in the pelvis. When a man is sexually excited, these muscles pull the penis into its erect position and blood rushes into the columns of spongy tissue, making them swell. The blood vessels leading away from the penis virtually close so that the blood is trapped and the penis becomes engorged and firm. As the penis becomes erect it not only changes in size, it also darkens; large blue veins stand out on its surface, and the shaft may become slightly curved. This curved shape helps the penis fit into the vagina. Although rare, an unusually curved penis may be due to a condition known as Peyronie's disease. Advanced age can affect the angle and firmness of a man's erection.

Average penis length when flaccid is between 2½ and 4 inches (6.5 to 10.5 cm) from the tip of the glans to the base. This length varies from one man to another, and is affected by conditions such as temperature. The average length of the erect penis is 6 to 7 inches (15 to 18 cm). The size of an erect penis can be affected by alcohol consumption, fatigue and degree of arousal. Penis girth and shape vary greatly: some have a wide base and taper to a point, whereas others are the same width throughout their length.

Contrary to popular myth, penis size has no effect on sexual ability or virility, nor does it correlate with body size or the size of the hands, feet or nose. In fact, sex therapists Masters and Johnson reported that penis size had less relation to the skeletal and muscular size of a man than any other organ in the body. Also, it is rare for an

X-ray of the penis During arousal the tissues inside the penis fill up with blood, making it hard and erect.

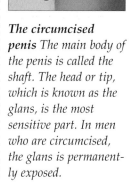

***The circumcised penis** The main body of the penis is called the shaft. The head or tip, which is known as the glans, is the most sensitive part. In men who are circumcised, the glans is permanently exposed.*

adult male not to have an erect penis within the usual size range. Nevertheless, many men worry that it is less "manly" to have a small penis. One reason men may perceive their own penis to be smaller than other men's is because when they look down they see a foreshortened view. Doctors advise men who are anxious about penis size to look at themselves in profile in a mirror.

The glans

The smooth, conical tip of the penis is the glans, and the opening of the urethra in the center of the glans is where urine and semen exit the body. The ridge where the glans joins the shaft of the penis is the coronal sulcus, and during infancy the foreskin is attached to this. There may be tiny white bumps in this area; these are quite normal, but they can be mistaken for genital warts. The skin of the glans has many sensory nerve endings, making it one of the most erogenous areas of the male body.

The foreskin

Also called the prepuce, the foreskin is the loose fold of skin covering the glans. When the penis becomes erect, the foreskin retracts to expose the glans. At birth the foreskin is still partially fused to the penis. It gradually separates and, by the age of four, more than 90 percent of boys can move the foreskin over the glans, even if it cannot be fully retracted. The foreskin should never be forcibly retracted because it can lead to scarring and permanent damage. After puberty, the foreskin attaches to the glans only at the frenulum, a small, triangular fold of highly sensitive skin on the underside of the penis. On rare occasions poorly lubricated sex can cause the frenulum to tear or bleed.

The foreskin is thin and hairless and has small glands on the inner surface that produce an oily substance which, when mixed with dead skin cells, is called smegma. Freshly secreted smegma is colorless and odorless, but if it is not washed away it becomes white and foul-smelling and can even become infected. Boys should be taught to gently retract the foreskin and wash underneath it with warm water.

Circumcision is the surgical removal of the foreskin, a procedure widely performed for medical, cultural and religious reasons.

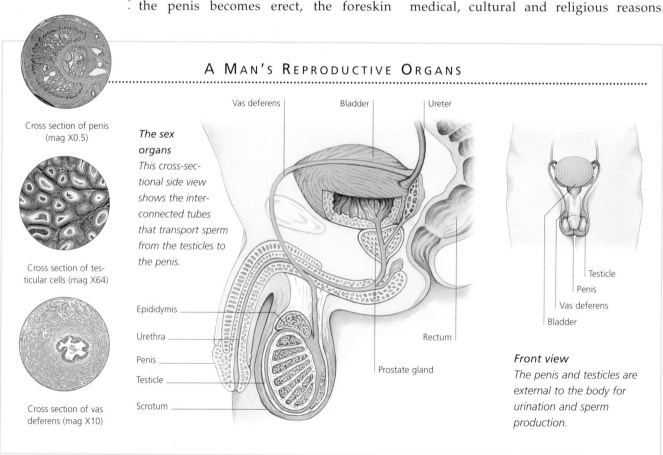

A Man's Reproductive Organs

Cross section of penis (mag X0.5)

Cross section of testicular cells (mag X64)

Cross section of vas deferens (mag X10)

The sex organs
This cross-sectional side view shows the interconnected tubes that transport sperm from the testicles to the penis.

Vas deferens

Bladder

Ureter

Epididymis

Urethra

Penis

Testicle

Scrotum

Rectum

Prostate gland

Testicle

Penis

Vas deferens

Bladder

Front view
The penis and testicles are external to the body for urination and sperm production.

According to a U.S. organization called NOCIRC, up to 3,000 circumcisions are carried out daily. Although this indicates a decrease over past years, circumcision remains common in the U.S. and Canada, particularly with newborns. In the U.K., the National Health Service abandoned the routine practice of circumcision of newborn boys in 1949. Circumcision is a traditional practice among Jews, Muslims and many African tribes. Female circumcision (see page 226), a much more brutal procedure, is still carried out in some African cultures.

THE TESTICLES

The male sex glands, or testicles, are two oval-shaped organs contained in a pouch of skin, the scrotum, and are the male equivalent of the female ovaries. The testicles hang loosely behind the penis, but in cold temperatures or during sexual arousal the skin of the scrotum contracts to draw them up close to the body. It is normal for the left testicle to hang lower than the right and for one testicle to be larger than the other. The skin of the scrotum is wrinkled and hairy.

The testicles produce sperm and the male sex hormone testosterone. To make sperm, the testicles must be slightly cooler than the rest of the body, which is why they hang just outside the body. Sperm formation begins in the seminiferous tubules—hundreds of tiny tubes that are tightly coiled inside each testicle. These tubules open out into the epididymis, which is another tightly coiled tube where sperm mature and are stored until ejaculation. Scattered between the seminiferous tubules are the cells of Leydig, where testosterone is made.

INSIDE THE BODY

Hidden inside the pelvic cavity is a complex system of ducts, tubes and glands that either carry sperm out of the body or bathe it in nutritious fluid to aid it in the journey through the female reproductive system (see page 125).

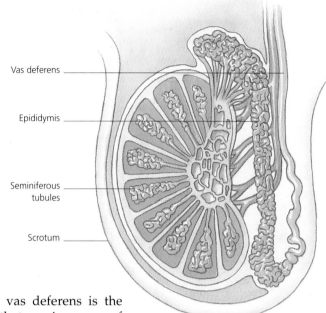

The vas deferens is the tube that carries sperm from the epididymis to the urethra. One such tube ascends from each testicle up and around the bladder and then descends to the urethra. A wider part of the vas deferens that sits just under the bladder—the ampulla—holds sperm just prior to ejaculation.

Both the prostate gland and the seminal vesicles secrete fluids that make up the whitish semen propelled from the penis during ejaculation. The seminal vesicles produce the bulk of the semen. The prostate gland contributes a small amount of fluid containing sugars, vitamins, minerals and enzymes, which all keep sperm healthy and help to stimulate movement.

Cowper's glands, also known as the bulbourethral glands, sit just below the prostate gland and secrete a clear, alkaline mucus that neutralizes any urine left in the urethra. This mucus lubricates the tip of the penis before ejaculation and may contain some sperm. When a man is about to ejaculate, the ampulla squeezes its sperm into the urethra, where sperm mix with the milky secretions. The semen is then pumped down the urethra, along the penis and out of the body.

Inside a testicle
Sperm are manufactured inside many tiny convoluted tubes known as the seminiferous tubules. They are then stored in the epididymis.

Vas deferens

Epididymis

Seminiferous tubules

Scrotum

*f*act or *f*iction?

Men should practice Kegel exercises.

Fact. Kegel exercises maintain the strength of the pelvic-floor muscles that surround the sex organs in both men and women. Men can exercise their muscles by repeatedly contracting and relaxing them (the pelvic-floor muscles are the same muscles used to stop the flow of urine).

The Sperm Cell

Sperm are the male sex cells that fertilize a female egg.
Each sperm carries information that will determine a baby's sex
and some of its physical characteristics. After puberty, millions
of sperm are made daily in the testicles.

Penetrating the ovum
This microscopic picture shows the sperm entering the outer layer of cells of the ovum.

Acrosome cap

Head containing chromosomes

Mature sperm *These healthy mature sperm cells are shown at 300 times their actual size.*

Midportion

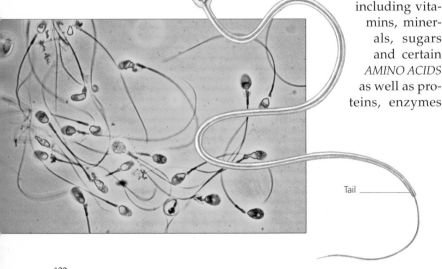

Tail

Every sperm cell has three parts: a head, a midportion and a tail. The oval or round head contains genetic information that, on fertilization, unites with the mother's chromosomes, ensuring that children inherit traits from both parents. The head of the sperm is capped by a structure called the acrosome, which contains enzymes to help penetrate the ovum.

The midportion of the sperm contains mitochondria, structures that convert nutrients in semen into energy the sperm can use to swim toward the ovum. The whiplike tail of a sperm is a protein structure that has a complex corkscrew motion, propelling the sperm forward at an average speed of 0.1 inch (3 mm) every minute.

SEMEN

A man ejaculates more than just sperm. In fact, sperm form only a fraction of the ejaculate. The milky fluid that sperm are bathed in is known as semen or seminal fluid. This liquid is very rich in nutrients, including vitamins, minerals, sugars and certain *AMINO ACIDS* as well as proteins, enzymes and alkaline substances. All of these components nourish and energize the sperm and help protect them from the acidic environment of the vagina.

The amount of semen released during ejaculation is roughly equivalent to one teaspoonful (5 ml) and usually contains 100 million to 500 million sperm.

Substances known as prostaglandins are found in semen. Experts believe that when semen comes into contact with a woman's cervix (see page 126), the prostaglandins soften the cervix, allowing the sperm an easier passage into the uterus. Prostaglandins may also increase contractions of the uterus, not only aiding sperm on their journey to the fallopian tubes but also possibly enhancing female orgasm. Other chemicals that play an important part in sexual reproduction are produced by the sperm. For example, the acrosome, covering the head of each sperm, produces chemicals called lysosomes that help the sperm to penetrate the ovum during fertilization.

THE DEVELOPMENT OF SPERM

Spermatogenesis, the creation of sperm cells, is a process that begins in the tight coils of the seminiferous tubules inside each testicle. The first stage is the production of germ cells—simple cells that are capable of evolving into highly specialized cells. These cells, which are also known as spermatogonia, develop into cells called spermatocytes. Spermatocytes divide in such a way that they contain only one-half of the normal pair of chromosomes. By spermatocyte stage the potential sperm cells are becoming increasingly specialized. After more divisions the spermatocytes become spermatids and finally sperm, at which point they move away from the supporting cells—known as Sertoli cells—and into the central cavity of the seminiferous tubules.

Next, sperm move to the epididymis, where they mature fully and grow their characteristic tails. Owing to the coiled length of the epididymis—20 to 23 feet (6 to 7 meters)—it takes sperm three weeks to complete their journey through it. Sperm then spend at least six days in the vas deferens, waiting to be ejaculated. If this does not happen, they die and are replaced by fresh ones. The development from germ cell to ejaculated sperm takes three months.

Sperm production first begins in puberty (see page 92) as a result of stimulation by hormones that are released from the pituitary gland in the brain. Thereafter, sperm production is continuous throughout a man's life, until he reaches old age, when his fertility gradually starts to decline. On average, each testicle manufactures approximately 1,500 sperm every second.

THE DIVERSITY OF SPERM

Research conducted on animals by Dr. Robin Baker, research biologist at the University of Manchester in the U.K., has led to the suggestion that men may produce several different types of sperm, each with a unique role to play in fertilization. "Killer" sperm are the most athletic—after ejaculation, they swim around the female's reproductive tract attempting to destroy alien sperm (those from another male) by producing a poisonous fluid. "Blocker" sperm also try to defeat alien sperm, but using a more passive technique: they become lodged around the cervix which prevents the entry of rivals. Both killer and blocker sperm exist to facilitate the relatively few sperm, known as the "egg getters," that are capable of fertilizing an ovum in the fallopian tube. Baker has also identified a fourth type of sperm known as "family-planning" sperm. These are thought to act as a natural contraceptive by destroying a male's own sperm. Males are believed to produce a particularly large amount of family-planning sperm when they are under stress. Baker's theory that sperm act as a kind of army—each type having a specific task—has challenged the notion that all sperm are capable of fertilization. His theories about the different roles of sperm remain controversial.

MALE SEX HORMONES

Hormones are chemical substances that are secreted into the blood by specialized glands or gland cells. They are transported in the blood to specific target sites in the body where they take effect. The male sex hormones, or androgens, are manufactured in the testicles and adrenal glands (located just above the kidneys). Several types of androgens exist, the main one being testosterone.

Testosterone is a steroid hormone that is made in the body from cholesterol. It is produced almost entirely (95 percent) in the testicles by the cells of Leydig (see page 121). If one testicle is lost or is badly damaged, the other testicle is still able to take over, producing twice as much testosterone when required.

Testosterone levels rise and fall during a man's lifetime. Although the hormone is very important in the development of the fetus, after birth its levels in the blood remain very low until puberty (see page 92). Hormone production then rises, peaking dramatically in the late teens and early twenties, as testosterone triggers the physiological changes of manhood. From the twenties on, testosterone levels gradually decline with age.

fact or fiction?

The male sex hormone testosterone is present only in men.

Fiction. Women manufacture testosterone in both their ovaries and adrenal glands. Testosterone is thought to be important in maintaining female sex drive.

Testosterone drives the development of sexual anatomy of the fetus.

Testosterone initiates male sexual development in puberty.

The sex drive (libido) in males and females is maintained by testosterone.

Testosterone stimulates the testicles to produce sperm.

Testosterone and other androgens stimulate muscle growth.

Testosterone may help influence sexual orientation early in fetal life.

Testosterone The most important male hormone is testosterone. It gives men some of the features associated with masculinity, such as body hair and muscles.

Female Sex Organs

In contrast to the breasts and buttocks, a woman's genitals and sex organs are mostly hidden from view. This may be why, in the past, knowledge of the vulva and vagina was shrouded in mystery. Even today, ignorance about the sex organs persists.

A woman's pubic and genital area is marked by a triangle of hair that first appears during puberty. Also at this time there is a thickening of the flesh over the pubic bone, causing the mound to protrude more. Pubic hair, which is coarser in texture and darker than head hair, may be sparse and neat, or cover a large area that stretches down to the upper and inner thighs.

The clitoris

At the front of the vulva is a soft fold or hood of skin that covers the clitoris. The clitoris is the erogenous center of the female body—it is packed with sensory nerve endings, and stimulation of it during sexual intercourse or masturbation can lead to orgasm.

The only visible part of the clitoris is the tip, or glans, which appears as a small pinkish bud under the clitoral hood. Internally, however, there is a large amount of erectile tissue. The clitoris and the penis both develop from the same structures in the embryo (see page 118).

The labia

The folds of skin that enclose the clitoral area and *VESTIBULE* are called the outer lips, or labia majora. Hairy on the outside and containing sweat glands on the inside, they protect the entrance to the urethra and vagina. The size of the labia majora varies considerably with age and from person to person. Although small in childhood and in old age, during the reproductive years the labia majora are full and fleshy.

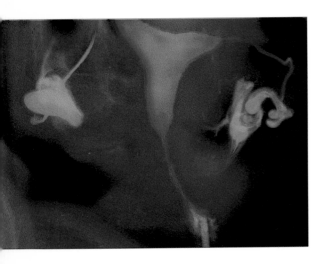

An X ray view of a woman's pelvic organs This colorized X ray shows the uterus in blue, the ovaries in red and the vagina as a pale blue tube. The fallopian tubes extend from either side of the top of the uterus.

THE EXTERNAL SEX ORGANS

The female genitals run from the pubic mound at the front of the body to the area behind the vagina known as the perineum. The vulva consists of two sets of lips, or labia (the labia majora and the labia minora), and includes the mons veneris (pubic mound), clitoris, and the vaginal and urethral openings.

The vulva The collective term for the female genitals is the vulva. The moist area enclosed by the labia minora is called the vestibule.

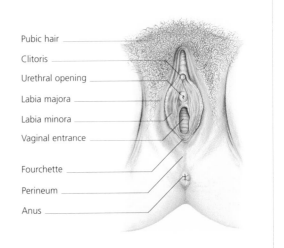

Pubic hair

Clitoris

Urethral opening

Labia majora

Labia minora

Vaginal entrance

Fourchette

Perineum

Anus

A Woman's Reproductive Organs

Cross section of cells lining fallopian tube (mag X1,100)

Cross section of vaginal wall cells (mag X50)

Cross section of uterine lining cells (mag X30)

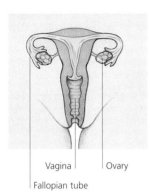

A front view of the female pelvic organs
The vagina extends upward and back into the pelvis. The top end of the vagina forms a curved vault around the cervix. The cervix leads into the uterine cavity.

The pelvic organs in profile
The vagina is situated between the urethra and bladder at the front and the rectum at the back.

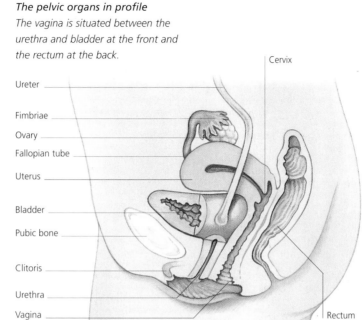

Ureter
Fimbriae
Ovary
Fallopian tube
Uterus
Bladder
Pubic bone
Clitoris
Urethra
Vagina

Cervix
Rectum

Flattened within the labia majora are the delicate, hairless inner lips, or labia minora. The labia minora extend from the clitoral hood to the back of the vulva, where they fuse to form the fourchette. They are full of sebaceous glands and apocrine (scent) glands that secrete lubricants that make the genitals smell sexually attractive.

In some women the labia minora extend outside the labia majora; this is a normal variation in size. The labia minora are very sensitive and when stimulated become engorged with blood and darker in color.

The hymen

This thin membrane, which surrounds part of the entrance to the vagina, is rich in sexual significance. Historically, an intact

The Language of Sex

The fleshy pad of fat at the front of a woman's genital area that cushions the pubic bone is known as the mons pubis, meaning "pubic mound," or the mons Veneris. In Latin, the word "mons" means "mound" and "Veneris" refers to Venus, the Roman goddess of love, so "mons Veneris" may also be translated as "mound of love."

hymen was a sign of virginity and chastity, whereas a broken hymen indicated lost virginity and promiscuity.

Some women, in countries such as Japan and India, have been known to have their hymens reconstructed with plastic surgery to indicate (or pretend) that they are virgins. A hymen may be ruptured through means other than intercourse—inserting tampons or engaging in strenuous physical activity, such as horseback riding. In some girls the hymen is absent at birth.

To allow vaginal secretions and menstrual blood to pass through, the hymen has a small opening. A very small number of girls have an imperforate hymen—one that completely obstructs the vaginal opening. Often not discovered until a girl fails to start menstruating at puberty, an imperforate hymen can be cut to allow the passage of menstrual blood. A thick hymen may prevent a girl from using tampons or having vaginal intercourse until surgically broken.

Occasionally the tearing or rupturing of the tissue may cause discomfort, slight pain or bleeding when a woman has sexual intercourse for the first time.

The vestibular glands

There are two small, rounded structures on either side of the vaginal opening known as vestibular, or Bartholin's, glands. During sexual arousal they secrete a few droplets of fluid to lubricate the vulva in preparation for sex. The vestibular glands occasionally become infected, making intercourse painful (see page 194).

The vagina

Its name derived from the Latin word meaning "sheath" or "scabbard" of a sword, the vagina is an elastic, muscular tube. It has three functions: to receive the penis during intercourse, to channel the flow of blood out of the body during menstruation, and as a birth canal during delivery of a baby.

In an adult woman the vagina is normally about 3.5 inches (9 cm) in length, but its elasticity allows the length and width to vary greatly. The ridged inner walls of the vagina are surrounded by strong muscles that can be contracted around the penis during intercourse. They contain an extensive network of veins that fill with blood during arousal. The vaginal walls also have many sensory nerves that respond to deep pressure (but none that respond to light touch). The vaginal walls thin out in old age.

The G-spot

First described by Ernst Grafenburg, a German obstetrician and gynecologist, the Grafenburg spot, or G-spot, is reputed to be a highly erogenous area located on the front wall of the vagina. Since Grafenburg's apparent discovery, there has been intense debate among doctors and sex therapists as to whether the G-spot actually exists.

Anatomists have failed to find any gland or any area of tissue that they can identify as the G-spot, even though it has been claimed that the G-spot contains glands and nerve endings involved in female ejaculation. It is possible that the G-spot is a remnant of a gland equivalent to the prostate in men (see page 120) and is present or partially present in only some women.

Some women claim that pressure on the G-spot, about 2 inches (5 cm) up on the front wall of the vagina between the back of the pubic bone and the front of the cervix, produces the urge to urinate, followed by sexual arousal. Continued stimulation of this area may result in engorgement of the G-spot, followed by orgasm. When stimulated in this way, the G-spot may be felt as a lump or protrusion that is roughly the size of a small bean. Women who do not appear to have a G-spot should not be considered abnormal. Sexual pleasure and orgasm are dependent on stimulation of the clitoris rather than the G-spot.

The cervix

The neck of the uterus is known as the cervix and can be felt 4 to 6 inches (10 to 15 cm) into the vagina. It is round and quite firm, with a very small dimple the size of a pinhead (in women who have not been pregnant), known as the cervical os, in its center. The cervical os is the opening into the uterus that allows sperm to enter and menstrual blood and other secretions to leave. During childbirth the os opens widely to allow the baby's head to pass out of the uterus. After she has had one or more pregnancies, a woman's os becomes slit-shaped instead of round. Just before ovulation, the cervix becomes softer and moves farther down in the vagina.

The cervix produces a special type of mucus that varies throughout the menstrual cycle. At ovulation, the mucus becomes clear and stretchy—women can identify their fertile days in each cycle by watching for this change (see page 145).

A Pap test (see page 198) involves taking a sample of cells from the cervix and examining them microscopically for abnormalities that may increase the risk of cervical cancer.

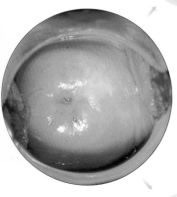

The cervix provides a passage for menstrual blood to leave the uterus.

The cervix softens and descends during a woman's most fertile days.

At ovulation the cervix produces mucus that is hospitable to sperm.

Contractions of the cervix during orgasm may draw sperm into cervical canal.

During pregnancy the cervix stays closed to protect the fetus.

During childbirth the cervix dilates to allow the baby into the vagina.

The cervix Situated at the top of the vagina, the cervix acts as the gateway to the rest of the female reproductive tract, and performs the numerous functions described above.

The uterus

Also known as the womb, the uterus is a hollow muscular organ the size and shape of an upside-down pear. It lies in the pelvic cavity between the bladder at the front and the rectum at the back. The primary functions of the uterus are to support and nourish a developing fetus during pregnancy. It can stretch by an incredible amount: enough to hold at least a 10-pound (4.5-kg) baby, plus the placenta and more than 2 quarts (2 liters) of *AMNIOTIC FLUID*.

The uterus has three layers: the lining, which builds up and breaks down each month in the menstrual cycle, is called the endometrium; the strong layer of muscle, which contracts to expel the baby during childbirth, is the myometrium; and the fibrous tissue, which forms the outer layer of the uterus, is known as the parametrium.

The ovaries

Located on either side of the uterus, the two small, almond-shaped organs called the ovaries produce female *GAMETES*, or ova. The ovaries are the female equivalent of the male testicles, and each measures about 1½ inches (3.8 cm) long and ¾ inch (2 cm) wide. In addition to producing an ovum during most menstrual cycles in a woman's reproductive life span (as a woman ages, some menstrual cycles are *ANOVULATORY*), the ovaries release the two sex hormones estrogen and progesterone.

The ovaries are as sensitive to pain as the male testicles. For example, deep penetration during sexual intercourse can bump them painfully into the pelvic wall. This problem can usually be overcome by a change in sexual position.

The fallopian tubes

Two fine tubes about 4 inches (10 cm) long, known as the fallopian tubes, run from close to each ovary and open into the upper part of the uterus. The ends of these tubes are bell-shaped and lined with fimbriae—fingerlike projections about 1 inch (2.5 cm) long. At ovulation, the ends of the tubes move toward the emerging ovum and the fimbriae wave in unison to sweep the released ovum into the tube. The ovum travels down the fallopian tubes to the uterus.

Externally, the fallopian tubes are the size of drinking straws; internally, the canals that carry the ova are the size of thin pieces of wire. The thick, muscular outer walls of the fallopian tubes protect the inner canals and their lining of cilia (hairlike projections) that beat rhythmically to move the ovum toward the uterus. An abundance of specialized cells in the inner lining of the fallopian tubes nourish the ovum or fertilized egg during the three-day journey to the uterus. Fertilization of the ovum most commonly occurs in the part of the tube nearest to the ovary.

The position of the uterus The uterus is usually tipped forward over the bladder, but about 20 percent of women have a retroverted uterus that lies backward against the rectum. Doctors once thought that this caused problems such as infertility. It is now recognized to be completely normal.

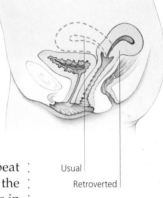

Usual

Retroverted

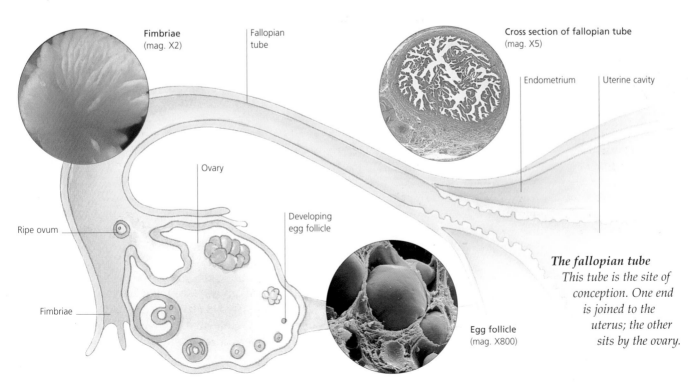

Fimbriae (mag. X2)

Fallopian tube

Cross section of fallopian tube (mag. X5)

Endometrium

Uterine cavity

Ovary

Ripe ovum

Developing egg follicle

Fimbriae

Egg follicle (mag. X800)

The fallopian tube
This tube is the site of conception. One end is joined to the uterus; the other sits by the ovary.

The Ovum

When a girl reaches puberty her ovaries begin to release egg cells, or ova. "Ova" refers to more than one egg cell; "ovum" is singular. Each tiny cell contains all the genetic material necessary to combine with a sperm cell and create a life.

Unlike the male body, which produces sperm continuously, the female body contains all the ova it needs at birth. The ova mature and are released at the approximate rate of one every 28 days.

As a female fetus is growing in the uterus, several million structures called primordial follicles are developing in her ovaries. Each one of these follicles has the potential to become a mature ovum, yet almost as soon as they are formed, thousands of follicles begin to die. In fact, by the time a baby girl is born, only about one million of several million follicles have survived. Thousands more degenerate before puberty, and this process continues throughout adulthood. Since only about 400 to 500 ova can be released in a lifetime—more than enough for a woman to become pregnant many times—this does not constitute a problem.

Only when a girl reaches puberty do the primordial follicles, present in her ovaries since she was a fetus, start to develop into ova. During puberty, the chemical follicle-stimulating hormone (FSH) initiates the development of these follicles each month. Around the beginning of each menstrual cycle, approximately 20 to 30 primordial follicles start to mature, producing the hormone estrogen as they do so. Follicular maturation is a complex three-stage process in which usually only one follicle ultimately develops into a mature ovum while the others degenerate.

OVULATION

A mature ovum is contained in a fluid-filled structure called a Graafian follicle. This moves toward the surface of the ovary and then, stimulated by a surge of luteinizing hormone (see page 129), bursts to release the ovum into the pelvic cavity. This is ovulation. The ovum is swept into the fringed, funnel-shaped end of its companion fallopian tube. The journey to possible conception (see page 148) has begun.

The remnants of the burst Graafian follicle undergo several important changes. First, they collapse. Then the space inside the fol-

INSIDE THE OVARY

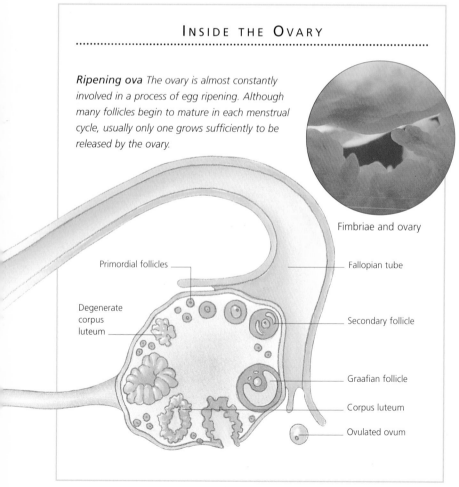

Ripening ova The ovary is almost constantly involved in a process of egg ripening. Although many follicles begin to mature in each menstrual cycle, usually only one grows sufficiently to be released by the ovary.

Fimbriae and ovary

Primordial follicles

Degenerate corpus luteum

Fallopian tube

Secondary follicle

Graafian follicle

Corpus luteum

Ovulated ovum

licle fills up with blood, and a glandular structure called a corpus luteum forms. This starts to secrete the hormone progesterone (it also secretes estrogen, but in lesser amounts), which helps the uterine lining thicken to receive a fertilized ovum. If conception does not take place, progesterone levels begin to fall in the last week of the menstrual cycle. The corpus luteum degenerates and the uterine lining starts to break down, to be shed during menstruation.

FEMALE SEX HORMONES

Hormones are chemical substances produced by parts of the brain, the ovaries, the endocrine glands and various other specialized cells in the body. Female sex hormones are secreted into the blood, where they circulate to target organs, affecting the development of *SECONDARY SEXUAL CHARACTERISTICS*, the menstrual cycle, pregnancy and breast-feeding.

Estrogens

Although people refer to estrogen as a single hormone, the estrogens are, in fact, a group of hormones. Types of estrogen include estradiol, estriol and estrone. Responsible for the development of female secondary sexual characteristics, they also help stimulate the development of the uterine lining each month for the possible implantation of a fertilized ovum. Estrogens are produced mainly by the ovaries but also by the placenta in pregnant women and in small amounts by the *ADRENAL GLANDS*.

Doctors prescribe synthetic estrogens in hormone replacement therapy (see page 108), the contraceptive pill and the so-called morning after pill. Doctors also use the synthetic estrogens in the treatment of certain prostate and breast cancers.

Progesterone

This hormone is released by the corpus luteum of the ovary after the ovum has been released. It is also produced by the adrenal glands and by the placenta during pregnancy. Like estrogen, progesterone prepares the uterus for implantation of a fertilized ovum, maintains pregnancy and causes development of the breasts during pregnancy. If fertilization does not occur, a fall in progesterone levels causes the shedding of the uterine lining during menstruation. Progesterone also affects the cervix and cervical mucus during the menstrual cycle and the production of sebum and deposition of fat on the body during puberty.

Progestogens are natural or synthetic forms of progesterone. In the U.S. and Canada they are used in the contraceptive pill; in the U.S., in some types of IUDs. Doctors also use progestogens in tests to find the cause of amenorrhea (see page 192). They may be combined with estrogens for use in hormone replacement therapy (HRT) and in the treatment of premenstrual tension and endometriosis (see page 195). Certain uterine cancers are treated with progestogens.

Prolactin

The secretion of prolactin, also known as lactogenic hormone, is regulated by the hypothalamus in the brain. Released by the *PITUITARY GLAND*, prolactin stimulates production of milk from the breasts after pregnancy. Sucking by the baby stimulates prolactin production during breast-feeding.

The gonadotropins

The term "gonadotropins" refers to any hormones that influence the functioning of the gonads (ovaries or testes). One of the main gonadotropins, follicle-stimulating hormone (FSH), is produced by the pituitary gland in the brain. In women, FSH stimulates the follicles in the ovary to become mature ova. It also promotes the secretion of estrogen.

The other main gonadotropin is luteinizing hormone (LH). This hormone triggers the release of the ovum from its ovarian follicle at ovulation and promotes the secretion of progesterone in women. In men, LH stimulates the production of male sex hormones (see page 123) in the testicles. Like FSH, LH is produced by the pituitary gland.

The hormone human chorionic gonadotropin (hCG) is produced in early pregnancy by the developing placenta. It prevents the corpus luteum from degenerating, so that progesterone continues to be produced and the uterine lining thickens to support a growing fetus. Most home pregnancy tests (see page 147) work by detecting the hCG that is excreted in urine.

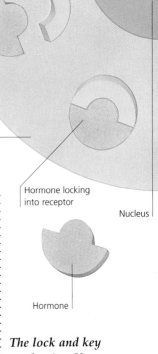

Receptor

Cell

Hormone locking into receptor

Nucleus

Hormone

The lock and key mechanism Hormones are able to affect only those cells that have receptors that exactly match the shape of the hormone molecule. This is known as the lock and key mechanism. Receptors may be inside or outside a cell.

The Breasts

*The breasts are one of the most erotically charged areas of
a woman's body and play a key role in defining her femininity.
Breasts also have an important biological function—to sustain
a child during infancy by producing milk.*

A woman's breasts will change during her lifetime and even, as part of her menstrual cycle, from month to month. The breasts are made up of fat cells, connective tissue and special secretory cells. During childhood the breast area is usually flat except for the nipple, which protrudes slightly from the surrounding skin. At puberty high estrogen levels lead to an accumulation of fat in the connective tissue beneath the nipple, causing the breasts to enlarge. During adulthood the skin and fine ligaments within the breasts gradually lose their elasticity, and after menopause the breasts may shrink and droop. Many women notice that their breasts swell each month immediately before menstruation.

THE FUNCTION OF THE BREAST

Secretory cells in the breast are responsible for milk production. In anatomical terms, the breasts are similar to sweat glands, except that they secrete colostrum and milk rather than sweat. Colostrum is a thin white liquid that is produced for the first few days after a baby is born. It is high in protein and antibodies and makes an ideal first food for a new baby's digestive system. Milk pro-

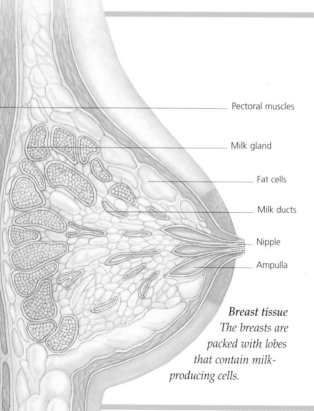

Pectoral muscles

Milk gland

Fat cells

Milk ducts

Nipple

Ampulla

Breast tissue
The breasts are
packed with lobes
that contain milk-
producing cells.

THE STRUCTURE OF THE BREAST

Within the breast there are 15 to 20 grapelike clusters of secretory cells, where milk is produced, divided by the supporting connective tissue into lobes. Each lobe contains a system of minute ducts that collect milk secretions. These join up to form about 15 larger ducts, all leading to the nipple. Just behind the nipple, each duct widens to form a collecting pouch called the lactiferous ampulla.

The breasts are made largely of fat cells and apart from the nipples, they do not contain any muscle. They sit outside the rib cage on top of the pectoral muscles, and the breast tissue merges into the surrounding body fat on the front of the body. The size and shape of a woman's breasts are determined by their fat content. Developing the pectoral muscles makes only a slight difference to breast appearance.

Cross section of
normal breast cells
(mag. X64)

Cross section of breast
cells during pregnancy
(mag. X64)

Cross section of lactating
breast cells
(mag. X64)

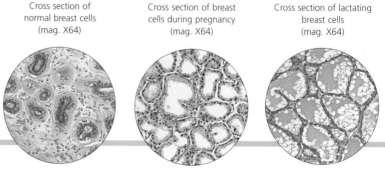

BREAST DENSITIES IN WOMEN OF DIFFERENT AGES

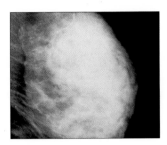

Under 30 years old
The younger a woman is, the denser her breast tissue (shown here on a mammogram as a white mass).

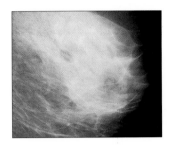

30 to 40 years old
Around this time, fatty tissue becomes more apparent. On a mammogram it appears as dark areas around the white mass.

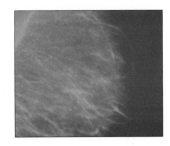

Mature (40-plus years old)
Approaching the menopause, breast tissue steadily decreases and any abnormalities can be more easily detected.

duction starts around the third day after birth. Milk provides all the nutrients needed for a baby's development. Milk also contains antibodies to protect the baby against disease. The lobes in a lactating breast become swollen with milk, giving breast-feeding women larger breasts than normal. When breast-feeding ceases, the breasts may return to their normal size, although from 30 to 50 percent of women have permanently larger breasts after breast-feeding.

THE NIPPLE

At the tip of the breast is the nipple, where a baby suckles breast milk. There are 15 to 20 milk-duct openings in the nipple, each bringing milk from the lobes. The shape of the nipple varies from woman to woman: it can be flat, protruding, cylindrical or conical. Some women have inverted nipples, a normal variant that can be corrected—if the woman chooses—with suction devices or cosmetic surgery. Inverted nipples do not impair breast-feeding (although cosmetic surgery does). If a nipple suddenly becomes inverted, however, it may be a sign of disease, such as breast cancer, and should be investigated immediately by a doctor.

The nipples contain many muscle fibers that contract during sexual arousal and breast-feeding and in response to cold temperatures. The contraction of these fibers makes the nipple elongated and hard to the touch. The nipple is an erogenous zone.

The areola

The area of skin around the nipple is the areola. Its color can vary from light to dark pink to almost black. It darkens during pregnancy and stays dark afterward. The tiny bumps on the areola are sweat and sebaceous glands that help to keep the nipple area lubricated during breast-feeding. When the muscles of the nipple contract, the areola also contracts, becoming small and puckered in appearance.

Can We Talk About It?

SEX AFTER A MASTECTOMY

A woman undergoing a mastectomy (surgical removal of a breast as treatment for cancer) experiences not only physical pain and a loss of sensitivity in a highly erogenous zone, but also frequently a loss of self-esteem and perceived sexual attractiveness. If you have undergone this procedure and are in a relationship, your partner may be feeling hesitant about initiating or expressing sexual intimacy and will need guidance and reassurance from you. It is important to discuss your feelings openly and honestly with him. Including your partner in your surgery and its aftercare—especially the moment when you see your scar for the first time—can also help to bring you closer together.

If you are single and have had a mastectomy, you may not want to date for fear of rejection. However, you need not discuss your surgery until the relationship is becoming serious or physical. Be prepared for some men to react with initial shock, and try to remember that breasts, or lack of them, should not determine the quality of a relationship.

The Sexual Response Cycle

The human sexual response cycle is a bodily process that begins with arousal. Before this physical arousal occurs, however, there must be a mental anticipation of sexual activity or the perception that something is attractive or stimulating.

Each person experiences sexual desire in a way unique to him- or herself, and many different stimuli can trigger the feeling. For some people simply sitting next to someone they find attractive will be enough to initiate sexual interest. It has been well documented that reading about sex or looking at photos or erotic movies can stimulate sexual feelings; but even the sound of someone's voice or the smell of their clothes may be enough to initiate feelings of sexual desire.

THE STAGES OF SEXUAL RESPONSE

Once the mind has recognized a conscious or subconscious sexual attraction, the sexual responses of the body follow. One explanation of sexual response, proposed by psychologist David Reed, concentrates on how the mind perceives and responds to arousal. He named this the Erotic Stimulus Pathway Model. In Reed's model, the psychological

changes that take place during arousal are more or less the same for men and women. The seduction stage consists of a person's experience of a conscious or subconscious sexual attraction to someone (whether a new or existing partner) and his or her attempt to interest or attract them. Sensation is the stage when the five senses—sight, hearing, taste, touch and smell—send signals of sexual pleasure and arousal to the brain. These sensations are then processed and can be acted upon consciously. The surrender stage describes the mental "letting go" that is necessary for orgasm to take place. Finally, the reflection stage involves thinking about the physical events that have taken place. If the feelings are positive, there will be a subconscious and conscious desire to repeat the cycle.

FEMALE SEXUAL RESPONSE

Sexologists Masters and Johnson (see page 257) were the first to explain in detail how human beings respond sexually. Their four-stage sexual cycle describes the physical changes that the body experiences at different levels of arousal. In their theory, after an initial period of desire, men and women go through four phases: excitement, plateau, orgasm and resolution. In females, the following changes take place.

Excitement

During the excitement phase, the clitoris and vagina become engorged with blood, and there are changes in the size and position of the vagina and uterus (see page 134). Changes also occur to the breasts—they enlarge slightly, while the nipples become erect and the *AREOLAE* swell and darken. Some women develop a skin flush or fine

Sexual responses in the mind and body
For every stage of physical sexual arousal, there is an associated cognitive or mental stage during which the brain responds to sexual stimuli.

Physical stages

Psychological stages

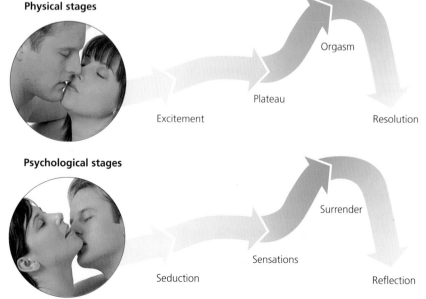

Orgasm

Plateau

Excitement   Resolution

Surrender

Sensations

Seduction   Reflection

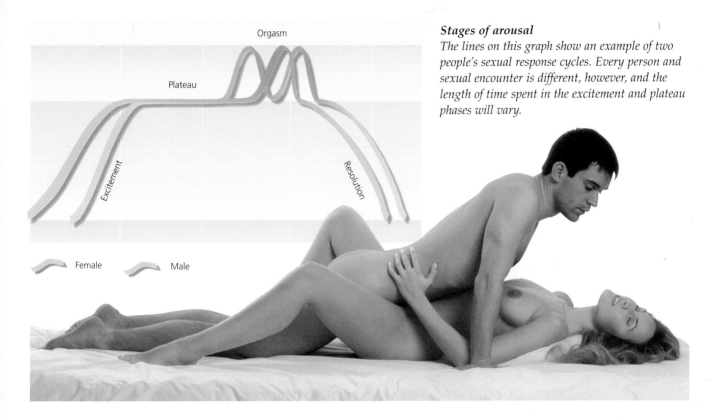

Stages of arousal
The lines on this graph show an example of two people's sexual response cycles. Every person and sexual encounter is different, however, and the length of time spent in the excitement and plateau phases will vary.

rash on the chest, known as a sex flush, that can appear at any time during sexual arousal. In addition, sexual excitement causes an increase in blood pressure, heart rate, breathing rate and muscle tension. Excitement lasts a variable length of time and may lead either to the plateau phase or to a return to rest.

Plateau

If sexual excitement and stimulation continue, a woman will enter the plateau phase. This is characterized by further blood flow to the entire genital area. The outer (or lower) third of the vagina decreases in diameter, which helps the vagina to grip the penis during intercourse, and the inner two-thirds of the vagina becomes more distended, providing a good receptacle for semen.

The uterus rises from the pelvic cavity and pushes into the abdominal cavity in a process called "tenting." Tenting results in the expansion of the vaginal cavity and creates an area where semen can pool after the man has ejaculated into the vagina. It also straightens the path from vagina to uterus to fallopian tubes, which facilitates the movement of sperm through the woman's reproductive tract. There is some evidence that stimulating the clitoris causes tenting.

Also during the plateau phase, the labia minora deepen in color, and the clitoris shortens and withdraws under the labial hood. A few drops of fluid may be secreted by the vestibular glands.

The duration of the plateau phase varies depending on the degree and type of sexual stimulation involved. The culmination of the plateau phase may be orgasm—the third and shortest of the four phases—or it may just slowly resolve. While some couples find this frustrating, others are comfortable with nonorgasmic resolution.

Orgasm

Although the intense, reflexive release of sexual tension that has built up during sexual stimulation and arousal may be centered in the genitals, it also affects the rest of the body. Female orgasms can feel intense, but they rarely last longer than 10 to 15 seconds. An orgasm begins with rhythmic contractions in the lower third of the vagina. The first contractions occur every 0.8 second—the same frequency with which the penis expels semen. After the initial contractions, the interval becomes progressively longer.

Penetrative sex
The penis fits snugly into the vagina, which becomes lubricated with slippery mucus during the excitement stage of female arousal.

Sexual Arousal and the Female Body

During sexual arousal, a woman experiences physical changes in and around the genitals. In a process called vasocongestion, blood rushes into the clitoris, which becomes erect; the labia minora flatten and move apart; the labia majora deepen in color and enlarge; the inner (or upper) two-thirds of the vagina lengthens; and the vaginal walls become moist and slippery.

EXCITEMENT

One of the first signs of sexual arousal in women is the wetness around the opening to the vagina. This allows penetration in a later stage of sexual response.

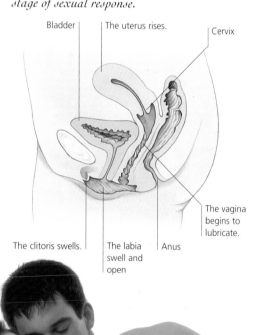

Bladder

The uterus rises.

Cervix

The clitoris swells.

The labia swell and open

Anus

The vagina begins to lubricate.

PLATEAU

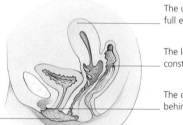

The upper part of the vagina is greatly expanded, while the lower part tightens up.

The genitals are fully engorged with blood.

The uterus reaches full elevation.

The lower vagina constricts.

The clitoris retracts behind its hood.

ORGASM

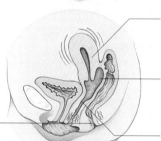

A series of contractions, or spasms, occur in the vagina and uterus.

The rectal sphincter contracts.

The uterus contracts.

The upper vagina balloons (a process called tenting).

The lower vagina contracts rhythmically.

RESOLUTION

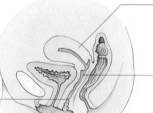

The uterus, vagina, clitoris and labia gradually return to their relaxed state.

The lower vagina relaxes.

The uterus lowers.

The upper vagina returns to normal size.

Postcoital glow
Following arousal, women experience the changes of the resolution stage. They may feel relaxed and tired or they may want to become aroused again. Unlike men, women do not have a refractory period.

Orgasmic contractions spread from the outer third of the vagina to the inner two-thirds and then up to the uterus. The uterine contractions start at the cervix and move toward the top of the uterus. These contractions may help to move sperm into the uterus and fallopian tubes and aid fertilization. The muscles of the pelvis and perineum and around the opening of the bladder and rectum also contract.

Some women may thrust their hips and pelvis as the muscles in the pelvis contract. Women usually experience 5 to 15 orgasmic contractions, depending on the intensity of the orgasm. The clitoris withdraws under its hood during orgasm, and although it may feel as though it is pulsating, it does not appear to contract rhythmically in the way the penis does.

Muscles in the back and feet may also undergo involuntary spasms during orgasm, causing the back to arch and toes to curl. The heart rate can rise to as much as 180 beats per minute and the breathing rate to as much as 40 breaths per minute. The blood pressure also rises. The pupils and nostrils dilate, and a woman may breathe rapidly or hold her breath for the duration of the orgasm. The more intense the orgasm, the greater the total body reaction. Masters and Johnson reported that immediately after orgasm, the area around the nipple starts to contract and wrinkle.

Outward behavior during orgasm varies from woman to woman. Some women have a contorted facial expression, as though they were in pain, and may moan or cry out. Other women clutch at the nearest object, be it their partner or a pillow, and some women make no sound and remain perfectly still, but report just as intense an orgasm.

Different types of female orgasm were first ranked by the Austrian psychoanalyst Sigmund Freud, who postulated that women experienced either a clitoral (or immature) orgasm or a vaginal (or mature) orgasm. He maintained that women who only had clitoral orgasms were sexually and psychologically immature.

This misconception survived for a long time, until Masters and Johnson used scientific equipment and many human volunteers to show that there is no physiological difference between an orgasm achieved by clitoral stimulation or vaginal penetration.

Subsequent research on the area known as the G-spot (see page 126) has shown that some women do seem to have two different types of orgasm. It is thought that one type of orgasm results from direct or indirect clitoral stimulation, whereas the other is achieved by G-spot stimulation.

Orgasms that originate from clitoral stimulation are sometimes referred to as tenting orgasms and lead to the contraction of the *PUBOCOCCYGEAL (PC) MUSCLES.* G-spot orgasms are sometimes referred to as uterine, or A-frame, orgasms and center around the uterus. They originate from stimuli carried by the pelvic nerve to the spinal reflex center. The deeper muscles of the pelvis and the uterus contract. Most women probably experience a combination of the tenting orgasm and the A-frame orgasm. Some women experience multiple orgasms (see below).

Resolution

After the last contractions of orgasm fade, the resolution phase begins. The breasts decrease in size, muscles all over the body relax, the heart rate and breathing pattern return to their resting state, and skin flushing begins to fade. The clitoris resumes its pre-excitement state within 10 to 20 seconds of orgasm, but the rest of the genital area takes longer—about 15 to 30 minutes.

If stimulation continues after orgasm, women can return to the plateau phase instead of entering resolution. This means they may be able to have more orgasms.

The stages of sexual response can vary between women and also from one sexual encounter to the next. On one occasion a woman may experience quick excitement and plateau phases, followed by orgasm and then resolution. On a second occasion the same woman may experience the excitement and plateau phases but not orgasm. This would be followed by a slow resolution. On a third occasion the woman may have repeated orgasms and keep returning to the plateau level before resolution.

MALE SEXUAL RESPONSE

The four stages of the male sexual cycle affect not only the penis and scrotum but also the internal sex organs and the blood flow and muscle tension in the entire body.

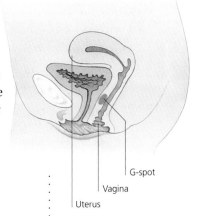

The G-spot There has been much debate about whether the G-spot exists. Some women report that they derive intense sexual pleasure from this area on the front wall of the vagina.

G-spot

Vagina

Uterus

MALE VERSUS FEMALE ORGASM

Advances in research and increased general knowledge about sex have made people much better informed about female sexuality and orgasm. One consequence of this is the expectation that women should experience orgasm as often as men. Women who are highly orgasmic may find this easy, but many women do not experience orgasm with each episode of sexual intercourse. Nonorgasmic intercourse can still be enjoyable.

Some fundamental differences exist between male and female orgasm. Female orgasm, unlike male orgasm, does not have a recog-

Nearing orgasm
Whereas men experience "ejaculatory inevitability," women can be distracted from orgasm right up until the last moment.

nized biological function. In fact, a woman can enjoy sex and conceive without ever experiencing orgasm. Psychological factors play a much greater role in determining whether a woman reaches orgasm. For example, if she is not completely relaxed, orgasm becomes difficult. Common psychological barriers to orgasm include feeling pressured to reach orgasm (or to reach orgasm quickly), worrying about something unrelated to sex, or concentrating on a partner's pleasure to the detriment of one's own. Whereas the thrusting movements of sexual intercourse cause many men to ejaculate easily, women may need additional or alternative types of stimulation. Intercourse does not always stimulate the clitoris enough to bring about orgasm.

FEMALE EJACULATION

Research suggests that a few women may ejaculate fluid at the time of orgasm in response to stimulation of the G-spot (see page 126). Those who analyzed the ejaculated fluid claim it resembles male prostatic fluid (see page 121) and is secreted by Skene's glands, near the urethral opening—the female equivalent of the male prostate gland. Female ejaculation is still controversial. It should not be confused with urine, which can leak when the sphincters of the bladder and urethra contract during orgasm, nor with vaginal lubrication.

Excitement

When a man becomes sexually aroused, there is a sudden increase in the blood flow to the penis and scrotum, and the penis becomes erect. The *ADRENAL GLANDS* also release adrenalin during the excitement phase, and this causes the heart rate, blood pressure and breathing rate to rise.

Plateau

If excitement or stimulation continues, the penis becomes more engorged, and the man has a full erection. The glans of the penis deepens in color, becoming deep red or purple, and there may be secretions of fluid from the *BULBOURETHRAL GLANDS*. The testicles increase in size by up to 50 percent and are pulled tightly against the body wall.

The series of events leading to ejaculation starts with the movement of sperm from the testicles to the ampulla, which is the flared end of the vas deferens. When the other constituents of semen have been squirted into the urethra by the seminal vesicles and the prostate gland, ejaculation is imminent. It is at this stage that a man experiences a sensation known as "ejaculatory inevitability." This means the man knows that even if all stimulation of the penis ceased, ejaculation would still occur. Ejaculatory inevitability lasts for about three seconds.

Orgasm

Ejaculation is the expulsion of semen through the penis, and it is usually, but not always, accompanied by orgasm. When a man experiences ejaculatory inevitability, the muscle sphincters at both ends of the urethra are closed and a pleasant sensation of pressure occurs. Then the outer muscle sphincter opens, and semen moves to the urethral bulb at the base of the penis. A man may experience orgasm without ejaculation, particularly if he experiences orgasm more than once in a short space of time.

Ejaculation occurs when several intense contractions of the muscles in the urethra and around the base of the penis pump semen out of the body. The contractions may be strong enough to expel the semen farther than 11 inches (28 centimeters). There are usually three to five main contractions at intervals of 0.8 second (this is the same interval as the vaginal contractions during female orgasm). These contractions may continue but become progressively weaker and irregular. Waves of contractions occur in the pelvic-floor muscles, and the inner thigh muscles may contract involuntarily. Male orgasm rarely lasts longer than 15 seconds and is generally between 4 and 10 seconds—this is shorter than most female orgasms.

Sexual Arousal and the Male Body

The first sign of arousal in men is penile erection, due to vasocongestion (engorgement with blood). The skin and muscles of the scrotum thicken as the testicles are drawn up toward the body, and secretions may leak from the tip of the penis.

EXCITEMENT

An erect penis is usually a clear sign of male sexual excitement. Erections occur very quickly after a man feels aroused or stimulated.

The penis becomes hard and erect.

Urethra

Bladder

Seminal vesicle

Prostate gland

Rectum

Partial erection

The testicles start to move up toward the body.

PLATEAU

At the plateau stage the man's body is preparing itself for ejaculation.

The glans deepens in color.

The testicles increase in size and the scrotum thickens.

Droplets secreted by the bulbourethral glands appear at the tip of the penis.

The testicles are drawn up tightly against the body.

ORGASM

Male ejaculation and orgasm are usually simultaneous. As semen is expelled, the penis rhythmically contracts.

The penis and urethra contract.

Semen is expelled from the tip of the penis.

The bladder sphincter closes.

The prostate gland contracts.

The seminal vesicles contract.

RESOLUTION

Blood flows away from the genitals, and the penis gradually becomes flaccid — this is called detumescence.

Blood flows out of the penile tissues and the erection slowly disappears.

The scrotum thins and the testicles descend.

Postcoital fatigue
It is common for men — and women — to feel relaxed and drowsy after making love.

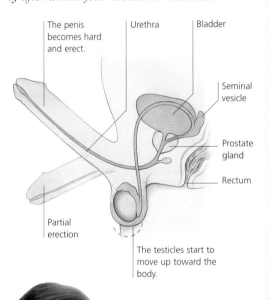

The average volume of semen expelled during ejaculation is usually about one teaspoonful containing 100 million to 500 million sperm. The volume of semen and the sperm count are markedly reduced by repeated ejaculation within the space of a few days. If a man has not ejaculated for some time, a relatively large volume of semen will be produced. It is thought that the more semen a man ejaculates, the more enjoyable his orgasm is. (This contrasts with the female orgasm. Many women claim to have smaller, less powerful orgasms if they have not experienced one for a while.) Changes in the body include a rise in the breathing rate, heart rate and blood pressure, all of which reach a peak at the moment of orgasm. The breath-

fact or fiction?

Men cannot urinate and ejaculate at the same time.

Fact. As soon as a man feels that he is about to ejaculate, the sphincter muscle at the neck of his bladder contracts tightly so that urine cannot pass through into the urethra, and he will not be able to urinate until after he has ejaculated. The closing of the sphincter muscle prevents the backward flow of semen into the bladder.

ing rate may go up to 50 per minute and also the heart rate may increase to around 180 beats per minute.

The sensation of orgasm can be overwhelming, starting in the pelvic region and then spreading through the whole body. Men characteristically begin to thrust their hips during intercourse when they feel they are about to ejaculate. At the moment of ejaculation a man may thrust his pelvis forward very hard, pushing the penis as deep into the vagina as possible. Some men make involuntary noises during orgasm and grimace and clutch at their partner. Men may clench their toes and arch their feet in the way that some women do during orgasm; this is less likely if the man is on top of his partner during intercourse. A few men experience dilation of small blood vessels in the skin, giving rise to a sexual flush or rash, but this is seen more often in women.

Resolution

After orgasm, the penis and testicles quickly decrease in size and return to their pre-aroused state within 10 minutes. This process is called detumescence. During this phase, a man's penis is relatively insensitive to sexual stimulation.

Most men are not thought to experience multiple orgasms with a single erection. The period between ejaculating and being able to have another erection is called the refractory period. Young men may have very short refractory periods (sometimes a matter of minutes) and potentially can achieve one erection after another in quick succession. In contrast, older men may find that the refractory period lasts much longer, so that it takes several hours or even days to achieve another erection after having sexual intercourse.

A man's breathing rate and heart rate slow down during the resolution period, and his blood pressure drops. It is common for men and women to feel relaxed and sleepy after orgasm.

SHOULD SEX BE SYNCHRONIZED?

The stages of arousal can take variable amounts of time, but generally, the younger a man is, the quicker he becomes aroused. Because of the slower arousal times of women, couples may find that their sexual responses are out of sync. For instance, this can create a situation when a man has reached an advanced stage of the plateau phase and his partner may only just be feeling aroused. Similarly, during penetration, when both partners are in the plateau stage, a man may progress rapidly to orgasm and ejaculation but his partner may need much more time and stimulation. Sex therapists Masters and Johnson suggest that: "In couples who have come to recognize that one usually reaches orgasm much more quickly than the other, deliberate alterations in their sexual routines may be called for to compensate for a discrepancy in timing."

Sexual timing
Sex can be prolonged by delaying penetration and concentrating on foreplay. The discrepancy between arousal times may diminish with age.

SEX &
REPRODUCTION

Human Fertility

The ability to reproduce is known as fertility. If a couple engage in a single episode of unprotected sexual intercourse around the time of the woman's ovulation, they have about a one-in-three chance that a sperm from the man will fertilize her ovum.

In recent years scientists have speculated that human fertility may be declining (see page 153). Whereas a few decades ago, most people took their fertility for granted, nowadays they are more likely to be concerned about issues relating to reproductive health. In the past, if couples had intercourse, pregnancy was hard to avoid, whether or not they wanted children. In fact, a marriage that did not produce children was considered remarkable and, in some cultures, grounds for divorce.

Today fertility has become a major issue. People spend millions of dollars annually on methods of contraception devised to prevent pregnancy. At the same time, researchers spend enormous sums of money seeking infertility treatments that will restore fertility to the increasing number of people who cannot conceive naturally.

Fertility is closely linked to age, particularly in women. Beginning at puberty, when boys and girls start to produce mature sex cells (sperm and ova), full adult fertility is established a few years after a girl's first menstrual period or a boy's first ejaculation.

Doctors estimate that a healthy woman who regularly has unprotected sexual intercourse will conceive in an average of two to three months if she is under 25 years old. She may need six months or longer if she is over the age of 35, because, as she ages, a woman's ova more frequently fail to mature and to be released by an ovary. This causes her fertility to decline. A woman will typically remain fertile until the age of 45 to 50, when her ovaries stop releasing ova altogether and she reaches menopause. Men continue to be fertile until a much later age, although the quality of sperm begins to deteriorate after age 40.

THE MENSTRUAL CYCLE

To know when conception is most likely, it is necessary to understand the complex fluctuation of hormone levels that controls ovulation and the entire menstrual cycle.

At birth a girl's ovaries contain as many as one million egg follicles, each of which has the potential to produce a mature ovum. By puberty, only 100,000 of these follicles remain. For the next 30 to 40 years, approximately every 28 days, one of these follicles will mature to become an ovum that is released from an ovary. The ovum then travels down the fallopian tube and into the uterus. If the ovum is not fertilized, the lining of the uterus begins to break down and is shed in a process called menstruation. This monthly cycle of ovulation and menstruation is the hallmark of a woman's fertile years.

While the average menstrual cycle is 28 days, women's actual experiences vary greatly. Many factors can influence the length and regularity of the menstrual cycle, including poor nutrition, obesity,

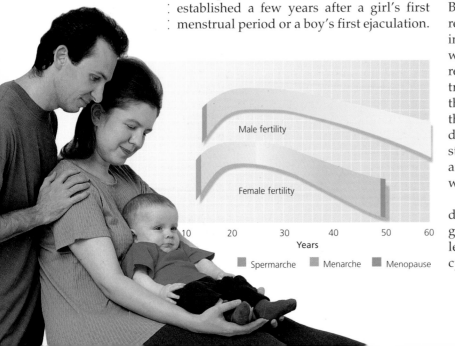

The rise and fall of fertility Men and women differ in their ability to reproduce. Whereas men's fertility stays reasonably constant throughout life, women's fertility starts to decline several years before menopause, at which time it ends permanently.

Male fertility

Female fertility

| 10 | 20 | 30 | 40 | 50 | 60 |

Years

■ Spermarche ■ Menarche ■ Menopause

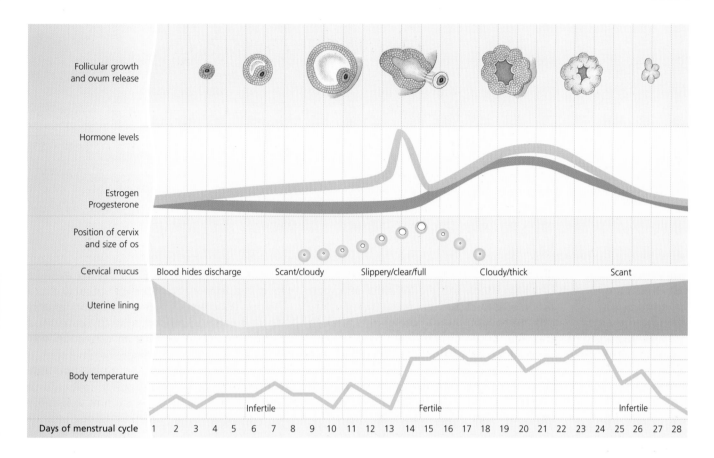

Follicular growth and ovum release		
Hormone levels		
Estrogen Progesterone		
Position of cervix and size of os		
Cervical mucus	Blood hides discharge	Scant/cloudy	Slippery/clear/full	Cloudy/thick	Scant
Uterine lining		
Body temperature		
	Infertile	Fertile	Infertile
Days of menstrual cycle	1 2 3 4 5 6 7 8 9 10 11 12 13 14 15 16 17 18 19 20 21 22 23 24 25 26 27 28	

abnormally low body weight, stress, emotional trauma, hormonal imbalance, travel, *ENDOMETRIOSIS* and *OVARIAN CYSTS*. The menstrual cycle is regulated by the hormones of the pituitary gland, hypothalamus, ovaries, uterus and corpus luteum (see below). Other hormones, such as thyroid hormone, can upset menstruation.

The menstrual period

A woman's menstrual period—when an unfertilized ovum and the uterine lining flow through the vagina and out of the body—marks the beginning of the menstrual cycle. The amount of blood loss varies from woman to woman and from cycle to cycle. An average menstrual bleed can last between one and eight days and involves a loss of 2 to 2½ ounces (60 to 75 ml) of fluid. Women may experience heavier bleeding as menopause approaches and lighter bleeding if they use oral contraceptives.

The proliferative phase

The next stage of the menstrual cycle begins when part of the brain called the hypothalamus secretes gonadotropin-releasing hormone (GRH). This causes the pituitary

gland in the brain to release follicle-stimulating hormone (FSH) and luteinizing hormone (LH). The egg follicles in the ovary respond to these hormones by maturing and producing estrogen. During this phase of the menstrual cycle, one egg follicle becomes dominant and the estrogen it produces causes the lining of the uterus to thicken in preparation for the implantation of a fertilized ovum.

The secretory phase

When an ovum is sufficiently mature, it is released from the follicle and is picked up by the fallopian tube. This is called ovulation, and it usually happens 14 days before a woman begins to menstruate (for many women this is around the middle of the menstrual cycle). A woman is most fertile and most likely to conceive in the days around ovulation.

Ovulation marks the beginning of the secretory phase of the cycle. The empty ovarian follicle that is left in the ovary develops into a structure known as a corpus luteum, which secretes the hormone progesterone. The corpus luteum also secretes estrogen but in lesser amounts. The uterine

The menstrual cycle
Each month an ovum matures in the ovary and is released at ovulation. Before and after this there are associated changes in hormone levels, body temperature, quantity and texture of cervical mucus and thickness of the uterine lining.

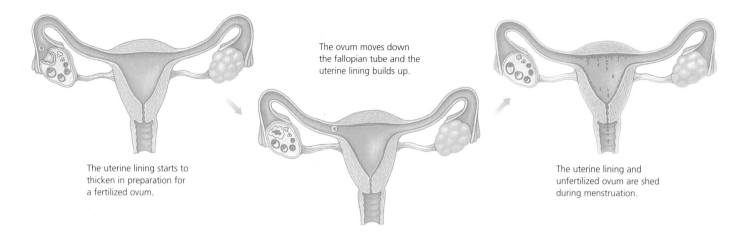

The ovum moves down the fallopian tube and the uterine lining builds up.

The uterine lining starts to thicken in preparation for a fertilized ovum.

The uterine lining and unfertilized ovum are shed during menstruation.

Inside the uterus In each menstrual cycle the uterus prepares itself to receive a fertilized ovum and support a growing fetus. It does this by growing a thick lining of blood vessels. When an ovum is not fertilized, the uterine lining falls away.

Family planning The majority of couples in their twenties should conceive within the first year of trying if they are in general good health and the woman has a normal menstrual cycle.

lining responds to these hormones by becoming thicker in preparation for implantation of a fertilized ovum.

If the ovum travels down the fallopian tube without being fertilized by a sperm, it degenerates, as does the corpus luteum. The estrogen and progesterone levels fall, while prostaglandins—substances produced by the uterus—rise, and this causes the uterine lining to break down and be shed.

CHANCES OF CONCEPTION

Many couples assume that with some basic knowledge about peak fertility times, the woman will easily become pregnant. In fact, even in healthy couples over the age of 25 who have a normal level of fertility, this may not be the case.

Doctors expect couples to try to achieve conception for an average of 6 months before it occurs. Doctors will not usually agree to investigate for difficulties until a couple have been trying for approximately 12 to 18 months.

Preexisting medical conditions may adversely affect fertility in a couple, but there are also several common reasons why a woman may not become pregnant as quickly as the couple would like. First, it is quite normal for a woman to have some menstrual cycles in which ovulation does not occur (this is especially true if she is in her thirties or forties). Second, ovulation can be temporarily suppressed by factors such as emotional upset, stress, sudden weight loss or stopping the use of the contraceptive pill. Third, without proper advice and correct monitoring, a couple may find it hard to pinpoint the exact time of ovulation (ovulation can be more obvious in some women than others). Furthermore, ovulation can happen at different points in different cycles, so depending solely on a menstrual calendar (see page 145), for example, would be unreliable.

Research carried out on couples who are trying to have a baby has produced the following statistics about the average amount of time it takes to conceive.

~ Approximately 80 percent of couples conceive after a year of trying.
~ Approximately 85 percent of couples conceive after 18 months.
~ Approximately 90 percent of couples conceive after two years.
~ After two years of trying to conceive, around 10 to 15 percent of couples are diagnosed subfertile.

Starting a Family

If a couple are planning to conceive, doctors advise that it is important to spend several months prior to conception paying careful attention to diet and general health. Good nutrition before pregnancy is important for producing a healthy baby.

If prospective parents want to maximize their chances of conception and ensure that a future baby will be as healthy as possible, they should be prepared to make lifestyle changes in the months before they start trying to conceive. Doctors recommend a healthy diet, stopping smoking, and avoiding alcohol and drugs (other than drugs that have been endorsed by a doctor). This is particularly important for women.

Caffeine, for example, is thought to reduce the chances of conception, and some studies have linked high caffeine intake with low-birth-weight babies. Therefore, women are advised not to drink more than four caffeinated drinks, such as tea, coffee or cola, per day. Cigarette smoking is notoriously damaging because of its adverse effect on sperm count and overall negative effect on general health. Chronic use of

THE PRECONCEPTION DIET — WHAT TO EAT AND WHAT TO AVOID

Doctors say that it is important that women receive adequate amounts of vitamin B_{12} and folic acid when they are planning to conceive. Vitamin B_{12} can be obtained from foods such as meat, eggs, fish and milk, which most people eat in their everyday diet. Folic acid is harder to obtain in sufficient amounts from diet alone, so doctors recommend that women take supplements

(400 mcg a day for at least three months before conception). Liver, caffeine, large amounts of alcohol, smoking and drugs or medications (except those approved by a doctor) should all be avoided preconceptually.

Men should give up smoking and heavy drinking and eat fruit, vegetables and whole-grain products that are rich in vitamins and minerals.

Taking folic acid
A pill a day will significantly reduce the risk of spina bifida in a future baby.

Enhancing the chance of conception
Vitamin B_{12} is found in animal products. Strict vegetarians, whose dietary intake of this vitamin may be limited, should seek advice from a dietician.

Reducing the chance of conception
Drugs, smoking and heavy drinking are habits that should be given up immediately. Some foods such as liver or liver pâté are known to be detrimental to fetal health.

A preconception consultation Some couples seek advice from their doctors when they are planning to conceive. This is particularly important for partners who suffer from hereditary illnesses or for women who have conditions that require regular medication usage or that might make pregnancy dangerous.

drugs such as marijuana inhibit sperm production in men and disturb the menstrual cycle in women.

An important vitamin in preconceptual care is folic acid, a B vitamin found in fresh green leafy vegetables, cereals, wheat germ, meat, oranges, potatoes, yeast extract and milk. It plays a crucial role in the prevention of spina bifida and other neural tube defects in babies. Women who are planning to conceive should take 400 mcg of folic acid a day. Since most people have an average intake of only 200 mcg per day, folic acid supplements are recommended. Women who have already had a baby with spina bifida or an associated condition such as anencephaly (partial or complete absence of the cerebral hemispheres of the brain) are at risk of having another baby with the same condition and should seek advice about the recommended daily intake of folic acid.

Women should take folic acid for three months before conception and throughout the first 12 weeks of pregnancy. If a pregnancy is unplanned, folic acid should be taken as soon as pregnancy is suspected or confirmed. Women should not take extra multivitamins to get an adequate intake of folic acid, because some of the vitamins in the combination can be toxic in high doses.

Vitamin B_{12}, present in meat, fish, eggs and dairy products, is also important in preconceptual care. It is vital for the production of the genetic material DNA and works alongside folic acid to prevent neural tube defects, such as spina bifida.

Some foods should also be avoided by pregnant women and women trying to conceive. These include liver and liver products which, although containing folic acid in large quantities, have been linked to an increased risk of spina bifida in babies.

Women planning to conceive are advised to have a thorough medical checkup by a doctor. This includes checking for immunity against rubella (German measles), through either previous infection or vaccination. Women who take prescribed drugs for conditions such as epilepsy, depression, acne or hypertension should have their treatments carefully reviewed—some prescribed drugs are known to be teratogenic. This means that they will cause damage to an embryo. For example, one drug marketed for the treatment of acne can cause severe birth defects. Doctors also advise that women be screened for sexually transmitted diseases (STDs)—most importantly HIV—especially if a woman or her partner has had an STD in the past or either of them has had many sexual partners.

MAXIMIZING THE CHANCES OF CONCEPTION

Most women are fertile for between two and seven days every month. By detecting ovulation and then having intercourse during the fertile period, couples maximize the chance of conception. They can identify these fertile days in several ways.

Keeping a menstrual calendar
If a woman has a menstrual cycle that is 28 days long, she can predict that she will ovulate around the 14th day. If menstruation is expected to begin, for instance, on the 25th day of the month, ovulation can be predicted to occur around the 11th.

Menstrual calendars

If a woman has a regular menstrual cycle, she can predict when she will ovulate by using a menstrual calendar. By marking the days when menstrual bleeding occurs, she can discern a pattern. The menstrual cycle begins on the first day of a period and ends on the last day before the next period. The average length of the menstrual cycle is 28 days. Ovulation usually occurs 14 days before menstruation, so in a 28-day cycle, this is day 14, the midpoint of the cycle. In a longer cycle of 32 days, ovulation would probably occur around day 18. In a shorter cycle of 24 days, it would occur around day 10. Keeping a menstrual calendar over several months familiarizes a woman with the length of her menstrual cycle and helps her predict ovulation.

Body temperature

Approximately two days after ovulation, a woman's body temperature rises by a few tenths of a degree. This rise remains until her next menstrual period. Women can identify changes in body temperature by taking their temperature first thing in the morning every day with a specially calibrated thermometer and by keeping a chart of the readings over a period of months to discern a pattern. However, as a rise in temperature indicates that ovulation has occurred already, this method cannot be adopted as a contraceptive technique by women who want to avoid pregnancy. Women charting their

temperature should also be aware that other factors, such as mild infections or colds, can cause a rise in body temperature.

Monitoring cervical mucus

Some discharge is a normal part of every woman's menstrual cycle, but around the time a woman is ovulating the mucus covering her cervix takes on special properties. Fertile mucus is similar to egg white in appearance and texture—it is clear and can be stretched between the thumb and finger. It is easily distinguishable from discharge at other times of the month, which is thick, white and nonelastic. Fertile mucus aids conception by forming a slippery passage for the sperm to swim through.

Body awareness

Various subtle signs exist that ovulation is taking place, but not all women find these easy to identify. A woman may notice that her sex drive increases and she is more likely to initiate sex with her partner. Another woman may experience pain when she ovulates. This ovulation pain, or mittelschmerz (literally, "middle pain"), may be a short burst of discomfort, mild in degree and duration, or a severe pain similar to menstrual cramps.

Ovulation-detection kits

A surge of a hormone called luteinizing hormone (LH) occurs before ovulation (LH causes the ripening egg follicle in the ovary to rupture and release the ovum).

fact or fiction?

A couple who are trying to conceive should make love throughout the month, not just during a woman's fertile period.

Fact. Regular sex during the rest of a woman's menstrual cycle will strengthen male fertility rather than weaken it. If a couple have intercourse only during a woman's fertile period, the man's semen is more likely to contain dead sperm.

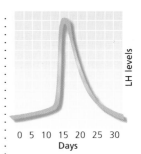

Rising LH levels A surge of luteinizing hormone from the pituitary gland is a sign that ovulation is about to happen. Ovulation-detection kits measure LH levels in urine.

Fluctuations in body temperature There is a small rise in temperature that occurs just after a woman ovulates. This can be detected using a special thermometer.

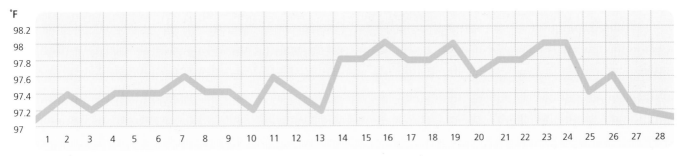

Bleeding   Mucus increases and becomes clearer

DETERMINING SEX

Practices that are claimed to influence whether a boy or a girl is conceived.

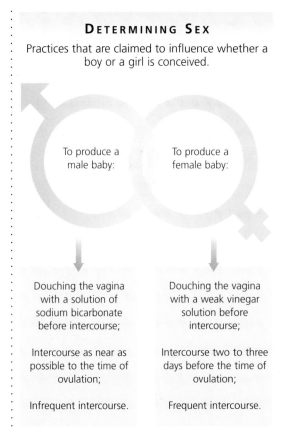

To produce a male baby:

To produce a female baby:

Douching the vagina with a solution of sodium bicarbonate before intercourse;

Intercourse as near as possible to the time of ovulation;

Infrequent intercourse.

Douching the vagina with a weak vinegar solution before intercourse;

Intercourse two to three days before the time of ovulation;

Frequent intercourse.

Pharmacists sell kits that detect LH in the urine and so give advance warning of ovulation. These kits are useful, but LH in the urine is not a guarantee of ovulation.

The timing of intercourse

Experts differ in their opinions about the correct timing and frequency of intercourse to maximize the chances of conception. Generally, they agree that couples should make love at least every other day around the time of ovulation. Most sperm are capable of fertilizing an ovum for up to 24 hours after ejaculation (although some are capable for longer), and an ovum remains viable for up to 24 hours after ovulation.

Sexual practices and conception

It is thought that the muscular contractions that women experience during orgasm may help to carry the sperm up the vagina and into the uterus. The timing of a woman's orgasm may also be significant. Recent research by biologists at the University of Manchester in the U.K. suggests that if a woman reaches orgasm at any time up to a

HOW CHROMOSOMES DETERMINE THE SEX OF A CHILD

Whether a baby is a boy or girl depends on the combination of chromosomes the child "inherits" from its parents. Chromosomes are structures that carry genetic material. Women's ova all contain one type of sex chromosome, known as X chromosomes. A man's sperm may contain either an X chromosome or a Y chromosome. If an X sperm unites with an ovum at conception, the resulting baby will be female. If a Y sperm fertilizes an ovum, the baby will be male. Geneticists use the shorthand XX to refer to female and XY to refer to male.

A girl

If the ovum, which contains an X chromosome, is fertilized by a sperm that is carrying an X chromosome, the result will be a baby girl.

A boy

If after ejaculation during sexual intercourse, a Y sperm from the male partner is the first to fertilize the ovum, the resulting embryo will have XY sex chromosomes and be male.

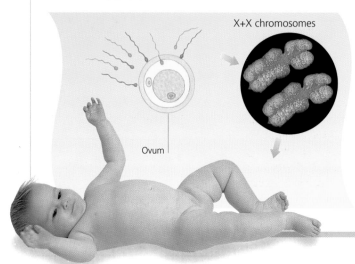

X+X chromosomes

Ovum

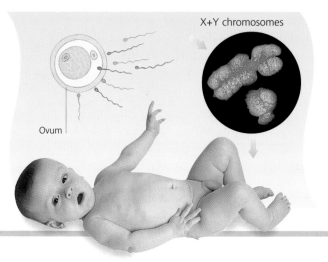

X+Y chromosomes

Ovum

minute before her partner ejaculates, or if she does not have an orgasm, she will retain relatively few of his sperm. In contrast, if a woman reaches orgasm at any time from a minute before her partner to 45 minutes afterward, she is likely to retain a relatively large number of sperm. However, the lack of female orgasm is not a barrier to conception—women who retain relatively few sperm can still become pregnant.

Specific sexual positions, such as the so-called missionary position (see page 78), are unlikely to enhance a couple's chances of conception. It is thought that as long as the sperm are deposited in the vagina, they will be able to penetrate the cervical mucus very quickly, regardless of the way in which a couple have intercourse. Such techniques as the woman tilting her pelvis up with the aid of a pillow after intercourse to stop the sperm from flowing out of the vagina are thought to help but are far from fail-safe.

Some couples employ techniques that are thought to influence the sex of a child. Since men produce equal numbers of X-carrying and Y-carrying sperm, the chances of producing boys or girls should be equal. There have been claims, however, that specific practices (see opposite page) do have an effect. The claims are based on the theory that X sperm travel slowly, are resilient and survive well in an acid environment, while Y sperm are light and agile and survive best in an alkaline one. These practices have not been rigorously tested and they may not work, but they are harmless.

Confirming pregnancy

Signs that a woman may be pregnant are breast tenderness and swelling, vaginal secretions, constipation, food intolerances, and nausea—some women experience these only a week after conception (around week three of a typical 28-day menstrual cycle). It is easy to mistake premenstrual syndrome (PMS) for signs of pregnancy.

A more reliable sign of pregnancy is a missed period at the beginning of the next menstrual cycle (although some pregnant women continue to have scanty bleeding). If a woman takes her temperature every day, and it is still raised 20 to 22 days after ovulation (well into the next menstrual cycle), she is probably pregnant. Pregnancy testing kits, purchased from drugstores, also give reliable results.

PREGNANCY TESTING KITS

Pregnancy testing kits can be used from the first day of a missed period and onward. They detect the hormone human chorionic gonadotropin (hCG), which is produced by the developing embryo and placenta and appears in the blood and urine of pregnant women. There are different types of kits—some have test wells that urine is dropped into, while others have sticks that are held directly in the stream of urine. All are highly effective.

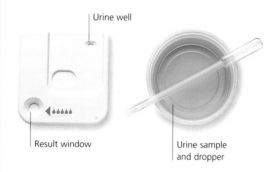

Urine well

Result window

Urine sample and dropper

Using a test well kit After a urine sample is collected, the dropper is used to drop urine into the test well. A specific color change in the result window indicates pregnancy.

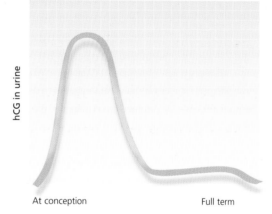

hCG in urine

At conception

Full term

The rise in hCG The levels of hCG rise dramatically in early pregnancy. The hCG level can be measured in the blood six days after conception and in the urine on the first day of a missed period.

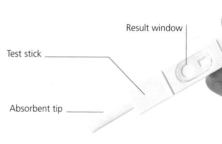

Result window

Test stick

Absorbent tip

Positive result

Negative result

Using a test stick
Test stick kits are very simple to use. The absorbent tip at the end of the stick is immersed in the flow of urine, and then the stick is laid flat while the result appears as a color change in the result window. Alternatively, urine can be collected in a clean dry container.

Fertilization

Fertilization, or conception, is the moment when a sperm cell penetrates an ovum, usually inside a woman's fallopian tube. As a result of fertilization, two sets of chromosomes—one set from each parent—combine, and a new life begins.

The route to the ovum *Sperm are deposited near the cervix during sexual intercourse. Here they begin the journey through the cervical canal, up through the uterus and then along the fallopian tubes.*

After being ejaculated into a woman's vagina, the sperm contained in a man's semen can take minutes or hours to make the comparatively short journey of 6 to 7 inches (15 to 18 cm) up through the uterus and into the fallopian tubes. If a woman has recently ovulated, an ovum will be waiting there.

Some sperm are fast swimmers and can reach their destination in just five minutes. The majority, however, will struggle to get to the fallopian tubes. Many will be destroyed or lost in the vagina or other areas of the reproductive tract.

Out of an average 300 million sperm that start the journey, only about 500 reach the correct fallopian tube and fewer still reach the ovum. Those that manage to reach the correct fallopian tube are transformed by substances in the cervix, uterus and fallopian tubes that make them capable of fertilizing the ovum. Despite this assistance, microscopic studies show that many sperm simply swim past the ovum, oblivious to its presence. If no ovum is present in the fallopian tube, the sperm swim to and fro, surviving for up to several days before they start to degenerate.

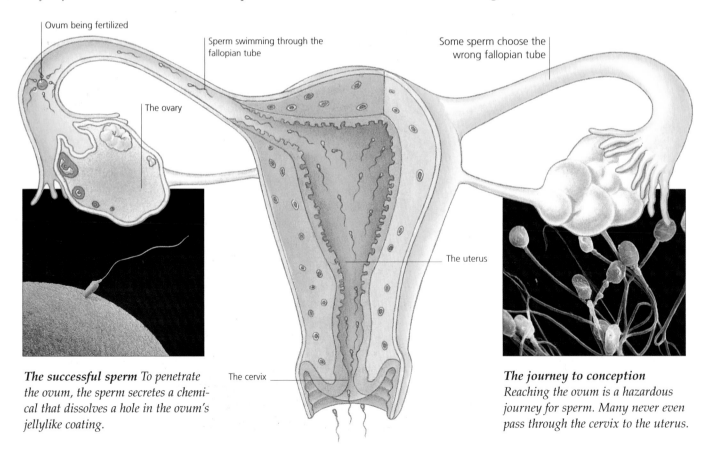

Ovum being fertilized

Sperm swimming through the fallopian tube

Some sperm choose the wrong fallopian tube

The ovary

The uterus

The cervix

The successful sperm *To penetrate the ovum, the sperm secretes a chemical that dissolves a hole in the ovum's jellylike coating.*

The journey to conception *Reaching the ovum is a hazardous journey for sperm. Many never even pass through the cervix to the uterus.*

SPERM MEETS OVUM

After being released from its follicle at ovulation, the ovum is picked up by the fimbriae at the end of the fallopian tube and starts its journey to the uterus. Because of the slow progress of sperm through the female reproductive tract, fertilization usually takes place hours rather than minutes after intercourse (unless there are sperm already present in the fallopian tubes). The ovum is usually fertilized in the outer to mid third of the fallopian tube.

When sperm come into contact with female secretions, a process known as capacitation takes place. The outer layer of the head of the sperm is stripped away so that the enzymes in the acrosome cap (see page 122) can create a hole in the outer membrane of the ovum. Only after capacitation has taken place can sperm penetrate and fertilize the ovum.

The moment a sperm breaks the membrane of an ovum, a chemical reaction occurs inside the ovum to make it impossible for another sperm to enter. When the sperm is safely inside the ovum, it sheds its tail. Fertilization (also known as conception) occurs when the head—or nucleus—of the sperm fuses with the nucleus of the ovum, uniting the CHROMOSOMES of the man and the woman.

Within minutes of fertilization, the fertilized ovum releases hormones important to the continuation of the pregnancy. Several hours after fertilization, the ovum divides for the first time and is called a zygote. After three or four divisions, it becomes a solid cluster of cells known as a morula. The cells of the morula divide every 12 to 15 hours until there are about 100 cells, at which point it becomes a blastocyst.

During fertilization and for several hours afterward, a number of sperm unsuccessfully attempt to penetrate the outer membrane of the ovum. Eventually, the loser sperm die and their frenzied activity ceases.

IMPLANTATION

The journey of the blastocyst from the fallopian tube to the uterus, where it will grow to become a fetus, begins about three days after conception. Once again, the journey is not straightforward. The blastocyst is hindered by a sphincter muscle between the widest and narrowest part of the fallopian tube, through which it cannot pass.

However, the increasing levels of the pregnancy hormone progesterone allow the muscle to relax and open so the blastocyst can continue its journey. A damaged or blocked fallopian tube causes particular concern at this stage because it may bar the blastocyst's route, resulting in an ectopic pregnancy in which the embryo starts to develop in the fallopian tube.

Assuming its journey is successful, the blastocyst will enter the uterus and then implant itself in the thickened lining of the uterus. Crucial hormones released from the blastocyst immediately alert the body to the fact that it is not a foreign body and should be nurtured rather than expelled. The growth of the fetus begins.

UNUSUAL SITUATIONS

In most cases a woman's ovaries release ova alternately. Occasionally a woman may produce two ova—one from each ovary—and each may be fertilized by separate sperm. This results in the birth of nonidentical siblings, or fraternal twins, each nurtured by his or her own separate placenta during pregnancy. Fraternal twins, even of the same sex, are no more alike than any two sisters or brothers in a family.

Another unusual situation occurs when a single fertilized ovum divides to produce two embryos. This results in identical twins (that is, siblings who share the same genes and therefore look exactly alike). The growing fetuses share the same placenta. Increased use of fertility drugs, which stimulate the ovaries to produce several mature ova in one menstrual cycle, has resulted in a greater incidence of multiple pregnancies, giving rise to triplets or quadruplets.

Zygote

Morula

Blastocyst

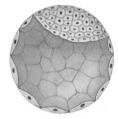

Cross section of blastocyst

The dividing embryo
After fertilization, the ovum is called a zygote. This divides to form the morula, which divides to form a structure known as a blastocyst. The blastocyst then implants itself in the uterine wall, and gestation begins.

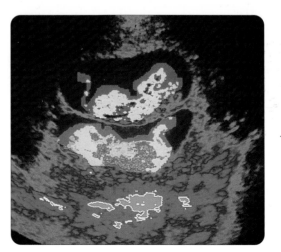

Conceiving twins
Twins can result from two separate ova being fertilized or from one ovum being fertilized and then splitting into two. Twins can be detected in an ultrasound scan around the eighth week of pregnancy.

Infertility

Infertility is defined as an inability to conceive and carry a fetus to term after two years of regular, unprotected intercourse. Total infertility is rare—more often couples suffer from subfertility, for which many treatments are available.

Long regarded as exclusively a woman's problem, doctors today estimate that roughly one-third of infertility problems are due to the female partner, one-third to the male partner and one-third to a combination of factors in both partners. However, this situation may change significantly in the future. There is growing concern that men's sperm counts may be falling—a phenomenon that biologists attribute to environmental chemicals—and this could have serious implications for future fertility (see page 153).

Usually there is an identifiable reason why a couple cannot have a baby, such as sperm defects or blocked fallopian tubes, but for approximately 10 to 15 percent of infertile couples, the reasons remain unknown. Although the term infertility tends to be used to describe anyone having problems with conception, infertility varies in degree. True infertility, or sterility, is a total inability to conceive without medical intervention. This is relatively rare—most couples suffer from subfertility, which is reduced fertility. Secondary subfertility is a condition in which couples who have conceived normally in the past encounter problems when trying for another child.

FEMALE INFERTILITY

Causes of female infertility fall into three main categories: first, the failure to ovulate; second, the failure of an ovum to unite with sperm (this could result from blocked fallopian tubes or hostile cervical mucus); third, the inability to sustain a growing fetus inside the uterus.

Female infertility The most basic requirement for conception is that a woman is ovulating regularly, but difficulty conceiving may also be caused by mechanical problems, such as blockages in the fallopian tubes.

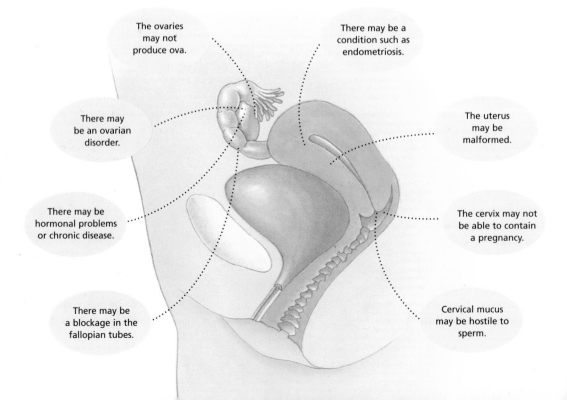

The ovaries may not produce ova.

There may be a condition such as endometriosis.

There may be an ovarian disorder.

The uterus may be malformed.

There may be hormonal problems or chronic disease.

The cervix may not be able to contain a pregnancy.

There may be a blockage in the fallopian tubes.

Cervical mucus may be hostile to sperm.

Failure to ovulate

If a woman is not ovulating (a condition known as *ANOVULATION*), natural conception is impossible. Absent, scanty or erratic periods are indications that a woman may not be ovulating, but the most reliable indicator of anovulation is a blood hormone test. This can pinpoint hormone levels at different times of the menstrual cycle. If there is no progesterone in a woman's bloodstream in the second half of her menstrual cycle, she has not ovulated.

The causes of anovulation include hormonal imbalances and disorders or diseases of the ovaries. The first line of treatment for anovulation is usually a drug called clomiphene. Clomiphene comes in pill form and is effective in restoring ovulation. It does have some side effects, however, such as hot flashes, nausea, depression, bloating and release of multiple ova.

Anovulation may also be caused by polycystic ovary disease (see page 194), a disorder resulting from hormonal imbalance. Treatment involving the surgical removal or destruction of small pieces of the surface area of each ovary may restore ovulation.

Damaged fallopian tubes

If the fallopian tubes are scarred, blocked or constricted, the sperm may be prevented from completing their journey to meet the ovum, or the fertilized ovum from reaching the uterus. Damage to the tubes can result from infection or previous abdominal surgery. Sometimes doctors can surgically open up the tubes and restore fertility. If the damage to the tubes is too severe for surgery, or if a woman has not conceived 12 to 24 months after an operation, a doctor may recommend in vitro fertilization (IVF) (see page 156).

Endometriosis

Fragments of the uterine lining may become attached to other pelvic organs, which can result in a condition known as endometriosis (see page 195). Some women with this condition have no difficulty sustaining healthy pregnancies, but others, especially those whose ovaries are affected, need to be treated before fertility is restored. Hormone treatment is usually successful, but in severe cases surgery may be required. Conversely, the birth of a baby has been known to ease endometriosis.

UTERINE ABNORMALITIES

Although rare, a few women do not possess a uterus; others are born with a malformed uterus; and still others have a condition, such as fibroids, that distorts the shape and size of the uterus. Even though women with uterine problems may be able to conceive successfully, the fertilized ovum is often unable to implant. If it does implant, the fetus and placenta may not develop properly.

Uterine malformations
There are various different types of uterine malformation. All are congenital, meaning that they are present at birth.

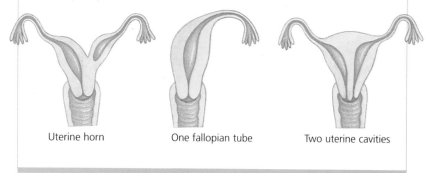

Uterine horn   One fallopian tube   Two uterine cavities

Cervical problems

Occasionally the mucus in the cervix is hostile to sperm cells, producing antibodies that kill or immobilize them. The sperm are thus prevented from traveling to the fallopian tubes, and conception is impossible.

Another cervical problem, known as incompetent cervix, does not impede conception but causes late miscarriage or very premature delivery. In a normal pregnancy, the cervix remains tightly closed until two to four weeks before delivery. This enables the fetus to grow safely in the uterus until it is ready to be born, at which time the cervix begins to dilate. An incompetent cervix opens prematurely, usually in the third or fourth month. About one in five women who have recurrent miscarriages has cervical incompetence. If a woman has had two or more miscarriages after the 14th week of pregnancy, doctors suspect the condition and use ultrasound scanning and internal examinations to diagnose it.

Doctors can treat an incompetent cervix, once the cervix starts opening, by threading a stitch around the cervix like a purse string. This is done using an epidural, which numbs the lower half of the body, or a general anesthetic. The stitch remains in the

Male infertility

Sometimes sperm counts may be lowered by an individual's behavior—activities such as smoking and frequent hot bathing have a detrimental effect on sperm count. Physiological causes include hormonal imbalances and testicular problems.

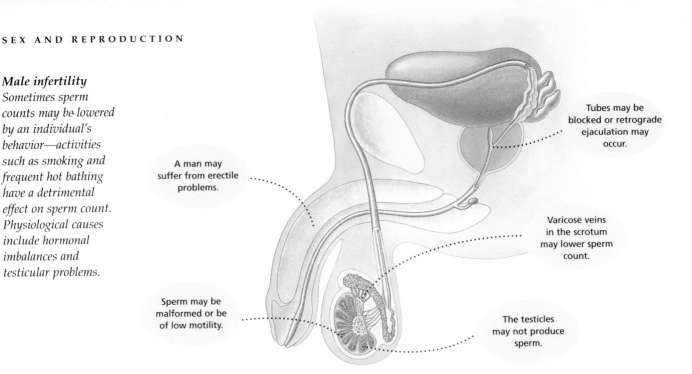

A man may suffer from erectile problems.

Tubes may be blocked or retrograde ejaculation may occur.

Varicose veins in the scrotum may lower sperm count.

Sperm may be malformed or be of low motility.

The testicles may not produce sperm.

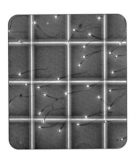

Normal sperm count

A healthy sperm sample does not just mean a minimum number of sperm. Their health and motility are also factors.

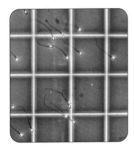

Low sperm count

Since a number of sperm are lost or destroyed on their journey to meet the ovum, a low sperm count will make conception even more difficult.

cervix until shortly before the end of the pregnancy, when it is taken out so that a normal delivery can take place.

MALE INFERTILITY

The World Health Organization publishes guidelines about what constitutes a healthy and fertile sample of sperm. First, there must be more than 20 million sperm per milliliter of semen. Second, more than half of the sperm in the sample must be of normal shape. Third, more than half of the sperm must be motile (able to swim effectively). Estimates for male infertility vary, but it is thought that one in 15 men fails to meet the above criteria.

Sperm problems

A number of men do not produce sperm in their semen—a condition called azoospermia. This may result from a physical blockage in the tubes leading from the testes to the seminal vesicles that prevents sperm from being ejaculated. In other cases, the muscles that pump semen through the penis may not function properly, to the extent that the sperm may even be pumped backward into the bladder (a condition known as retrograde ejaculation).

There may be primary testicular failure, which means that the testicles do not produce sperm. This rare condition, accounting for less than 5 percent of cases of infertility in males, may be due to hormonal disturbances, undescended testes in childhood,

Can We Talk About It?

INFERTILITY

If you are receiving infertility treatment, make sure that you and your partner are kept fully informed of what is happening and what your options are at each stage. When discussing these options together, listen to what your partner is trying to tell you, and insist on your right to be heard also. Ensure that your decisions are joint decisions. If either of you makes choices alone, they may have negative consequences for your relationship.

It is vital that you and your partner share your feelings—hopes and fears—with each other. Sexual intimacy and intercourse may soon start to feel like a clinical exercise, so try to find ways to keep your sex life enjoyable. Suggest that you also make love at times other than at ovulation, and remind each other that your relationship must be nurtured as something separate from your attempts to have a child.

It is important to talk about painful or embarrassing feelings—many people feel shame, anger, guilt or a loss of masculinity or femininity when they discover they are infertile, but may find it difficult to express. Talking candidly, without blaming each other, will help bring you closer and ease the stress associated with infertility.

chromosomal disorders like *KLINEFELTER'S SYNDROME*, physical injury, genetic diseases such as cystic fibrosis, mumps if contracted in adulthood, or a reaction to treatment with certain drugs. Men may also suffer an immunological condition in which they produce antibodies that attack and destroy their own sperm.

Oligospermia—low sperm count—is also a cause of male infertility. This is most frequently due to a problem known as a varicocele, which is the collection of large swollen veins, rather like varicose veins, in the scrotum (see page 201). Varicocele can often be successfully treated with surgery. Sexually transmitted diseases (STDs) such as gonorrhea and chlamydia (see page 185) can reduce sperm production or may even block the tubes that transport sperm from the testes, leading to azoospermia.

A man's sperm count may also be lowered by stress, cigarette smoking, excessive consumption of alcohol, treatment with certain drugs (especially drugs for cancer and ulcerative colitis) or exposure to certain toxins. Infertility may likewise result from sperm that are defective, with abnormally large heads, double heads or double tails.

If a couple seek help from a fertility specialist, one of the first tests that a man will undergo is a sperm count. This involves masturbating and ejaculating into a sterile glass container. The semen is then examined in a laboratory and a doctor compiles a report about the volume and consistency of the semen, the number of live sperm in the sample, the shape and health of the sperm, and their ability to swim.

A sperm count or semen evaluation is likely to be repeated more than once, since there are a number of factors—such as sexual intercourse several times a day prior to the test or a high fever a few weeks previously—that can result in a temporarily low sperm count. A doctor will also check semen for infections.

Depending on the type and severity of sperm problems, specialists are sometimes able to collect some sperm from the male partner to be used in assisted conception.

◄ *Abnormal sperm*
Healthy sperm should be tadpole shaped. Abnormalities manifest themselves in many different ways: sometimes sperm have two heads or no tail. The head of the sperm cell at the top of the picture is deformed and therefore incapable of fertilizing an ovum.

THE RISE IN MALE INFERTILITY

Over the past 20 years, male sperm counts have been falling by about 2 percent each year, and more sperm abnormalities are now apparent than ever before. Studies conducted in the early 1990s in Denmark, Scotland and France claim that the incidence of testicular cancer is rising, as is the number of boys born with a misshapen penis or testicles. Although much controversy exists regarding the causes of these problems, a number of scientists believe that environmental chemicals are to blame.

Some chemicals are thought to mimic the natural female sex hormone estrogen when they enter the body, causing men to undergo slight feminization. This has a direct effect on the testicles, causing fewer sperm to be produced. A long list of chemicals has been implicated, including substances found in a diverse range of products, from paints, inks, herbicides and adhesives to babies' pacifiers and food packaging. At one stage scientists believed that the estrogen in contraceptive pills was entering the water system and polluting drinking water.

Although the environmental-estrogens theory is popular, scientists also seek other explanations for the rise in male infertility. One theory focuses on the fact that optimum sperm production occurs when the testicles are at a lower temperature than that of the rest of the body. Modern heated home and work environments, hot tubs and saunas, and wearing tight underpants and jeans may overheat the testicles and have an adverse effect on sperm count. Both obesity and stress have also been linked to low sperm count.

Current theories
Research into the apparent drop in sperm counts suggests that industrial chemicals may mimic estrogens in the male body, contributing to this phenomenon.

INVESTIGATING INFERTILITY

TEST	PROCEDURE	RESULT
Microscopic analysis of sperm	Sperm are collected and examined under the microscope.	This gives information about sperm count, motility and quality.
Testicular biopsy	A tiny piece of tissue is removed from the testicle and examined under a microscope (this is done only after other reasons for sperm problems have been eliminated).	This establishes that sperm are forming normally.
X-rays with dye	In women dye is introduced into the uterus and fallopian tubes and X-rays are taken.	This reveals any blockages in the fallopian tubes and abnormalities in the uterus.
Blood tests	In women blood samples are taken and may be tested for the presence of follicle-stimulating hormone, luteinizing hormone and progesterone.	The presence or absence of different hormones at various stages in the menstrual cycle reveals whether or not ovulation is taking place. Blood tests can also detect chronic diseases that affect fertility.
Ultrasound scan	High-frequency sound waves are directed through the abdomen, and reflected echoes are viewed on a screen.	This provides information about the development of ovarian follicles and the size and shape of the uterus.
Laparoscopy	A tiny telescope is inserted into the abdomen.	This reveals abnormalities of the fallopian tubes and ovaries and whether ovulation has taken place.
Endometrial biopsy	A piece of the uterine lining is removed and analyzed microscopically.	This reveals whether uterine lining responds adequately to changing hormone levels.
Postcoital test	A sample of cervical mucus is taken shortly after intercourse.	This reveals whether cervical mucus is hostile to sperm.

But some problems with sperm quality and motility have no cure. In such a case the only way a couple can fertilize the woman's ovum is to accept sperm from a donor for an assisted conception.

UNEXPLAINED INFERTILITY

The approximately 10 to 15 percent of infertile couples whose bodies are functioning entirely normally—that is, the woman is ovulating regularly and has a healthy uterus and fallopian tubes, and the man produces normal sperm in sufficient amounts—are said to have unexplained infertility. Sometimes, such couples find that unexplained infertility resolves itself spontaneously with no medical intervention. Doctors are investigating whether stress and other psychological factors may play a part in suppressing fertility.

OVERCOMING SUBFERTILITY

When a couple realize that conception is proving more difficult than they had anticipated, they may decide to seek the help of a fertility specialist. A number of tests are undertaken to determine the cause of subfertility. Once the cause is determined, there are various methods that can be tried in order to achieve conception. Around 60 percent of couples undergoing fertility treatment eventually have a baby.

Artificial insemination

To increase the odds of sperm reaching the fallopian tubes, sperm can be placed in the cervix or uterine cavity by a means other than sexual intercourse. This method, called artificial insemination, is suitable for couples who have normal or near-normal fertility but have a physical problem in getting the sperm to the right place. Problems may include congenital abnormalities of the penis, injury to the penis, *RETROGRADE EJACULATION* or psychosexual difficulties that prevent intercourse. If a man has a markedly abnormal semen analysis, a couple may decide to use donor sperm from a sperm bank for artificial insemination.

There are two types of artificial insemination. The first is intracervical insemination (ICI); the second is intrauterine insemination (IUI). In both cases the man produces a sperm sample by masturbation (or a frozen sample from a donor is thawed) near to the time that his female partner ovulates. In ICI, the semen is inserted high up in the vagina and into the cervix (a small plastic cap may be used to hold the sperm in place). This is the place where sperm normally pools after intercourse, but ICI ensures that more sperm are in the right place and stay there for longer. In IUI, the sperm are injected directly into the uterus. Both methods are helpful for couples where the man has a low sperm count.

Since sperm placed in the uterus do not pass through the cervix, IUI is recommended for subfertility caused by hostile cervical mucus. Injecting sperm into the uterus has two disadvantages; it carries a small risk of infection, and hormone-like substances in the semen, *PROSTAGLANDINS*, can cause uterine cramps. Doctors try to overcome this problem by washing sperm before injection to remove the prostaglandins. Nevertheless, 10 percent of women who have IUI experience cramps.

Drugs such as clomiphene that stimulate ovulation to take place may be used in conjunction with artificial insemination.

Sperm donation

If a male partner is infertile because of severe sperm problems, then the healthy sperm of another man—a donor—can be used to fertilize the female partner's ovum.

Inside a sperm bank
Technicians store sperm in microtubules and freeze it in a protective fluid at a temperature of -292°F/-144°C. The sperm can survive indefinitely in this way.

The Language of Sex

Infertility treatments are often categorized by confusing acronyms such as IVF, IUI, ICI, GIFT and ICSI. Some of these refer to the techniques used to unite sperm with ova—inside or outside the woman's body. Others refer to the place where sperm or fertilized ova are put back into the body—the cervix, uterus or fallopian tube. Fertilization outside the body is referred to as in vitro (hence IVF), which in Latin means "in glass."

A couple who are considering this option need to think carefully about the impact it may have on the male partner and about the effects donor insemination may have on the child when he or she is told.

There are some people who consider sperm donation a form of adultery, and some men may worry that they will not feel that a baby resulting from sperm donation is truly their child. However, in their book *Heterosexuality*, Masters, Johnson and Kolodny argue that evidence shows that "almost all couples who achieve a pregnancy using donor sperm find the experience brings them very close together and that the husband's excitement at fatherhood is genuinely felt." Donor insemination has also provided a way for lesbian couples and single women to have children.

Sperm banks store frozen semen that is supplied by carefully selected donors. The donor is matched to a recipient couple's physical characteristics and blood group, but the recipients usually are given no additional information about the identity of the sperm donor. The recipient couple will be advised that the donor's sperm can be used

ASSISTED CONCEPTION—IVF AND ZIFT

Mixing selected sperm and ova in a laboratory dish maximizes the chances of fertilization. The resultant embryos are placed inside the woman's body.

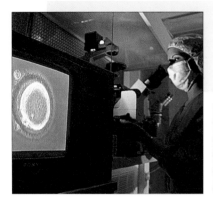

STAGE 1

Fertility drugs stimulate the ovaries into producing several ova. The ova are then extracted and examined microscopically to determine whether they are suitable for IVF.

STAGE 2

A sample of semen is examined and a fine needle is used to extract the healthy sperm best suited to fertilization.

STAGE 3

The sperm are washed from the semen and then united with the ova in a petri dish. The sperm and ova mixture is placed in an incubator.

STAGE 4

The sperm in the petri dish compete to penetrate the ova in the way that they would in the fallopian tube. One or all of the ova may be successfully fertilized. Fertility specialists closely monitor progress.

STAGE 5

After fertilization has taken place, the embryos remain in an incubator. Later on, usually when the embryos have divided a couple of times, fertility specialists select a maximum of three to place into the woman's body. The embyros that are not used may be frozen for future use.

IVF METHOD
Up to three fertilized ova are placed directly into the uterus in a procedure known as embryo transfer.

ZIFT METHOD
In the ZIFT method, fertilized ova are placed in the fallopian tubes—this is the site of natural conception.

to produce a maximum of 10 live births from different women, and they will be given the option of using a further sample from the same donor for a future sibling.

Semen donors are comparatively hard to find—50 percent of men who apply to be semen donors are rejected by clinics because they are unhealthy, have genetically linked disorders or do not have a high enough sperm count. Applicants have to have sperm counts in the top 2 percent in order to be accepted on a donor program.

Men who are prepared to donate their sperm receive counseling before they begin. Clinics make sure potential donors have thought about all the issues involved. For example, will they want children of their own in the future? How will they feel about having biological children who are unknown to them? How will their family and present or future partners feel?

The donor is thoroughly screened for HIV, other sexually transmitted diseases and hereditary problems. The semen, which is collected by masturbation, then goes into quarantine for six months before it is used. The donor has to have another negative screen for HIV before the frozen semen is released.

In vitro fertilization (IVF)

Whereas artificial insemination allows the sperm and ovum to unite naturally in the fallopian tube, in vitro fertilization (IVF) is a technique in which the sperm and ovum meet outside the body, in a test tube or petri dish. IVF is recommended for many types of infertility, including blocked or absent fallopian tubes, poor-quality sperm, unexplained infertility, hostile cervical mucus and *ENDOMETRIOSIS*.

IVF treatment begins with drug treatment that stimulates ova production. In a normal menstrual cycle, only one ovum is released from the ovary, but drug treatment ensures that several ova reach maturity. These ova are usually extracted from the ovarian follicle using an ultrasound-guided needle through the top of the vagina.

Each collected ovum is placed in a laboratory dish in a solution of nutrients designed to resemble the natural environment of the fallopian tubes. A sample of sperm washed from semen obtained by masturbation are then added to the dish, and doctors wait to see if fertilization occurs. To maximize the chance of a sperm fertilizing an ovum, doctors screen semen and choose only the most active sperm.

The ova that are fertilized are placed in the uterus through a thin tube inserted through the cervix. Up to three fertilized ova may be put into the uterus, but usually only one of these, if any, will develop into a baby. Younger IVF candidates have a greater chance that all the placed fertilized ova will develop into babies. For this reason, doctors may decide to place two fertilized ova instead of three.

It is hoped that one of the fertilized ova placed in the uterus will implant in the wall of the uterus and develop as it would in a conventional pregnancy. If this fails to happen, couples can repeat IVF treatment in the next menstrual cycle.

IVF is most successful in women who are under 35, have normal menstrual cycles and have partners with a normal sperm count. This is the ideal situation, but many women who seek IVF treatment are doing so because their fertility has declined with age. As the technique has improved, more and more couples have gone on to have babies, but the procedures involved in IVF are notoriously stressful and expensive. The seemingly endless cycle of hope and disappointment that accompanies each treatment cycle can be emotionally draining for both partners. Because insurance often does not cover infertility treatment, the procedure may be a financial drain as well.

Zygote intrafallopian transfer (ZIFT)

Since the development of IVF, other assisted-conception techniques have evolved. One of these is called zygote intrafallopian transfer (ZIFT).

The first step in ZIFT is collecting ova from the woman. Three ova are selected and mixed with a sample of the male partner's healthy sperm. When fertilization takes place, the embryos or ZYGOTES are transferred into the fallopian tubes. ZIFT differs from IVF in that embryos are placed into the fallopian tubes instead of into the uterus.

Because more than one embryo is replaced in the fallopian tube, there is a chance that a multiple pregnancy may occur. A woman under the age of 30 whose partner's sperm quality is high may have only two ova replaced to reduce the chance of this happening.

Women are asked to return to a clinic two weeks after they have received ZIFT treatment to find out whether a pregnancy has been established. If a woman begins to menstruate within these two weeks, an embryo (or embryos) has not implanted in her uterus and she will have to wait until her

THE LOUISE BROWN STORY

The U.K. scientist Robert Edwards first became interested in fertilization outside of the body in the 1960s. He experimented on mice and rabbits and discovered that if sperm and ova were united outside the body, and a fertilized ovum was then implanted into the female uterus, a healthy pregnancy would ensue and the female could go on to give birth naturally.

In 1968, Edwards shared his knowledge with Patrick Steptoe, a U.K. gynecologist. Together they investigated using in vitro fertilization treatment in humans; by 1971 they were successfully growing human embryos to the blastocyst stage (see page 149) in test tubes. Eventually, they transferred an embryo into the uterus of a woman named Lesley Brown, and it implanted successfully.

On July 25, 1978, after experiencing a normal pregnancy, Lesley gave birth to a 5lb. 12oz. baby daughter, whom she named Louise. Louise Brown was the first test-tube baby in the world, and, although her birth was considered highly controversial at the time, the IVF method that was used paved the way for many thousands of assisted-conception babies in the future.

Childhood fame
When she was born, Louise received worldwide media coverage and was featured in nearly every newspaper in the Western world.

Monitoring progress Before a fertilized ovum is placed in the uterus, a scientist checks the progress of the embryo.

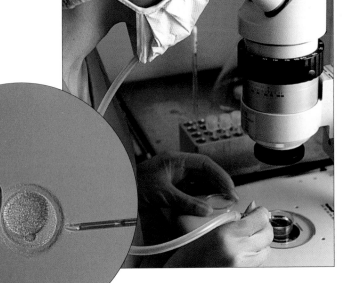

Artificial fertilization A single sperm cell is injected into an ovum. The needle on the right introduces the sperm into the ovum, while the pipette on the left holds the ovum steady. This technique, known as ICSI, ensures that fertilization takes place.

next treatment cycle begins to attempt pregnancy again. For this treatment, unlike IVF, women need to have at least one intact fallopian tube. ZIFT is thought to be a useful technique when sperm and ova have difficulty meeting in the fallopian tubes, perhaps because the cervical mucus is hostile to sperm or the man has a low sperm count. Gamete intrafallopian transfer, or GIFT, is a technique that is similar to ZIFT, but in this case a mixture of ova and sperm rather than embryos is returned to the fallopian tube.

Other infertility treatments

Developed by scientists in Brussels, intracytoplasmic sperm injection (ICSI) is a technique that leaves almost nothing to chance. Rather than placing ova and sperm in an optimum environment and allowing them to unite naturally, ICSI involves injecting a single sperm directly into an ovum. This technique bypasses all the barriers that the sperm would normally have to overcome before fertilizing an ovum.

ICSI is particularly suitable in cases of male infertility caused by a low sperm count or poor sperm motility. The procedure involves extracting an ovum from the ovary and removing its outer layer of cells. A semen sample, obtained by masturbation, is washed, and a single sperm is selected. Using a needle that is finer than a human hair, the sperm cell is injected into the ovum. Once fertilization has occurred, the process of transferring the ovum back to the uterus is the same as for conventional IVF.

Although ICSI seems to ensure fertilization, it does not necessarily ensure that a fertilized ovum will go on to implant itself in the uterine wall—so treatment with this technique does not guarantee pregnancy (this point also applies to other assisted-conception techniques). The success rate of ICSI is largely dependent on the age of the woman and the quality of the semen.

A technique known as subzonal insemination (SUZI) differs from ICSI in that between three and five sperm are injected into the space between the covering of the ovum and the ovum itself, instead of just one.

Infertility treatments also include embryo transplant and embryo freezing. Embryo transplant uses a man's sperm to artificially inseminate a donor woman, the resulting embryo is then removed from the uterus of the donor woman and transplanted into the man's partner. Embryo freezing preserves fertilized ova, which are defrosted later and used to facilitate pregnancy.

The sperm used in assisted-conception techniques is usually obtained by masturbation. A few men, however, do not produce enough sperm in the fluid they ejaculate. This may be because a man has had a vasectomy (see page 172) or because he was born with an abnormality of the reproductive tract (although rare, the vas deferens, or tubes that carry sperm from the testicles, are absent in some men). In these cases special techniques are needed to extract sperm. A clinic that specializes in infertility treatments may be able to do this by opening up the epididymis (the tightly coiled tube where sperm are stored in the testicle) and removing sperm with the aid of a high-powered microscope. The SUZI procedure has been almost completely replaced by ICSI as it yields superior pregnancy rates.

Egg donation

For women who cannot ovulate, do not have ovaries or are over the age of 40, egg donation may be a way of overcoming infertility. Egg donation also provides an alternative to women who want to avoid passing on a genetic abnormality to their children. Egg donation is similar in theory to sperm donation and involves using the ova donated by a fertile woman. The ova are collected and then fertilized with the husband's sperm in the laboratory and then placed into the woman's uterus using IVF techniques. The woman receiving the fertilized ovum is given special hormone treatment so that her uterus is prepared to accept a pregnancy.

The donor woman may be anonymous (but matched for physical characteristics with the recipient), or she may be a relative or personal friend. Donated ova can then be used in an IVF program.

The success of ovum donation depends on a number of factors, an important one being the age of the egg donor. The success rate of treatment for a woman over 40 who receives ova from a 25-year-old woman will be the same success rate as that of a 25-year-

old woman. It is the biological quality of the egg and the sperm that determines the health and viability of an embryo.

Surrogacy

In some countries, couples overcome childlessness by finding a woman who is willing to bear a child for them. Using IVF or GIFT, the host mother can carry the embryo made up of the ovum and sperm of the commissioning couple. This is called full surrogacy. The commissioning mother may be incapable of sustaining a pregnancy—she may even have had a hysterectomy—but as long as she has functioning ovaries, her fertilized ova can be placed in another woman's uterus. This means the resulting baby is genetically "hers." As an alternative to full surrogacy, an ovum belonging to the host mother may be fertilized with the commissioning father's sperm. Fertilization can happen through sexual intercourse or artificial insemination.

CONSULTING AN INFERTILITY SPECIALIST

Couples visiting an infertility specialist may be able to speed up diagnostic procedures by providing information about their own fertility. Women can take detailed charts of their temperature readings in each menstrual cycle (these are called basal body temperature, or BBT, charts). Couples can mark on their BBT records the days on which they had intercourse. Some women also keep the date-marked results of their ovulation prediction tests. Men who are having semen analysis should not have sex for 24 to 72 hours before visiting a clinic.

THE STORY OF BABY M

The case of Baby M in the U.S. illustrates very well the controversy and legal complications that surround a surrogacy.

Baby M was born by full surrogacy. The commissioning parents, William and Elisabeth Stern, both 41, decided that a normal pregnancy would be a health risk for Elisabeth, who suffered from multiple sclerosis. They sought out a host mother to carry the Sterns' embryo to a full-term pregnancy and give birth.

The host mother, Mary Beth, had initially agreed to the surrogacy, but she changed her mind shortly after handing the baby over to the Sterns. Mary Beth returned to the Sterns' and begged them to let her keep the child.

Although the Sterns complied and handed the baby over to Mary Beth, they undertook legal proceedings to recover Baby M. The judge hearing the case of Baby M decided that the Sterns would make the better parents and awarded them full custody of the child; Mary Beth was not given any right of access to the baby. Then, two years after Baby M's birth, the New Jersey Supreme Court overturned this ruling and made the buying and selling of babies—by surrogacy or any other means—illegal. Mary Beth was given regular visiting rights, and, although the Sterns kept the baby, Elisabeth Stern was refused the legal right to be the child's adoptive mother.

Whose baby?
The ethics of surrogacy are complex. Who has most right to a child—the genetic mother or the woman who carried the baby to term? Also, what are the psychological implications for a surrogate child?

Contraception

Although women are highly fertile for only a short time every month, much research is devoted to trying to prevent conception from occurring. Effective methods of contraception have been sought not only in modern times but throughout history.

The ability to control fertility has been a great liberating force, particularly for women in the 20th century. Before effective contraceptives were available, efforts concentrated on identifying ovulation and avoiding sexual intercourse during this time. Nowadays, sophisticated hormonal contraception can totally suppress a woman's ovulation.

HISTORY OF CONTRACEPTION

Despite limited physiological knowledge, people throughout history have connected the ejaculation of sperm into the vagina with pregnancy. In the ancient world, coitus interruptus (the withdrawal of the penis from the vagina before ejaculation) was the most widely practiced form of contraception, although its effectiveness was limited.

By the 19th century coitus interruptus, although widely used, was beginning to lose popularity as a birth control method,

perhaps because alternatives were becoming available. Men felt that it destroyed their pleasure in sex and so found it difficult; women felt that it allowed them no control over their fertility; and physicians argued that it led to physical and psychological illness.

Abstinence from sexual intercourse was also widely used to control the number of pregnancies a woman had. People who practiced abstinence sometimes used herbal anaphrodisiacs to suppress their libido or searched for alternative sexual outlets, such as oral or anal sex, homosexual sex and, occasionally, bestiality.

Some couples tried to abstain from sex when they believed that a woman was in her fertile phase—the practice now known as the rhythm method. However, women's fertile periods were often miscalculated. For example, the ancient Greeks believed that conception was most likely to take place immediately before or after menstruation; the Romans thought that the days just after menstruation were the riskiest; and in 1847 a French physician claimed that women were safe from conception from the 12th day after menstruation to the beginning of their next period. A woman's fertile period was not accurately plotted until the 1920s.

Over the centuries, numerous suggestions for contraceptive practices, potions or mechanical devices have been recorded. In ancient Rome, the Greek physician Soranus of Ephesus suggested that a woman should squat down and induce sneezing after having sexual intercourse. Centuries later Casanova was reported to have placed half a squeezed lemon over a woman's cervix—presumably it acted as a crude forerunner of the diaphragm.

The 19th-century family Compared with the small nuclear families of today's society, 19th-century families tended to be extensive. Although having many children was the social norm, unreliable methods of contraception undoubtedly played a part in determining family size.

160

The condom

The design of the first condom is attributed to the Italian anatomist Gabriello Fallopio (after whom the fallopian tubes were named). In 1564 Fallopio designed a small linen covering to put over the glans of the penis during sexual intercourse. Fallopio intended his condom to protect the wearer against venereal disease, however, and not against pregnancy.

By the 19th century condoms were made from sheep's intestines. They did not fit well, had to be put on very carefully and were secured at the open end with a ribbon. Because condoms were stocked only in brothels or by specialist wholesalers, they were hard to obtain. At least one advice book provided instructions on how to make condoms from intestines.

It was not until the discovery of the process to vulcanize rubber in 1844 that condoms became available. By the 1850s they were easy to buy, but had a negative image, condemned as inconvenient, unesthetic and unsafe. Some birth control advocates warned of condoms bursting and advised people to inflate them with air or water before use. There was also a lingering assumption that condoms were to prevent promiscuous men from contracting syphilis.

During the 1920s and 1930s condoms became increasingly popular and sales began to surge and did not fall off until the advent of the birth control pill. Today, with the increase in sexually transmitted diseases such as HIV, condom sales have risen again. Refinements in design have resulted in condoms varying in thickness, shape, size, color and even flavor. The female condom, which is now widely available, was first introduced in 1992.

The diaphragm

Stopping the passage of sperm by blocking the cervical opening is an age-old method of contraception, but a scientifically designed diaphragm was not proposed until 1838. Its German pioneer, Friedrich Adolphe Wilde, suggested making a wax mold of the cervix and using this to make a rubber shield. Unlike today's diaphragm, which is inserted only before intercourse, the rubber shield was worn by a woman all the time when she was not menstruating. Perhaps because diaphragms had to be individually fitted, the idea failed to take off.

OLD CONTRACEPTIVE DEVICES

Before hormonal contraceptives were invented, most birth control devices aimed at preventing pregnancy either by covering the penis with a condom or by shielding the cervix with a sponge or a crude cap or diaphragm. Douches were devices that propelled water into the vagina after intercourse in an attempt to wash away the semen. They have since been proved ineffective, but barrier methods of contraception (see page 165) are still used today.

Sheep-gut condom
Before the vulcanization of rubber, people had to use other materials, such as animal intestines, to make condoms.

The sponge
A small piece of sponge attached to a ribbon was widely used as a contraceptive at the beginning of the 20th century.

Tortoiseshell condoms
Condoms made from tortoiseshell were used in 19th-century Japan. The smaller ones were designed to cover the glans.

Vaginal douche
Made from rubber and vulcanite, this vaginal douche was used in the early 20th century.

U.S. Patent Office records from the 1850s show many patents for rubber pessaries. These were mainly doughnut-shaped devices that were prescribed by doctors to correct a malpositioned or a prolapsed uterus (conditions now believed to have been very common at the time). Before long, however, these pessaries were modified to act as contraceptives.

In 1864 a rubber device known as a womb veil was introduced. The literature that accompanied the womb veil described its benefits: "Conception cannot possibly take place when it is used. The full enjoyment of the conjugal embrace can be indulged in during coition. The husband would hardly be likely to know that it was being used, unless told by the wife."

Natural methods
Plants, oils and substances such as honey and lemon were once used as spermicides.

The two main selling points—invisibility and infallibility—may have been appealing to women in the 19th century, but limited knowledge of anatomy may have made them uncomfortable with the idea of inserting a diaphragm and fearful that, once inserted, it would be irretrievable. The devices did not achieve major popularity until the 20th century.

The sponge

Mention of the contraceptive sponge appears in birth control literature dating back to the 14th century, and it became a popular method of contraception in the 18th and 19th centuries. Women would take a small piece of sponge, dampen it with water, tie a ribbon around it and insert it high in the vagina before sexual intercourse. They hoped that the dampened sponge would absorb the man's semen during intercourse. After intercourse the sponge was withdrawn, washed and stored for next time. With the sponge, women believed that they gained unobtrusive control over fertility.

Advice about the way sponges should be used varied immensely. Some 19th-century birth control experts advised moistening the sponge with chloride of soda or other chemicals. Others recommended that it be repeatedly reinserted and rinsed after intercourse in order to soak up all the semen. Another suggestion was that the sponge be left in for several hours after intercourse.

Many doctors told women to use a douche after withdrawal of the sponge. Women in the 19th and early 20th centuries often douched routinely with water and a spermicidal agent, such as vinegar, baking soda or bichloride of mercury. Many relied on this as their sole contraceptive.

The intrauterine device (IUD)

The first known intrauterine device was a pebble placed in the uterus of a camel to prevent the animal from becoming pregnant during long trips across the desert.

Research on the IUD for humans was first carried out by German scientists early in the 20th century. The prototypes were made of silk, then later of gold and silver (birth control advocate Marie Stopes called her early IUD device the gold pin). However, they caused severe internal irritation, and research on the IUD soon stopped. Not until the early 1960s did development of the IUD recommence. The first of the new generation of IUD devices, the Lippes Loop, was made of plastic. More recent types contain copper or hormones, which are slowly released over a period of 1 to 10 years.

Hormonal contraceptives

When the oral contraceptive pill first became available in the early 1960s it was embraced wholeheartedly by both women and the medical profession. It was

THE WORK OF MARGARET SANGER

The most influential figure in the history of U.S. family planning, Margaret Sanger was born in New York in 1879 to a middle-class family of 11 children. Sanger was thus aware of the many health problems associated with large families.

During her career as a nurse she saw the terrible problems women faced—including fatal self-performed abortions—in their attempts to control their fertility. The Comstock Act of 1873 made it a criminal offense to distribute material that even mentioned birth control.

Frustrated at this lack of information, Sanger traveled abroad to learn about family planning. In 1914 she founded the National Birth Control League, and, with gathering support from doctors, she founded the National Committee on Federal Legalization for Birth Control in 1923.

The campaign for contraception
When Sanger opened her first birth control clinic in New York in 1916, she was promptly arrested. It was not until the 1950s that U.S. laws were revised to allow contraception and the provision of contraceptive advice.

CONTRACEPTION

considered revolutionary because, for the first time, women were given total control over their fertility.

The first research into hormonal contraceptives was a U.S.-funded project in Austria in the early 20th century. The results showed that ovulation in animals could be prevented with estrogen injections.

In the late 1930s an American, Gregory Pincus, continued the research. By the early 1950s he had gained the support of Margaret Sanger, who organized more funding for him. As early as 1951 Pincus proved that progesterone inhibited ovulation, and he began a search for a synthetic hormone to emulate it.

In 1956, extensive clinical trials of a combined estrogen-progesterone contraceptive pill were undertaken in Boston and Puerto Rico by John Rock, a Harvard gynecologist. Finally, in 1960, the U.S. Food and Drug Administration approved the pill as an oral contraceptive, and it was released onto the American market.

Since the advent of the contraceptive pill, there have been intermittent scares about its possible side effects, such as an increased risk of blood clots, heart attacks, high blood pressure and breast cancer. Despite this, the pill remains one of the most popular forms of birth control for North American women under the age of 30.

Research into hormonal contraception has led to the introduction of injections and implants that deliver hormones to the body.

Abortion and infanticide

Throughout history, abortion and infanticide have been used as last resorts when contraceptive measures have not been used or have failed. In some early civilizations abortion was a punishable offense, while infanticide was acceptable—perhaps because it targeted female babies, whereas abortion put the more highly valued male fetus at risk. Other societies accepted abortion in the belief that fetuses were not human—in ancient Greece the philosopher Aristotle taught that human life did not begin until 40 days after conception.

In the 19th century there was an upsurge in the number of abortions, presumably because people saw advantages in limiting family size. In 1869 (until 1969) abortion was a criminal code offense in Canada. Canadian women continued to have abortions during this period, however, these illegal abortions were clandestine and usually unsafe, posing a considerable threat to women's health.

CONTRACEPTION TODAY

The large variety of contraceptive products available from doctors and pharmacies today allows couples to choose the method that best suits their sexual needs, age and reproductive history.

Hormonal treatments

The two main hormones that rise and fall each month in a woman's menstrual cycle are estrogen and progesterone. When a woman becomes pregnant, the levels of

THE BODY'S RESPONSE TO THE PILL

Progesterone
Women who take the pill have artificially high levels of this hormone. Usually progesterone is released only after ovulation.

Estrogen
In non-pill users estrogen is released by developing egg follicles in the ovary.

How the pill works
Increased levels of the hormones estrogen and progestogen stop the pituitary gland in the brain from releasing FSH and LH (see page 129). This stops ova from maturing in the ovary, thus preventing ovulation. It also temporarily changes the fallopian tubes, uterine lining and cervical mucus to make conception and implantation of a fertilized ovum unlikely.

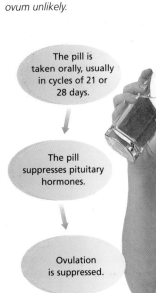

The pill is taken orally, usually in cycles of 21 or 28 days.

The pill suppresses pituitary hormones.

Ovulation is suppressed.

Cervical mucus becomes hostile to sperm.

Contraceptive pills
Doctors will prescribe the pill with the individual needs of the woman in mind. Some pills have very low doses of hormone, some have variable amounts, and some contain the hormone progestogen, but not estrogen.

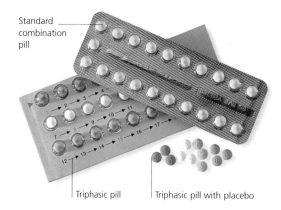

Standard combination pill

Triphasic pill   Triphasic pill with placebo

Implants *Silicon rods are inserted under the skin of the upper arm. Once in place, they are invisible, although most women can feel them through the skin.*

these hormones remain high instead of rising and falling. Hormonal contraception works by using synthetic versions of natural hormones to trick the body into thinking it is already pregnant. This prevents ovulation and makes fertilization impossible.

Hormonal contraception also makes the cervical mucus hostile to sperm and alters the uterine lining to prevent the implantation of a fertilized ovum. Hormonal methods of contraception are among the most effective and are available in several forms.

The combined pill contains both progestogen (a synthetic type of progesterone) and estrogen. If it is taken in the correct way, the combined pill is 99 percent effective in preventing pregnancy. Women who do become pregnant while taking the pill may have taken it irregularly or taken medication (antibiotics, for example) that interferes with the pill's efficacy. Stomach upsets that cause vomiting and diarrhea also make the pill unreliable.

There are three types of combined pill. These are the monophasic pill, in which each pill in the pack contains the same dose of progestogen and estrogen; the biphasic pill, in which the first 7 pills contain less progestogen than the remaining 14; and the triphasic pill, in which there are three different types of pills in each pack. Particular types of hormonal combinations suit some women and not others.

Contraceptive pills can be taken in 21- or 28-day regimes. In a 21-day regime, a pill is taken daily for 21 days, followed by a pill-

free break of 7 days. During the pill-free break a withdrawal bleed occurs. This is similar to menstruation, but it is not the same as a true menstrual period because it is the body's response to the withdrawal of the hormones found in the pill. A withdrawal bleed is usually lighter and shorter than a menstrual period.

Women who follow a 28-day regime take pills continuously, but the pills they take between day 21 and day 28 are placebos (they do not contain any hormones). The women experience a withdrawal bleed while they are taking the placebo pills in just the same way as women who follow a 21-day regime. Following a 28-day pill regime prevents the woman from becoming confused about when to stop and start taking pills in each cycle.

The combined pill allows convenience and spontaneity in lovemaking, lighter and more painfree and regular periods as well as some protection against various disorders, such as ovarian and endometrial cancer, ovarian cysts, endometriosis and pelvic inflammatory disease (see pages 194 to 198).

Although it rarely causes any undesirable side effects, some women do experience nausea, headaches, increased appetite, weight gain or a slightly increased risk of heart problems and high blood pressure. Unlike barrier methods of contraception, the pill does not protect against sexually transmitted diseases.

The progestogen-only pill (POP) is also known as the mini-pill. The POP does not contain estrogen, and only 10 percent of pill users take it. Unlike the combined pill, the POP does not prevent ovulation. Instead, it works by turning the cervical mucus into a barrier against sperm, making the uterine lining inhospitable to a fertilized ovum and interfering with the muscular action of the fallopian tubes so that the journey of the ovum is made difficult.

The POP has fewer side effects and health risks than the combined pill and is suitable for smokers, women over 40, diabetics and breast-feeding women. The main disadvantage of this contraceptive is that a pill must be taken within the same 3 hours every day, compared with the 8 to 12 hour range for the combined pill. Also, many women taking the POP can develop amenorrhea (see page 192) or spotting.

USING A MALE CONDOM

It is important to remember that a condom should be put on as soon as the penis becomes erect. It should then be worn during any penis-vagina contact, whether or not this includes penetrative sex.

1 Carefully remove a condom from its packet and pinch the air from the teat between thumb and forefinger.

2 Still pinching the teat with one hand, hold the condom in place on the glans of the penis and, using the other hand, slowly roll the rim of the condom down the length of the shaft.

3 Roll the rim as far down the shaft of the penis as possible. Remember to hold the rim in this position during withdrawal after intercourse, before the penis becomes flaccid.

Implants come in the form of six small silicon rods that are inserted under the skin of the upper arm. Once in position they release a low dose of progestogen into the bloodstream and provide contraception for up to five years. Fewer than 1 in 100 women become pregnant while using implants. The insertion, which is carried out in a doctor's office, involves making a small incision in the skin of the arm under local anesthetic. If a woman wants to conceive during the five-year life span of the implants, they can be removed by a doctor.

Although implants provide very effective contraceptive cover, a number of side effects, such as irregular bleeding, mood swings, weight gain, nausea and hair loss,

have been reported. Some women have also experienced discomfort and scarring when the silicon rods are removed.

Injectable hormones work on similar principles to the pill, but they are injected rather than taken orally. The injection contains one of two long-lasting progestogens, which prevent ovulation, thicken cervical mucus and thin the uterine lining. Depending on the type, women are given repeat injections at two- or three-month intervals.

While injected hormones provide freedom from menstrual pains and allow sexual spontaneity, they occasionally produce irregular periods, acne, mood swings and loss of interest in sex.

Barrier methods

Condoms, diaphragms and caps—all barrier methods of contraception—provide a physical barrier that prevents sperm from completing their journey to the fallopian tubes. Barrier methods afford very effective protection against disease and infection. The condom in particular has come to be associated with safe sex and helping to prevent transmission of the HIV virus.

The condom is made of thin latex rubber. It is unrolled onto a man's erect penis before intercourse and contains the semen when he ejaculates. After ejaculation, the man should immediately withdraw his penis, holding on to the rim of the condom, and dispose of the condom. If this is done after the erection subsides, the condom can slip off and semen can leak into the vagina. Condoms are the most popular method of contraception—45 million couples worldwide use them as their main contraceptive.

Condoms are readily available in most countries; they have no side effects and offer good protection from sexually transmitted diseases. Although many couples use condoms successfully, some find putting them on disruptive. Couples also complain that they have to plan ahead to use them; some men claim a loss of sensation during intercourse; and condoms can occasionally split or slip off on withdrawal.

Condoms should always be used with a water-based lubricating jelly rather than an oil-based one, since latex breaks down when in contact with oils (see page 178). Some people are allergic to the latex used in

The range of condoms Condoms come in many different colors and flavors. The latest type is made from plastic rather than latex, which means it will not degenerate in the presence of oil.

condoms. A relatively recent innovation is the plastic condom, which is made from strong, thin polyurethane. This is suitable for men and women with allergies to latex, and, it is claimed, because the polyurethane is so thin, it does not decrease sensitivity during sexual intercourse. The plastic condom is as effective at preventing pregnancy and protecting the user against sexually transmitted diseases as the conventional latex condom.

The female condom is a loose polyurethane tube designed to line the inside of the vagina. It has two flexible rings, one at each end of the tube. The top ring fits high inside the vagina against the cervix and the bottom ring lies flat against the labia. The condom is inserted before intercourse and gently removed after the man has ejaculated. As long as the penis remains inside the condom during intercourse, no semen will escape into the vagina. The female condom also protects against most sexually transmitted diseases (STDs).

Female condoms are less likely to interrupt lovemaking than male condoms, but a woman using one for the first time may have difficulty inserting it properly and is advised to practice alone a couple of times.

Caps and diaphragms, unlike male and female condoms, allow semen to enter the vagina but prevent it from passing through the cervix. The diaphragm is a soft latex dome with a flexible metal rim that fits around the cervix and holds the diaphragm in place against the pubic bone. The cap is a smaller rubber device that covers the opening in the cervix that leads to the uterus. There are three types of cap: the cervical cap is thimble-shaped; the vault cap, which is not available in Canada, is shallow and semicircular, more like the diaphragm, but without the metal rim; and the vimule cap is a combination of the other two. Although both cervical and vimule caps stay in place by suction, cervical caps are rarely used because they are harder to insert, and few doctors and nurses are trained to fit them.

Diaphragms and caps come in different sizes to suit individual women. They must be fitted by a nurse or doctor and refitted if a woman loses or gains weight or has a baby. During fitting, the doctor or nurse teaches a woman the correct procedure to insert her cap or diaphragm. The woman follows this procedure before every episode of sexual intercourse. The device must be used with spermicidal jelly or cream and left in place for at least six hours after inter-

INSERTING A FEMALE CONDOM

It takes practice to insert a female condom. New users may find it helpful to use the hand to guide the penis into the vagina. This avoids the penis missing the condom or causing the condom to bunch up.

The condom for women
Made from fine polyurethane, the female condom ensures maximum sensitivity.

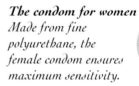

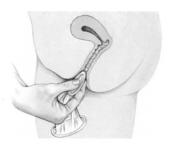

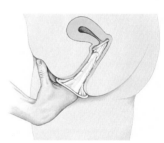

1 Hold the condom at the closed end, squeezing the inner ring between a thumb and middle finger.

2 Still squeezing the inner ring, gently push the condom into the vagina and then up past the pubic bone.

3 Let one inch of the condom sit outside the body. Check that the outer ring is lying flat against the labia.

course. Caps and diaphragms are reasonably durable and, if properly cared for, can last for up to two years.

Diaphragms and caps are often recommended for women who live with their partners. They have few long-term health risks and are suitable for women who cannot use hormonal contraception. They can be left in for renewed lovemaking, but extra spermicide is necessary after three hours.

Some women dislike the intrusiveness of inserting a device every time they have intercourse. Caps and diaphragms also carry a risk, although extremely low, of toxic shock syndrome if left in for too long, and some women using the diaphragm find they suffer frequently from *CYSTITIS*.

Intrauterine devices (IUDs)

The IUD is a small plastic device wrapped in thin copper wire that is inserted into the uterus by a doctor. Once fitted, it can provide contraceptive protection for up to 5 years. The IUD appears to work by making the uterine lining hostile to both sperm and fertilized ova. Even if conception does take place, the implantation of a fertilized ovum cannot.

Most women who use IUDs are older women who do not want to have any more children. While the IUD offers complete sexual freedom, it is associated with a slight risk of pelvic infection (see page 194), which can cause complications such as damaged fallopian tubes. Insertion of an IUD may be uncomfortable for a couple of hours afterward, and some IUD users complain of heavy and painful periods. IUDs may cause cramping and significant discomfort in women who have not had a baby.

Progestogen-containing IUDs are small T-shaped plastic devices that are inserted into the uterus, where they release the hormone progestogen. Progestogen thickens the cervical mucus, which prevents sperm from traveling to the fallopian tubes. It also thins the uterine lining, making pregnancy difficult to achieve, and causes some women to stop ovulating.

Unlike conventional IUDs, progestogen-containing IUDs cause periods to become light and often painless. They are effective immediately and give protection for one to three years. Progestogen-containing IUDs are available in the U.S. but not in Canada.

HOW TO INSERT A DIAPHRAGM

Find the easiest position for insertion. This may be lying down, squatting or with one foot raised on the edge of the bath or toilet.

1 Hold the rim between thumb and forefinger and squeeze spermicide into the diaphragm.

2 Squeeze the rim into an oval shape and insert it into the vagina. Push the diaphragm as high into the vagina as possible so that its front lies behind the pubic bone.

3 To check that the diaphragm is sitting in the correct position, insert the middle finger high up into the vagina. The cervix should be felt as a firm rounded shape through the latex.

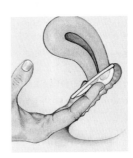

Can We Talk About It?

USING A CONDOM

Knowing when to raise the issue of using a condom with a new partner is difficult. You may worry that if you broach the subject very early, you are making the assumption that intercourse is definitely going to happen. If you broach the subject when you are already in bed together, however, it may be too late to take precautions. The best idea is to talk about the issue when you feel sure that you and your partner want to have sex but before you become too intimate.

Your partner may feel relieved that you have broached the subject. If not, point out that using a condom will make you feel safer and able to relax and enjoy yourself. If your partner resists, you may need to reconsider your relationship. Remind yourself and your partner that condoms are not optional but are a vital form of protection against pregnancy and STDs (see page 184). Don't be made to feel selfish.

THE MALE PILL

Men produce vast numbers of sperm. In order for a male contraceptive to work, it must stop the production or the delivery of every single sperm. (Preventing ovulation in women is comparatively simple, since only one ovum is released every month.) Current research centers around injecting male hormones (androgens) into the bloodstream. This would halt the sequence of events that leads to sperm production, since high levels of androgens instruct the brain to secrete less gonadotropin-releasing hormone (GRH). The problem with this method is that it causes such side effects as irritability and acne, although adding a female hormone, progestogen, may eliminate these problems. Scientists are also looking at the possibility of blocking gonadotropin-releasing hormone with molecules other than androgens.

Disadvantages may include slight bleeding between periods and temporary side effects such as acne, headaches and tenderness of the breasts. Cysts can sometimes appear on the ovaries during the first few months after insertion of the progestogen-containing IUD. These are not considered dangerous and usually disappear without treatment.

Chemical methods

In North America, spermicides are available as creams, foams and gels, and in the U.S. as suppositories and film. Although they chemically destroy any sperm they come into contact with, they are not effective contraceptives on their own and should always be used in conjunction with a cap or a diaphragm. The contraceptive sponge—a round piece of polyurethane foam that is inserted high in the vagina—is also impregnated with spermicide. Some women use the sponge as their sole method of contraception, but this is not recommended unless they have low fertility.

The active ingredient in most spermicides is nonoxynol-9, which increases protection against some sexually transmitted diseases, including human immunodeficiency virus (HIV). Some types of condom are impregnated with nonoxynol-9. Men and women who have an allergic reaction to nonoxynol-

9, resulting in irritation to the vagina, vulva or penis, are advised to choose a different spermicide and check condoms before use.

Natural methods

Understanding the way that conception occurs allows people to use natural methods to prevent it. This can mean avoiding sex during fertile periods or not ejaculating during intercourse. The latter, however, is notoriously ineffective.

The rhythm method, also known as the safe period method, has a reputation for being highly unsafe. However, if couples are taught by an experienced family-planning expert, they can become quite skilled in recognizing the bodily changes associated with ovulation. It is essential that a couple either avoid intercourse during the entire period around ovulation, when a woman may be fertile, or use a barrier method of contraception. The main clues to ovulation are changes in cervical mucus, the position and firmness of the cervix, changes in body temperature, and predictions based on a menstrual calendar. As the technology available to detect ovulation improves (see page 170), the rhythm method may become more widely used. The rhythm method may be easiest for those women who have regular, established menstrual cycles.

HAVING AN IUD FITTED

An IUD should be fitted and removed by a doctor. The device is inserted into the uterus via the cervical canal through a special inserter tube. Threads attached to the IUD hang down into the vagina. IUDs can be fitted at any time, but some doctors prefer to fit them at the end of a period, when the cervix is softer and pregnancy is unlikely.

What are IUDs made from?
IUDs are small plastic devices wrapped with pure copper. Some contain progesterone.

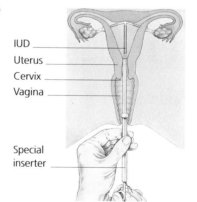

IUD
Uterus
Cervix
Vagina

Special inserter

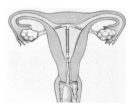

Checking an IUD
Insert a finger high into the vagina to feel the threads of an IUD at the entrance to the cervix.

Inserting an IUD
The IUD is gently pushed through the hollow tube into the uterine cavity. It springs into its normal shape and sits high up in the uterus. The inserter tube is then removed and disposed of.

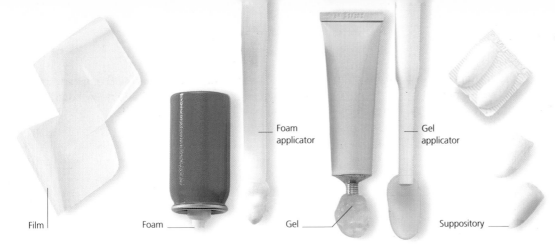

Film | Foam | Foam applicator | Gel | Gel applicator | Suppository

Types of spermicide
Spermicides are chemi-
cals that destroy sperm.
Spermicides should be
used in conjunction
with barrier methods of
contraception.

The withdrawal method, also known as coitus interruptus, is an ancient practice involving withdrawal of the penis from the vagina immediately before ejaculation. Because the semen is deposited outside the body, people have routinely assumed that conception could not occur. During arousal, however, men release drops of pre-ejaculatory fluid that contain sperm, making coitus interruptus highly unreliable as a method of contraception. A recent Oxford University study showed that 6.7 percent of married women between the ages of 25 and 39 using the withdrawal method for a year became pregnant. Other studies have put this figure at as high as 25 percent.

Breast-feeding fully—that is, giving two- to four-hourly feedings to a baby day and night—is thought to protect a woman from becoming pregnant. This is because breast-feeding helps to raise levels of the hormone prolactin, which prevents ovulation. This form of protection is not always reliable, however, and most doctors would recommend using an additional contraceptive during breast-feeding.

Emergency contraception

A woman who has had sex without using contraception or who thinks her method of contraception might have failed has two emergency options.

The postcoital pill is a type of hormonal medication given after unprotected sex. It is popularly referred to as the morning-after pill. "Morning-after" is slightly misleading, however, because the first dose can actually be taken at any time within 72 hours of having unprotected sex. If unprotected sex has resulted in conception, the postcoital pill will prevent the fertilized ovum from becoming implanted in the uterus.

The postcoital pill must be prescribed by a doctor. Four pills are taken—two right away and two 12 hours later. The hormones are of the same type contained in the normal contraceptive pill, but the doses are much higher, which can make some women vomit or feel nauseous. The treatment is not designed for regular use, and patients must have a follow-up checkup. The postcoital pill is 95 to 99 percent effective.

The IUD can be fitted within five days of unprotected sex (the sooner the better) to prevent pregnancy. It can also be used as an ongoing method of contraception if desired. Insertion of an emergency IUD requires a follow-up checkup.

Contraceptive reliability

The efficiency of any contraceptive method depends on the diligence and care that is taken when using it. All forms of contraception are more effective for couples who are highly conscientious (remembering to take the pill every day, for example). Methods that need practice, such as the diaphragm, may have an above average failure rate during the first year of use.

THE FUTURE OF BIRTH CONTROL

The ideal contraceptive is safe, inexpensive and 100 percent effective. It should have no side effects, be unobtrusive to lovemaking and be easi-

Prolonged breast-feeding In some developing countries, women breast-feed their children for several years. This ensures ongoing nutrition for the child and some degree of contraception.

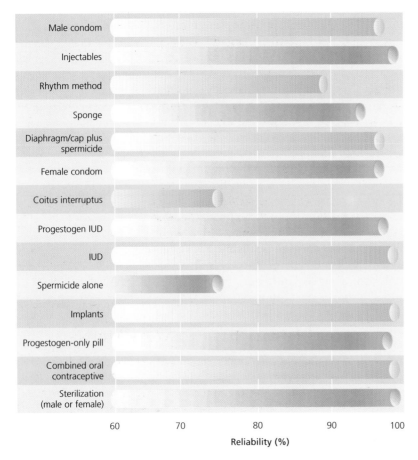

Contraceptives compared The efficacy of a contraceptive is measured by how many women out of 100 using that method become pregnant in one year.

ly reversible. At the moment no single contraceptive meets all of these criteria, but researchers continue to look for one that does. The following methods of contraception for women are all being investigated.

The personal contraceptive system is a small handheld monitor that stores the results of urine tests and calculates the days on which a woman should avoid sex because she is ovulating.

Injectable microspheres and implanted microcapsules are placed under the skin, where they release hormones into the body at a constant daily rate. They cannot be removed, but they dissolve harmlessly and are designed to provide contraceptive protection for up to 18 months.

The vaginal ring is a soft plastic ring impregnated with progestogen. It is placed in the vagina and can be worn either continuously or for 21 days out of 28, during which time it releases a steady amount of the hormone into the body. The ring contains enough of the hormone for use up to

six months. A ring containing estrogen and progestogen is also being researched.

Patches would deliver contraceptive hormones transdermally (through the skin) in the same way that hormone replacement therapy (HRT) patches do.

Nasal sprays would contain contraceptive hormones that prevent ovulation.

Contraceptive vaccines are being researched. A vaccine could work by disrupting the implantation of a fertilized ovum, by causing a man to make antibodies to his own sperm, by causing a woman to be immune to a man's sperm or by preventing the sperm from fertilizing an ovum. All of these vaccines are thought to be a long way from actual use.

Copper fix is a copper IUD that would be inserted into the wall of the uterus and have fewer side effects than current IUDs.

The abortion pill is being tested as a once-a-month method of contraception.

STERILIZATION

When a couple have completed their family or are convinced that they will never want to have children, they may decide that sterilization is a sensible alternative to using contraception for their remaining fertile years. Sterilization involves surgery to the reproductive organs that will permanently prevent pregnancy. Couples may also opt for sterilization for health reasons—some medical conditions make pregnancy dangerous—or to prevent the genetic transmission of serious diseases. The decision to be

fact or fiction?

The older the woman, the more effective the contraceptive.

Fact. As women get older, especially as they approach menopause, they ovulate less frequently. This means that even women who use contraception carelessly are less likely to become pregnant.

sterilized should not be taken lightly, since although it is sometimes possible to have a reversal operation, this may be associated with complications.

Female sterilization

Sterilization is a popular method of contraception in women over age 35. It is extremely effective in preventing pregnancy, it does not stop the menstrual cycle, and it has no impact on sexual enjoyment. Some women are sterilized because pregnancy would mean passing on a serious hereditary disease to their children or because pregnancy would pose a threat to their own health.

Sterilization works by blocking or cutting the fallopian tubes so that sperm cannot reach the ova, and conception can no longer take place. Sterilized women continue to ovulate each month, but the ovum no longer passes into the uterus to be shed during menstruation. Instead, it moves as far along the fallopian tube as it can and then stops, dies and is reabsorbed. Menstruation occurs as usual.

Sterilization can be carried out at any time during the menstrual cycle, but conception may occur if an ovum has been released before surgery takes place. For this reason, women should use a barrier contraceptive such as a condom until their first menstrual period after sterilization. Although it is rare, pregnancy can sometimes occur if one of the fallopian tubes has not been successfully blocked by surgery.

A quarter of sterilized women complain of heavier periods and worse premenstrual symptoms after the operation. These are usually women who used birth control pills before sterilization, who then return to their natural menstrual cycle. Studies measuring amount of blood loss and ovarian hormone levels before and after women have received surgery show no change.

The latest advance in sterilization procedures involves inserting a tiny tube into the fallopian tube via the cervix. The tube deposits a blocking device that prevents sperm from coming into contact with ova.

Hysterectomy

The most extreme example of female sterilization is hysterectomy (see page 196), which is the surgical removal of the uterus and, in some cases, the fallopian tubes and ovaries (which is called a hysterectomy and bilateral salpingo-oophorectomy). Obviously, without these organs, conception and pregnancy become impossible. Because hysterectomy involves major surgery, it is not recognized as a sterilization procedure; nevertheless, permanent sterilization is the result. By the age of 75, an estimated one in five women will have had her uterus removed.

If a doctor suggests that a woman should have a hysterectomy for a non-life-threatening condition such as *FIBROIDS*, she must bear in mind that she will no longer be able to have children. If a woman has any doubts about the necessity of a hysterectomy, she should seek a second or third opinion.

WHAT FEMALE STERILIZATION MEANS

Sterilization is usually performed under general anesthetic. There are various techniques for blocking or sealing the fallopian tubes so that sperm is prevented from meeting an ovum. Sterilization is rarely reversible, and should be considered a permanent step.

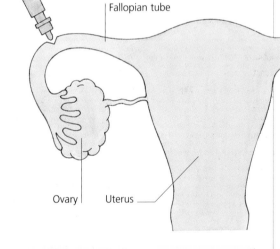

Cautery
A high-frequency electric current is directed at each fallopian tube via a surgical instrument. The current burns through and seals the tubes. This sterilization process is known as cautery.

Fallopian tube

Ovary | Uterus

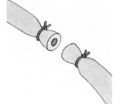

Cutting
A small section of each fallopian tube is cut away and the cut ends are tied and cauterized.

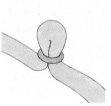

Constriction
The fallopian tubes are pulled up into a loop that is constricted with a tight band.

Clipping
A special clip made of plastic or metal is applied to each fallopian tube.

WHAT MALE STERILIZATION MEANS

A vasectomy does not impede ejaculation or orgasm, but it does mean that the fluid a man ejaculates is sperm-free. Since the tubes that need to be cut are just below the skin, they can be reached easily, making vasectomy a quick and straightforward procedure. The only problem men may experience is slight bruising or discomfort.

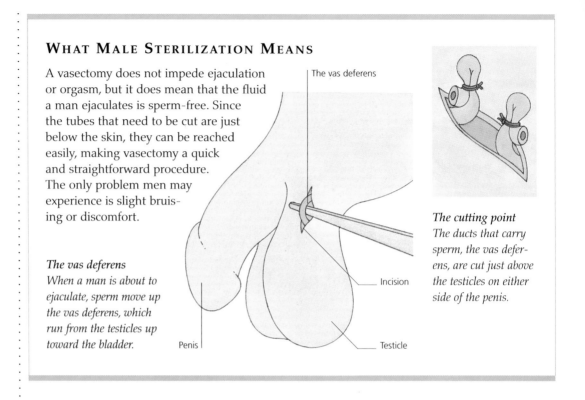

The vas deferens
When a man is about to ejaculate, sperm move up the vas deferens, which run from the testicles up toward the bladder.

The vas deferens

Incision

Penis

Testicle

The cutting point
The ducts that carry sperm, the vas deferens, are cut just above the testicles on either side of the penis.

Male sterilization—vasectomy

Vasectomy is a minor surgical procedure that provides almost 100 percent contraception. It involves cutting and tying the vas deferens (the tubes that carry sperm). This means that men can still ejaculate, but there is no sperm present in the semen (the sperm are reabsorbed within the testicles).

Vasectomy is a safer surgical procedure than female sterilization, with fewer postoperative complications, and it is estimated that a third of North American men will eventually undergo one. Surgery takes a few minutes and is performed by a doctor on an out-patient basis under local anesthetic.

Two to three months after vasectomy men are asked to provide samples of semen produced by masturbation—this is to ensure that any sperm remaining in the vas deferens before surgery have cleared. Until sperm have cleared (usually after about 20 ejaculations), men are advised to continue using another contraceptive.

Sterilization reversal

Fewer than 50 percent of women who have undergone sterilization reversal surgery will go on to become pregnant. The success rate depends mainly on the type of sterilization that was originally performed. Constriction and clipping are the steriliza-

tion procedures that are most likely to be reversible. They also have lower rates of contraceptive failure.

Before a doctor will consider a woman for a reversal, he or she will check that the woman's partner's sperm count is healthy, since reversal surgery may be a waste of time if it is not. A doctor will also perform a *LAPAROSCOPY* to check that there is enough fallopian tube to make the reversal possible and that the tubes are not so badly scarred that they would hinder pregnancy.

One of the main problems with sterilization reversal is the 10 to 15 percent chance that the woman will later have an ectopic pregnancy (one in which the fetus develops in the fallopian tube). The sperm may be able to swim into the fallopian tube to fertilize the ovum, but the *BLASTOCYST* may be too big to pass through the fallopian tube into the uterus to implant.

Surgery to reverse a vasectomy is expensive and complicated, taking about two to three hours to perform. It involves rejoining the cut ends of the vas deferens. The results are unpredictable, and approximately half of the men who have a vasectomy begin to produce antibodies to their own sperm, rendering them infertile anyway. The success rate of reversal surgery is about 50 percent, but this decreases considerably over time.

Maintaining Sexual Health

Sexual Health

Today people are more informed about sexual health than ever before. Safer sex practices, good sexual hygiene and awareness of how infections are spread have enabled individuals to take control of their sexual and reproductive health.

For those who think they may be at risk of contracting a sexually transmitted disease, sexual health means having regular checkups—the sooner a disease is diagnosed, the sooner it can be treated and the fewer the people who will become infected. For others, sexual health means practicing good day-to-day personal hygiene. The importance of this cannot be overstated. For example, poor genital hygiene can be a risk factor for some male genital cancers (see page 202), especially if a man works with substances such as oil and soot or is not circumcised.

GENITAL HYGIENE

People are taught that cleanliness and hygiene are an important part of staying healthy. To a large extent this is true, but over the past few decades, cosmetic and deodorant companies have exploited this fact, making many individuals believe that their natural body smells are unhygienic and should be washed away or disguised with other smells.

Women in particular have been targeted by the companies that manufacture fragranced feminine hygiene products, such as vaginal deodorants and scented genital wipes and sanitary napkins. The message conveyed by these products is that the normal smell of the vulva and vagina is unpleasant and undesirable. In fact, as long as a woman does not have a gynecological infection, the natural odors and secretions produced by her genitals are not only healthy and natural but also important for sexual desire and arousal.

The tissue lining the labia and the vagina is very sensitive; it provides a home to the healthy bacteria that help keep the vagina—and to some extent the inner labia—clean. Using deodorants or highly perfumed soaps upsets the pH and delicate bacterial balance around the vulva and the vagina, making yeast infections more likely. Even adding bubble bath or bath salts to bath water can upset the bacterial balance in the vagina, killing the "good" bacteria and encouraging the growth of "bad" bacteria. In fact, doctors have reported an increase in the number of women complaining of yeast infections just after the holiday season, when such products are widely received as gifts.

All that a woman needs to do for daily genital hygiene is to wash the vulval area with plain water and the anal area with unscented soap and water. Using soap on the vulva is unnecessary, although many women say that plain water does not make them feel clean. If women do wash with soap, they should choose an unscented

Disrupting the pH balance in the vagina
Certain bacteria live in the vagina and keep the area clean. These bacteria produce lactic acid, which kills unwanted bacteria and yeasts. If the balance of healthy bacteria is changed—by highly fragranced bath products, for example —a woman becomes more prone to vaginal infections.

These factors alter pH and upset bacterial balance

- Bubble bath
- Spermicide
- Douching
- Infection
- Synthetic underwear
- Antibiotics
- Chlorinated pools
- Unusual increase in dairy consumption

- Healthy diet
- Cotton or silk underwear
- Specific medications for vaginal infections
- Avoiding scented hygiene products

These factors maintain healthy pH and bacterial balance

Sanitary Protection

The two most common methods women use to absorb the menstrual flow are sanitary napkins and vaginal tampons. Many girls begin by using napkins and later move on to a combination of napkins and tampons. Some women use napkins at night and tampons during the day, especially when playing sports or swimming. Modern napkins are very slim and absorbent, attach to underwear with a peel-back adhesive strip, and are invisible through clothing.

Women of any age can use tampons, as long as insertion causes no discomfort. Girls and women who have never had intercourse may find it easier to use small tampons.

Different absorbencies of tampon should be worn to suit the degree of blood flow. Super-absorbency tampons may be needed for the start of a period, followed by regular or light absorbency for subsequent days. Tampons should be changed every four to six hours and removed before sexual intercourse.

Fragranced tampons may cause irritation and lead to vaginal infection. A tampon that is left in the vagina too long eventually produces a strong-smelling, colorless discharge. This form of bacterial vaginosis (see page 193) should go when the tampon is removed, but a doctor should be consulted nonetheless.

Some women use contraceptive caps and diaphragms to catch menstrual blood flow during their period. Although convenient, this practice can cause abrasions in the membrane that lines the vagina and increase the risk of toxic shock syndrome (see page 176). For sex during menstruation, however, caps and diaphragms with spermicide will conveniently reduce the blood flow.

Some women use natural sea sponges to absorb menstrual blood flow as an alternative to tampons. Doctors discourage this method of protection because it is difficult to ensure that sponges are adequately free of pollutants, both natural and man-made.

Sanitary napkins
Napkins come in many different shapes and thicknesses.

Padded for heavy flow

Shaped for comfort

Wings for extra security

Slim for light flow

Applicator tampons
Cardboard or plastic applicators help guide the tampon into the vagina.

Tampon for heavy flow

Tampon for medium flow

Plastic-applicator tampon

Fragranced tampon (may cause irritation to the vaginal lining)

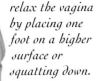

Finding the best position
Often it helps to relax the vagina by placing one foot on a higher surface or squatting down.

INSERTING A TAMPON

Tampons are inserted high into the vagina, where they absorb the menstrual blood that flows through the cervical opening. Once it is inserted, a woman should be unaware that she is wearing a tampon. If it is uncomfortable, then it has probably been incorrectly inserted.

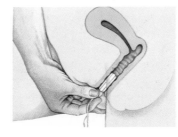

1 Push the applicator-free tampon into the vagina with the fingers. Aim toward the small of the back.

WITH AN APPLICATOR

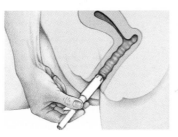

1 Holding the outer tube where it meets the inner one, insert the tampon into the vagina.

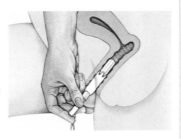

2 Push in the plunger with the index finger and then remove both tubes.

TOXIC SHOCK SYNDROME

This rare but life-threatening illness occurs primarily in women using tampons. If a tampon is too absorbent for the degree of menstrual flow or is left in too long, it can dry out the vagina and cause abrasions. These tiny cuts allow the *Staphylococcus aureus* bacterium to enter the body, where it starts producing poisonous toxins. Symptoms of toxic shock syndrome include high fever, sore throat, aching muscles, vomiting, diarrhea and a reddening of the skin. The illness can also lead to kidney failure. Doctors treat toxic shock syndrome with antibiotics.

To prevent occurrence of toxic shock syndrome, women should use tampons of the correct absorbency for the degree of menstrual flow and change them at least every four to six hours. Tampons made of cotton or non-enhanced rayon are least likely to cause the illness.

Menstruation in other cultures In northern Nepal, a menstruating woman is believed to pollute those around her and is segregated from everyone except her younger children.

brand and make sure the soap lather is completely rinsed away. Postmenopausal women in particular should try to avoid soap, since the skin of their *UROGENITAL TRACT* becomes thin and sensitive and more susceptible to infection (see page 111).

It is important that girls and women are aware that some amount of vaginal discharge is normal and not a sign of poor hygiene or infection. There is cause for concern only if a vaginal discharge becomes profuse, discolored or smelly.

Male genital hygiene is very straightforward. Uncircumcised men—and boys old enough to retract the foreskin—should gently wash under the foreskin with water every day. They may or may not need to use soap depending on how much *SMEGMA* they produce. Some men find that soap dries the sensitive skin of the glans and causes rashes and irritation. Circumcised men usually need only to use water on the glans. All men should wash the anal area with soap and water daily.

The type of underwear worn also plays a role in the general health and cleanliness of male and female genitals. Both men and women should avoid underwear made from synthetic fabrics because these encourage sweating in the genital area, which in turn encourages the growth of bacteria and yeasts. Natural fibers such as cotton and silk absorb sweat and allow air to circulate. Some women who suffer from recurrent yeast infections (see page 193) can avoid the problem by wearing pure cotton underwear and stockings instead of pantyhose. Men's tight-fitting polyester or nylon briefs have also been found to lower sperm count.

MENSTRUAL HYGIENE

Menstruation has been perennially shrouded in myth: some women still believe that menstrual blood is dirty; some are superstitious about what they can and cannot do while they are bleeding. In some Arab cultures, women are forbidden to prepare or cook food while they are menstruating, and some orthodox Jewish and Muslim women undergo elaborate cleansing rituals after each menstrual period. Although myths and taboos persist, no medical or scientific reason exists why menstruation should be thought of as dirty.

The volume of fluid loss varies from woman to woman and month to month, averaging between two and six fluid ounces (60 and 175 ml). The fluid that is lost is a mixture of unclotted blood, mucus and cells. Enzymes inside the uterus unclot the blood, which allows it to drip through the cervical canal. Sometimes the blood reclots in the vagina and passes out of the body in that state—a menstrual flow with some blood clots is normal. An unusually heavy blood flow with many large clots, however, should be investigated by a doctor.

No specific hygiene needs to be practiced during menstruation beyond washing with unperfumed soap and water and using plenty of water around the entrance to the vagina. Women who use douches around the time of their period may actually encourage yeast infections.

PREVENTING SEXUALLY TRANSMITTED DISEASES

Sexually transmitted diseases (STDs) are diseases that are passed on by sexual contact (see page 184). The most threatening STD—HIV—is passed on by unprotected sexual intercourse (sex without a condom). While a definitive cure for HIV continues to elude researchers, experts have known how to treat other types of STD, such as *SYPHILIS* and *GONORRHEA*, for some time. But whether or not STDs are treatable, they should be avoided—they are frequently uncomfortable and can cause dangerous health complications, including infertility.

STDs can be communicated in a number of ways: genital-to-genital contact (such as vaginal sex); genital-to-oral contact (oral sex); genital-to-anal contact (anal sex); and oral-to-oral contact (kissing). Some types of sexual intimacy pose more of a risk than others (see page 179). There are also non-sexual ways of passing on diseases; for example, HIV can be transferred by sharing infected needles, and *CHLAMYDIA* and *TRICHOMONIASIS* can be passed on by a mother to her child during childbirth.

While antibiotics can cure many STDs, no existing vaccines prevent infection. The only way to avoid catching an STD is to be confident about the sexual history and health of sexual partners, though most doctors working in the field of sexual medicine would argue that even this is impossible. Some barrier contraceptives such as male and female condoms (see page 165) can help to protect against infection, but people whose behavior is considered to be particularly high-risk (see page 179) should have regular checkups at a clinic.

STD testing

People may attend a clinic specializing in sexual medicine for any of a variety of reasons. They may have had casual sex (on one occasion or frequently) and want to eliminate the possibility that they have been infected with an STD. They may have symptoms that they suspect are due to an STD, or they may have been warned

by a sexual partner that they could be infected. Some people have checkups just to be reassured about their sexual health.

It is important to investigate a suspected STD as soon as possible—the longer an infection goes untreated, the greater the chances of permanent damage to the infected individual (for example, untreated gonorrhea can go on to cause infertility) and transmission to other people.

Most clinics will ask for a full sexual and medical history, including details of any travel abroad, before checking for STDs. It is important to provide information on all sexual contacts to be sure they can be informed if need be. People should not urinate for at least two hours before attending a checkup so that no bacteria are washed away. In some U.S. states and Canadian provinces, teenagers can request diagnosis and treatment of STDs without parental permission.

A number of STD clinics now have resident counselors who can help patients come to terms with the fact that they have an STD. Counselors can give advice on safer sex and the repercussions of an STD and will discuss with the patient any lifestyle changes that are considered to be necessary.

Culturing a swab
Many STDs are caused by bacteria. A swab allows a small sample of bacteria to be grown, or cultured, on an appropriate medium in a test tube or dish and identified under a microscope. The doctor takes a swab, using a metal loop or a cotton-tipped stick, from the urethra, the vagina, the cervix, the anus, the rectum or the throat.

DIAGNOSING STDS

Depending on the patient's symptoms and sexual history, various tests will be carried out to determine sexual health.

Checkups for women may include some or all of the following:

Examining the breasts

Taking a swab from the cervix and vaginal walls

Palpating the uterus from inside the vagina

Checkups for both men and women may include some or all of the following:

Taking a swab from the throat (when oral-to-genital contact has taken place)

Taking a swab from the urethra

Feeling the lymph glands in the neck, armpits and groin

Examining the pubic region for parasites, ulcers, abnormal lumps, bumps and rashes

Taking a urine sample

Examining the anal area and inside of the rectum

Taking a swab from the anal area and/or rectum

Taking a blood sample

Examining the external pubic and genital area

Checkups for men may include some or all of the following:

Examining the testicles for abnormal lumps or signs of tenderness

Examining the penis for visible discharge, ulcers or growths

Taking a swab from the tip of the penis

Safer Sex

Wearing a condom during penetrative sex is the single most important measure that an individual can take to prevent the transmission of diseases such as gonorrhea, herpes, genital warts and, most important, HIV.

Safety first *Be careful not to damage the condom when tearing open the packet, and squeeze it out gently, rather than pulling it.*

The term "safe sex" became popular in the late 1980s to describe sexual practices thought to have a lower risk of transmitting HIV (see page 180). "Safer sex" has now replaced the earlier term, because no sexual practice involving body fluids can be completely free of risk. Safer sex practices offer protection not only from HIV but also from other sexually transmitted diseases and unplanned pregnancies.

CONDOMS

Using condoms during oral, vaginal and anal sex helps to protect against HIV as well as common STDs (see page 184), such as gonorrhea, herpes, genital warts and chlamydia. The condom provides a physical barrier to viruses and bacteria that may be carried in semen, vaginal secretions and other body fluids. Condoms should be used with nonoxynol-9, a substance that was developed as a spermicide but later found to kill some bacteria and viruses, among them HIV. A few people are allergic to nonoxynol-9, in which case condoms using alternative spermicides are available.

The amount of protection offered by a condom (from both disease and pregnancy) depends on how carefully it is used. Men who have not used a condom before should practice putting one on before they use one for sexual contact (see page 165). Likewise,

USING A CONDOM SAFELY

GUIDELINES	REASONS
Store condoms away from heat, light and damp.	Latex deteriorates in adverse conditions.
Check the expiration date before use.	Latex deteriorates over time.
Avoid any genital-to-genital contact until the condom is on.	Fluid is released from the penis during foreplay before ejaculation.
When putting the condom on, squeeze the tip between thumb and forefinger to expel air.	Air trapped in the tip during intercourse can cause the condom to split.
Use condoms only with water-based lubricants or jellies.	Oil-based products can damage latex. For example, baby oil destroys up to 95 percent of a condom's strength after only 15 minutes. Even substances such as suntan oil and lipstick can cause rubber to deteriorate.
Withdraw the penis and condom before the penis becomes flaccid after ejaculation.	If the penis becomes flaccid, there is more chance that the condom will slip off and semen will leak out.
Handle condoms carefully.	A tiny hole in the latex, caused by a ring for example, will allow semen to leak out.

women should familiarize themselves with the insertion technique for female condoms before they have intercourse (see page 166).

WHO IS MOST AT RISK FROM HIV?

When AIDS was first identified as an illness in the Western world, it predominantly affected young homosexual men. Today it affects heterosexuals and homosexuals in all cultures and from all walks of life. Nevertheless, it is still possible to identify groups who are considered to be high-risk.

Homosexual and bisexual people who have had casual sex or multiple partners are at risk, especially those who have had unprotected receptive anal intercourse. High-risk groups among heterosexuals include people who have or have had unprotected sex with multiple partners (or even just one infected partner) and men who have or have had unprotected sex with prostitutes (particularly in Africa, Asia and South America).

Drug users who share needles, snorting tubes (which can cause the nose to bleed) or other equipment that comes in contact with blood are a very high risk group.

HEMOPHILIACS who received blood products before products were tested for HIV are a risk group, as are people working or traveling in developing countries who received blood transfusions before blood was screened for HIV (some countries still do not screen blood). The sexual partners of people classified as high-risk are in danger themselves, and HIV-positive mothers can transmit the virus to their unborn babies.

CHANGES IN SEXUAL BEHAVIOR SINCE AIDS

Because no effective vaccines or cures for HIV exist, control of the virus has so far been limited to behavioral changes by individuals. Studies of the gay male population in the U.S. have shown a distinct change in sexual practices since HIV was first discovered in the 1980s. Most gay men have reduced the number of their sexual partners and in particular the number of unfamiliar sexual partners. Research carried out in San Francisco showed a decline in the number of newly infected individuals.

Trends in the heterosexual population have not been as encouraging. Because the transmission of HIV was first associated with homosexuality and intravenous drug

Highest-risk activities are unprotected anal, vaginal and oral sex or any activity that involves the exchange of blood.

Less risky activities are protected penetrative sex or protected oral sex (using a male or female condom).

RISKY ACTIVITIES
Because HIV is carried in body fluids, levels of risk are determined by the chances of exchange or mingling of those body fluids.

Very low-risk activities are dry kissing and mutual masturbation.

Risk-free activities are solo masturbation; massage without genital contact; unshared sex toys; hugging; and holding hands.

Levels of risk Doctors now agree that some sexual practices are less risky than others. Although it is possible, in theory, for HIV to be transmitted through the exchange of saliva during kissing, this has not been found to be a common route of transmission. In contrast, unprotected anal sex is an established and common way for the virus to be transmitted.

use, many heterosexuals failed to perceive themselves as "at risk." According to the World Health Organization (mid-1996 estimates), 70 percent of HIV infections in adults worldwide are transmitted by heterosexual sexual contact. Male homosexual sexual contact accounts for between 5 and 10 percent of HIV cases.

Globally, teenagers and young adults between the ages of 15 and 24 are considered to be most affected by HIV/AIDS—more than 50 percent of new infections occur in this age group. At present rates, about 13 young people are infected every 5 minutes. An estimated 21 million people live with HIV/AIDS worldwide. Evidence that heterosexuals have not adjusted their behavior also comes from an increase in other STDs (see page 184) such as gonorrhea, syphilis, chlamydia and chancroid in urban areas of the U.S. In Canada, gonorrhea and chlamydia rates are disturbingly high among young women aged 15 to 19 years.

HIV and AIDS

*The acronym HIV stands for human immunodeficiency virus.
A person infected with HIV suffers progressive damage
to the immune system until the body can no longer
defend itself against infection.*

Memorial quilt for AIDS victims *Since AIDS was first identified in 1981, thousands of people have died as a result of HIV infection in the U.S. alone. The AIDS memorial quilt, assembled at Washington, D.C., is part of the "Names Project," which aims to remember the victims of this devastating disease.*

The doctors in the U.S. who witnessed the first reported cases of AIDS in 1981 were stunned to see rare, life-threatening illnesses such as Kaposi's sarcoma repeatedly affecting young homosexual men. Such illnesses were previously limited to older men from Africa and the Mediterranean region, and to people with suppressed immune systems. Kaposi's sarcoma is a malignancy of the skin capillaries and connective tissue that causes disfiguring purple skin blotches.

Young homosexual men also began to show an increased incidence of another unusual condition—*PNEUMOCYSTIC PNEUMONIA*.

While doctors suspected immediately that a virus was responsible, it took them a couple of years to isolate and identify it. In the meantime arguments and accusations filled the media. The Soviet press accused the U.S. Army of genetically engineering the virus, while some members of the gay community accused the CIA of deliberately infecting the waters in New York City bathhouses.

In 1983 Dr. Luc Montaigner at the Institut Pasteur in Paris finally identified the virus. He named the virus "lymphadenopathy associated virus" (LAV). At the same time,

THE HISTORY OF HIV

When the first cases of AIDS were diagnosed in 1981, scientists believed that they were witnessing a completely new disease. Since then research has shown that HIV has been around much longer than originally thought. In fact, people arriving in Europe from West Africa in the early 1970s were becoming sick with AIDS-like symptoms, and evidence of HIV has been traced back to blood samples taken from Africans in 1959. Scientists hypothesize that the original source of the virus was the African green monkey. This species may have carried the virus—albeit in a different form—for thousands of years.

The origins of HIV *Monkeys are thought to carry a virus known as simian immunodeficiency virus (SIV). It is only comparatively recently that SIV may have mutated to cause fatal illness in humans.*

HIV CASES WORLDWIDE—THE MOST COMMON ROUTES OF INFECTION

Sexual intercourse
Penetrative sex is the most common route of transmission for HIV. It accounts for 70 to 85 percent of cases.

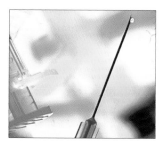

Needle sharing
Five to 10 percent of HIV infections result from contaminated injection equipment. Intravenous drug users are at high risk.

Blood transfusion
Blood or blood products (this includes organ donations) that are infected with HIV account for 5 to 10 percent of cases.

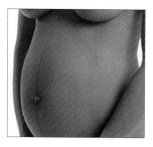

Mother to infant
Five to 10 percent of HIV cases are attributable to mothers passing the infection to their children.

another researcher, Dr. Robert Gallo, also identified the virus, naming it human T-lymphotropic virus (HTLV-III). A long dispute began between the two research teams over which had isolated the virus first.

Eventually, in 1986, the International Committee on Taxonomy of Viruses was called upon to decide the correct name for the virus. After much debate, the dispute was finally settled when U.S. president Ronald Reagan and Prime Minister Jacques Chirac of France announced that researchers had agreed that the official name for the virus would be human immunodeficiency virus-1 (HIV I) and that the royalties from tests developed for HIV I would be shared.

THE SPREAD OF AIDS

HIV spread very quickly through the gay community in the U.S. in the early 1980s. Experts blamed the speed of the spread on the promiscuity of gay men, and HIV and AIDS gained a reputation as the "gay plague." But the notion that linked the disease solely to the gay community had to be revised when people who exchanged blood in some way also became prone to infection. Such people included intravenous drug users and *HEMOPHILIACS* who received infected blood products. It was not long before non-drug-using heterosexuals began to test positive for HIV. Scientists, doctors and governments realized that anyone could become infected.

Unprotected sex, whether homosexual, heterosexual, anal or vaginal, is now the main method of HIV transmission worldwide. In Africa, Thailand and India, the large numbers of prostitutes and the high incidence of untreated sexually transmitted diseases have accelerated the rate of spread. The sores and inflamed membranes that characterize STDs such as *SYPHILIS* and *CHANCROID* make it easier to both transmit and become infected with HIV.

HOW HIV CAUSES AIDS

Despite controversy in the past, most scientists now believe that HIV is the cause of AIDS. Not everyone who is infected with HIV, however, goes on to develop AIDS. Some studies show that as many as 35 percent of people infected with HIV still have no symptoms after 10 years. Some of these people may never develop AIDS. This may be because they are protected in some way by their own genetic makeup or because the virus infecting them is flawed (has mutated) and is weaker than the usual HIV. Some children who were born with HIV have apparently succeeded in clearing the virus from their bodies.

HIV is known to enter the body through cuts, sores, tears and tiny breaks in the skin or mucous membranes. Sexual intercourse provides the usual route, and anal sex is particularly dangerous because of the abrasions and small tears that occur. The other main route of infection is needles that are contaminated with infected blood, then reused. Once inside the body, HIV begins its attack on the immune system by targeting T-helper cells, a crucial part of the body's immune defense.

HIV attaches itself to macrophages and T-helper cells—their surface receptors allow HIV to quite literally lock on to them—and then injects its core into the T-helper cell, incorporating its own genetic material into the cell's DNA. After HIV has entered the nucleus and changed the genetic structure of the T-helper cell, the virus can then start to replicate itself.

It is thought that as soon as T-helper cells become infected with HIV and the amount of virus circulating in the body—known as the viral load—starts to increase, the body's immune system mounts a massive response. From this moment on the immune system is locked in battle with the virus. Researchers estimate that HIV can multiply at the rate of a billion new viral particles every day, thereby overwhelming the immune system. HIV may also outwit the immune system and drug treatments by mutating into different forms.

The immune system sometimes successfully contains HIV for many years, but there usually comes a point when so many T-helper cells have been destroyed that the immune system can no longer function adequately and the person becomes ill. The combinations of infections that then afflict the body are traditionally referred to as AIDS and AIDS-related complex. Doctors are now trying to make this terminology simpler and increasingly refer to people as HIV symptomatic or HIV asymptomatic, and use the term "HIV disease" to cover all stages of the infection.

Stages of the infection

HIV infection progresses in stages. The first stage is the initial infection, when HIV enters the body—an undetectable process that leaves a person feeling well and without signs of any ill health. If a person has an HIV test too soon after becoming infected, no antibodies will be apparent and he or she will test negative. Antibodies are substances that appear in the blood in response to invaders such as bacteria or viruses; their role is to neutralize or destroy the invader.

It takes between 6 and 10 weeks (and occasionally longer) for the body to produce antibodies in sufficient numbers for an HIV antibody test to become accurate. Because of this period, known as the "viral window," doctors advise people to wait 12 weeks after possible exposure to HIV before being tested. The production of antibodies, known as seroconversion, goes unnoticed in many people, while in others it causes a short illness similar to flu or infectious mononucleosis. Symptoms include malaise, fever, swollen lymph glands and a rash over part or all of the body.

The second stage of HIV infection, called the asymptomatic carrier state or the dormant or latent stage, can last for years. Although HIV is busy replicating and mutating, the body's immune system keeps it in check, and the infected individual suf-

Infected T-cell T-cells *infected with the HIV virus have a characteristic lumpy appearance, with irregular surface protrusions (seen here as white nodules). Budding out from the surface are thousands of tiny new HIV particles (colored green), ready to infect and destroy new T-cells.*

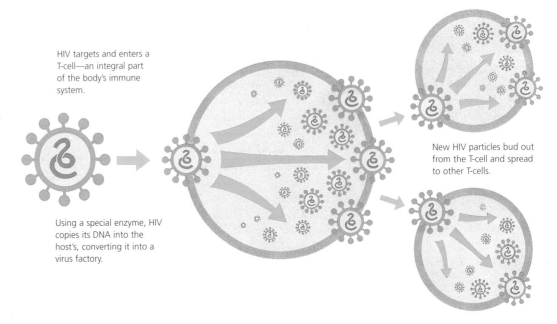

Replication of HIV Viral particles use special proteins to lock on and gain entry to the target T-cell. Once inside, they incorporate their DNA into the host's genetic material, turning the infected T-cell into a virus factory, churning out millions of new HIV viruses.

HIV targets and enters a T-cell—an integral part of the body's immune system.

Using a special enzyme, HIV copies its DNA into the host's, converting it into a virus factory.

New HIV particles bud out from the T-cell and spread to other T-cells.

HIV gets into bloodstream through:	Viral window		HIV negative	
	HIV asymptomatic		HIV asymptomatic (T-cell count can stay constant)	
			HIV symptomatic	
• unprotected sex • blood transfusion • sharing needles • the placenta	The viral window is the period between infection and the production of sufficient antibodies to detect that virus is present.	The immune system is keeping the virus in check, but the T-cells are gradually being depleted.	Some sufferers manage to clear the virus from blood; others keep it in check indefinitely.	In 90% of sufferers, the immune system loses its battle and the victim is susceptible to a range of infections.

1000   500   200   T-cell count per ml of blood

fers no symptoms of ill health. During this so-called healthy stage of the infection, the virus can be passed on unwittingly. The duration of the second stage varies from person to person. Some people succumb to the virus a few years after infection; others stay healthy for a decade or more.

To determine the stage of an infected individual, doctors measure numbers of T-helper cells in the blood. In a healthy person there will be an average of 1,000 such cells per milliliter of blood. In an HIV-infected person nearing the end of the asymptomatic stage, there will be approximately 500 T-helper cells per milliliter of blood. Although a person may remain asymptomatic with a T-helper cell count lower than 500, the next stage of HIV is considered to have begun.

A diagnosis of AIDS used to be made when the T-helper cell count dropped below 200. As doctors found more and more people who remained healthy despite a count below 200, they began to review this criterion for diagnosis. Now an apparently healthy person with a low T-helper cell count is more likely to be described as having asymptomatic HIV. Doctors are now able to measure the amount of HIV itself in the blood, and this is proving to be a better indicator of health and long-term prognosis than the T-helper cell count.

Apart from measuring T-helper cells or HIV levels, doctors can also interpret physical symptoms as signs that the infection is progressing. People with symptomatic HIV commonly experience fever, night sweats, diarrhea, weight loss, chronically swollen lymph glands, disturbance of vision and mental function, and a persistent cough (these symptoms can also be due to infections that are unrelated to HIV). Sufferers may become ill with atypical pneumonia,

oral yeast infections, persistent *HERPES SIMPLEX*, fungal skin infection, hairy *LEUKOPLAKIA* and Kaposi's sarcoma. These are typical in people with some kind of immunodeficiency or other underlying condition, but they are not always caused by HIV.

HIV progression
This chart shows the course of HIV and how the T-cell count can drop, weakening the immune system.

TREATING HIV INFECTION

Doctors treat HIV disease in a variety of ways. They use anti-HIV drugs to directly attack the virus's enzymes or its ability to attach to cells. These drugs block receptors on the host cell or deactivate the attachment mechanism of the virus. Treatment is also given to boost the immune system, specifically the T-helper cells. Lastly, treatment of individual infections is attempted.

A person with HIV disease may be given a cocktail of drugs designed to beat the virus's ability to mutate and become resistant. There are a large number of these drugs, and recommendations change monthly. On top of this, HIV-related infections—which can be bacterial, viral or fungal—must be treated, perhaps several at a time. With these drug cocktails people are remaining free of symptoms for more than 10 years after becoming HIV positive. So far an HIV vaccine has proved elusive; the best hope may be a drug that can attack the virus while it is in the lymph nodes.

Living with HIV
The likelihood of an HIV-infected person developing AIDS increases as time goes past. Many people keep the virus in check for 5 to 10 years; some indefinitely.

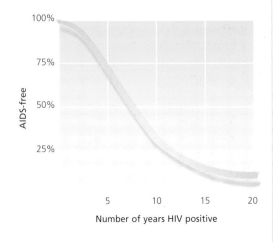

Other STDs

Sexually transmitted diseases are usually passed on by unprotected sex with an infected partner. While some diseases produce obvious symptoms, others, such as chlamydia, may be symptomless, meaning that they can be passed on unwittingly.

I f a sexually transmitted disease (STD) is suspected, it is important to visit a physician or clinic immediately to get a professional diagnosis and receive prompt treatment. Many STDs are easily treated if they are detected at an early stage.

SYPHILIS

Syphilis can spread by vaginal or anal intercourse, oral sex, kissing, and skin-to-skin contact. It can also be passed on by infected blood transfusions and through the use of needles shared by drug abusers. Left untreated, it can be fatal.

Between 9 and 90 days after infection with syphilis, a small lump appears at the site of infection, usually on the genitals or around the anus, but sometimes inside the vagina or on the cervix. This lump develops into a firm sore or ulcer with raised borders, which is known as the primary chancre.

Several weeks after the chancre disappears, the disease moves into its second stage, in which lymph nodes all over the body may enlarge and dusky red spots appear on the skin, particularly on the hands and the feet. There may be sores on the hands and the feet; painless, wartlike growths on the genitals; headaches; low-grade fever; sore throat; and hair loss. Distinctive mucous patches known as snail-track ulcers may appear inside the mouth and throat. Complications, including a mild form of hepatitis, meningitis, kidney abnormalities and eye infections, may also occur.

Without treatment, these symptoms last about six weeks. Then syphilis enters a latent period in which the infected person feels healthy. Through some of the latent period syphilis continues to be infectious, and a woman can infect her unborn child for 8 to 10 years after becoming infected.

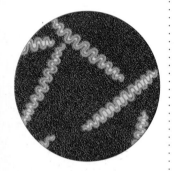

Treponema pallidum
Syphilis is caused by a bacterium that enters the body through mucous membranes and cuts in the skin.

Neisseria gonorrhoeae *The bacterium responsible for gonorrhea can live in the vagina, cervix, urethra, rectum and eyes.*

VENEREAL DISEASES IN THE 19TH CENTURY

T reatment for STDs has advanced considerably in the last century. In the 19th century, doctors believed that syphilis and gonorrhea were the same disease at different stages. Patients were treated with mercury, which was painful and often ineffective. In 1909 doctors claimed that a derivative of arsenic was a cure for syphilis. Unfortunately, they would occasionally prescribe too much by accident, sometimes with fatal consequences. Today doctors rely on antibiotics to treat bacterial STDs.

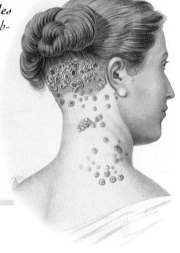

Syphilis pustules
An engraving published in 1885 depicts chronic skin abscesses on the neck and base of the skull resulting from syphilis.

Some people are lucky enough not to enter the third stage of syphilis, but those who do suffer from brain damage, paralysis and cardiovascular problems, and finally die from the disease.

Syphilis can be diagnosed by microscopic examination of a smear from the primary chancre. In the later stages of syphilis, blood tests or spinal fluid examination is needed for diagnosis. High doses of antibiotics can cure syphilis, but any damage already done to the body cannot be reversed.

GONORRHEA

Neisseria gonorrhoeae is the bacterium responsible for gonorrhea. It can be passed on during unprotected anal or vaginal sex. Oral sex and deep kissing with an infected partner can cause throat infections.

Many people with gonorrhea have no symptoms and can pass on the infection unwittingly. Sometimes people discover they have gonorrhea only when they infect a partner who then experiences symptoms.

Typically, men infected with gonorrhea notice a discharge from the penis or anus and pain when urinating or defecating. The discharge is milky at first and becomes thick and yellow. Women are more likely than men to have symptomless gonorrhea. If there are symptoms, they may include a yellow vaginal or urethral discharge and frequent, urgent and painful urination. Unless gonorrhea is symptomless, signs of infection usually appear within two weeks of being exposed to the bacterium.

Untreated gonorrhea in men can lead to infection of the prostate gland, the epididymis and the seminal vesicles (see page 121). In extreme cases this can result in infertility, scarring of the urethra and problems with erections. In women untreated gonorrhea can spread through the cervix and uterus to the fallopian tubes, causing pelvic inflammatory disease (see page 194) and fertility problems.

In rare cases bacteria can spread into the abdominal cavity and cause inflammation of the membrane surrounding the liver. If bacteria enter the bloodstream, general illness, fever and arthritis may develop. Gonorrhea may also lead to eye infections, since an infected person can pass the bacteria from the genitals to the eyes on their hands. Babies born to infected mothers may develop serious illness or become blind.

Can We Talk About It?

DISCUSSING YOUR SEXUAL HEALTH

Most people find it hard to know where to start when broaching the subject of a sexually transmitted disease. Raise the subject before you become physically intimate, in a place where you can talk privately and without interruption. Presenting your partner with the facts about your STD and its method of transmission makes it easier for him or her to understand its implications. You may feel ashamed, confused and guilty, or you may worry that your relationship could end when you talk to your partner, but try to be strong minded. If you put off telling the truth, you will betray your partner and you may put his or her health at risk.

Your partner may respond with anger or shock, but both of you should try to avoid making hasty decisions until the information has sunk in. If your partner wants to ignore the dangers of an STD, don't be persuaded; if you have unprotected sexual intercourse you will face responsibility later for passing on the disease. In a relationship that is worth maintaining, sexual pleasure should be able to wait until you find out about the necessary precautions.

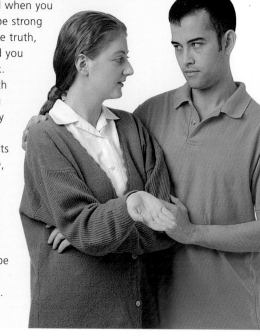

Doctors may take swabs from the vagina, urethra and anus (and sometimes the throat). The secretions are then cultured and examined microscopically. If the gonorrhea bacterium is present, antibiotics are prescribed. Some strains of gonorrhea have proved resistant to specific antibiotics. A strain of the infection known as Vietnam Rose, for instance, has evolved to produce an enzyme called penicillinase that inactivates penicillin. In such cases alternative antibiotics are prescribed.

NONSPECIFIC (NONGONOCOCCAL) URETHRITIS AND CHLAMYDIA

Nonspecific urethritis (NSU) is a condition that causes inflammation of the male urethra. It most commonly develops from a bacterium-like microorganism called *Chlamydia trachomatis* (other causes are shown on page 186). Chlamydia infections are transmitted by vaginal, anal and oral sex.

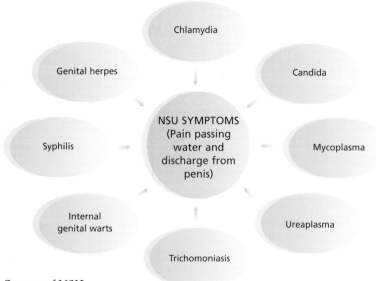

Causes of NSU
Nonspecific urethritis is very common. It can be caused by a wide range of the microorganisms responsible for STDs. Chlamydia is the usual cause.

In men the symptoms of chlamydial urethritis are burning pains when urinating and a urethral discharge that may be clear and watery or thick and yellow. Symptoms usually appear between one and three weeks after exposure to the infection. Some men may not have any symptoms.

Chlamydia in women is almost always symptomless, or the symptoms are so slight that they go unnoticed.

It is very important that chlamydia is treated promptly. In men it may lead to infections of the epididymis, prostate gland and rectum (see page 121). Occasionally it causes Reiter's syndrome, one of the main causes of arthritis in young men.

Because chlamydia is often symptomless in women, it may only be a complication of the infection that alerts a woman to the fact that something is wrong. As with gonorrhea, chlamydia can cause pelvic inflammatory disease (see page 194), which can result in blocked fallopian tubes and infertility. Chlamydia can be passed from mother to baby during childbirth.

The presence of a chlamydia/NSU infection in men is confirmed from swabs taken from the urethra. A slide is made from the swab and examined for pus cells. The

The Language of Sex
An old-fashioned term for sexually transmitted disease is venereal disease—in Latin "venereus" means "dedicated to Venus," the goddess of love and beauty. "The clap," a slang term for venereal disease, comes from the French word "clapoir," meaning "genital sore."

specimen may also undergo special tests to try to distinguish chlamydia from the other causes of NSU. Samples of a man's urine are also examined for pus cells, and a rapid urine screening test can identify likely chlamydia infection. Female partners of men with NSU must always be screened and treated—they will rarely have symptoms of infection. Doctors will prescribe antibiotics to treat the disease.

CHANCROID

A common STD in tropical countries, chancroid is becoming more and more common in the U.S. and Europe. Caused by the bacterium *Hemophilus ducreyi*, chancroid should not be confused with a chancre, which is one of the main symptoms of the first stages of syphilis.

The infection usually starts with a small painful spot or pimple that develops into one or more ulcers. In men the ulcers appear on the foreskin or around the glans of the penis and in women around or inside the vagina. In both sexes there may be swollen, tender lymph nodes in the groin. Chancroid may appear around the anus if anal sex with an infected partner has taken place. The first signs of infection appear about a week after contact, and the ulcers can grow rapidly if not treated. If women have ulcers inside the vagina, they may not be aware that they are infected.

On rare occasions, the lymph nodes in the groin become large and swollen and rupture to release thick pus. Because chancroid causes large open sores, it may facilitate HIV transmission. Chancroid is diagnosed by physical examination and analysis of material from the ulcer under a microscope. Antibiotics are used to treat the disease.

TRICHOMONIASIS

Caused by a single-celled parasite called *Trichomonas vaginalis*, trichomoniasis is usually passed from person to person by sexual intercourse, although transmission is thought to be possible via moist objects such as towels and washcloths. The parasite may be able to survive on damp or wet cloth for periods of up to 24 hours.

Men do not usually experience symptoms beyond mild urethral irritation. Women, in contrast, may have profound symptoms, such as a copious, foul-smelling, greenish yellow vaginal discharge. This can cause intense irritation and itching around the vaginal area. Intercourse may also become painful. Symptoms usually become apparent anywhere from a few days to a few weeks after contact with an infected person.

Trichomoniasis has been known to cause inflammation of the prostate gland in men. The infection can be passed from mother to baby during childbirth.

Trichomoniasis is diagnosed by identifying one of the parasites on a microscope slide, made when a swab is taken (see page 177) from the vagina or urethra. Treatment relies on antibiotics.

GENITAL WARTS

The virus responsible for causing genital warts is known as the human papillomavirus (HPV). More than 60 strains exist, a quarter of which cause warts that are sexually transmitted and appear only on the genitals. Genital warts are one of the most common STDs.

The wart virus can exist in a dormant or an active state. Warts can appear weeks or many months after initial exposure to infection—doctors do not know exactly what causes HPV to become active.

Genital warts start as tiny hard lumps on the penis, scrotum, vulva or anus that can be felt rather than seen (there may be one or several). They can also occur inside the vagina, urethra and rectum. Warts may stay the same size for weeks or months, or they may grow rapidly, becoming cauliflower-like in appearance. Rarely, they can grow large enough to block the vagina, urethra or anus.

Five types of the wart virus have been linked to cancerous growths of the genitals—particularly the cervix. A woman who has genital warts should have a Pap smear every six months to a year so that any abnormalities can be detected early. A test can confirm the presence of HPV on the cervix.

Warts on the external genitals can be diagnosed by physical examination. It takes a doctor experienced at recognizing genital warts to make a conclusive diagnosis, because there are other conditions, such as *Molluscum contagiosum* (a virus that causes small pearly lumps on the skin around the genitals and groin), that can resemble warts. Sometimes even normal lumps and bumps can be mistaken for genital warts. Wiping the potentially infected area with acetic acid (a vinegar-like liquid) can make the warts more easily visible.

The treatment for genital warts depends on how large they have grown, how persistent they are and whether they are internal or external. The first line of treatment for external warts is usually podophyllin solution applied directly to the warts and washed off later (podophyllin should never be applied to internal warts). Alternatively, a strong acid called trichloroacetic acid can be used. Large, internal or persistent warts

LYMPHATIC SYSTEM

The body's lymphatic system reacts to sexually transmitted disease in the same way as it does to other infections. Lymph nodes in the lymphatic system trap bacteria and viruses and then proceed to neutralize or destroy them. Sometimes the lymph nodes become enlarged in the process, which accounts for swollen glands.

Fighting infection
Lymphocytes attack and engulf foreign organisms that get past the body's outer defenses.

Lymphatics carry the protective fluid, lymph, around the body.

Lymph capillaries carry lymph into larger vessels.

Spleen produces antibodies and white blood cells that are carried around the body in the lymph.

Lymph nodes become swollen when the body is fighting infection.

187

SCABIES

Since it is not transmitted by sexual intercourse, scabies is not classified as an STD. However, most cases are acquired through skin-to-skin contact. Scabies is a microscopic mite that burrows under the skin, forming a small bump. It lays eggs and the new mites form thin, wavy burrow lines extending from the original site. The main symptom of the infection is intense itching. The preferred body areas of scabies mites include such warm, moist creases as in the armpits and on the genitals or the tops of the thighs. Scabies is treated with topical medications.

CAUSES AND TREATMENTS OF COMMON STDS

STD	CAUSE	TREATMENT
Syphilis	Treponema pallidum*	Antibiotics
Gonorrhea	Neisseria gonorrhoea*	Antibiotics
NSU/NGU	Multiple causes (see diagram page 186)	Antibiotics
Chancroid	Hemophilus ducreyi*	Antibiotics
Trichomoniasis	Trichomonas vaginalis**	Antibiotics
"Crabs"/pubic lice	Pediculosis pubis**	Topical insecticide
Scabies	Sarcoptes scabiei**	Topical insecticide
Genital warts	Human papillomavirus***	Podophyllin, trichloroacetic acid, electrocautery, cryotherapy, laser surgery
Genital herpes	Herpes simplex 1 and 2***	Antiviral drugs
Hepatitis B	Hepatitis B virus***	No specific treatment; bed rest, nutritious diet, preventive vaccine
Hepatitis C	Hepatitis C virus***	Interferon may prevent or slow progression of the disease.
HIV/AIDS	Human immunodeficiency virus***	Combinations of antiviral, immune-boosting and antibiotic drugs

*Bacterium **Parasite ***Virus

Pubic lice *Specially adapted claws allow the pubic louse to cling firmly to the hair of its host, where it feeds on the host's blood and lays its eggs.*

can be treated with cryotherapy (freezing), electrocautery (destroying tissue using an electric current) or laser surgery.

PUBIC LICE

Also known as "crabs," pubic lice are usually passed between people during sexual intimacy—not necessarily intercourse—but can also be caught from infested bedding, clothing, saunas and tanning beds.

Pubic lice feed on blood and can survive in a warm environment away from the body for up to 24 hours. Most people notice itching from lice bites between 5 and 14 days after infection. How quickly the infection is noticed depends on how many lice are present and how long it takes to become sensitized to the bites. People may also see small, brown, flat objects attached to their pubic hairs. The eggs are tiny and pale. Excessive scratching of the pubic area can lead to a secondary bacterial infection of the skin.

Pubic lice are easily recognizable under a microscope and can be treated with applications of prescription lotions or shampoos. Sexual partners should be treated, and bedding and clothes should be washed in very hot water or dry-cleaned.

GENITAL HERPES

There are two types of herpes virus, Herpes simplex 1 and Herpes simplex 2. Herpes simplex 1 typically causes cold sores around the mouth, and Herpes simplex 2 is usually responsible for the sexually transmitted herpes sores that affect the genitals. However, both types of virus can infect the lips and genitals.

Herpes viruses live in nerve cells, either lying dormant for the whole of a person's life or reactivating sporadically, causing new outbreaks of sores. Lowered immunity, stress, fatigue, strong sunlight and tanning beds can all cause the virus to reactivate.

The herpes virus is unpredictable. Some people become infected and never have symptoms, others experience an outbreak of sores within two days to two weeks of being infected, while still others suffer herpes attacks months or years after first becoming infected. It is generally accepted that the first attack of herpes is the worst and that subsequent attacks diminish in severity and occur further apart with time.

First symptoms include a tingling or itching sensation in the genital area, general malaise, a slight fever and swollen, tender lymph nodes. Sometimes there is discomfort on passing urine. Within hours, small painful blisters appear on the glans of the penis and the foreskin in men and the vagina, cervix or perineum in women. The blisters also appear on the anus and on the skin around the genitals. The blisters burst or are scratched open to reveal painful ulcers that can take between two days and three weeks to heal. Open blisters are highly infectious.

Genital herpes can spread to other parts of the sufferer's body—not just to the area around the lips and nose but to the eyes and throat as well. Women with herpes sores can pass the virus to their babies during delivery, and in the most serious cases this can cause brain infections and blindness.

A doctor can usually identify herpes sores by physical examination. The virus can be cultured from a swab taken from an ulcer.

Herpes is a chronic disease with no absolute cure. At the first signs of infection, doctors usually prescribe an antiviral drug such as acyclovir, which effectively limits the intensity and duration of symptoms and can be taken to prevent recurrence. If herpes attacks are linked to stress, relaxation therapies may help to prevent outbreaks.

HEPATITIS B

Like HIV, the hepatitis B virus lives in blood and body fluids and can be transmitted sexually, by sharing needles or by receiving an infected blood transfusion. It can also be transmitted on unsterilized needles used for acupuncture or tattoos. Hepatitis B is much more infectious than HIV, and researchers have isolated the virus in body secretions such as tears and sweat.

The hepatitis virus causes inflammation of the liver. Symptoms appear between six weeks and six months after infection (although the disease can sometimes be symptomless). Generalized aches and pains, mild fever, pain in the small joints of the hands and feet, tenderness in the liver area, nausea, loss of appetite, and jaundice may all be symptoms of hepatitis B.

Chronic forms of hepatitis B can lead to progressive liver damage and eventually cirrhosis (a condition in which the liver can no longer effectively remove toxic substances from the blood) and cancer of the liver. In places where hepatitis B is very common, such as Southeast Asia, tropical Africa and parts of China, it is estimated that 1 percent of those infected die from acute liver failure; 25 percent die from cirrhosis of the liver, and 5 percent die from cancer of the liver. There is an 80 percent chance that a woman carrying the hepatitis B virus will pass it on to her children at the time of their birth.

Hepatitis B can be diagnosed by a blood test. There is no cure, and treatment consists of bed rest and a nutritious diet. Doctors recommend vaccination for people who are at high risk, such as health-care workers, people who have multiple sexual partners and intravenous drug users.

HEPATITIS C

Hepatitis C is a highly aggressive strain of hepatitis. Like hepatitis B, it is transmitted in blood and semen, can stay in the body for life, and may cause liver damage. It does not, however, seem to be as easily transmitted sexually as hepatitis B or HIV. Twenty percent of hepatitis C sufferers develop cirrhosis, liver failure or cancer (10 percent die from these complications). There is no vaccine against hepatitis C. Worldwide, there may be 500 million hepatitis C carriers.

INFECTION WITH THE HEPATITIS B VIRUS

Hepatitis B can be symptomless, but an illness similar to influenza accompanied by jaundice and localized swelling is common. The virus may remain in the body and become chronic (persisting for a long time), so that the liver cannot function properly, and the risk of liver cancer is increased.

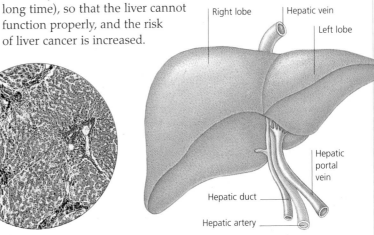

Right lobe • Hepatic vein • Left lobe • Hepatic portal vein • Hepatic duct • Hepatic artery

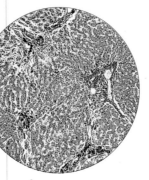

Damaged liver cells
Chronic hepatitis B can cause structural changes to the liver.

Inflammation of the liver
When inflamed the liver cannot fully perform its normal functions of regulating the levels of blood chemicals and removing toxins.

Female Disorders

Certain changes occur normally as part of a woman's reproductive life cycle: irregular bleeding around the time of puberty and menopause; amenorrhea during pregnancy; and premenstrual syndrome in the days leading up to menstruation.

If symptoms of female disorders do not coincide with certain stages of a woman's reproductive cycle, they may be signs of an underlying gynecological condition. Anything that is unusual or that does not have a straightforward explanation should be investigated by a doctor.

PREMENSTRUAL SYNDROME (PMS)

During the days leading up to menstruation, many women experience a combination of physical and emotional symptoms that have come to be known as premenstrual syndrome (PMS). For most women, the symptoms are minor, but in 10 percent of cases the symptoms are severe enough to disrupt normal life. PMS usually occurs between 5 and 12 days before a period and disappears within 24 hours before or after menstruation begins. The wide range of symptoms includes emotional instability, anxiety, depression, angry or tearful outbursts, bloating and swelling, constipation, headaches, breast tenderness, eating disturbances, changes in sexual desire, fatigue, and clumsiness.

Eating disturbances such as binge eating and craving sweet foods are typical PMS symptoms. These may be caused by low blood sugar that results from changes in the way the body processes carbohydrates.

Doctors have not identified exactly what causes PMS, but they believe it possible that high estrogen levels at the end of the menstrual cycle have a negative effect on the efficiency of the kidneys. This results in the retention of salt and water and the swelling of body tissues. Swollen tissues in the intestines may cause constipation and a bloated abdomen; swelling in the brain may cause headaches and emotional symptoms; breast swelling causes breast tenderness.

Some experts attribute PMS symptoms to an imbalance of progesterone and estrogen. Suppressing ovulation seems to cure PMS, which has led doctors to prescribe the contraceptive pill to sufferers. Another treatment is diuretic medication to eliminate excess fluid, but it has little effect.

Apart from prescription drugs, various natural remedies have proved effective for PMS symptoms. Many women report that homeopathy and yoga are helpful, as are high doses of vitamin B_6 (pyridoxine). High estrogen levels are thought to lead to reduced levels of vitamin B_6 in the body, which can cause low levels of certain brain chemicals, resulting in depressed mood and irritability. Gamma linoleic acid, found in evening primrose oil, is also recommended.

Easing breast discomfort *Simple massage techniques can ease premenstrual breast pain. Using the backs of the fingers, make gentle circling movements between the breast and the armpit.*

In addition to symptom relief, women suffering from PMS also need support and understanding from their partners and family.

MENORRHAGIA

Abnormally heavy menstrual loss of blood is known as menorrhagia. Blood loss can vary from woman to woman and even from one menstrual cycle to the next, but a woman suffering from menorrhagia loses more than 2.5 fluid ounces (80 ml) of blood per cycle. Heavy periods are not only uncomfortable, they can also cause iron deficiency anemia (in which the oxygen-carrying pigment in the blood falls below normal levels).

Menorrhagia is sometimes caused by the use of an intrauterine device (IUD) or by an imbalance of the hormones estrogen and progesterone (see page 129). Some women experience heavy bleeding around the time of menopause. Because heavy bleeding may also be caused by fibroids, polyps, endometriosis or malignancies, a doctor should always be consulted. Treatment for menorrhagia depends on the cause; doctors may recommend *DILATATION AND CURETTAGE (D&C)*, hormone treatment or, in severe cases, removal of the uterus.

DYSMENORRHEA

"Primary dysmenorrhea" is the term for the cramps that often accompany menstruation. It is common in teenage girls and young women and is thought to be due to a high level of the hormone prostaglandin, which is secreted by the uterine lining. Prostaglandin makes the muscular wall of the uterus contract, causing acute cramplike pains. Women who experience severe dysmenorrhea may secrete 15 times as much prostaglandin as women who do not suffer from period pain.

The pain of primary dysmenorrhea is usually centered in the lower abdomen and may radiate down the inner thighs and into the back. The standard treatment is pain-killing medication. Aspirin, which acts directly on prostaglandin, is often more

fact or fiction?

PMS is a psychosomatic problem.

Fiction. In the past some doctors believed that PMS was a psychological condition and treated women with tranquilizers. Today PMS is recognized as a problem with a physiological cause: tranquilizers should never be prescribed as a treatment unless there are other disorders.

effective than much stronger painkillers. Other antiprostaglandin drugs, such as the fenamic acids and naproxen, are prescribed specifically for painful periods.

Suppressing ovulation with the contraceptive pill is another way to control period pain. Some women also find that self-help measures, such as exercise or calcium supplements, alleviate pain.

Secondary dysmenorrhea is menstrual pain that arises for the first time in an adult woman whose menstrual cycle is well established. A medical reason usually surfaces for the sudden onset of menstrual pain, and secondary dysmenorrhea should always be investigated by a doctor. Common causes of the condition include endometriosis, fibroids and pelvic inflammatory disease (PID).

Menstrual cramps The muscular wall of the uterus, the myometrium, contracts to cause cramping pains during a menstrual period.

Uterine cavity

Myometrium

Endometrium

THE BODY'S HORMONE-PRODUCING SITES

The hormones responsible for sexual development and function are produced and secreted into the bloodstream by a number of different endocrine glands. The pituitary gland is known as the master gland, since it coordinates the activities of other endocrine glands.

Some menstrual disorders result from over- or under-production of hormones by the endocrine system.

Menstrual control Hormones that can influence the menstrual cycle are released by the brain, the ovaries, and the adrenal and thyroid glands.

Hypothalamus

Pituitary gland

Thyroid gland

Thymus

Adrenal gland

Kidney

Ovaries

CYSTITIS—AN INFLAMMATION OF THE BLADDER

Cystitis is one of women's most common complaints. The main symptom is frequent, urgent urination—typically a small amount of urine is passed and there is stinging or burning pain in the urethra. Sometimes blood or pus may be visible in the urine. Pain in the lower abdomen and back, and fever and malaise, may indicate that the infection has spread to the kidneys.

The causes of cystitis include infection, allergies and physical trauma. The bacterium that is often responsible for cystitis lives naturally in the bowel and rectum, but it can easily be transferred to the vaginal area or the urethra. Some women suffer cystitis symptoms in response to highly perfumed products such as vaginal deodorants or soap. Cystitis may also be caused by trauma to the urethra. Sometimes during sexual intercourse the penis hits the opening of the urethra, causing tiny abrasions. This can happen when the vagina is insufficiently lubricated.

Cystitis can become recurrent, but symptoms are often moderated by drinking large amounts of water. Over-the-counter medications that make the urine more alkaline will reduce pain on urination and render the urine less hospitable to bacteria.

If self-help measures for cystitis fail, a doctor may prescribe antibiotics. A urine sample will be taken to confirm that cystitis is due to bacteria and, if it is, which bacterium is responsible.

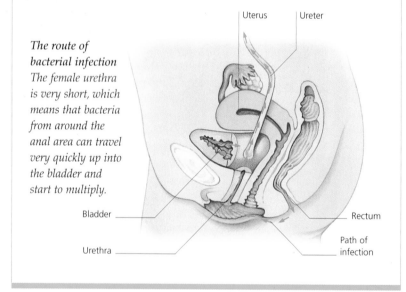

The route of bacterial infection
The female urethra is very short, which means that bacteria from around the anal area can travel very quickly up into the bladder and start to multiply.

Uterus | Ureter

Bladder

Urethra

Rectum

Path of infection

IRREGULAR BLEEDING

By their late teens, most girls have established a regular pattern of menstrual bleeding—they have a menstrual period at regular intervals and bleed for approximately the same number of days each month. If bleeding is erratic for three months or more, menstruation is termed irregular. During some stages of a woman's life, such as puberty and menopause, this is normal, but irregular menstruation at other times may be a sign of an underlying problem. Common causes of irregular menstruation include stress, hormonal imbalances and overweight or underweight. More serious causes include ectopic pregnancy, miscarriage, polycystic ovaries, cervical or uterine cancer, polyps, fibroids, thyroid gland problems, and endometriosis.

The treatment for irregular menstruation depends entirely on the cause. Unusual bleeding should always be investigated by a doctor, who may perform diagnostic techniques such as an endometrial biopsy or dilatation and curettage (D&C). These procedures will allow diagnosis of any abnormality or malignancy.

Contraceptives such as the pill and IUDs can cause some bleeding or spotting between periods. This is not true menstrual bleeding but a recognized side effect of these contraceptives. If bleeding is heavier than occasional spotting or persists for more than three months, a doctor should be consulted about the possibility of changing contraceptives.

AMENORRHEA

When a woman never menstruates, her condition is termed amenorrhea. There are two types of amenorrhea: primary amenorrhea, when menstruation has not started by age 16, and secondary amenorrhea, when a woman with an established menstrual cycle suddenly stops menstruating.

Primary amenorrhea may be caused by low body weight or a family tendency of late menarche (first menstruation). Rarely, primary amenorrhea is caused by a physical or hormonal abnormality.

Secondary amenorrhea is a normal result of pregnancy and a permanent result of hysterectomy and menopause unless hormone replacement therapy (HRT) is prescribed (see page 108). It can also signal problems such as endocrine or ovarian disorders, or *ANOREXIA NERVOSA*.

The contraceptive pill may cause temporary amenorrhea—when a woman stops taking the pill it can be months before her menstrual cycle returns to normal.

Amenorrhea should be investigated by a doctor. If no cause is apparent from either a woman's gynecological history or physical examination, then her thyroid, pituitary and ovarian hormone levels will be measured.

If a woman suffering from diagnosed amenorrhea wants to become pregnant, a doctor may need to prescribe a fertility drug that will induce ovulation.

CANDIDIASIS

This yeast infection occurs around the vulva and vagina and occasionally in the mouth. The symptoms of candidiasis are soreness around the vulva and vagina and a thick, white odorless vaginal discharge. There may be mild or severe vulval irritation.

Candidiasis occurs only when the normal, healthy environment of the vagina is disturbed. Taking antibiotics and using highly perfumed soaps on the genital area are two common ways of acquiring a yeast infection. An increase in the intake of dairy products has also been claimed to cause candidiasis. Rarely, candidiasis is a symptom of a serious illness, such as *DIABETES*.

Self-help techniques include gentle washing with warm water (never soap) and wearing loose cotton underwear. A tampon dipped in live yogurt and inserted into the vagina may be helpful, but some women say it is unlikely to help once the infection is established. Medical treatment for yeast infections consists of antifungal suppositories or creams or oral medication.

Candidiasis is not considered an STD, and can occur in women who are virgins. It can, however, be passed to a woman's sexual partner—a recurrent infection may mean that the couple is passing it back and forth.

FIBROIDS

Also known as myomas, fibroids are benign growths of the muscle tissue in or on the wall of the uterus. Fibroids may be symptomless, unless they have grown large enough to press on nearby organs, such as the bladder or the bowel, causing problems such as frequent urination or constipation. If a fibroid grows inward to the cavity of the uterus, it may result in heavy or irregular menstruation. Fibroids can develop to the size of a grapefruit or even larger, but they usually exist as small discrete lumps inside the wall of the uterus. Small fibroids should not have any effect on fertility or pregnancy. They should be monitored by a doctor, but do not normally require treatment.

The cause of fibroids is not known, but their growth seems to depend on estrogen stimulation. When estrogen levels fall at menopause, fibroids stop developing and typically decrease in size. Therefore, menopausal women with large fibroids may not be prescribed HRT.

Large fibroids that cause symptoms or present a danger during pregnancy because they obstruct the birth canal need medical attention. Occasionally fibroids can become infected or start to degenerate, causing pain. Rarely, fibroids can grow on stalks that can twist and cut off the fibroid's blood supply, causing acute pain. Severe fibroids may be treated by hysterectomy or by myomectomy (a surgical technique that removes the fibroids but leaves the uterus intact).

BACTERIAL VAGINOSIS

A vaginal infection known as bacterial vaginosis is caused by an overgrowth of the normal vaginal bacteria. The main symptom is a thin, gray discharge that has a fishy odor. Sometimes there may be vulval burning or itchiness, but the infection can also be symptomless.

Some women who use a diaphragm or condoms and spermicide (or women who have genital warts) experience repeated episodes of bacterial vaginosis—this suggests that the infection may occur more readily when there is a change in the acidity of the vagina.

Treating bacterial vaginosis with antibiotics usually eliminates the problem.

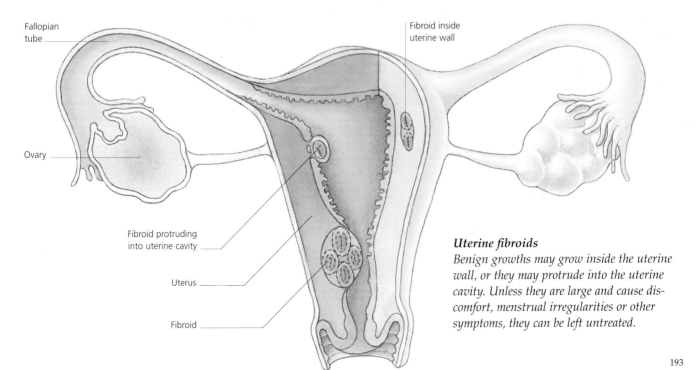

Fallopian tube

Ovary

Fibroid inside uterine wall

Fibroid protruding into uterine cavity

Uterus

Fibroid

Uterine fibroids
Benign growths may grow inside the uterine wall, or they may protrude into the uterine cavity. Unless they are large and cause discomfort, menstrual irregularities or other symptoms, they can be left untreated.

Bartholin's glands
Most women are not aware that they have Bartholin's glands unless these glands become infected and form a painful abscess that requires treatment. Situated on either side of the vagina, they secrete some of the lubrication produced during sexual arousal.

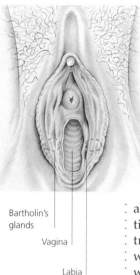

Bartholin's glands

Vagina

Labia

POLYCYSTIC OVARY

Also known as Stein-Leventhal syndrome, polycystic ovary is a condition in which the ovaries enlarge and contain multiple cysts. Sufferers experience scanty menstrual periods or do not menstruate and are often infertile. About 50 percent of women with polycystic ovary have excessive body and facial hair and a tendency to obesity. Typically, a girl with polycystic ovary disease menstruates normally for about two years after MENARCHE, then her periods become increasingly irregular and may cease completely.

Polycystic ovary is caused by an imbalance of the hormones that control ovulation. This imbalance prevents ovulation and causes excess production of testosterone. The condition is diagnosed from its symptoms and by physical examination, ULTRASOUND scans, LAPAROSCOPY and blood hormone tests.

Doctors usually prescribe hormone-based drugs to treat polycystic ovary—sometimes the contraceptive pill can effectively regulate a woman's menstrual cycle. Occasionally a wedge of ovarian tissue is removed surgically. The type of treatment depends on the severity of a woman's symptoms and whether or not she wishes to become pregnant in the future.

BARTHOLINITIS

There are two pea-sized glands on either side of the entrance to the vagina known as Bartholin's glands. Their normal function is to secrete lubricating fluid during sexual arousal. Occasionally they become infected, resulting in a condition called bartholinitis, which causes the glands to swell and become sore, sometimes to the extent that even walking becomes painful. If the duct from the gland becomes blocked as a result of infection and subsequent scarring, a Bartholin's cyst forms. This is a painless swelling of the gland, but the cyst is vulnerable to repeated infections.

Bartholinitis can be treated with antibiotics. In the case of a severe infection where an abscess forms, it may be necessary to drain the abscess surgically. If a Bartholin's cyst develops, it may be surgically removed or the duct leading to the gland may be turned into an open pouch. Even if both Bartholin's glands have to be removed, the vagina will still produce adequate lubrication during sexual intercourse.

CERVICAL AND UTERINE POLYPS

Polyps are small, fingerlike growths that occur on the mucous membrane of the uterine lining and the cervical canal. There may be one or many, and they are usually benign rather than malignant. Polyps may be symptomless, or they may cause bleeding between periods or bleeding after intercourse. If they ulcerate, they can become infected, causing a vaginal discharge.

Doctors treat polyps that cause troublesome symptoms with dilatation and curettage (D&C) or electrocautery (in which an electric current is used to destroy tissue), depending on whether they are in the uterus or the cervix. If a malignancy is suspected, the polyps will be removed and examined for evidence of cancer.

PELVIC INFLAMMATORY DISEASE (PID)

Infection or disease of the pelvic organs results from a variety of causes, most commonly sexually transmitted diseases (STDs; see page 184) such as chlamydia and gonorrhea. Less commonly, pelvic inflammatory disease (PID) may occur after miscarriage, abortion or childbirth. It is a serious infection that can permanently affect fertility. Infections can enter

OVARIAN CYSTS

Cysts in or on the ovaries are common and, in most cases, benign. They are usually fluid-filled sacs, although they can be solid growths. Many women who have ovarian cysts do not experience symptoms and may not know they have them. Most cysts need no evaluation or treatment. When symptoms occur, these are likely to be abdominal discomfort, pain during intercourse and irregular menstrual bleeding or amenorrhea. If a cyst twists or ruptures, there may be pain, nausea and fever. If a cyst causes discomfort or needs to be investigated for malignancy, it may be viewed or biopsied through a laparoscope or surgically removed.

Treating large cysts
Occasionally, when a cyst is very large, the whole ovary may need to be surgically removed.

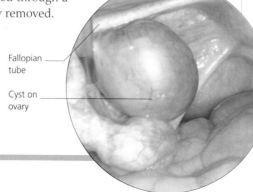

Fallopian tube

Cyst on ovary

the reproductive tract through the vaginal entrance and then travel up through the cervix and uterus to the fallopian tubes. The cervix is usually an effective barrier against any infection, but infecting organisms can enter when carried by sperm. Infection is also more likely during menstruation, when the cervical canal is not filled with protective mucus. Inserting objects into the uterus or the cervix (during abortion or the insertion of an intrauterine device, for example) increases the risk of PID. Occasionally PID can result from infection occurring elsewhere in the pelvis, such as the appendix.

PID should always receive medical attention. It can cause mild or intense abdominal pain, pain during intercourse, fever and vaginal discharge. Menstrual bleeding may be heavier, and spotting may appear between periods. Alternatively, there may be mild symptoms or none at all.

Treatment for PID consists of a course of antibiotics and bed rest. Taking time to rest and recover is important to minimize the possibility of scarring inside the fallopian tubes. In severe cases, a woman may need an operation to drain pus from the fallopian tubes, but this is unusual.

ENDOMETRIOSIS

The tissue lining the uterus is called the endometrium. Endometriosis is a painful gynecological condition in which fragments of endometrial tissue adhere to other parts of the body. Sites where this can happen include the fallopian tubes, the bladder, the ovaries, the lining of the abdominal cavity and even the intestines.

Displaced endometrial tissue is not malignant, but it does respond to a woman's menstrual cycle as if it were inside the uterus. This means it builds up and breaks down and bleeds in a monthly cycle. Because the blood cannot escape from abnormal sites, it may cause inflammation, pain and cyst formation. Scar tissue may form over the site of inflammation, causing adhesions in the abdomen.

Common symptoms of endometriosis are abnormal menstrual bleeding, abdominal pain and bloating, lower back pain, and pain during menstruation, intercourse and bowel movements. Endometriosis is also associated with infertility, and, as with other chronic painful conditions, sufferers may experience insomnia and depression.

The symptoms of endometriosis are relieved during pregnancy and frequently disappear permanently after a woman gives birth. Doctors often advise sufferers to try to conceive sooner rather than later if they know that they want children. Treating endometriosis with hormonal drugs can be successful, as can surgical treatments. Hysterectomy used to be recommended for women who did not want to become pregnant in the future, and many women have obtained relief in this way. If a surgeon removes the ovaries in addition to the uterus, a woman will go on to experience premature menopause (hormone replacement therapy is usually prescribed in such cases). Unfortunately, if the ovaries are not removed, any remaining endometrial tissue may still respond to the hormones they produce.

UTERINE PROLAPSE

The uterus normally rests in the abdomen, supported by muscle and connective tissue, and only the cervix projects down into the vagina. When the muscles and ligaments become weak, the uterus can sag, causing a condition called uterine prolapse.

Prolapse occurs in degrees. In a mild case of prolapse the uterus descends slightly, so that the cervix sits lower down in the vagina than usual. In more severe cases the

The complications of PID Infection can travel through the female reproductive tract, with consequences such as infertility.

The complications of PID

Blocked fallopian tubes, leading to subfertility

Blocked fallopian tubes, leading to ectopic pregnancy

Transmission of infection to baby at birth

Recurrent episodes of PID that do not respond to treatment

Spread of infection to blood, leading to septicemia

Possible sites of endometriosis Endometrial growths may occur on any of the pelvic organs. One explanation of endometriosis is that menstrual fluid, containing fragments of endometrium, flows backward into the fallopian tubes and into the pelvic cavity.

Bladder
Fallopian tube
Ovary
Vagina
Cervix
Uterus
Bowel

cervix moves a long way down the vagina— this can be extremely uncomfortable and penetration during sexual intercourse can become difficult or impossible. In very severe cases the cervix and part of the uterus can actually protrude outside the vaginal opening. There may be no symptoms of prolapse or there may be a dragging sensation in the lower abdomen. Backache may occur, and sometimes stress incontinence (leaking small amounts of urine on sneezing, coughing or exertion).

Overstretched, weakened muscles can be caused by pregnancy and frequent births. Weak pelvic muscles can be further weakened by heavy lifting, obesity, constipation or a chronic cough (all of which increase intra-abdominal pressure). Uterine prolapse is more common in postmenopausal women, as this is when pelvic muscles and ligaments slacken.

TYPES OF HYSTERECTOMY

The surgical removal of the uterus is known as hysterectomy. It is carried out when the uterus is severely prolapsed, when conditions such as endometriosis have not responded to other treatments or when cancer is present. In some types of hysterectomy a woman's ovaries are removed. This brings about premature menopause (unless the woman is postmenopausal).

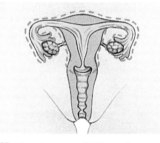

Hysterectomy and bilateral salpingo-oophorectomy
The fallopian tubes and ovaries are surgically removed as well as the uterus and the cervix.

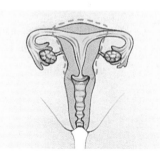

Hysterectomy
The uterus and cervix are removed, and the fallopian tubes and ovaries are left intact.

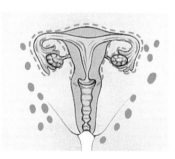

Radical hysterectomy
If a reproductive cancer has spread, the pelvic lymph nodes are removed as well.

In mild cases of prolapse, exercising the PUBOCOCCYGEAL (PC) MUSCLES by repeatedly contracting and relaxing them can help. Alternatively, a device called a ring pessary may be used to support the uterus, but this can erode the already thin urogenital tissues of postmenopausal women.

In severe cases surgery can repair the front and back walls of the vagina or repair defects in the muscles and connective tissue supporting the uterus. A hysterectomy may be advised for postmenopausal women.

CERVICAL CANCER

Early cervical cancer is symptomless and invisible to the naked eye. It is not until the cancer has progressed that symptoms such as bleeding between menstrual periods or after intercourse appear. Occasionally the malignant area becomes infected, causing a vaginal discharge. Pain is not a symptom until late into the disease, when the cancer has spread to other pelvic organs.

There are cell changes in the cervix, known as precancerous changes, that precede malignancy, and these can be easily detected by a Pap test. This involves collecting some cells from the cervix and examining them microscopically (see page 198). If more severe abnormalities are present, a colposcopy (a detailed examination using a magnifying device) may be recommended.

Treatment depends on the stage of the disease, whether it has spread and whether a woman is planning to have children in the future. Destruction of cancerous cells on the cervix can be carried out using heat (electrocautery and laser treatment) or cold treatment (cryosurgery). Hysterectomy is not usually performed unless the cancer has spread beyond the cervix.

ENDOMETRIAL CANCER

Cancer of the uterine lining, often referred to as uterine or endometrial cancer, is most common in postmenopausal women. Symptoms are irregular menstrual periods, spotting between periods or after sexual intercourse, and, if a woman is postmenopausal, a bloodstained discharge.

Endometrial cancer is diagnosed from a sample of endometrial tissue. It is often treated with a full hysterectomy (removing the ovaries, fallopian tubes and uterus). If the cancer has spread, RADIATION THERAPY and CHEMOTHERAPY may be given.

Breast Cancer

In its early stages breast cancer is usually detected as a small, painless lump found in the upper, outer quadrant of the breast (although it can be in any part of the breast). Occasionally the skin overlying the lump appears puckered or dimpled, and in advanced stages there may be ulceration. Other warning signs include a bloody discharge from the nipple or a nipple that is becoming inverted. Only one in five lumps is malignant, but regular breast self-examination is an important part of breast care and, if any unusual changes are noticed, immediate medical attention is critical.

The best time to conduct breast self-examination is just after the end of a menstrual period (the breasts are often lumpy in the days prior to menstruation). Women should look carefully at their breasts in a mirror as well as feeling them manually.

One way to detect breast cancer early is by mammography, which provides an X-ray image of the breasts. If a solid lump is detected, doctors will perform a biopsy, in which a piece of

tissue is removed to establish whether it is malignant. If it is, a biopsy of the lymph nodes will reveal whether the cancer has spread this far.

Radiation, chemotherapy and hormonal treatment may be recommended, and surgery (see below) will aim to preserve as much breast tissue as possible. Women may also be offered cosmetic surgery and breast reconstruction. With early detection and treatment of breast cancer, about 85 percent of women survive for at least five years.

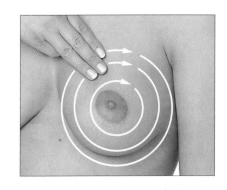

Looking at the breasts
Use a mirror to study the contours of each breast. Do this with the arms beside the body and then raised behind the head. Look for abnormalities.

Feeling the breasts
Pressing gently with the middle three fingers, trace large circles around each breast. Feel for unusual lumps. Check under the collarbone and armpits.

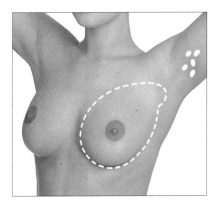

TYPES OF COMMON BREAST SURGERY

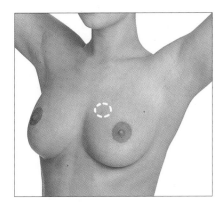

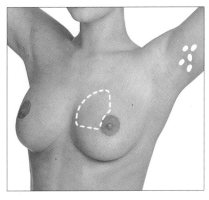

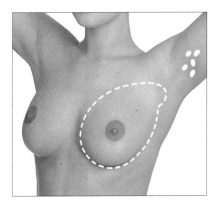

Lumpectomy
Removing a lump from the breast is a straightforward operation that leaves the whole of the nipple and most of the breast intact. As well as the lump, a surgeon will usually remove a small area of surrounding tissue.

Partial mastectomy
When a cancerous area is not confined to a small discrete lump, a partial mastectomy is usually carried out. A sample of the lymph nodes in the armpit may also be taken. Alternatively, they may be removed.

Total mastectomy
The whole breast, including the nipple and areola, and sometimes the lymph nodes, is removed. The only breast surgery that is more extensive than this is a radical mastectomy, involving the removal of muscles. This is rare.

THE PAP TEST—AN EARLY WARNING FOR CERVICAL CANCER

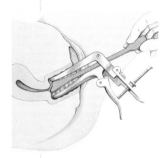

A Pap test is carried out in a doctor's office. The woman lies on her back or on her side with her knees bent, and an instrument called a speculum is inserted into the vagina. By opening the speculum inside the vagina, the doctor has a clear view of the cervix. A sample of cells is collected and transferred onto a glass slide for microscopic examination.

A woman should have her first Pap test when she turns 18 or after she starts to have intercourse. Women should discuss with their physicians how often the test should be done. Most physicians recommend annual tests to age 35 and, if there has been no abnormality, tests every two or three years until age 69.

Having a Pap test
A small spatula or brush is used to collect cells from inside the cervical opening.

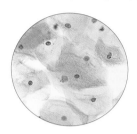

A healthy result
Cells taken from a healthy cervix are all roughly the same size and have small central nuclei.

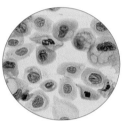

Signs of abnormality
Cancerous or precancerous changes include enlarged cell nuclei and coarse clumps and strands.

EARLY DIAGNOSIS

In the U.S., cancer of the genital organs accounts for approximately 250,000 deaths per year. It has been estimated that if women had Pap smears at least every two years and sought early medical advice about abnormal bleeding during and after menopause, around 100,000 lives could be saved over the next five years. Early diagnosis and prompt treatment are essential. Early diagnosis depends largely on women getting regular checkups and seeking early advice about unusual symptoms.

OVARIAN CANCER

Cancer of the ovaries is less prevalent than cervical or endometrial cancer, but it is responsible for more deaths each year than any other pelvic cancer. Although ovarian cancer can affect any age group, women aged 50 and over are most at risk. Ovarian cysts (see page 194) are not usually cancerous.

Ovarian cancer is often symptomless until it spreads elsewhere. Sometimes the first warning signs are digestive symptoms such as nausea. Alternatively, if the tumor spreads, fluid may collect in the abdomen, causing swelling.

A doctor will look for a diseased ovary using *LAPAROSCOPY*. He or she will examine ovarian tissue removed from an enlarged ovary to make a diagnosis. If malignancy is discovered, surgery involving the removal of the ovaries, fallopian tubes and uterus will probably be recommended. Radiation therapy and *CHEMOTHERAPY* are often recommended following surgery.

VAGINAL CANCER AND DES

Vaginal cancer was once almost unknown. Rarely was a woman diagnosed with the disease, and she was almost certainly in the 50-plus age range. When the incidence of vaginal cancer began to rise in the 20th century, especially in younger women, doctors realized that it was an iatrogenic disease (medically induced) caused by a synthetic hormone called diethylstilbestrol (DES).

DES was given to pregnant women by obstetricians to prevent miscarriage. Unfortunately, not only did it have no impact on rates of miscarriage, but it also became linked with an increased risk of a particularly rare form of vaginal cancer. The increased numbers of women who were being diagnosed with vaginal cancer more commonly had mothers who had been given DES during pregnancy.

The symptoms of vaginal cancer include a bloodstained vaginal discharge and spotting after intercourse. If the cancer has spread, other symptoms may include pain on intercourse, when urinating and when passing a bowel movement. Treatment depends on the extent of the disease, but hysterectomy and removal of the upper vagina and pelvic lymph nodes, followed by radiation therapy, is usually necessary.

OTHER FEMALE CANCERS

Two less common types of cancer affect the fallopian tubes and the vulva. Both affect postmenopausal women. Abnormal vaginal bleeding is the usual sign of cancer of the fallopian tubes. Persistent vulval itching or irritation can be a sign of cancer of the vulva. Sometimes there may also be a lump, an area of discoloration or an ulcer on the vulva. Some women delay seeking help about vulval irritation because of embarrassment, but if it is detected early, survival rates for vulval cancer are good.

Male Disorders

Although not susceptible to the same range of urogenital infections as women, men still need to be vigilant about genital health from a young age. While prostate cancer affects older men, testicular cancer is a young man's disease.

A combination of simple self-examination techniques and medical tests—particularly in relation to the testicles and prostate gland—should ensure that any disorders that threaten fertility or the health of the body are detected early.

PROSTATE PROBLEMS

The function of the prostate gland is to secrete a milky fluid just before ejaculation. This secretion helps to make semen liquid. The two most serious health problems that can affect the prostate gland are enlargement and prostate cancer (see page 202).

Enlarged prostate gland

The prostate gland begins to enlarge in men over the age of 50 and is a common source of problems in later life. When the prostate gland enlarges, it can put pressure on the urethra, making it harder for urine to flow from the bladder out of the body. A man may notice that it takes him a long time to begin urinating or that his stream of urine is very weak. The medical name for a normal enlarged prostate is benign prostatic hyperplasia (BPH). BPH is induced by a form of the hormone testosterone.

Other symptoms typical of BPH are frequent urination, especially in the middle of the night, and terminal dribbling: the flow of urine trickles out slowly at the end of urination rather than stopping abruptly. Men may experience abdominal discomfort and swelling if the bladder is not able to empty itself completely, and they may have difficulty in postponing urination. If the condition is more serious, bladder or kidney infections and kidney stones may develop, accompanied by fever, a burning sensation when urinating and blood in the urine.

A man complaining of urinary symptoms should be examined by a doctor, who will feel the prostate gland manually through the front wall of the rectum.

Treatment of BPH depends on the severity of symptoms. Although most older men have some degree of prostatic enlargement, the obstruction this causes to the urethra varies. Moderate symptoms may be treated with hormones or drugs that decrease the size of the prostate or relax muscles to increase urine flow. Men suffering from severe symptoms may need surgery to remove the prostate gland.

EXAMINING THE PROSTATE GLAND

Prostate examination
The walnut-sized prostate gland encircles the urethra just under the bladder. A doctor can examine the prostate manually through the front rectal wall.

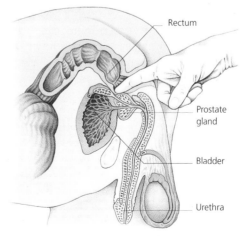

Rectum

Prostate gland

Bladder

Urethra

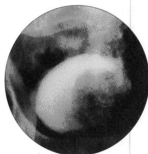

X-ray showing an enlarged prostate
The gold area in the center is the bladder. The violet circle in front of the bladder is the enlarged prostate gland.

TORSION OF THE TESTICLES

At puberty the testicles become more mobile and occasionally twist around on themselves, cutting off the blood supply. This is called torsion of the testicles and causes acute pain and sometimes discoloration and swelling in the scrotum. Urgent medical intervention is required to save the testicle and preserve fertility, as irreversible damage can be done in a matter of hours. If medical help is delayed, a doctor may have to surgically remove the damaged testicle. Fortunately, one testicle is sufficient for a man to remain fertile.

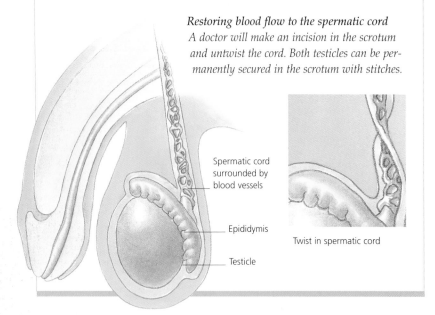

Restoring blood flow to the spermatic cord
A doctor will make an incision in the scrotum and untwist the cord. Both testicles can be permanently secured in the scrotum with stitches.

Spermatic cord surrounded by blood vessels

Twist in spermatic cord

Epididymis

Testicle

SWOLLEN TESTICLES

The testicles are two oval-shaped organs that hang in the scrotum behind the penis. They are fragile and highly sensitive and, due to their position, prone to injury. Swelling of the testicles or scrotum is usually harmless, but if caused by a bacterial or viral infection, it may lead to a lowered sperm count. Swellings should be investigated by a doctor whether large or small, uncomfortable or painless.

Prostatitis

Inflammation of the prostate gland, known as prostatitis, is usually caused by a bacterial infection that has spread from the urethra. It can affect men of any age. Bacteria from the rectum, and chlamydia (see page 185) are just some of the many organisms that can cause prostatitis.

The symptoms of prostatitis include pain when passing urine and increased frequency of urination. There may be fever, a discharge from the penis, and pain between the anus and the penis (the perineum) and in the lower back and genitals.

Prostatitis is diagnosed by physical examination of the prostate gland, analysis of urine, and milking of the prostate during digital rectal examination in order to push secretions into the urethra, where they can be collected on a swab. Prostatitis can take some time to clear up and tends to recur. Treatment for the condition includes long courses of antibiotics, bed rest and anti-inflammatory painkillers.

Prostatodynia is a relatively common problem characterized by the presence of prostatitis symptoms but the absence of any infection. Treatment is difficult, and painkillers may not help. The sufferer may find symptom relief by increasing the frequency of ejaculation, taking regular exercise, eating sufficient fiber to keep bowel movements regular, and avoiding cigarettes and alcohol. Hot baths and direct heat treatment to the prostate may also be soothing.

TESTICULAR PROBLEMS

The most serious problems include torsion of the testicles and cancer, both of which can necessitate surgical removal of the testicle. Other problems may cause subfertility.

Orchitis

Roughly 25 percent of men who have mumps as adults go on to develop orchitis—infection and inflammation of the testicles. The testicles become painful and swollen, and the man may run a fever. Orchitis sometimes leads to permanent damage of the testicle. If both testicles are affected, subfertility (see page 152) may result. Treatment of orchitis consists of painkilling drugs and ice packs to relieve pain. A physician should be consulted.

Inflammation of the testicle and epididymis—the network of tubes at the back of the testicles—is a separate condition called epididymo-orchitis, usually resulting from bacteria that have spread from an infection in the urethra. Doctors prescribe antibiotics to treat this condition.

Swellings

A painless swelling of the scrotum caused by fluid collecting in the tissues surrounding the testicles is known as a hydrocele. It usually occurs in men between age 45 and 60. A hydrocele can be small or large, sometimes growing to the size of a small melon.

Diagnosis involves physical examination and shining a light through the testicles to see if the swelling contains clear fluid. The hydrocele may be an abnormality that has existed from birth, or it may be due to an injury or an infection. On rare occasions, the cause is a tumor of the testicle.

If a hydrocele is large enough to cause discomfort, it can be drained using a needle and syringe. An irritant substance can then be introduced between the two layers to

fact or fiction?

Not ejaculating when sexually aroused causes pain and damage to the testicles.

Not ejaculating can cause temporary physical discomfort, but it does not cause damage. When men become extremely aroused but do not ejaculate, they may suffer from a harmless condition known as testicular ache or "blue balls." This occurs because of vasocongestion (increased blood supply to the genitals).

cause scarring where the hydrocele formed, which will prevent recurrence. If a hydrocele is found to be present at birth and does not disappear spontaneously, it may be surgically repaired by removing a small amount of tissue.

Another type of swelling in the scrotum is a hematocele. This results from an injury, such as a fall or blow to the testicles. The injury causes bleeding within the scrotum, and the subsequent buildup of blood causes the swelling. An operation is necessary to drain the blood.

Testicular swelling can also result from a varicocele—this is a collection of varicose veins, usually on the spermatic cord above the left testicle. It occurs when the blood cannot drain properly from the testicle. About 10 to 15 percent of all men suffer from this condition.

A varicocele may be painful, and it raises the overall temperature of the testicles, increasing the likelihood of male subfertility by lowering the sperm count. Doctors diagnose varicoceles through physical examination or from a heat-sensitive detector wrapped around the testicles. The latter can reveal a varicocele before it can be felt on clinical examination. In the presence of great discomfort, or if subfertility is a problem, surgical treatment may be carried out to remove the varicocele.

Sometimes painless swellings occur in the *EPIDIDYMIS*. The swelling, known as a spermatocele, is a harmless cyst filled with sperm and fluid. Spermatoceles need surgical removal only if they are very large or uncomfortable.

Undescended testicles

When a male baby is born, his testicles are examined by a pediatrician to see if they have descended into the scrotal sac. In about 3 percent of full-term and up to 30 percent of premature male babies, however, one or both testicles fail to fully descend—a condition known as cryptorchidism. Sometimes the condition resolves itself spontaneously after a few months. Hormone therapy may promote normal testicular descent. When hormone treatment fails, surgery may be recommended, usually before two years of age. The main risks associated with cryptorchidism are testicular cancer and possible subfertility later on during adulthood.

PENILE PROBLEMS

Although there are several sexually transmitted diseases (see page 184) that can cause a penile rash or discharge, everyday problems are relatively few.

Balanitis

Inflammation of the glans of the penis is called balanitis. The skin may feel sore and itchy and look red and moist.

There are several causes of balanitis. Yeast infections or trichomoniasis (see page 186) may infect the glans of the penis and, if not treated, can be passed back and forth between sexual partners. Allergic balanitis results from contact with a substance to which the skin is sensitive, such as spermicide, soap or laundry detergent. Other causes include poor hygiene and a tight foreskin that cannot be retracted to wash the glans. If the latter causes recurrent balanitis, circumcision may be necessary. Balanitis can also cause the foreskin to tighten by causing scarring within the foreskin.

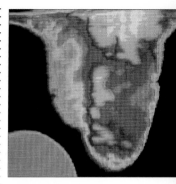

Taking testicular temperature A temperature map of a testicle containing a varicocele shows how this condition raises the temperature in and around the scrotum (orange and purple show hot areas). This can lower a man's sperm count.

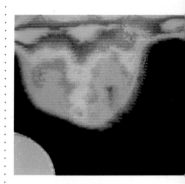

Normal temperature A healthy testicle shows a cool, even temperature pattern.

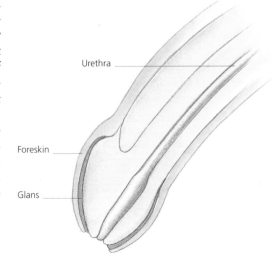

Urethra

Foreskin

Glans

Inflammation of the glans The area of the penis that is affected by balanitis is the glans. The glans is the smooth-skinned tip of the penis, which is covered by foreskin in uncircumcised men.

201

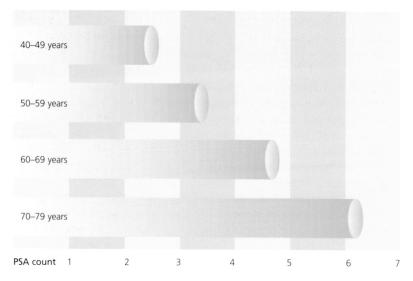

40–49 years

50–59 years

60–69 years

70–79 years

PSA count 1   2   3   4   5   6   7

Normal PSA levels
There is a substance in a man's blood known as prostate specific antigen (PSA). Although PSA levels increase naturally with age, there is a sudden jump if cancer develops in the prostate gland. By routinely measuring PSA levels in a man's bloodstream, a doctor can detect any malignancy early and take appropriate action. But many other things can elevate the PSA besides prostate cancer. Talk to your doctor about the pros and cons of PSA testing. Newer more specific prostate cancer tests are being developed.

Rarer, but more serious, causes of balanitis include diabetes (the excess sugar in the urine encourages bacteria to multiply, giving rise to infection) and malignant changes in the penis.

Diagnosis of balanitis is from physical examination and swabs (see page 177). The way a doctor treats balanitis depends on diagnosis. Yeast infections are treated with antifungal medications, and allergies are minimized by avoidance of the allergen. Symptoms can be relieved by bathing in a warm saltwater bath.

Doctors advise balanitis sufferers about personal hygiene. They recommend that men should clean the glans and foreskin regularly with plenty of warm water and gentle, non-perfumed soaps to avoid the possibility of future infection.

Phimosis

When the foreskin of the penis is so tight that it cannot be drawn back, the condition is referred to as phimosis. In very young, uncircumcised male babies, phimosis is quite normal. After six months, however, the foreskin should be able to be partially retracted. If it cannot, boys may experience difficulty urinating and recurrent infections such as balanitis. If phimosis persists into adulthood, it can make erections painful, and circumcision may be necessary to rectify the condition (see page 120).

MALE CANCERS

Malignant changes can affect the penis, the testicles, the scrotum or the prostate gland, but the latter type of cancer is the most common as men get older.

Prostate cancer

Cancer of the prostate gland is the most common type of malignancy in men. Screening for this type of cancer involves regular manual examination of the prostate. Blood tests and *ULTRASOUND* scans are controversial, and the pros and cons of these tests should be discussed with a physician. The blood test identifies a substance called prostate specific antigen (PSA). The presence of PSA in the blood can detect small cancerous changes before there are any symptoms, but it often gives a positive result in many men who do not need treatment. The risk of developing prostate cancer is three times greater than normal if an immediate relative has suffered from it.

Prostate cancer is slow-growing and does not normally produce symptoms until late in the disease. In fact, symptomless prostate cancer is often discovered during treatment for an enlarged prostate gland. If prostate cancer spreads, it usually moves to the lymph nodes and bones. Late symptoms are bone pain, *ANEMIA*, weight loss and blood in the urine or semen.

The treatments for prostate cancer include surgery, *RADIATION THERAPY*, *CHEMO-THERAPY* and hormone treatment to counter the action of testosterone.

Cancer of the testicles

Testicular cancer occurs most commonly in men between the ages of 20 and 35. Malignant tumors occur more frequently in the right rather than the left testicle, although in approximately 2 percent of cases tumors are present in both testicles.

The first sign of a problem is usually a firm, painless swelling in the testicle, although some men experience pain and inflammation. An undescended testicle that was not corrected before age two constitutes one of the main risk factors for testicular cancer. Another is having a brother with testicular cancer. The incidence of testicular cancer has risen dramatically over the last 30 years. It is the third leading cause of male deaths in the age group 20 to 40.

An ultrasound scan, which can usually discern a malignant tumor, is necessary for diagnosis. Blood tests are also used in diagnoses, since tumors may produce abnormally high levels of certain chemicals. A biopsy then confirms the diagnosis, and if there is cancer, the affected testicle is surgically removed. Radiation therapy and chemotherapy may also be implemented, especially if the cancer has spread.

If only one testicle is removed because of malignancy, the other testicle will continue to produce sperm, so that fertility should be restored to normal some two years after treatment. When detected early, testicular cancer is curable in most men.

Cancer of the penis

Penile cancer is quite rare and seen mainly in men over 50 years old. The tumor can start anywhere on the head of the penis as a small painless lump, often rough and wartlike in appearance. Sometimes the tumor may appear on the foreskin as a painful ulcer. The tumor gradually develops into a cauliflower-like mass. A highly malignant tumor may spread quickly, affecting the lymphatic glands in the groin within a few months.

Circumcised men have a slightly lower risk of penile cancer. Smoking and poor personal hygiene are risk factors for penile cancer. Other risk factors are thought to be phimosis and exposure to certain viruses and skin conditions.

Biopsy of the tumor will allow a doctor to diagnose penile cancer. Because penile cancer tends to spread slowly, small tumors require only removal of the tumor and radiation therapy. If the tumor is advanced, then more extensive surgery, involving removal of part or all of the penis, is required.

The worldwide incidence of cancer of the penis varies widely. In Europe and the U.S. it accounts for about 5 percent of all cancers, while in Asiatic countries it accounts for approximately 20 percent of cancers.

Cancer of the scrotal skin

Malignant changes in the scrotum have been directly linked with cancer-causing chemicals found in oil, soot and tar. Men, such as mechanics, who work with these materials are at risk if these substances repeatedly come in contact with the scrotum. Such workers are advised to wear protective clothing and to wash all residue off their hands before handling their genitals.

The cancer starts as a painless lump or ulcer on the scrotum. Lymph nodes in the groin may swell if the cancer spreads. Treatment includes surgery, radiation therapy and chemotherapy.

TESTICULAR SELF-EXAMINATION

Men should carry out monthly examinations of their testicles beginning at age 14 to 16. The exams enable them to detect lumps and swellings that may be signs of cancer. Testicular cancer, if diagnosed early, is one of the most easily cured forms of cancer.

During or after a bath or shower is the best time to examine the testicles, as the scrotal skin is relaxed. It should be loose and move freely over the testicles, making it easy to feel the normally smooth surface of the testicles between the thumb and the forefinger.

The epididymis should be identified as the small, soft, slightly lumpy area at the back of the testicles. Signs to look out for are lumps, areas of pain or discomfort, swelling in either testicle, or ulceration of the scrotal skin. All of these should be considered worthy of medical examination. All young men should be taught self-examination procedures, just as young women are taught to conduct a breast self-examination.

The site of a possible tumor
Tumors are most likely to be found in the right testicle. Cancerous lumps usually feel firm to the touch and are not tender when pressed.

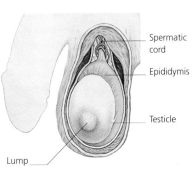

The examination technique
Palpate each testicle in turn, with the index and middle finger below the testicle and the thumb on top. Gently rolling the testicle between fingers and thumb will reveal any abnormalities.

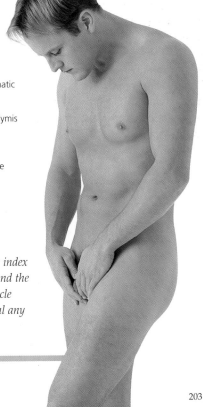

Abnormal Sex Organs

Rarely, something happens to a developing fetus that results in sexual abnormalities, such as the presence of both male testicles and female ovaries. Usually a defect in the chromosomes or a hormonal imbalance is responsible.

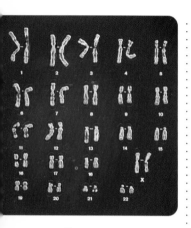

Chromosome pairs
Defects with chromosomes are rare: most people have the full complement of 23 pairs.

FETAL MASCULINIZATION

A rare condition known as congenital adrenal hyperplasia occurs in female fetuses with overactive adrenal glands (see page 191). Adrenal glands produce steroids, some of which have a similar effect to male sex hormones. Baby girls may be born with a penis and scrotum. Corrective surgery and hormone treatment ensure normal female development.

Sexual abnormalities may be obvious as soon as a child is born, but others may not be discovered until puberty. Surgery on the sex organs and hormonal treatment can often help assign a gender to people whose physical sex is ambiguous.

HERMAPHRODITISM

A person with both male and female genitals, or ambiguous gender, is known as a hermaphrodite. Hermaphroditism is present from birth and is caused by an imbalance of hormones in the mother's uterus during fetal development. The condition is treated with surgery and hormone therapy.

There are four general types of hermaphroditism. True hermaphrodites, a rarity, have ovaries and testicles, and also ambiguous external genitalia that seem to be both male and female. An affected child is usually raised as a boy.

In agonadal hermaphroditism the testes and ovaries are absent or underdeveloped. The genitals are clearly male or female, but the chromosomal sex of the individual (see page 146) is opposite to the genital sex.

Male pseudohermaphrodites have testicles and female genitals, whereas female pseudohermaphrodites have ovaries and male genitals. The most common cause of male pseudohermaphroditism is androgen insensitivity syndrome (AIS). This occurs when the fetus is insensitive to the male sex hormones that are produced by the developing testicles. Therefore no penis forms and the baby has the outward appearance of a girl. Surgery can remove the testicles and construct or lengthen the vagina. Menstruation and conception are impossible, but hormone therapy ensures an otherwise normal life as a woman.

TURNER'S SYNDROME

Girls with Turner's syndrome have only one sex chromosome: X instead of XX (see page 146). They are clearly female at birth but may have other physical abnormalities, such as webbed neck, short stature or congenital heart disease. At puberty, these girls do not menstruate or grow breasts. Female hormones may improve growth and breast development.

KLINEFELTER'S SYNDROME

Rarely a boy may have an extra chromosome: XXY instead of XY (see page 146). Klinefelter's syndrome may pass unnoticed until puberty. Boys who are affected have small testicles that produce little or no sperm. They may also have a female body shape with wider than average hips and enlarged breasts. Surgery to remove breast tissue, combined with testosterone therapy, helps to enhance a masculine appearance.

The Language of Sex

The word "hermaphrodite" derives from the minor Greek god Hermaphroditus, the son of Hermes, messenger of the gods, and of Aphrodite, the goddess of love. The nymph Salmacis fell in love with him, and the gods answered her prayers by uniting them in one body with both male and female qualities.

OVERCOMING PROBLEMS IN LOVE & SEX

Causes of Sexual Problems

Sexual problems can be caused by physical factors such as tiredness, illness or alcohol intake, or psychological factors such as anxiety or depression. Sometimes the physical and psychological causes of problems are intertwined.

When a person is in poor or reduced physical health, his or her body cannot respond to sexual stimuli in the normal way. General fatigue and hormonal disorders can reduce sexual drive, and damaged nerves and fibrous tissues, or malfunctioning valves in blood vessels, can interfere with normal sexual response. Sex drive is also closely linked to an individual's psychological state.

Sex books There is a diverse range of sex books available. Some aim to be titillating; others take a self-help or educational approach. Looking at a sex book with a partner is one way to initiate a conversation about sex.

SEX AND MEDICATION

A number of prescription and over-the-counter medications have side effects that can be detrimental to a person's sex life. Many of the medications that are prescribed for high blood pressure (hypertension) can reduce libido. Ten to 15 percent of men taking methyldopa, one of the most commonly used drugs for hypertension, have re-duced libido and erection problems. High doses of methyldopa are known to cause orgasmic problems in women.

Medication for angina reportedly causes erection difficulties in about 10 percent of users. More everyday medications such as antihistamines, which dry up nasal secretions in cold and hayfever sufferers, can inhibit vaginal lubrication in women, making sex painful (see page 216). Diuretics, which are commonly prescribed for congestive heart failure, can decrease sexual desire and cause erection problems in 20 to 25 percent of male users. Medication for peptic ulcers (such as cimetidine) can reduce testosterone levels and cause impotency problems in about 12 percent of male users; and medication used to treat epilepsy can cause sexual dysfunction and reduce sexual desire in both men and women.

For people who experience sexual problems when taking a new prescription drug, a doctor may reduce the dosage or even change medications. Individuals react differently, and not everyone will experience the same side effects from the same medication. In most cases, a drug can be found to treat a particular illness that does not affect sexual behavior and response.

SEX AND ALCOHOL

Although alcohol consumption can decrease sexual inhibition in men and women, its negative effects on sexual performance have been widely documented. Alcohol depresses the nervous system, so men and women who have had several or more drinks have impaired sexual responses, making it difficult to achieve an orgasm. Alcohol also dilates small blood vessels all over the body, which means that there is less engorgement of blood in the penis and in the walls of the vagina. This can inhibit sustained erection in men and vaginal lubrication in women. Decreased vaginal lubrication is also caused by the dehydrating effect of alcohol consumption.

According to sex therapists Masters, Johnson and Kolodny, 40 to 50 percent of all male alcoholics have low or nonexistent sex drives. This is because the toxins in alcohol directly affect the male sex hormone testosterone; the testes shrink, and the production of testosterone is greatly decreased. In addition, these smaller amounts of testosterone are quickly broken down in the body by increased levels of liver enzymes, another side effect of alcoholism. In female alcoholics, 30 to 40 percent report that they have problems with sexual arousal, and about 15 percent report an inability to reach orgasm or a significant reduction in the intensity or frequency of orgasm.

LONG-TERM ILLNESSES

Multiple sclerosis, *DIABETES*, arthritis, heart disease and circulatory problems can all have adverse effects on sexual function and desire. Multiple sclerosis (MS), in particular, is a progressive, serious condition of the nervous system. About 25 percent of male MS sufferers experience problems in erection and orgasm, and about the same number of women suffer from reduced sensitivity in the genital area. Long-term illnesses do not necessarily prevent sexual intercourse, but patience, understanding and an ability to be flexible, especially by a sexual partner, are necessary.

PSYCHOLOGICAL PROBLEMS

Although some sexual problems, such as vaginismus (see page 216) or impotence, may seem to be physical in nature, they are often psychologically induced, with fear, anxiety or guilt at their root.

Sexual satisfaction is closely linked to an individual's state of mind. When a person is confident and happy, he or she is usually able to appreciate the positive and pleasurable aspects of life, including sex. To enjoy sex, an individual must be able to let go of inhibitions, be intimate with a partner and feel relaxed and confident about his or her body. However, when someone is unhappy,

insecure or subconsciously distracted, his or her sexual behavior will be adversely affected. Worries about work or money may create feelings of anxiety, as may relationship problems—not getting along well with one's partner, doubting his or her faithfulness, or feeling guilty about being unfaithful oneself.

Problems may arise as well from low sexual self-esteem. A person who perceives himself or herself as unsexy, unattractive, inexperienced, too old or too overweight to give or receive sexual pleasure is likely to find that pleasure elusive.

Negative views about sex can also impede enjoyment. Parents, for example, may pass on the belief to their children that sex is immoral. Masters and Johnson, who say that men from strict religious backgrounds often have erection problems, stress that it is not the religious teachings that cause problems but the associated attitude that sexual pleasure is sinful.

Feelings of chronic stress or anxiety

Fear of sex resulting from past sexual trauma or abuse

SEXUAL PROBLEMS
State of mind can have a profound effect on an individual's sexual responses. There are many psychological causes of low libido and other problems.

Nervous disorders or depression

Relationship problems, including boredom

Childhood trauma
One of the most compelling reasons for sexual problems in adulthood is sexual violation in childhood. Children who have been abused need sensitive counseling from a specialist.

Some individuals may have unresolved feelings about childhood situations—parents divorcing, being unpopular or bullied at school, or simply feeling unloved by the people around them when they were growing up. Although these issues may not seem to be directly related to sex, they can have a profound effect on self-esteem and behavior during adulthood.

Men and women who felt unloved, abandoned or rejected during childhood, for example, may try to compensate for such loneliness by becoming sexually promiscuous. For them, many sexual partners may be required before they can feel desired, needed and loved, and even then the satisfaction may be only temporary. Promiscuity works as a defense against loneliness, but although the individual acts of sex might be enjoyable, an ongoing sexual relationship will be difficult to maintain when fueled by insecurity. Sex can become a way of convincing oneself that a relationship exists,

fact or fiction?

Good sex cannot be planned.

Fiction. Although sex is a natural human activity, sexual pleasure is not always as easy and spontaneous as people expect it to be. Good sex is often a result of knowledge and planning: knowledge about the way the body works sexually and about the sexual needs and responses of you and your partner; planning for sex by thinking about mood, setting and practical considerations as contraception.

rather than being an expression of that relationship. Alternatively, people who have had problematic childhoods may withdraw from sexual relationships completely.

Sex and depression

Doctors and psychologists make a distinction between depression and depressed mood. The former refers to a clinical illness, while the latter refers to the downcast feelings that most people temporarily experience in response to everyday bad news. Depressed mood does not have a profound effect on an individual's ability to function sexually in the way that clinical depression does. Clinical depression can be emotionally, socially and physically incapacitating and, in extreme cases, can lead to suicide. Often treated as a medical condition because of its physical symptoms and the feelings of malaise it produces, depression causes the disturbance of an individual's psychological well-being. Depression can develop as a response to certain life events, such as the breakup of an important relationship, bereavement or unemployment, or it can appear for no clear reason.

The feelings of melancholy, hopelessness and inadequacy that characterize depression can cause a sufferer to stay at home alone all day. A depressed person may lose interest in life to the extent that such previous desires as food, sleep, socializing and sex no longer hold any appeal.

Although having no interest in sex does not necessarily mean that someone is depressed, it is one of the hallmarks of depressive illness. A doctor suspecting that a patient suffers from clinical depression may well ask questions about the individual's libido.

Depression is an illness that can have a marked effect on a person's sense of self—how he or she values or feels about himself or herself. The ability to derive pleasure from sexual activity is closely linked to feelings of self-esteem and self-worth. Any kind of depressive illness is likely to have a negative effect on sexual behavior.

Although lack of sexual desire is a common symptom of depression, the situation may work in reverse, so that the sexual problem precipitates the depression. For example, a man who is suffering from impotence and whose sexual partner is unsympathetic can begin to doubt his masculinity. As his self-esteem falls, feelings of rejection and worthlessness increase, and depression may set in.

Past sexual trauma

Intimacy can make both men and women feel vulnerable. Successful sexual relationships depend on partners who feel relaxed, secure and trusting with each other. In healthy adult relationships, trust and security evolve over a period of time, but people who have had damaging sexual experiences in the past may find it difficult to relax enough to allow a normal sexual relationship to develop.

If a child is abused, his or her natural instinct to trust will be damaged, and later sexual development and adult relationships may be adversely affected. This is especially so when the childhood abuse includes sexual abuse.

Childhood sexual trauma can range from indecent physical exposure to experiences of violent adult sex. Although more girls than boys are known victims of childhood sexual abuse, boys may also be targets of adult sexual interests.

Children who have been involved in adult sexual activity of any kind frequently find themselves confused about sex and sexuality when they become adults. They may harbor great anxiety about sexual behavior, or they may suffer unresolved guilt and shame as a result of their past experiences. Either feeling can make normal sexual relationships difficult or impossible.

Sexual trauma also occurs during adulthood. Men and, more often, women may find themselves the subject of unwanted sexual attention—from verbal harassment to physical molestation or rape. Whether these events are psychologically or physically invasive, or both, the resulting sexual trauma can be extremely difficult to overcome. Rape victims commonly have a sense of acute violation and loss of control over

their own bodies and lives. Sometimes sexual trauma can be so great that long-term psychological help is needed; even then the effects of abuse may last, causing depression and sexual and emotional problems.

Stress and sex

A certain amount of stress in life is normal. In order to face certain challenges, the body's chemical balance alters and a surge of adrenalin is released into the bloodstream. The body can cope with this altered chemical balance for a short period of time, but when everyday pressures build up without relief, stress becomes chronic. For men and women in such circumstances, life is so stressful that any sort of spontaneous enjoyment can become impossible.

Chronic stress especially damages good sexual relationships. Its effects are slow and insidious. Sexual interest, desire and activity may decrease to such an extent that a partner begins to doubt his or her attractiveness. Male sufferers often find themselves experiencing erection problems.

When the cause of stress is obvious—for example, the sudden loss of employment by the main earner in a household—a strong personal and sexual relationship may be a source of strength and reassurance. More often than not, however, sudden stress can expose the weaknesses in a relationship. Issues that have never been addressed or properly resolved, such as how to manage money or to cope with strained family relationships, become a focus of tension that inhibits sexual interest.

The stress scale
Different life events bring about different levels of stress. People who are experiencing extreme emotional stress should expect their libido to be adversely affected. The Holmes-Rahe stress scale (summarized below) is one attempt to quantify the amount of stress associated with different life events.

High
- Death of a husband or wife
- Death of a family member
- Divorce
- Marital separation
- Jail sentence or being institutionalized
- Illness or injury

Medium
- Marriage
- Loss of job
- Retirement
- Health problems of close member of family
- Major change at work
- Change of financial status

Low
- Child leaving home
- In-law problems
- Trouble with employer
- Change in working hours
- Change in social activities
- Holiday season

Sexual boredom

The ancient Greeks recognized boredom as a very dangerous state, one that created a desire to act impulsively in ways otherwise considered foolish, simply to escape from a mundane state of inactivity. An educated and thoughtful man prided himself on having enough interests to prevent him from sinking into boredom.

Can We Talk About It?

SEX IS BECOMING ROUTINE

Instead of blaming your partner for being no good in bed, discuss the routine nature of your lovemaking as a problem you both have. Start by acknowledging that you also contribute to the boredom by not introducing anything new. Then ask your partner to tell you specifically what he or she would like you to do to make sex more interesting. Remind each other of the early days of your relationship and what you then found erotic. Recall your early sexual encounters with each other, where they happened and who initiated them. Ask each other what you enjoyed most during that time. Be completely honest in your responses. Agree with your partner to give each other a pleasant sexual surprise in the coming week. This could be sharing a bath or finding a new place to enjoy a seduction. These experiences should appeal to you and your partner's senses of taste, smell, touch, sight and hearing. Anything unusual could arouse both partners' interest. At the end of the week, tell each other what you enjoyed about each other's surprises and why.

Many good books and videos exist on sexual behavior, with advice about specific sexual techniques and ways to keep romance and eroticism alive in your relationship. Ask your partner to buy one with you and look at it together, discussing what you like and don't like; then make a date to try out some new ideas.

Sexual boredom usually results from lovemaking that has become routine and predictable. If one or both partners lose interest, lovemaking soon becomes unimaginative and unfulfilling. Either partner may look elsewhere for sexual excitement and embark on an affair. The sexual excitement surrounding an illicit relationship very often forms its basis. When the relationship becomes more established or legitimate, the sexual excitement disappears, leading to boredom yet again.

The key to preventing boredom is to consciously maintain an interest in a sexual partner and exercise variety, fun and spontaneity in the relationship. Sexual excitement comes naturally at the beginning of a relationship but frequently declines when a couple stop making time for each other or start taking each other for granted. Initial sexual excitement may lead a couple into cohabitation and marriage, but if they do not devote time and energy to their relationship, sex may become a low priority.

Sexual ignorance

Masters and Johnson believe that there are two main causes of sexual problems—ignorance and fear. Their published works have done a great deal to dispel both, but many people remain ignorant on both an emotional and a physical level.

People do not necessarily find sex naturally easy or instantly fulfilling. Lack of knowledge about the sexual anatomy or physical response of a sexual partner can provoke intense anxiety, which can hinder spontaneous sexual expression.

Sexual ignorance is common—and virtually inevitable—in people who are having sexual relations for the first time; but lack of sexual knowledge can cause problems at other times of life as well. Many men and women are ill informed about the sexual changes associated with aging. Men may not realize that slower and weaker erectile responses coupled with a decreased urgency to ejaculate are entirely normal. Similarly, women may be unaware that they will produce less vaginal lubrication as they get older. If men and women respond to these changes with anxiety, they may exacerbate or even create sexual problems.

Individuals may also feel reticent about having sex if they are ignorant about such issues as contraception or STDs.

Male Problems

At some time in their lives, most men will experience some anxiety about their sexual performance, or temporarily lose interest in sex. Two common sexual problems are an inability to maintain an erection and premature ejaculation.

Some sexual problems can be a short-lived response to nervousness or an overconsumption of alcohol. Others may prove to be long-term or chronic and need to be diagnosed and treated by a professional, such as a doctor or sex therapist.

LOW SEX DRIVE

Men vary greatly in the frequency of their sexual activity. Some men claim to think about or desire sex almost all the time; others feel satisfied by making love every other week. Throughout a man's life, sexual desire increases and decreases, depending on his age, his life situation, his stress levels, his relationships and many other interconnected factors. In terms of age, a man's sexual peak usually occurs around his late teens and early twenties.

Male sexual drive is determined by both physiological and psychological factors. Sexual desire can be suppressed with drugs that inhibit the production of sex hormones—this treatment has been used for male sex offenders. Similarly, people with disorders such as Klinefelter's syndrome (see page 204), which causes low levels of sex hormones, have low libidos.

Occasionally men have sexual phobias that inhibit their libidos. Such phobias can result from past unpleasant sexual experiences (including sexual abuse), low self-esteem, a fear of physical intimacy, or the entrenched belief that sex is wrong or dirty.

In many cases men simply have a naturally low sex drive that cannot be linked to a hormonal disorder or a sexual phobia. This need not be treated as a problem unless the man's partner has a significantly higher sex drive and their different sexual needs give rise to tension and disagreement.

The treatment for low sex drive depends on whether the underlying cause is physical or psychological. If a man and his partner are happy with relatively infrequent intercourse and do not perceive lack of libido as a problem, no treatment is necessary.

Reduced sex drive

Although low sex drive is not necessarily a problem, reduced sex drive may be. Reduced sex drive indicates that a man's libido was once satisfactory to him and his partner but has now dropped to a dissatisfying level. This drop can be precipitated by such factors as relationship difficulties, a new baby in the family, work or financial worries, fatigue, or grief. Ill health and poor diet can also reduce sex drive.

A good counselor or sex therapist can help to restore sexual desire by identifying the underlying causes of reduced sex drive and working through them with a client.

ERECTION PROBLEMS

An inability to have or maintain an erection is known as erectile insufficiency, but the term "impotence" is still the most widely used when erection problems are described. Although an erection may not be an

Sources of stress
Men who are stressed may find they become less interested in sex. Such multiple commitments as meeting work deadlines and childcare can have a detrimental effect on an individual's personal life.

Treating Erection Problems

Many treatments are available for men who cannot achieve a natural erection for physical reasons. Some doctors recommend injecting the penis with such drugs as papaverine. Drugs like this dilate the penile arteries, causing a sudden increase in blood flow to the penis and, therefore, an erection. Men are taught to inject themselves at home, and the resulting erection typically lasts between one and two hours. Penile injections do not work in all cases of erection problems, however, and they sometimes cause pain and scarring.

One alternative is an implant, which is surgically installed by a urologist. Some implants can be inflated with air when an erection is desired. Others consist of flexible rods that leave the penis in a perpetual state of semi-erection. The most sophisticated (and expensive) implant consists of three pieces: a squeeze pump in the scrotum, a reservoir of liquid stored under the abdominal skin and an implant in the penis. A less invasive method is the penile splint, a sheath reinforced with plastic "ribs" that covers the penile shaft but not the glans.

USING A PUMP DEVICE

A common device that men with erectile problems can use to induce an erection is a vacuum pump. The penis is lubricated with a water-soluble jelly and then inserted into the pump. The air is drawn out of the pump, and the resulting vacuum causes blood to rush into the penile vessels, making the penis erect. A penile ring placed on the end of the pump is then slipped onto the penis to maintain the erection. The ring should not be left on for more than 30 minutes at a time.

The vacuum pump
This device can enable lovemaking by producing an erection (ejaculation may not occur as heavily as usual). It is used in conjunction with a penile ring that stops blood from flowing out of the penis.

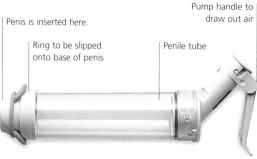

Pump handle to draw out air

Penis is inserted here.

Ring to be slipped onto base of penis

Penile tube

Side loops help positioning and removal of ring.

Penile rings
Rubber rings can be used independently of vacuum-pump devices by men who can gain but not maintain erections. They come in various sizes.

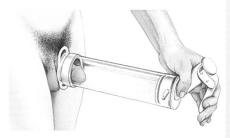

1 The penis is inserted into the cylinder, which should be held tightly against the body to make an airtight seal. The cylinder handle is pumped up and down.

2 Once an erection has been achieved, the penile ring is eased off the plastic sleeve and onto the base of the penis. This prevents the penis from becoming flaccid.

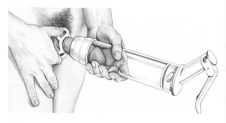

3 A release valve is pressed to allow air to fill the vacuum so that the cylinder can be removed. After sexual intercourse, the ring is removed from the penis.

absolute requirement to prove a man's potency, it is considered by many men and women as the clearest sign of a man's strength, virility and sexual identity. This is why difficulty in attaining an erection evokes feelings of embarrassment, shame, anxiety and inadequacy in a man.

An erection occurs when blood flow increases and swells the spongy tissues of the penis (see page 119). The increase in blood flow is triggered by physical or psychological stimulation. A man's inability to achieve or maintain an erection can occur as a result of such physical factors as impeded blood flow (as in the case of diabetes), overconsumption of alcohol, acute fatigue or a drug side effect.

Erections generally decline in frequency and firmness as a man ages, but, depending on his lifestyle, a 70-year-old man may still be able to achieve an erection regularly. Heavy smoking, eating and drinking, however, all have adverse effects on the erectile tissues in the penis.

Psychological causes of erection problems can range from boredom and lack of interest in a partner to feelings of guilt and anxiety. Any activity, such as putting on a condom, that draws attention to the firmness of an erection can lead to self-consciousness and *DETUMESCENCE*. Sometimes a physical cause can develop into a psychological one. For example, a man who on one occasion fails to achieve an erection because he has drunk too much alcohol may feel that he has failed sexually and be anxious on subsequent occasions when he tries to perform.

As with other sexual difficulties, diagnosing the cause of erectile insufficiency requires knowledge of both physical and psychological causes and their interdependency. An erection that subsides on penetration, for example, may have a different cause from an erection that is lost after penetration or an erection that was never full in the first place. A man who has erections in his sleep is unlikely to be suffering from an underlying physical problem. A man can find out whether he has erections during his sleep by placing a paper ring around the base of the penis—if he finds the ring broken when he awakes, he has probably had an erection during the night.

It is not known how widespread erection problems are. It is generally agreed that most men experience unwanted loss of or

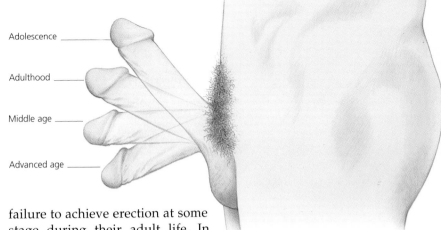

Adolescence

Adulthood

Middle age

Advanced age

failure to achieve erection at some stage during their adult life. In 1992, the U.S. National Consensus Conference on Erectile Dysfunction estimated that over 10 percent of adult men may suffer from serious erection problems.

PREMATURE EJACULATION

Ejaculating before or quickly after sexual penetration is described as premature ejaculation. Like low sex drive, it may be a problem only if a couple perceive it as such. Some couples cope easily with early ejaculation, especially if a woman reaches orgasm quickly or reaches orgasm before or after intercourse via masturbation.

Angle of erection
Although penile length and girth determines the angle of a man's erection, age also has a big impact. In men of advanced age, the erect penis is more likely to point downward than upward. This is not a sign of erection problems.

TREATING PREMATURE EJACULATION

Premature ejaculation can be treated using two types of squeeze technique. When a man is feeling highly aroused and close to ejaculation, pressure applied to the top or the bottom of the penis will temporarily diminish his erection.

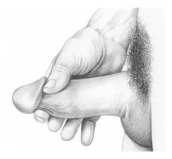

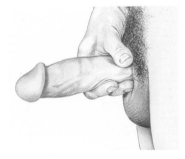

The "top" squeeze
The thumb and fingers are used to squeeze the penis just below the glans. Either the man or his partner can apply pressure until the feeling of intense arousal passes.

The "bottom" squeeze
The man or his partner should apply firm pressure around the base of his penis. This variation of the squeeze technique is useful when the man's penis is inside the vagina.

The more highly arousing a sexual situation is, the more easily ejaculation is triggered. Sometimes prolonged foreplay that includes manual or oral penile stimulation can result in hyperarousal, so that a man ejaculates soon after penetration. Young men who are just becoming sexually active often suffer from premature ejaculation, as do men with new sexual partners or men who are having sex for the first time in a long while. Anxiety about being able to perform adequately also hastens ejaculation.

Ejaculation occurs in the late stages of sexual arousal, when rhythmic contractions occur in the muscles of the pelvic floor and at the base of the penis. To treat premature ejaculation, contractions need to be controlled so that ejaculation is delayed.

Many men suffer from premature ejaculation, but it is one of the most successfully treated problems.

Treating premature ejaculation

Some drugs delay ejaculation and help give men a feeling of ejaculatory control. However, a more common treatment for premature ejaculation is the squeeze technique.

The squeeze technique requires a partner's cooperation. She has to manually stimulate her partner to erection. As she continues stimulating him, her partner must recognize the feelings of imminent ejaculation—this is called ejaculatory demand—and ask her to stop. She then places her thumb on the frenulum and her forefinger around the coronal ridge (see page 120) and applies strong pressure to this area for four to five seconds. The man should lose the sensation of ejaculatory demand and his erection may wane. The woman can then continue manual stimulation.

The exercise should be repeated five times a day for a few weeks or until it is possible for the man to have longer periods of stimulation where his ejaculatory sensation is under control. Some men may ejaculate the first or second time the squeeze technique is being performed. This is quite common and should stop after a few sessions.

A similar method is the stop-start technique (sometimes called the stop-and-go technique), which does not require a partner's participation. A man masturbates until he gets an erection, then simply stops stimulation. He continues with this exercise until he can gradually stimulate himself for longer periods, stopping when he recognizes he is close to ejaculatory demand.

When a man feels confident that he has gained sufficient ejaculatory control, the woman should guide his penis into her vagina and let it lie there without any thrusting movements for 10 seconds or so. This is called the "quiet vagina" technique, and the side-by-side or woman-on-top position is best for this.

If ejaculatory feelings are still under control using the quiet vagina technique, then thrusting movements can gradually commence. If ejaculatory demand builds up so much that the man feels he cannot control it on a stop-start basis, he should withdraw his penis and he or his partner should apply the squeeze technique.

RETARDED EJACULATION

When a man has an erection but fails to ejaculate or ejaculates only after a considerable length of time (between 30 minutes and one hour of repeated thrusting), this is known as retarded or inhibited ejaculation. This can become a source of frustration and physical pain for both him and his partner.

The causes of retarded ejaculation are uncertain. The problem tends to occur in high-achieving men who strive for perfection. It may also occur in men who fear their own sexual power and unconsciously try to inhibit it, in men who dislike the messiness of ejaculation and in men who are afraid of making their partners pregnant. If any of these is the underlying cause, sex therapy may be necessary.

Heavy alcohol consumption or taking tranquilizers, antidepressants or medication used to treat high blood pressure may also delay ejaculation in some men.

Arousal patterns
Normal sexual arousal (see top graph) is a joint sequence of excitement, plateau, orgasm and resolution. When a man ejaculates prematurely, however, his arousal and orgasm (see bottom graph) takes place very quickly and his partner's level of arousal can remain slight for the duration of the sexual encounter.

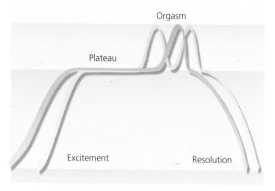

Normal sexual arousal

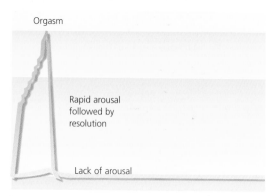

Premature ejaculation

Female arousal

Male arousal

Female Problems

Before the sexual revolution of the 1960s, women's sexuality was not widely discussed. Today people have a greater understanding of female sexual response and problems related to female libido and orgasm.

Whereas ejaculation is a reflex response in men, the female orgasm is far more elusive. The inability to reach orgasm (anorgasmia) is just one sexual problem that many women experience and seek help for.

LOW AND DECREASED SEX DRIVE

A woman's sex drive depends on her emotional and physical health, and changes in these will affect her libido. Libido can also be affected by the menstrual cycle, most typically increasing around ovulation or before menstruation.

Sex drive, however, can decrease during times of stress or fatigue, or when there is frustration, anger or poor communication in a relationship. Sex drive is usually at its height at the beginning of a relationship and gradually decreases as the initial excitement wears off.

A woman's sexual desire reaches its peak later in life than a man's; this is believed to result from women taking longer to learn about their sexual response patterns (see page 100). Sex drive is more complicated in women than men because orgasm is not so closely linked to intercourse.

Pregnancy almost certainly affects a woman's sex drive. Desire may be increased by the rise in circulating hormones, while debilitating symptoms such as morning sickness and fatigue may reduce it. After childbirth, many women find that their libido diminishes. This may be due to the fatigue and extra effort involved in caring for a newborn baby, or to tears and stitches resulting from the birth, which make sexual intercourse temporarily painful. A fear of pregnancy can likewise have a negative effect on a woman's libido.

The onset of menopause, with its decrease in the body's production of estrogen, can also reduce sex drive. Taking hormone replacement therapy (HRT) can boost it, but some menopausal women experience a natural revival of sexual interest and energy without HRT. This may be because sex is no longer associated with reproductive responsibilities and can be enjoyed without the inconvenience of contraception. The same is often true after a hysterectomy (see page 196).

A woman concerned about a lack of, or decrease in, sexual desire should consult her doctor. Treatment for lack of libido will depend on the underlying cause. If the problem is physical, hormone replacement therapy may be appropriate. If low sex drive has a psychosexual cause, or is linked to emotional or relationship difficulties, counseling or sex therapy may help.

The impact of stress Working long hours in a stressful job can cause emotional and physical problems, including diminished sex drive.

Self-image Women often report that their sexual desire is affected by how they feel about themselves physically. If a woman feels attractive, she is more likely to feel sexy.

CAUSES OF PAINFUL SEX

CAUSE	TREATMENT
Penis bumping the cervix or an ovary through the vaginal wall	Change in sexual position
Vaginal dryness	Artificial lubricant (as a temporary measure) or HRT for postmenopausal women (not all women can take HRT)
Gynecological infection (such as bartholinitis)	Appropriate treatment from a doctor
Recently performed episiotomy	Healing time before having intercourse
STD (such as herpes)	Appropriate treatment from a doctor (herpes treatment may not always involve medication)
Unstretched hymen	Gently encouraging hymen to stretch or seeking medical help if penetration is impossible
Allergic reactions to spermicide or latex	Change in spermicide, condom or diaphragm, or, if problem persists, change in method of contraception
Irritation due to prolonged intercourse	Avoiding intercourse until soreness goes away
Vaginismus	Counseling and sex therapy

THE IMPACT OF VAGINISMUS

Vaginismus is a female problem, but it can also affect male partners. If the pain of vaginismus forces a woman to avoid penetrative sex, her partner may see this as emotional rejection and, in extreme cases, begin to suffer erectile problems. The woman may try to satisfy her partner in other ways, and the couple become accustomed to sex that does not include penetration. As a result, the man suffers from "conditioned erectile dysfunction."

VAGINAL DRYNESS

One of the first signs of female sexual arousal is vaginal and vulval wetness. As a woman becomes aroused, the vaginal walls respond by secreting moisture, which aids penetration and prevents penile thrusting from causing abrasions to the vaginal wall. In terms of arousal, vaginal lubrication is the female equivalent of the male erection.

If a woman does not produce enough lubrication before intercourse, penetration can be uncomfortable or painful. The simplest reason for lack of lubrication is that the woman is not sufficiently aroused. This may be because foreplay has been short or nonexistent or because she does not want sexual intercourse at that particular time.

Vaginal dryness can also be due to low estrogen levels—a common occurrence after childbirth (especially if a woman is breast-feeding) and at menopause (see page 106). Hormone replacement therapy (HRT) helps to restore the estrogen balance after menopause. Heavy alcohol consumption can cause vaginal dryness as a direct result of the dehydration produced by alcohol.

Short-term remedies for vaginal dryness include artificial lubricants in the form of water-based lubricating jellies (oil-based products should not be used with condoms because they destroy rubber) and saliva. When the problem persists, a doctor or sex therapist may be able to diagnose and treat an underlying cause.

PAINFUL INTERCOURSE

Pain during sexual intercourse may have a physical cause that should be diagnosed and treated by a doctor. It helps if a woman can describe the location and type of pain and the stage of sexual intercourse at which it occurs: on penetration, during thrusting or during orgasm. One cause of extreme pain during intercourse is a gynecological condition called bartholinitis, an inflammation of the Bartholin's glands on either side of the vaginal entrance (see page 194).

VAGINISMUS

Occasionally, women cannot have sexual intercourse because their vaginal muscles go into spasm whenever penetration is attempted. This condition, known as vaginismus, not only makes penetration difficult or impossible but also causes pain from the muscle spasm and extreme pain when penetration is attempted.

Vaginismus is a psychological condition involving deep-rooted fears or anxieties about sex. It can result from a past traumatic sexual experience, such as rape; a careless first vaginal examination; or a subconscious fear of sex, pregnancy and childbirth. Some postmenopausal women whose vaginal tissue has shrunk and does not lubricate sufficiently develop vaginismus because they learn to associate sex with pain.

When penetration is attempted, a woman with vaginismus has an expectation of pain, and her body automatically tenses in anticipation. At first this reaction may be a protective mechanism, but it later becomes an automatic reflex after the source of pain or trauma is removed.

If sensitively managed, treatment for vaginismus is highly successful. A therapist will discuss a woman's attitudes toward sex and try to unravel any deep-seated fears she may have. The therapist will also teach the woman about her body's sexual responses and how to relax her pelvic-floor muscles. The woman is encouraged to use a mirror to explore her genitals with her fingers and, when she is ready, to practice dilating the vagina with a series of "vaginal trainers." A woman continues using vaginal trainers until she feels comfortable and relaxed enough for sexual penetration. She should then attempt intercourse in a woman-on-top position, which will give her control over the depth and speed of penetration.

INABILITY TO REACH ORGASM

To reach orgasm, a woman needs to be relaxed and free of distractions. This means feeling comfortable about her surroundings and her partner and relaxed about her body and sexual responses. Any sort of inhibition, whether psychological or physical, can make orgasm difficult. For many women, losing control is not an easy thing to do, especially in the presence of another person, when they feel at their most vulnerable.

Women are orgasmic to different degrees. Some women reach orgasm easily during intercourse. Others reach orgasm only in specific sexual positions. Others can reach orgasm through masturbation only, not

through intercourse. Still others never reach orgasm under any circumstances. The latter problem is true anorgasmia. Orgasmic responses—or lack of them—constitute a problem only if a woman or her partner perceives them as such.

Lack of orgasm does not necessarily indicate that there is anything physically or psychologically wrong with a woman, or that she cannot enjoy sex. Many women have learned to put other people's needs and pleasures before their own; since reaching orgasm requires that a woman exclude all other stimuli and focus on her own sexual pleasure, she may feel selfish. In other words, she may worry that by concentrating on herself, she is denying her partner sexual pleasure. If a woman believes that she has

SELF-HELP FOR VAGINISMUS

A woman can treat vaginismus under the guidance of a sex therapist using her fingers or vaginal trainers. Vaginal trainers are plastic devices that come in graded sizes. The woman practices inserting the smallest trainer first; when she has mastered this, she moves on to larger-sized trainers.

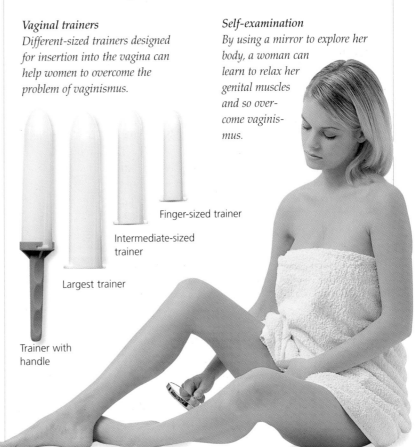

Vaginal trainers
Different-sized trainers designed for insertion into the vagina can help women to overcome the problem of vaginismus.

Self-examination
By using a mirror to explore her body, a woman can learn to relax her genital muscles and so overcome vaginismus.

Finger-sized trainer

Intermediate-sized trainer

Largest trainer

Trainer with handle

SEX ADDICTION

Affecting both men and women, sexual addiction is uncommon and defined as a compulsive dependence on frequent, ritualized sexual activity. The addict is preoccupied with sexual matters and carries out special rituals to intensify sexual arousal and excitement. Addicts engage in sexual activity irrespective of the risks, but their desire for sex is marked afterward by dissatisfaction and hopelessness as the compulsion interferes with everyday life. Sex addicts are thought to be motivated by low self-worth or a fear of loneliness. They gain a sense of power from sexual conquests, even though the feeling is short-lived. They may crave an intimate relationship but not know how to achieve it.

no rights to sexual pleasure, or lesser rights than her partner, she will be prevented from learning about her own sexual needs and responses. She will lack necessary knowledge about the way her body works. Alternatively, a woman may know how to reach orgasm by masturbation but feel too inhibited to tell her partner how to incorporate this into their lovemaking.

If a woman has never experienced an orgasm, she should start by exploring her own body to discover what type of touch or other sexual stimulation feels good. Time alone, unhurried and without any pressure to perform, is a vital factor for this task. Some women find a relaxing bath an ideal setting. Sexual aids such as vibrators are helpful for stimulating orgasm, and fantasizing or reading an erotic book can enhance arousal and help to eliminate distracting thoughts. Sex therapists believe that nearly all women who suffer from anorgasmia can be taught to achieve an orgasm through masturbation.

A significant number of women can reach orgasm on their own or when their partner uses manual or oral stimulation but find it difficult to climax during intercourse. If this is the case, the bridge technique may be helpful. In this technique, clitoral stimulation is provided by the woman's partner—or by the woman herself—up to the point of orgasm, then it is stopped and penile thrusting is used to trigger orgasm. The side-by-

Can We Talk About It?

NOT REACHING ORGASM

Start by telling each other how important orgasm is to you. Do you feel that it is an essential part of intercourse; that it is sometimes important, but not always; or that sex is a fulfilling experience without orgasm? Tell your partner whether you want to change your joint expectations of intercourse or change the way you have sex so that orgasm becomes more likely. If you take the latter approach, tell your partner how he can help you reach orgasm. If you do not know, suggest to your partner that seeing a sex therapist would help you to learn more about your sexual responses.

If you have been faking orgasm, make clear your reasons for doing so: perhaps you wanted to live up to your partner's expectations. Explain that you never intended to deceive him and that now you are being honest because you want to find new ways of interacting sexually with him.

side and woman-on-top sexual positions are recommended for the bridge technique because they allow easy access to the clitoris. A vibrator can be used to provide clitoral stimulation.

The bridge technique
For women who find it difficult to reach orgasm during intercourse, the bridge technique can help by providing extra stimulation.

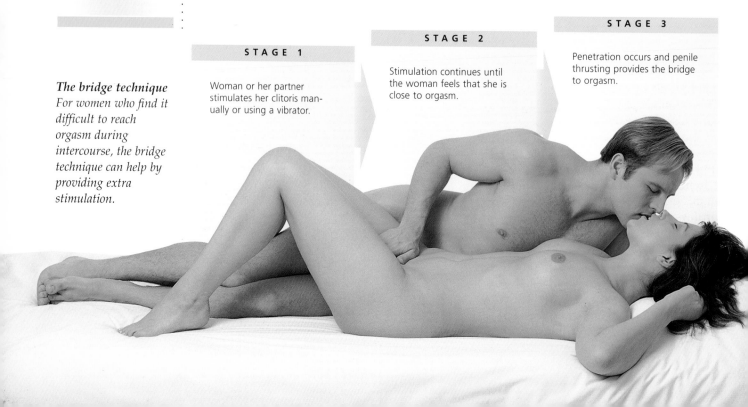

STAGE 1
Woman or her partner stimulates her clitoris manually or using a vibrator.

STAGE 2
Stimulation continues until the woman feels that she is close to orgasm.

STAGE 3
Penetration occurs and penile thrusting provides the bridge to orgasm.

Treating Sexual Problems

A bewildering array of therapies exist to treat sexual and emotional problems, but not all practicing therapists have received recognized training and accreditation. Seeking a doctor's advice about sexual problems is always advisable.

When deciding on a treatment for a sexual problem, it is important to understand its cause. Does the sexual problem have a psychological cause, or could it have a physical basis, in which case it should be treated by a doctor? If the problem is definitely a psychosexual one, is it due to emotional or relationship difficulties that would be treated best by a relationship counselor? Or is it a long-standing anxiety about sexual technique or performance that sex therapy could address? Sometimes people manage to treat minor sexual problems at home with self-help techniques and a supportive partner.

Anyone offering treatment for sexual problems must have a knowledge of both the physical and psychological aspects of sexual behavior or be part of a team covering all aspects of treatment. In approximately one-third of people seeking help for what seem to be psychological difficulties in their sex lives, an underlying physical disorder is present. The possible physical causes of sexual problems should always be eliminated first of all.

In most large communities, there are professional therapists, clinics and programs that specialize in treating sexual dysfunctions and deviations, gender identity problems, sexual addic-

tions, and the effects of sexual abuse. For more information, contact the American Association of Sex Educators, Counselors and Therapists (AASECT) or the Sex Information and Education Council of Canada (SIECCAN).

SEX THERAPY

A sex therapist treats problems in three main areas of the sexual response cycle: desire, arousal and orgasm. Therapists can also treat problems of sexual technique or phobic responses such as vaginismus (see page 216).

Sex therapists aim to help an individual or couple discover how to enjoy their sexuality free of difficulties and inhibitions. Some single people approach sex therapists because a sexual problem is preventing them from entering a relationship. Others go into sex therapy as couples because their sex life is no longer satisfactory (or has never been satisfactory).

Virtually everyone has the natural ability to be sexual. Yet as people grow up they may develop inhibitions that prevent the natural or spontaneous expression of sexuality in adulthood. Even simple reprimands made by an adult to a young child about touch-

Dr. Ruth Well known for her candid no-nonsense advice, Dr. Ruth Westheimer is a famous television and radio personality as well as a trained psychotherapist specializing in sexual dysfunctions.

fact or fiction?

Sex therapists recommend masturbation for sexual problems.

Fact. Masturbation is a good way to gain sexual self-knowledge. Women can build up their sexual confidence by using self-stimulation—a woman who knows that she is capable of reaching orgasm on her own will feel more confident about reaching orgasm with a partner. Sex therapists suggest using masturbation as a type of self-directed sensate focus (see page 220). Specific masturbation exercises can also help men overcome premature ejaculation.

THE ORIGIN OF SEX THERAPY

The principles of sex therapy were first explained by Masters and Johnson in their groundbreaking 1969 book *Human Sexual Inadequacy*. Their work was extended by Helen Singer Kaplan, who, in *The New Sex Therapy* (1974), moved the subject into the mainstream of good psychiatric and medical practice. Treatments have, except for some minor modifications in practice, remained largely unchanged, although knowledge about the chemistry of sexual function has increased.

ing his or her genitals may instill in the child the belief that there is something forbidden or naughty about this body part. People may feel great pressure to be sexually attractive and to perform sexually. As a result, women feel inadequate if they do not have coital orgasms, and men feel inferior if they cannot sustain repeated erections.

Sex therapy helps redirect people's thoughts from those that obstruct or inhibit sexual arousal and pleasure. A sex therapist encourages clients to stop judging and evaluating their sexual experiences, and instead to concentrate on the physical sensations and sensual aspects of sex.

A good sex therapist will compile a complete picture of a sexual problem. What were the initial triggers? In what context did symptoms first arise? How did the client's sexual partner respond? Does the problem occur only in specific circumstances? What impact does the sexual problem have on a client's relationships?

When to see a sex therapist

Deciding when to seek professional help for a sexual problem can be difficult, especially since problems such as erectile difficulties can often be treated at home with self-help programs. Sex therapists Masters, Johnson and Kolodny suggest that if any of the following are present, a person should consider sex therapy rather than home treatment.

- Sex drive is absent or little thought is ever given to sex.
- A relationship is characterized by anger, bitterness and conflict.
- Ejaculation occurs through a flaccid penis more than 10 percent of the time.
- Feelings of sexual guilt are having a negative effect on sexual behavior.
- Either partner is uptight about sex.
- Sexual abuse that took place in childhood is having a negative impact on adult sexual behavior.
- Either partner is uncomfortable about touching the other's genitals.
- Obsessive and troubling sex urges are occurring.

Surrogate partners

Sex surrogacy is a branch of sex therapy first suggested and adopted in the 1970s by Masters and Johnson in the treatment of men and women with sexual problems. The

TREATING SEXUAL PROBLEMS WITH SENSATE FOCUS

A sequence of exercises known as sensate focus is used to help couples learn or relearn how to interact sexually. Before a couple embark on sensate focus, a sex therapist will conduct detailed interviews with both partners about their sexual histories and their responses and attitudes toward sex. Sensate focus aims to restore the sensual pleasure of sex by teaching individuals to concentrate on pleasurable sensations instead of anticipating and worrying about intercourse. It is helpful for orgasmic problems and reduced sex drive.

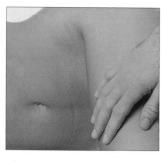

1 Touch your partner's skin but omit sexual parts of the body. Ask your partner to tell you what he or she enjoys.

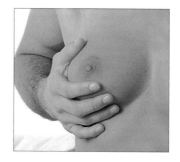

2 Experiment with touching sexual areas of the body, such as the breasts, nipples and genital area.

3 A therapist will advise you about the next stage, suiting it to the particular needs of you and your partner.

surrogate partner is trained in the principles of sex therapy and attempts to treat a client's problems by having sexual intercourse or being sexually intimate with him or her. Surrogate partners are also known as body work therapists. Sex surrogacy was surrounded by controversy from its outset and was soon abandoned by Masters and Johnson. Today it is largely discredited and its use confined mainly to work with young, physically impaired clients.

There are numerous practical and ethical problems associated with surrogacy, including the risk of HIV infection. Sex surrogates by definition must have multiple partners, and even practicing safer sex (see page 178) cannot eliminate the risk of infection. Also, it may be difficult for clients and surrogate partners to maintain a professional relationship with each other: sexual intimacy can have a profound emotional impact, and it may become difficult for sex surrogates and their clients to distinguish successfully between sex and emotional involvement, which can lead to further problems.

Sensate focus

One of the basic principles of sensate focus is that individuals with sexual problems become "self-spectators" during sex. For example, both a woman who has problems reaching orgasm and a man who tries to stop himself from ejaculating too soon will be so preoccupied with assessing their own performance that the sensual pleasure of sex will be lost.

Through conversation, a sex therapist builds up a picture of a couple's sexual problems. He or she will then give the couple an assignment to do at home. In many cases this begins with partners learning to touch themselves while alone to discover their own sensitive areas. The initial assignment together requires the couple to undress and simply take turns touching each other. The partner who is "giving" the

The Language of Sex

Sex therapy, like other types of therapy, rarely produces instant results. Sex therapists respond to this fact by using "repetition," "insight" or "bypass." Repetition involves frequently practicing a task; insight is understanding the emotional issues that can block therapy; bypass means changing the type of task that the clients do.

ment gives couples the opportunity to touch each other in an enjoyable way without the pressure or anxiety that sexual intercourse can provoke.

After reporting to the sex therapist about the success of the first assignment, a couple will be given a second assignment. This time they extend the touching to the entire body, including the breasts, nipples and genitals. The receiving partner gives specific feedback about what he or she enjoys most. He or she can also give specific instructions or place his or her hand on top of the giving partner's hand to offer guidance about the speed and pressure of touch. Sex and orgasm are still forbidden.

touch is forbidden to touch the breasts, nipples and genital area (sexual arousal and intercourse are not the aims at this stage), and the partner who is "receiving" the touch must try to relax and enjoy the experience (he or she should report anything that feels distracting or uncomfortable). This type of assign-

The cycle of sexual problems When treating sexual problems, sex therapists aim to break down the sequence of negative thoughts that turn sex into a chore and make individuals feel as though they are failing.

He or she obsessively monitors "progress" during sex.

He or she feels enormous pressure to perform.

Sex becomes less spontaneous and more inhibited.

Individual becomes very self-critical.

Sex becomes goal-oriented—a matter of success or failure.

Identification of a problem such as premature ejaculation or anorgasmia.

The original sexual problem becomes worse.

COUNSELING

Whereas sex therapy usually involves sexual exercises that people practice on their own at home, counseling is based on conversations with a trained person in an office context. In a counseling session the counselor listens to the emotional problems of a client and helps the client to resolve his or her current difficulties and find better ways to cope in the future.

Counseling is typically recommended when sexual problems are coupled with deep-rooted emotional anxieties. For example, erectile difficulties that have come about because a man has lost his sense of sexual confidence may respond well to sensate focus, but erectile difficulties that are caused by a lifelong conviction that sex is wrong or dirty may be better treated by counseling.

Using fantasies ▶
Many people are aroused by dressing-up or role-playing games, especially when dominant and submissive roles are involved.

After a couple have completed the first two stages of sensate focus, they move on to the third. This varies according to the sexual problem that the couple are experiencing. For example, if the woman has difficulty reaching orgasm, her partner will spend the next stage concentrating on her genital area. The aim is not for her to reach orgasm but to experiment with different forms of touch without feeling pressured. The woman should make clear what feels good and what does not. Further exercises then help a couple to apply the knowledge they have gained to full penetrative sex.

The third stage of sensate focus for a couple suffering from erectile problems involves the basic touching—in turn—of the second stage but requires the man to gain an erection and then lose it. Masters and Johnson say: "Tell your partner to deliberately stop touching the penis once an erection occurs and to move her touch elsewhere on your body. The reason behind this maneuver is simple: you need to discover for yourself that it's not a tragedy when an erection peters out, because erections come and go pretty much by their own volition."

Once a man has discovered the different sensory inputs that he needs to gain an erection, a sex therapist will recommend further sensate focus exercises to transfer this knowledge to mutual touching and, eventually, to full sexual intercourse.

Sensate focus encourages people to open up all their sensory channels—touch, taste, smell, sight and hearing—so that sex becomes a sensual and erotic experience.

Fantasy as therapy
Erotic fantasies (see page 77) are often viewed as self-indulgent or confined to arousal during solitary masturbation. In fact, sexual fantasies can be used therapeutically in all kinds of sexual situations, including inter-

course with a partner. Fantasies can be especially useful in overcoming problems of sexual arousal or reaching orgasm, and sex therapists who employ sensate focus techniques frequently recommend that their clients fantasize.

Sexual fantasies are unique to the individual, although as Nancy Friday demonstrated through her collections of sexual fantasies, *My Secret Garden* and *Men in Love*, there are common themes. Many people fantasize about previous sexual experiences that they found particularly erotic. These fantasies may involve a person's current partner or an old lover and consist of reliving the encounter or sometimes embellishing it. Other fantasies involve imaginary settings or imaginary lovers. Sometimes fantasies include elements beyond the experience of the individual (such as homosexual sex). Or they may include elements that a person would never want to experience in real life (such as sex involving force or strangers, or being watched having sex).

Fantasy may be particularly helpful for women who have difficulty reaching orgasm. It can boost arousal levels, and women who feel inhibited, self-conscious or easily distracted during intercourse may find that it helps them concentrate on their own sexual pleasure.

Some women worry that fantasizing during intercourse is disloyal to their partners. They may be accustomed to fantasizing during masturbation but are reluctant to do so during intercourse because they feel guilty or inadequate. Sex therapists reassure clients about the value of fantasy. Indeed, the brain is often described as the single most important organ of sexual pleasure. Therapists characterize fantasies as the equivalent of daydreams or "private aphrodisiacs" that are a useful aid to arousal. Without them, women could be putting themselves at a sexual disadvantage. Fantasies can be private or shared. For some partners, acting out fantasies together can heighten arousal and increase openness and intimacy.

SEX &
SOCIETY

Sex Around the World

Sexual relationships in non-Western cultures can differ markedly from the North American and European ideal of monogamous love between two equals. The practice of marrying more than one person still exists in some parts of the world.

A man or a woman who is married to more than one partner simultaneously is said to practice polygamy. The gender-specific term polygyny describes a situation in which a man has more than one wife at a time; "polyandry" refers to a situation in which a woman is married to two or more men.

POLYANDRY

The practice of women having multiple husbands is believed to be fairly unusual, although recent field studies have found polyandry to be more widespread than originally thought. It is known to occur in Tibet, Africa and the Philippines. In Tibet and among the Toda, who live in the Nigril hill area of India, the number of men is far greater than the number of women, a phenomenon that is believed to have resulted from the practice of female infanticide (see page 163). Polyandry has developed as a practical adaptation to this shortage of women, and it is often brothers who share a wife and apparently live together with her without friction or jealousy.

A special kind of polyandry existed among the Nayar of southern India, a tribe of professional soldiers who spent most of their lives away from home. Every girl would be ritually married before puberty to a man of a lineage linked to her own. After the marriage ceremony, no further contact with the man she married was required, and after puberty she was allowed to have sexual intercourse with other men. If she had a child by one of these men, he was expected to acknowledge paternity by paying the midwife but not by taking responsibility for the child—this duty rested with the mother's family. This kind of polyandry worked, apparently, because the men were away fighting for the majority of their lives and in many cases never returned.

POLYGYNY

Polygyny is much more common and acceptable in many cultures than polyandry. In most societies women outnumber men, and this disparity is greatest in the poorer countries of the world, where men may be more often involved in warfare or dangerous hunting exploits. Polygyny is practiced among the Zulu of South Africa, the Thonga in Mozambique, and societies in northeastern Asia, Papua New Guinea, the New Hebrides and the Solomon Islands.

In many parts of rural Africa, where polygyny was once common, the practice has declined because of the influence of Christian missionaries. This has not always led to improvements in quality of life for women. A woman who does not marry and has no children is a social anomaly in these rural areas. She has no way to support herself and little autonomy, particularly when she gets older. Polygynous marriage gives such a woman a home and a meaningful place in her community, even if she does not have her own children.

Fraternal polyandry
To prevent the division of land and to maintain family wealth, brothers share wives in the Nyinba tribe, who farm the borders of Tibet and Nepal. Here 12-year-old Tarilal stands with three of her five husbands. The youngest is just 5 years old.

Rural African women have often approved of polygyny. Only an important man in a village has more than one wife, and his importance confers a superior social status on his wives. Two or more wives can ease the burden of domestic chores, which is highly significant in parts of the world where the women do nearly all the work. The Nyakyusa tribe of southern Tanganyika (now Tanzania) found that their traditional values of hospitality were incompatible with the Christian value of monogamy. They could not fulfill their obligations of hospitality and generosity with only one wife to make all the food and beer.

Although the relationship between co-wives in polygynous marriages is typically friendly and cooperative, most polygynous societies explicitly recognize the potential instability of such a marriage and establish guidelines to minimize problems. Among some of the Bantu tribes, for example, the wives live in a designated hierarchy because the Bantu believe that there is less conflict among wives who do not see each other as equals. The senior wife in the hierarchy is always shown great respect, while the husband must obey strict rules about bestowing his attentions equally and impartially on all his wives.

Despite rules and guidelines, polygyny is not always harmonious: among the Rwanda people the word for "co-wife" means "jealousy." In many tribes a wife who finds herself infertile will blame this on the sorcery and witchcraft of the other wives, inciting such bad feeling that the conflicts have been known to lead to suicide and murder.

In the West, polygyny has been practiced by religious groups such as the Church of Jesus Christ of Latter-day Saints, also known as Mormons. They believe that polygyny ensures salvation for women and a favored place in heaven, especially for those marrying a prominent member of the Mormon Church. The practice was opposed,

and eventually, antipolygyny laws were passed in North America. The Mormon Church did not officially disavow the practice until 1890, and there are some splinter groups that continue to recognize polygynous marriages.

The Jewish religion accepted polygyny until it was banned in Europe in the mid-11th century, but Sephardic Jews continued the practice up until the mid-20th century. Polygyny is recognized and practiced by many Muslims today; the Muslim holy book, called the Koran, which sets out Islamic law, allows a man to have up to four wives at a time.

Polygynous marriages occur in patrilineal societies, where the lineage is passed through the male rather than the female. This means that if all the children have the same father, it does not matter how many mothers are involved: the children are part of the same descent group.

Wife hospitality

Some cultures share wives. For example, it is said that the Inuit offered their wives to special visitors for the night. This is known as wife hospitality and may have been a way of demonstrating that a visitor is a friend rather than an enemy.

The Language of Sex

There is a practice required by Old Testament law that upon the death of a man, his brother must marry the widow. Any children born to the widowed women and her brother-in-law are considered to be those of the dead man. Among the Nuer people of Sudan and the Bedouin of North Africa, this is known today as "levirate" marriage.

A Mormon man and his wives Although the Mormon religion no longer recognizes polygyny, it was practiced in previous centuries. This painting of French Mormons dates back to the mid-1880s.

Co-wives in Sudan These women are participating at a Sudanese wedding festival. They are all married to the same man.

ARRANGED MARRIAGES

Many societies view marriage as a union between two family groups rather than a union between two individuals. Because of this, an individual's relatives often involve themselves in the selection of a marriage partner. When families have complete control over the choice of partner, the resulting union is known as an arranged marriage.

Arranged marriage is common in India and other parts of Asia, where parents decide on a suitable spouse often without consulting their son or daughter. The couple may be betrothed, or promised to each other, at a very young age and may never see each other before the marriage ceremony takes place. Arranged marriages are frequently successful; the couple grow to love each other and report being happily married. Problems occur more often when Asian families in Europe or North America attempt to maintain the tradition of arranged marriages in a society where their children are surrounded by couples who have chosen each other for romantic love. In some cultures that typically practice arranged marriage, it is acceptable for the husband to have a mistress.

DOWRY AND BRIDEWEALTH

A dowry is money or property that is given to the groom by the bride's family at the time of engagement or marriage. In developing countries such as India, this custom has been made illegal because greater and greater demands were being put on the bride's family. This custom still exists to some extent today in Western societies, where the father of the bride is traditionally expected to pay for the wedding. The huge cost of modern weddings has caused a shift, however, and it is not unusual for both families, as well as the bride and groom, to contribute equally to the expense.

Bridewealth, or bride-price, is a widespread custom in rural Africa and Eastern countries, in which the groom or the groom's family presents money, property or other gifts to the bride's family. Cattle are the most common bridewealth, but in some societies, gifts of beer, animal skins, honey or jewelry are traditional.

Early missionaries saw bridewealth as a buying price for a woman in a society that viewed women as possessions. Today the importance of bridewealth is understood as a complex arrangement between two families. The husband is expected to behave with great respect toward the people who have made him such a priceless gift of their daughter or sister. Also, the bridewealth received when a sister marries is often necessary for her brothers to find a wife and so replace the woman who has been lost by the group. Bridewealth may also serve to ensure the good behavior of the bride and her husband. If the bride behaves badly, the husband can divorce her and demand the return of the bridewealth. If the groom misbehaves, the bride's family can refuse to return the bridewealth, and the man stands to lose both bride and property.

There is evidence from areas of South Africa that where missionaries have succeeded in eliminating bridewealth, couples who marry without it frequently do not perceive themselves as married, and their relationship does not last.

FEMALE CIRCUMCISION

The practice of surgically removing parts of the female genitalia such as the clitoral hood, the clitoris, the labia or the vulva is known as female circumcision. It has been reported in over 20 countries in regions as widely separated as Asia, Africa, the Middle East, and Central and South America. It has recently been found that female circumcision is also being performed in places in Europe, by communities of people originating from countries where the practice is common. The World Health Organization estimates that as many as 100 million

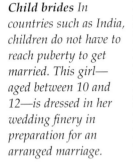

Child brides In countries such as India, children do not have to reach puberty to get married. This girl—aged between 10 and 12—is dressed in her wedding finery in preparation for an arranged marriage.

women around the world have undergone some form of circumcision.

Many experts say that removal of the clitoris, which has an important function in women, is not comparable to male circumcision and should be more correctly referred to as "female genital mutilation."

The first female circumcisions to be recorded took place over 4,000 years ago in Egypt, where circumcision is believed to have been a sign of distinction among the aristocracy. Evidence of infibulation (see below) has been found on Egyptian mummies, and historical records suggest that it was practiced in ancient Rome and pre-Islamic Arabia.

In the simplest form of female circumcision, the clitoral hood (see page 124) and all or part of the clitoris, with or without the labia minora, are removed. In its most extreme form, known as infibulation, two-thirds of the labia majora is removed and the remaining third is stitched together, apart from a tiny hole for urine and menstrual blood to pass through. This opening is later widened to allow consummation of marriage, an operation that causes the woman further pain. This form of circumcision is widely carried out in Chad, Djibouti, Somalia and Sudan.

In 90 percent of cases, female circumcision is performed with primitive tools, such as small penknives, and little or no anesthetic. It is not uncommon to hear stories of five or more women holding down a girl during the operation because she is in such pain.

Apart from immediate complications from the operation, such as infection and hemorrhage, girls may have permanent problems with urination, intercourse and childbirth. Circumcised women are unable to experience sexual stimulation or pleasure in the same way as uncircumcised women.

The age at which girls are operated on depends on the tribe or community and the number of girls ready to be initiated. The average age is usually between 8 and 10 years, or around puberty, but it may be done as early as 5 years and sometimes even a few days after birth. In some cultures, circumcision is performed just before marriage, and in parts of Nigeria, during the seventh month of the first pregnancy.

The operation is normally done by an older woman. In Sierra Leone this is an old, experienced professional called a *sowe,* who is believed to be endowed with special powers. The girls leave home, usually with girls of their own age from other families, and stay in a hut with the *sowe* for many months. There, while recovering from the operation, they receive instruction in wifely and motherly duties. Sometimes the operation is done in the home, but in more recent times it has increasingly been performed in private clinics and hospitals.

The operation does not have a medical basis; rather, it is a traditional rite of passage marking the changing status of the pubescent girl as she enters womanhood and prepares for marriage. In some cultures male circumcision is also considered an initiation into adulthood, although the long-term results are very different.

Infibulation ensures the preservation of virginity until marriage, and one reason for perpetuating the practice seems to be that women believe their daughters will not be accepted for marriage if they have not undergone the operation. The Masai of Kenya believe that an uncircumcised woman will become self-centered, rather than devoting herself to her family, home and group.

Among the Temne people of Sierra Leone, much attention is lavished on girls who have been circumcised. They receive deferential treatment when they return home, as well as elaborate gifts from relatives, and they wear special clothes and ornaments, indicating that they are ready for marriage.

◀ Circumcision rituals This young Pokot girl from northern Kenya wears a skin cloak and clay makeup as part of a post-circumcision ritual.

BODY EXPOSURE AND CULTURE

Islamic dress
In strict Muslim countries it is forbidden for women to reveal their bodies in public. Dress consists of loose robes and sometimes a yashmak—a veil that conceals the face.

Western dress
In the West, exposing the body is considered acceptable, although a woman who wears very revealing clothes may be perceived as making a statement of sexual availability.

to hysteria, insanity, epilepsy and sterility. He therefore advocated removal of the clitoris. Brown claimed that the procedure would help women to overcome "distaste for marital intercourse" and prevent them from "going for walks in the woods and coming back exhausted." Baker Brown did not have much support from the medical profession, but he nonetheless practiced female circumcision for many years. Eventually the medical profession stopped him because he failed to explain to his patients or their families exactly what the operation entailed.

It has been estimated that more than 90 million women worldwide have suffered this form of genital mutilation; usually before they reach the age of seven. It occurs in Africa, Asia and South America, and some ethnic communities in the West.

NUDITY AND EROTICISM

Certain parts of the body have different erotic connotations in different parts of the world. Many Arab women, for example, cover their entire bodies and faces and are perplexed by the way Western women routinely expose their faces, shoulders, arms and legs. In ancient China, the exposure of upper-class women's tiny feet was regarded as indecent. Even to talk about feet was forbidden in polite society, since they were considered the most erotic and sexually stimulating part of the female body. In Japan, the same was true of the back of a woman's neck, which in traditional dress is still covered by a large collar. Covering the whole or part of the body, however, is common to many cultures worldwide, which may suggest that concealment helps to create a mystery that contributes to the body's eroticism.

Female circumcision has become a human rights issue, but many cultures resent this and believe the attention paid to the practice is out of all proportion to other problems faced in developing countries, such as poverty and famine. They are angered by the perception of their cultures as self-mutilating and primitive—even opponents of circumcision feel it should be the women in the groups practicing it who lead the campaign for its abolition. Often, however, these are the very women who perpetuate the practice.

In mid-19th century England a notorious gynecologist, Baker Brown, wrote about the link between the clitoris and masturbation. He proposed that masturbation led, among other things,

fact or fiction?

Kissing is not a global practice.

Fact. Kissing on the lips is not a universal way of showing affection for or sexual interest in a partner. Among the Inuit people, nose rubbing was the customary way to show affection. The Maori people of New Zealand press noses and foreheads together.

An amusing story from the Dutch East Indies relates how a Dutch governor, shocked by the East Indian women's exposed breasts, ordered women to cover their breasts in public. This led to the women lifting their skirts over their heads whenever they saw a Dutch official, exposing the more embarrassing naked lower half instead. In some countries, the fingertips are considered erotic and must be kept covered; in other countries, it is the knees or the navel.

Nudity also has various definitions from culture to culture. A Nuer man considers himself naked if he does not have the scars across his forehead that tribesmen receive when initiated into manhood. The Seka people of New Guinea believe it is improper for a man not to wear a grass sheath on his penis when in public. The Tupari people of Brazil believe that it is indecent even to bathe without a covering on the penis and were apparently shocked when they learned that Western men bathe and shower completely naked. The men of the Pongo, in the former French West Africa, refused to allow their women to wear clothes, saying that the women would become more beautiful and be desired by men in other villages. Among some tribes where nudity is habitual, clothes are worn on certain occasions with the express purpose of provoking sexual excitement in dances and traditional rites.

In Japan, the naked body is still considered unerotic and faintly disgusting. The 18th-century Ukiyo-e school of Japanese art produced prints to express the pleasure of sex. These showed nearly all the figures covered with clothes or drapes, with only their genitals—often very enlarged and exaggerated—exposed.

The Japanese custom of both sexes bathing together naked is said to decrease sexual stimulation. Nudists make the same argument in North America and Europe, and some people have suggested that Western pressure on indigenous cultures to wear clothes, where none were worn previously, has led to a moral decline.

Sexual intercourse is generally considered to be a very private activity in the West. This contrasts starkly with practices in other societies, such as Papua New Guinea, where there is a taboo against making love

Japanese erotica
Many figures in Japanese erotica are depicted wearing clothes. This reflects the belief held in such cultures that a covered or partially covered body is more provocative than a nude one.

indoors. In Polynesia, where large families share open rooms and live in close proximity, couples have sexual intercourse openly without embarrassment or worries about offending family members. Some societies in Oceania include sexual intercourse in their ceremonial festivals.

Male adornment In cultures where few clothes are worn, men often temper their nudity by wearing body paint, headdresses, tattoos or penis sheaths.

Jewelry

Face paint

Penis sheath

Headdress

Sexual Statistics

How often do most people have sex? How often do they masturbate? Who has oral and anal sex? This kind of information interests people because it helps them understand where their own practices fit into their society's norms.

The last sexual event
Laumann and colleagues asked people what sort of activities they performed in their "last sexual event." This sort of question provides a snapshot of people's sexual behavior. This graph shows the percentage of people of different ages who engaged in oral sex in the "last sexual event."

According to *The Social Organization of Sexuality* (1994), by Edward Laumann and others—one of the latest and most comprehensive research studies into adult sexual behavior in a long line of sex surveys—frequency of sex increases once a couple enters a monogamous cohabiting relationship. Perhaps surprisingly, the media-perpetuated idea that young single people have active and exciting sex lives is an exaggeration. Even married people who have extramarital affairs make love less often than those who remain faithful to one partner, whether married or cohabiting.

Aside from running counter to the impression given by the media, this finding was deeply ironic. The researchers had their initial funding withdrawn after North Carolina's Senator Jesse Helms and others forced through a change in the law to prohibit state financing of sex surveys, partly on the grounds that the information such studies uncovered would damage the moral fabric of society. Instead, the survey suggests that traditional moral values are as strong (and satisfying) as ever.

Most people, according to the Laumann study, want to settle down in a long-term relationship—usually marriage—once they reach adulthood and to remain faithful to that partner for life. While a significant number of marriages do end in divorce, with infidelity cited as the main reason in many cases, the evidence suggests that the underlying cause of marital breakdown is irreconcilable differences between the couple rather than any lack of commitment to the principle of monogamy.

In the Laumann survey, 80 percent of those questioned—the participants ranged in age from 18 to 59—had had a maximum of one partner in the previous 12 months (some had had no partner in that time). Half of all the adults questioned in the study had had no more than three partners over their entire lifetime.

Just 3 percent of adults reported having had five or more partners over the previous 12-month period. Clearly, most people are not promiscuous. The study found that the average length of a marriage among this age group is 25 years, with 4 years being the average interval between marriages.

Surveys such as the Laumann study, which attempt to chart the demographics of human behavior, can give only a "snapshot" of current social behavior during the period in which the research was carried out. Another survey, conducted 10 years before or 10 years after, may produce a different picture. This simply confirms that human behavior, especially sexual behavior, changes over time.

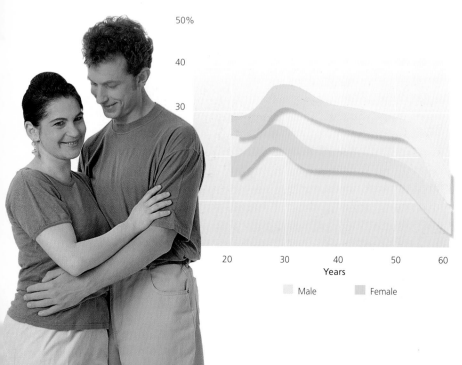

50%

40

30

20   30   40   50   60
Years

Male   Female

CHANGING ATTITUDES

Cohabitation, once called "living in sin," is now common practice as a prelude or alternative to marriage, and, to many people, it is morally acceptable. Yet 30 years ago living together out of wedlock was almost unheard of, and even 20 years ago it was still generally frowned upon. Those couples who chose to cohabit rather than marry would often assume the outward appearance of respectability, even to the extent of wearing wedding rings. Today many couples choose to live together for a year or more as a form of trial marriage. Some couples reject the institution of marriage altogether, considering it outmoded and unnecessary.

Sex surveys may also influence society's attitudes toward sex and generally encourage more openness about sexual issues. Research by Kinsey, and Masters and Johnson (see page 257) shocked society by suggesting that sexual practices such as oral sex and mutual masturbation were more widespread, and therefore by implication more acceptable, than had previously been thought. For these researchers, just getting people to talk about these kinds of subjects was a major battle.

In the Laumann study, however, most of those surveyed were willing to discuss their sexual preferences, and few people found such activities morally wrong when practiced by consenting adults, even if they did not engage in them themselves.

Laumann discovered that in the previous year, 90 percent of male participants in the study and 86 percent of female participants had had vaginal intercourse, but only 27 percent of men and 19 percent of women had had oral sex. For most people questioned, oral sex was placed well below "watching partner undress" as a popular sexual activity. Even fewer had bought erotic videos to spice up their love lives (23 percent of men and 11 percent of women), and only 10 percent of men and 9 percent of women had had anal sex.

OTHER SEXUAL OUTLETS

When Laumann's team questioned the study's participants about masturbation, they made a surprising discovery. Conventional wisdom has been that masturbation is a substitute for sex with a partner; a way to relieve sexual tension among those—particularly teenagers and young adults—who are not currently in a sexual relationship. In fact, the evidence suggests that masturbation is practiced most often by men and women in their late twenties and thirties who are also enjoying regular sex with a partner.

In the Laumann study, 85 percent of men and 45 percent of women who were living with a sexual partner said that they masturbate. This social group also thought about sex more than did other groups. The findings also showed that women are more likely to begin masturbating after they have begun a steady relationship than before.

The results suggest that having a relationship with one person, whether through marriage or cohabitation, creates such a highly charged erotic environment that couples become more preoccupied with sex and therefore desire additional sexual outlets, such as masturbation.

FEMALE ORGASM

Laumann found that despite the many magazine articles explaining in detail how women can obtain sexual satisfaction, the majority of women do not regularly reach orgasm during sex. While 75 percent of men questioned always had an orgasm during sex, only 29 percent of women did. Yet over 40 percent of married or cohabiting women and 50 percent of married or cohabiting men said they were satisfied by sex. This suggests that, despite the media hype, there is much more to sex than achieving orgasm.

◀ *The drive to marry Although cohabitation is increasingly popular as a test of compatibility, most couples eventually marry. Even older people who are beyond childbearing age and have been married before return to marriage as a way of expressing their love for one another.*

How long does sex last? The length of time people devote to each sexual episode is a sensitive subject. The Social Organization of Sexuality *study found that most people spent from 15 minutes to one hour making love, but as Laumann and his colleagues point out, many people overestimate the time that activities take.*

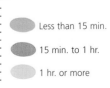

Less than 15 min.

15 min. to 1 hr.

1 hr. or more

Sex and the Media

Sex permeates the media. Magazine covers announce sex features; newspapers run stories on celebrities' sex lives; advertising sells products using sexual imagery; and film and TV bombard the viewer with sex in a multitude of ways.

The media, in a wide variety of forms, have become a dominant force in developed countries in the 20th century. Advertisements, newspapers, magazines, films, books, radio, television and on-line services are part of daily life. This constant presence gives the media great power to define as well as reflect social attitudes and behavior.

The positive aspect of media coverage of sex is that both men and women are better informed than ever about issues such as sexual response, fertility, contraception, the risks of unprotected sex (most important, HIV) and sexual health. Sex and sexuality are no longer seen as embarrassing, dirty or unmentionable. Open discussion of sex has encouraged people to become more broad-minded and tolerant, especially in relation to controversial issues such as homosexuality, bisexuality and HIV. Through media discussion, for example, the image of masturbation has been rehabilitated. Once seen as a dangerous and harmful addiction, masturbation is now widely regarded as an important means of sexual self-expression and knowledge.

On the downside, media openness makes soft- and hard-core pornography widely available. The effect of pornography on its viewers has been hotly debated. Is it a valid outlet for sexual tension, or does it degrade people by encouraging them to perceive one another as sex objects? Some parents worry that they have no control over the messages their children receive from the media.

CENSORSHIP

Since their invention, film and television have been major forces in shaping what is deemed suitable for public consumption. Because they reach such a wide segment of the population, their regulation has also become a source of great controversy.

The development of video led to a huge expansion in the pornography industry by enabling individuals to produce sex movies simply and cheaply, but access to video porn was still clandestine and relatively easy to control. The advent of cable, satellite and public access television, however, has raised the question of how we control what is transmitted via this medium. "Adult" channels may be available by subscription or transmitted after a certain time at night to prevent young children from being exposed to sexually explicit material, but the Internet (see page 260), which allows the almost unrestricted transmission of pornography, is very hard to regulate.

Too much sex? Many people argue that the media have reached saturation point when it comes to sex. There are, however, both advantages and disadvantages to media openness.

Advantages to media coverage of sex issues

- Sex has ceased to be a taboo.

- Exposure to subjects such as homosexuality encourages tolerance and awareness.

- Media coverage facilitates discussion between parents and children.

- Information encourages knowledge and responsibility about subjects such as contraception.

- Pornography is widely available (see page 246).

- Overexposure to idealized forms of male and female beauty exists.

- Media messages about sex may override parental messages.

- Teenagers feel pressured to have sex at an ever-younger age.

Disadvantages to media coverage of sex issues

MOVIE RATINGS

The law assumes that most adults can tolerate exposure to explicit sex scenes in movies without any serious harm, but many people feel concern about the possible effect that such imagery might have on children. In the United States, the movie industry, in 1969, set up the Motion Picture Code of Self-Regulation, a voluntary system that has since been amended three times (most recently in 1990). This code aims to limit children's access to strong language and sexually explicit and/or violent films and to provide guidelines for parents.

Similar codes—based on the appropriate viewing age for a movie—are also in effect in Canada, although the ratings vary according to province or territory. Before any movie is released for public viewing in Canada, a provincial censor—or board of censors—must review the movie and approve its content.

Fascination with the famous
Pop megastar Michael Jackson is just one example of a publicly hounded celebrity. Rumors about his sex life have been rife.

Many films that are made today contain sexual language together with explicit sex scenes and extensive nudity. The graphic depiction of sex on screen has only gradually become acceptable within the last few decades. In the 1930s and '40s it was considered indecent to show the female navel. Until the 1960s—a decade renowned for its permissiveness—nothing more explicit than a kiss was shown.

NEWSPAPERS AND MAGAZINES

Sex is common currency in today's mainstream newspapers and magazines, and this increased sexual content is controversial, whether it is intended to titillate or educate. Some people fear that frank sex talk in teenage magazines may encourage people to experiment sexually at too young an age. Questions from readers to advice columns can give the impression that sexual activity is common among young teens. Conversely, counselors argue that magazines can help to educate young people and demystify sex.

Magazines can perpetuate ideas about what is sexually attractive. The consumer is bombarded with images of "perfect" bodies that conform to standards dictated by the fashion and advertising industries. This acts to overrate physical appearance and underrate character—many people can only dream of a "model" figure, and pressure to conform produces feelings of inadequacy.

SEX AND ADVERTISING

Sex can be used to sell almost anything. The female body has long been used to advertise a wide range of products to men, who until recently had the greater spending power. In the 1990s, as women have come into their own as consumers, male sexual images are more visible in advertising designed to sell to both sexes. The portrayal of the body as a sex object is seen by many as exploitive—the issue remains controversial.

◀ *Sex on film This screen kiss between Alla Nazimova and Rudolph Valentino, in the 1921 film Camille, would have been seen as raunchy at the time. Today, when graphic depictions of sex are commonplace, it is considered tame.*

SEX SCANDALS

Interest in the sexual behavior and relationships of others is not a new phenomenon, but until the 20th century most people had little access to information about other people's private lives. Media coverage of the romantic and sexual lives of the rich and famous has created a huge public appetite for sexual scandals, especially those involving prominent figures such as movie and pop stars, politicians, and statesmen.

The media routinely expose sexual indiscretions to public opinion, and sex scandals abound. Political careers have been ruined when public exposure has turned the tide of popular support. Famous people's intimate sex lives have become part of the public domain.

Sex and Religion

Long before the introduction of civil laws on sexual behavior, almost every religion in the world imposed strictures on the sex lives of its followers. Today many religions place strong emphasis on sex in the context of marriage.

While pronouncements on sex vary from religion to religion, the issues are broadly the same—they include marriage, the purpose of sexual intercourse, the use of contraception, abortion, celibacy and homosexuality. Most religions traditionally extol the virtues of premarital chastity, heterosexuality, monogamy and the idea that sex is intended within marriage and for reproduction.

Many societies are becoming less religion-centered, yet attitudes about sex and sexuality still reflect the influence of the largest religions in the world. For example, while sex within a monogamous heterosexual relationship is almost universally accepted, sex outside this context is often frowned upon or forbidden.

CATHOLICISM

Millions of people all over the world look to the Roman Catholic Pope for guidance on matters of love and sexuality. They believe that the Pope, a Catholic priest required to be celibate as part of the Catholic ethos, is God's representative on Earth, and, as such, his word is law. The Catholic Church teaches that sexual intercourse outside of marriage is wrong and within marriage should be for procreation and

Pope John Paul II ▶
Elected as the head of the Catholic Church in 1978, Pope John Paul II is just one of the numerous religious leaders known for supporting the traditional Catholic ban on the use of artificial means of birth control.

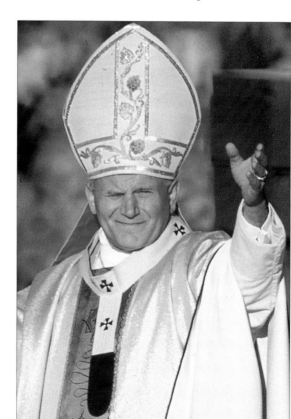

as a demonstration of love. For this reason, therefore, using any form of contraception, "before, at the moment of, or after the sexual act," is forbidden. Theoretically, the Catholic Church condemns even the rhythm method of contraception, in which couples abstain from sex during the woman's fertile days (see page 141), although in practice this method seems to be less repugnant because it is considered natural. Abortion, for any reason whatsoever (even for the victims of rape), is regarded as murder.

The Catholic doctrine teaches that marriages are indissoluble, which means that divorce is not allowed. A marriage can be annulled, but only in circumstances where the Church finds it invalid (for example, if the couple are too closely related by blood).

As a result the Church demands a fairly rigorous examination of Catholic couples who are planning to get married so that any grounds for a future dissolution have a good chance of being discovered beforehand. Indissolubility of marriage applies to marriage partners who are both baptized. If either marriage partner has not been baptized, then divorce and remarriage are permissible, but any subsequent marriage ceremony may not be held inside a Catholic church.

The Catholic religion condemns certain sexual practices. Among those considered to be sinful are homosexuality, masturbation and the use of pornography. Priests, monks and nuns are traditionally supposed to practice celibacy, although the Catholic Church has recently allowed Anglican priests who have become Catholics to remain with their wives.

Pope John Paul II rigorously adhered to the strictures of his predecessors, but the practices of many modern Catholics have changed. In the U.S. and Europe, where population control has been emphasized and the cost of raising and educating children has skyrocketed, many Catholics use some form of contraception. In South America, a Catholic stronghold, concern about the threat of AIDS has led to the ready availability of condoms.

Catholic marriages, like others, sometimes break down, and some Catholics divorce, even at the cost of leaving the Church. Some priests also find it difficult to live up to their vows of celibacy, and recently pressure has mounted to allow priests to marry. Priests were not forbidden to marry until the 12th century, and even the first Pope, Saint Peter, was a married man with at least one child.

PROTESTANTISM

Today the Protestant churches exhibit a wide range of views on sex. While the laws of morality that they preach have for the most part not changed, attitudes within the churches, especially the more liberal denominations, have.

Premarital sex is not universally condemned, provided that it occurs within a long-term, loving relationship. Divorce, even for clergy, is permitted, although in some churches, divorced clergy may not remarry in church if their first spouse is still alive. Some churches permit services blessing a second or subsequent marriage.

The Protestant churches have traditionally allowed the use of birth control, although many so-called fundamentalists, especially in the U.S., are strongly opposed to abortion. Fundamentalists tend also to be strongly opposed to the practice of a homosexual lifestyle. Although most Protestant

Can We Talk About It?

MARRYING OUTSIDE YOUR RELIGION

Today marrying or having a relationship with someone of a different culture or religion is no longer a rare occurrence, but it often has emotional repercussions for the couples and families involved, especially if one or both partners come from strict religious backgrounds.

If this is true for you, you may decide to conduct your relationship in secret. This may seem practical when the relationship begins, but hiding a serious, long-term relationship can lead to enormous guilt and stress for you and, when the truth emerges, a sense of betrayal on the part of your family. In any relationship leading to marriage, honesty from an early point can pave the way to the family's acceptance.

Families respond in many different ways. They may be in denial (refusing to acknowledge the fact that the relationship exists). They may refuse to accept that the relationship is important. Or they may show open hostility (some families threaten to ostracize their children if they refuse to conform to religious conventions). However your family responds, bear in mind that they react as they do because you seem to be rejecting their religion and the traditions that are important to them.

If you choose to marry someone who does not share your religion, make sure you discuss all the issues involved. Is "marrying out" an escape route, a personal rebellion or a way of demonstrating independence from your parents? How important is the support of your family? How important is the support of your partner's family? What issues will arise if you have children?

churches prohibit the ordination of admitted practicing homosexuals, homosexuality itself is sometimes tolerated.

Sex scandals

One of the arguments for allowing members of the clergy to marry is the belief that it can help pastors and priests to resist other sexual temptations. Inevitably sexual misconduct of religious leaders hits the news. For example, in the U.K. in 1995, the Reverend Chris Brain admitted sexual wrongdoing with young women who attended his "Nine

RELIGIOUS ATTITUDES TOWARD SEX

RELIGION	ATTITUDE
Buddhism	Sexual activities that do not harm or exploit others are permissible. Monks, nuns and Buddhists on meditation retreat must be celibate.
Islam	Relationships outside marriage are forbidden. No religious leader has to be celibate. Adulterers face the death penalty in some countries.
Protestantism	Sex should ideally be within the context of a lifelong marriage. No member of the clergy is required to be celibate.
Catholicism	Sex is prohibited outside of marriage. Sex inside marriage is for love and procreation. Catholic priests and nuns must be celibate.
Judaism	Sex is for pleasure and procreation inside of marriage. No member of the Jewish community is required to be celibate.
Hinduism	Sex before marriage is forbidden. Hindu monks (sadhus) are required to practice lifelong celibacy and be lust-free, ego-free and attachment-free.

A changing society
Western Protestant society is becoming less influenced by tradition and religion. More and more people are marrying in civil ceremonies, and those who do marry in church often have a less traditional approach to the ceremony—this bride is forgoing the traditional white wedding gown, for example.

O'clock Rave" services in Sheffield, England, and was forced to step down. There has been a long tradition of radical sexual attitudes among fringe Protestant sects in North America. Joseph Smith, the founder of Mormonism (also known as the Church of Jesus Christ of Latter-day Saints), espoused polygamy and had 27 wives. The Mormon Church outlawed polygamy in 1890, although a hundred years later it was estimated that there were still 35,000 polygamists in Utah, Arizona, Colorado and Mexico.

Around the same time that Mormonism sprang up in the early 19th century, other religious communities in New England practiced free love and "complex marriage." The most well known of these was the Oneida Community in upstate New York, which was founded in 1848 by a Congregationalist minister, John Humphrey Noyes. It began, essentially, as a wife-swapping arrangement, but things grew more complex when a second generation came of age. Adolescents in the Oneida Community were initiated into the mysteries of love by an older member of the opposite sex. Press campaigns and legal actions against the Oneida Community forced its members to publicly renounce their sexual practices in 1879, and the community broke up three years later.

JUDAISM

Unlike some religions, Judaism attributes no importance to the practice of celibacy. On the contrary, all members of the Jewish community, including rabbis, are encouraged to marry and procreate.

Judaism does not permit sexual intercourse before marriage, although a bride is not required to prove her virginity. After marriage, sexual intercourse is very important, and a man may not deny his wife sex, since it is the couple's responsibility to reproduce. Having sexual intercourse on the eve of the Sabbath is considered to be particularly meritorious.

Sex is for pleasure, however, as well as procreation. In fact, a husband is obliged by Jewish law to satisfy his wife sexually throughout her life, including during pregnancy and after menopause.

Sex is forbidden, though, when a woman is menstruating. In biblical times, contact with a menstruating woman was regarded as a source of ritual impurity. Today a Jewish woman is considered ritually impure until she has had a ritual bath, or *mikvah*, after the end of her period. This should take place seven days after the end of her period. During the ritual bath, the woman immerses herself in a pool of water and recites a blessing. Only after she has had a *mikvah* can she recommence sexual intercourse with her husband.

Orthodox Jews consider the act of masturbation to be wrong, and rabbis recommend various measures to help members avoid self-arousal. For example, according to the strictest rules, a man should not touch his penis at any time, even when he is urinating. Instead, he should direct his penis by lifting his scrotum. Liberal Jews, however, take a more relaxed view of genital touching and masturbation.

Jewish people are expected to marry other Jewish people, and intermarriage is frowned upon. Most Jews meet their future marriage partners through friends and family, but some Orthodox Jewish families practice arranged marriage.

To divorce her husband, an Orthodox Jewish woman needs to acquire both a civil divorce and a religious divorce, which, in some circumstances, her husband can refuse to grant her. A woman who has been refused a religious divorce by her husband

Jewish rites of passage A father teaches his son from the Jewish scriptures in preparation for the boy's bar mitzvah, a ceremony that marks the passage from boyhood to manhood.

is known as an *agunah*. Any subsequent marriage cannot then take place in a synagogue, and any children by the second marriage will be subject to a certain amount of religious stigma. Religious authorities have suggested the use of binding prenuptial agreements that will force men to grant a religious divorce in the event of a breakdown of the marriage.

Jewish baby boys are circumcised when they are eight days old. The rite of circumcision—*berit mila*—is accompanied by benedictions and ceremonies, including the naming of the child.

ISLAM

Adultery is a serious crime in the Islamic world. The minimum punishment, according to the Muslim holy book, the Koran, is one hundred lashes, although some Islamic countries consider adultery a crime punishable by death. In July 1977, in Saudi Arabia, Princess Mishaal was put to death on the orders of her grandfather Prince Muhammad ibn Abdul. She had been forcibly married to an older cousin who abandoned her. Later, in London, she met a young Lebanese man, Muhammad al Shaer. They returned to Jeddah to seek permission to marry, but her grandfather condemned Princess Mishaal as an adulteress, and she was stoned to death. Her lover, who was judged to have committed a lesser crime, was beheaded.

The Moonies
Mass weddings are a feature of some religious sects, such as the Unification Church. More commonly known as the Moonies, this group was founded by Sun Myung Moon in 1954.

GANDHI AND HINDUISM

Mahatma Gandhi, a holy man and scholar who campaigned for Indian independence from Britain, was married at the age of 13 to a child bride. By the time he was 16, he was a father. At 18 he went to England to study law, vowing at that time never to have sexual intercourse again, but failing for some years. Finally, at the age of 37, after fathering five sons, Gandhi took the Hindu vow of celibacy, partly because he thought that abstinence was the only morally acceptable form of birth control but also because he wanted to devote all his energy to the struggle for India's independence. Celibacy, he said, was a form of nonviolence between the sexes.

Mahatma Gandhi
Gandhi's wish came true in 1947 when India became independent. He was killed just a year later by a Hindu fanatic.

WHY CELIBACY?

Celibacy is seen as a way of maintaining the purity of those who intercede with God or the gods and as an aid to spiritual enlightenment. In primitive religions, shamans were often unmarried and avoided sex so that they did not sully their communication with the gods. Some Greek thinkers, notably the mathematician Pythagoras, believed that celibacy was conducive to the detachment required in a life of contemplation.

Despite worldwide condemnation of this execution, the death penalty for the act of adultery remains—in fact, just eight months after the showing of a film portraying the saga of Princess Mishaal, another Saudi prince asked King Khalid to execute his adulterous daughter. Nervous of another international scandal, the king told the prince he could not help and that the prince should handle the problem himself. He did: he took his daughter to a swimming pool in his palace and drowned her. The lover had been married 36 times.

Under Islamic law, a man can divorce his wife by repudiating her three times, but a woman can divorce her husband only if she proves to a religious court that he has committed some matrimonial offense—such as cruelty, desertion or failure to maintain her.

According to the Koran, a man may have as many as four wives, if he can afford them. This custom is known as "tetragamy" and is widespread. Wealthy sheikhs may also choose to keep concubines, provided they do not actually marry them.

Homosexuality is condemned by the Koran. After the Islamic revolution in Iran in 1979, homosexuals were publicly put to

death. Under strict Islamic law, anal sex is a crime against nature and is, again, punishable by death. The Koran endorses both male and female circumcision, although in most countries, civil law prohibits the circumcision of women and girls, and an international human rights campaign has developed in opposition to the practice.

Purdah

The word "purdah" means "screen" or "veil," and in the West it describes the Muslim practice of keeping women from the gaze of men who are not their husbands. Women in purdah are typically confined in high-walled enclosures and behind screens and curtains in the home. When a woman goes out, she covers her face with a veil, or yashmak, and her body with a special black garment known as a chador. She sometimes wears a mask with slits for the eyes. Purdah is widespread only among the very orthodox or in countries where Koranic law is strictly adhered to.

HINDUISM

The ancient Hindu text called the *Kama Sutra* is the most famous sex manual in the world. Written by the poet Vatsyayana in the 4th century A.D., the *Kama Sutra* classifies the sexual organs according to their dimensions and describes which male and female organs are compatible. It also describes various sexual positions and techniques. The *Kama Sutra* was given to girls at puberty to prepare them for a full sex life.

Hinduism also has a strong ascetic element. Hindu holy men spend their days in celibacy, poverty and self-denial in the hope of escaping from earthly desires. Only in this way, they believe, can they perfect themselves and escape the cycle of death and rebirth, with all the suffering it entails. Some very strict Hindu holy men—known as *naishthik brahmacharis*—practice the vows of eightfold celibacy. This means that they must never be in the company of women and must never think about women, even when they are dreaming.

BUDDHISM

Buddhism began when the Buddha, an Indian prince, believed he had discovered the path to enlightenment. It started as a celibate order of monks, but when it became a world religion, the requirement for celibacy was dropped. Young Buddhist men are still expected to spend a year in a monastery and abstain from sex during this time.

In contrast, the Indian Tantric cult, which has Buddhist origins, views sex as the road to enlightenment. It aims mystically to unite the female and the male sexual energy. A man and a woman have to perform sexual intercourse slowly for hours on end, while reciting sacred words or mantras and meditating on mystical diagrams. Both partners exercise great care not to reach orgasm, because this causes energy to be dispelled. It is said that although few devotees have attained enlightenment in this way, those who have gain supernatural powers and spiritual transcendence.

RELIGIOUS CULTS

Modern religious cults often use sex to recruit members. In the 1970s, for example, a group calling itself "Hookers for Jesus" sent out young women to seduce men into joining the sect. The followers of the Indian mystic Bhagwan Shree Rajneesh, who established an ashram in Oregon in the 1980s, were expected to indulge in sex orgies as a way to enlightenment. "Sex is one of those activities given by nature and God in which you are thrown again and again to the present moment," explained the Bhagwan. "Ordinarily you are never in the present—except when you are making love, and then too for a few seconds only."

The Bhagwan prescribed exercises to raise sexual energy. Devotees had to shower and go to the toilet surrounded by other naked people. People were blindfolded before having sex with each other. This, it was said, rid an individual of jealousy and helped to dissolve the ego. After allegations of fraud and attempted murder in 1985, the Bhagwan left Oregon and returned to India.

The Movement of Spiritual Inner Awareness, founded by American John Roger, also promotes sexual freedom as a path to spiritual enlightenment. Roger suggests that celibacy, on the other hand, leads to psychiatric illness. He maintains that only regular sex can lead to inner peace.

It is more common for cult leaders to advocate celibacy for their followers while indulging in an active sex life themselves. The Aum cult, which was believed to have staged the nerve-gas attack on the Tokyo subway in 1995, recruited nubile young women to lure sexually repressed young men into the sect. But once they had joined, they were required to be celibate on the grounds that "base desire saps vital energy." Men were required to give their girlfriends to the cult's leader, Shoko Asahara, and married couples were required to divorce. Asahara would summon female cult members to him at night. Once freed from the Aum cult, the women involved claimed they had been raped.

The Reverend Jim Jones, who convinced 914 members of his People's Temple to swallow poison in Guyana in 1978, also had sexual intercourse with members of his congregation—both men and women—while forbidding others any sexual outlet at all. Jones would force members to confess their sexual fears and fantasies. Jones himself claimed to take no pleasure in sex. He said that for him, it was a "revolutionary tool."

RELIGIOUS CULT LEADERS

Bhagwan ▶
Shree Rajneesh
This Indian guru set up a religious commune in the U.S. in the 1980s. He saw free love as the route to enlightenment.

Shoko Asahara ▲
The blind leader of the Japanese cult Aum Sinrikyo (The Supreme Truth) demanded that members have sex with him on a frequent basis.

David Koresh ▶
Leader of the fanatical Branch Davidians, David Koresh, shown here on television, died in a shoot-out with the FBI at Waco, Texas, in 1993. Koresh claimed to have had sex with 400 virgins.

Sex and the Law

Historically, U.S. sex laws have been strongly influenced by the religious tradition that only sexual intercourse within marriage is acceptable. Other forms of sexual activity have typically been regarded as sinful and illegal.

Traditionally, U.S. law has tended to divide sex offenses into "unnatural acts"—sometimes referred to as "crimes against nature"—and other prohibited sexual acts. The category of unnatural acts includes not only deviant practices such as sex with animals (bestiality) and children (pederasty) but also more accepted practices such as oral sex, anal sex, homosexuality and lesbianism.

Included in the category of other prohibited sexual acts are prostitution (see page 254), indecent exposure, indecent

assault, and the unlawful abduction or detention of a woman or child for prostitution or any other purposes relating to sex.

Many states still have laws aimed at restricting the availability of contraceptives or literature concerning their use, especially to minors (see page 242). Until 1965, Connecticut prohibited married couples from using contraceptives, at which time the restriction was held to be unconstitutional by the U.S. Supreme Court.

Various sexual activities that many people would not regard as criminal are still technically illegal in many states, although the law is not usually enforced. These include premarital sex (fornication), extramarital sex and cohabitation. Studies indicate that at least 90 percent of adult American males have committed a "sex crime" at least once in their lives.

It is often argued that lawmakers should not seek to legislate on matters of sexual morality, especially when these touch on the activities of consenting adults in the privacy of their own homes. Furthermore, the fact that crimes such as underage sex are frequently and flagrantly committed without any attempt by the authorities to prosecute the offenders simply encourages a contempt for the law.

The American Law Institute has developed a Model Penal Code that recommends that laws relating to sexual activities performed in private between consenting adults should be abolished. According to the Model Penal Code, activities such as premarital sex, adultery, oral-genital sex, and all consensual sex acts between husband and wife should be decriminalized. Violent crimes such as rape and the sexual abuse of children, and offenses such as

Amsterdam's red light district
Prostitution—engaging in sexual activity for payment—is legal in some parts of the world. In Amsterdam prostitutes use red lights to advertise their services.

indecent exposure and voyeurism—which are damaging to the individual or constitute a public nuisance—would continue to be treated as crimes.

Legal opinion is divided on issues such as prostitution and pornography, however. Some experts feel that these crimes should still be penalized because they are demeaning to the way in which society perceives women (some feminist writers argue that pornography is tantamount to violence). Some people believe that pornography and prostitution encourage the perception of sex as a crude physical act rather than a demonstration of love between two people. As such, they believe that this damages the moral fabric of society.

Other groups believe that by continuing to criminalize offenses such as these, society is encouraging a criminal subculture that allows the spread of more serious problems —drug abuse, child exploitation and police corruption, among others. In the case of prostitution, authorities also fear that sexually transmitted diseases, including HIV (see page 180), may be more difficult to control if prostitutes are discouraged by fear of harassment or prosecution from seeking medical checkups.

OBSCURE SEX LAWS

In all parts of the world, including some parts of the U.S., there are laws that were made many years ago that now seem particularly outmoded, obscure or bizarre. The following are a few examples of unusual U.S. sex laws:

~ In Harrisburg, Pennsylvania, it is illegal to have sex with a truck driver while in a tollbooth.
~ In Tremonton, Utah, having sex in an ambulance is illegal.
~ In Willowdale, Oregon, it is illegal for a husband to talk suggestively in his wife's ear while they are making love.
~ In Clinton, Oklahoma, there is a law against masturbating while watching two people have sex in a car.

~ In Alexandria, Minnesota, it is illegal for a man having sex with his wife to smell of onion, sardines or garlic.
~ In Newcastle, Wyoming, sex in the freezer of a butcher's shop is illegal.

THE AGE OF CONSENT

The age at which an adolescent can legally consent to have sex is a controversial subject. It covers issues of morality and health, and also raises the question of when a person can be considered old enough to accept the responsibilities of parenthood and marriage that underpin consent laws.

Although all parts of the U.S. have age of consent laws for heterosexuals— ranging from 14 to 18 years, depending on the state—these are rarely enforced, even in the presence of clear evidence (such as an underage pregnancy).

According to figures compiled by the Alan Guttmacher Institute in New York during the mid-1990s, a majority of adolescents begin to have sex in their mid- to late teens—55 percent of young women and 73 percent of young men by the age of 18.

A reluctance to enforce consent laws reflects the view held by many health-care organizations that making an example of

Strange sex laws In Ames, Iowa, there is a law prohibiting a man from taking more than three slugs of beer when in bed with a woman.

fact or fiction?

Age of consent laws exist because sex can damage young people.

Fiction. Underage sex is not illegal because it is physically damaging (although it can be), but because maturity is needed to face such possible consequences as STDs and pregnancy.

The age at which peo-
ple in the West can
legally consent to
homosexual acts is
often two or three
years older than that
for heterosexual sex,
although in most
European countries,
the age limit is the
same. In some parts of
the world homosexual-
ity is altogether out-
lawed, and offenders
face severe penalties.

Young mothers
Age of consent is less
important in some cul-
tures than others. This
13-year-old girl is from
the Akha hill tribe in
Thailand.

some young people would only discourage
others from seeking advice about contraception and, in the case of sexually transmitted diseases and pregnancy, early medical attention from a doctor.

13th-century English law

U.S. statutes covering the age of consent
were originally based on 13th-century
English common law. Under English law it
was illegal to "ravish" a maiden under the
age of 12, with or without her consent.
Three hundred years later, in 1576, the age
of consent was lowered to 10. The early lawmakers in America followed the English
example by adopting this same age of consent. Throughout the 19th century, however,
all the states steadily increased the age of
consent, with some opting for age 21. Now
the age of consent varies throughout the
U.S., ranging from 14 to 18, with more than
half the states opting for 16 years.

Age of consent in other countries

In most developed nations, the age at which
individuals can consent to heterosexual sex
is between 15 and 18 years, although in
some countries it is lower. Austria,
Germany, Italy and Iceland, for example, set
the age of consent at 14, while in Spain and
Malta it is only 12 years, provided the sexual partner is not in a position of power
or influence over the girl.

In the U.K., the age of consent is 16,
and the sexual partner of a female
below this age—but not the young
woman herself—can be prosecuted
for "unlawful sexual intercourse."
In practice, however, provided the
young woman is at least 13 years
old, a prosecution is extremely
unlikely to occur. Women are infre-
quently prosecuted for having sexual
intercourse with boys, although in 1997
an English woman was deported
from the U.S. back to the U.K.
and prosecuted for eloping
with her 14-year-old lover.

In many developing
countries, the age of
consent is either
much younger than
in developed coun-
tries, does not
exist or is not
enforced. Child

brides as young as 10 years old are common
in the poorer Asian nations, such as India
and Bangladesh, and in sub-Saharan Africa.
In fact, some parts of sub-Saharan Africa
encourage early sexual relationships
because young girls are expected to prove
their fertility before they will be considered
suitable marriage partners.

Teenage contraception

The right of underage women to seek contraception is a controversial issue in the U.S.
There have been two attempts in Congress
to ensure the involvement of parents in a
minor's decision to seek contraception, but
both have failed.

The idea of free access to contraception
for teenagers first surfaced as a political
issue in the early 1970s, when President
Richard Nixon signed Title X of the Public
Health Service Act. This law provided for
family planning clinics and other contraception advice services on a nationwide basis.
It followed studies in the 1960s that showed
that, because of inequalities in access to contraception, low-income women were twice
as likely as more affluent women to have
unplanned pregnancies. Title X required
that every woman have the freedom to seek
family planning services, regardless of age
or marital status. As a result, clinics funded
by Title X provided contraception to adolescents on a confidential basis.

In 1982 the Reagan administration pushed
through a law requiring that parents be
notified if their children were obtaining
contraception services. Supporters of the
move wanted more family participation in
adolescent family planning advice, arguing
that the current situation encouraged
underage sex. The law was blocked by two
federal appeals, however, and it was subse-
quently withdrawn.

Opponents of reform said that studies
showed that the majority of adolescents
who seek contraception services have
already had an active sex life for a year. Any
change in the confidentiality rule, it was
argued, would discourage adolescents from
seeking contraception without stopping
them from being sexually active. It was also
pointed out that family planning clinics
serve other important health functions for
underage clients, such as providing advice
and screening for gynecological disorders
and sexually transmitted diseases.

A further reform attempt, in 1996, which required family planning clinics to obtain written consent from parents before providing contraception to adolescents, failed to pass through Congress.

HOMOSEXUALITY

In most states in the U.S., it is not treated as a crime to be homosexual—that is, to feel sexual attraction toward another person of the same gender. For many years, however, laws were enacted to prohibit any physical expression of those feelings. Under public order laws, same-sex couples could be prosecuted for being physically demonstrative to each other.

On the books, at least, sexual acts between men, such as fellatio (oral-genital sex), mutual masturbation and sodomy (anal sex), were regarded as felonies, which meant that a convicted person could face imprisonment. In general, the law took the view that punishment would discourage homosexuals from engaging in sexual activity, and a prison term would "rehabilitate" them into a heterosexual way of life.

Many experts now accept that sexual orientation, whatever its origins (see page 50), cannot be altered or suppressed by legal sanctions. In recent years, society has moved toward accepting homosexuality as a way of life and liberalizing the laws concerning homosexual sex. Approximately half of all the states in the U.S. have decriminalized all sex acts, including sodomy, between consenting adults, and other states are considering following suit.

Where laws against homosexuals still exist, law enforcement officials most often arrest individuals for such offenses as loitering in a public place with the intention of committing an indecent act, or solicitation—approaching a stranger and offering to have sex for money. In order to obtain evidence for an arrest, plainclothes police officers may pose as homosexuals and encourage suspects to perform an illegal act. The crime has to be witnessed by another police officer to provide corroboration.

It is still illegal in some parts of the U.S. to operate a business catering to homosexuals. Some police forces try to discourage homosexuals from meeting openly by raiding venues where homosexual men and women are known to gather, such as private clubs and bars, and closing them down.

The gay rights movement

Society's views of homosexuality changed significantly after the Stonewall riots of 1969 (see page 244), when a police raid on a gay bar in New York erupted into violence. This event became a cause célèbre among the gay community, and a major turning point in the movement to establish equal rights for homosexual men and lesbians. Homosexual rights organizations adopted the term "gay" both as a label indicating their sexual orientation and as a political statement.

Before the Stonewall riots, the only public campaigns for improved rights for homosexuals were annual demonstrations in front of the White House and outside Independence Hall, in Philadelphia, every July 4. The protesters, in what they called "Homosexual Reminder Day," demanded that homosexuals be given the right to hold government jobs.

After Stonewall, campaign groups formed in major cities across the U.S. to mark the anniversary of the riots with demonstrations for gay rights. The original demand of

Public demonstrations Since the 1970s homosexuality has achieved a public face. To mark the yearly anniversary of the Stonewall riots (the beginning of gay liberation in the U.S.), gay men and women from all over the U.S. join together to parade in the streets and celebrate gay pride and identity.

Public affection Openly displaying affection to a gay lover may sometimes meet with homophobia, but it is very rarely treated as a criminal activity.

THE TRIAL OF OSCAR WILDE

Playwright, poet and wit, Oscar Wilde (1854–1900) is perhaps the most famous figure to be jailed for homosexuality. The author of such works as *The Importance of Being Earnest*, *Lady Windermere's Fan* and *The Picture of Dorian Gray*, Wilde scandalized late-Victorian society with his flamboyant lifestyle and candid relationship with his young lover Lord Alfred Douglas.

Lord Douglas's outraged father, the marquess of Queensberry, left a card on display at Wilde's London club accusing the writer of being a "sodomite," a practicer of buggery. Wilde tried to sue the marquess for libel and lost. In the trial that followed, testimony—including much of that given by Wilde himself—led to his subsequent imprisonment for homosexuality.

Wilde served two years' hard labor at Reading Gaol. He wrote as the legacy of his time in prison the narrative poem *The Ballad of Reading Gaol* (1898), inspired by the story of a soldier who was hanged for killing his wife. Wilde died a few years after his release in self-imposed exile in France, a broken man.

Oscar Wilde
Born Oscar Fingal O'Flahertie Wills in Dublin, Wilde attracted criticism for his extrovert lifestyle even before accusations of sodomy.

the Reminder Day protesters has now been absorbed into a much broader campaign that includes the repeal of all homosexual sex laws, the right to serve in the armed forces, and the right of homosexuals to marry or to receive legal treatment equal to that afforded heterosexual couples.

Laws have changed to some extent on all of these issues, although many restrictions remain. The federal government still bans homosexuals from holding jobs in the CIA and the FBI, even though the U.S. Civil Service Commission has ruled that gays must not be barred from federal posts.

A number of large corporations have lifted the ban against employing homosexuals. But in many U.S. states, openly practicing homosexuals cannot hold teaching posts, even though court rulings make it clear that sexuality alone is not sufficient grounds for refusing an individual a job. Only the state of Hawaii has passed a law making gay marriage legal; it is still outlawed in all other U.S. states.

In the early part of Bill Clinton's first term as president of the U.S. (1992 to 1996), his administration attempted to repeal the law banning homosexuals from holding posts in the military. Following protests from senior military figures, this move was abandoned in favor of a relaxation in the requirement that members of the armed forces admit to being homosexual. In effect, gays can join the military as long as they keep their sexual orientation secret.

Homosexuals still encounter discrimination in all spheres of daily life, including being barred, without legal redress, from private housing in many cities. The gay movement continues to campaign for equal legal treatment until such infringements of civil rights have been eradicated.

The Stonewall riots marked the origins of the modern gay rights movement. On the night of June 27, 1969, police raided the Stonewall Inn, a popular gay bar in Greenwich Village, New York City. Members of the New York Tactical Police Force and agents of the Alcoholic Beverage Control Board entered the bar, ostensibly on the grounds that alcohol was being sold on unlicensed premises.

All the patrons were promptly evicted, but instead of dispersing, they barricaded the officers inside. A crowd that included many heterosexual sympathizers grew until it numbered several hundred, and someone tried to set the building on fire. Police reinforcements arrived, and after several hours of rioting, the crowd was finally dispersed.

The first "Gay Power" rally was held one month later, on July 27, in New York's Washington Square. After a number of speeches, participants made a candlelight march to the Stonewall Inn. In the following year, a new generation of organizations appeared that included the Gay Liberation Front and the Gay Activists Alliance. The anniversary of the riots is now commemorated nationally every year with demonstrations, parades and "Gay Pride" marches in New York, London and other cities.

STATE-SPONSORED SEX EDUCATION

Most state legislatures accept the need for some form of school-based sex education, especially to combat teenage pregnancy and sexually transmitted diseases. In the past people have feared that information about the dangers of underage sex will encourage promiscuity. The Joint UN Programme on HIV/AIDS countered this fear with its survey of sex education and behavior in 10 countries. In all cases, education effectively discouraged underage sex—the number of unwanted pregnancies and STDs were cut.

Since the mid-1980s, the spread of HIV and AIDS has caused many U.S. schools to follow a comprehensive program of sex education on the premise that ignorance about sex is potentially fatal. Some states, most notably Florida, now offer cash incentives to schools to encourage them to set up AIDS awareness programs. Parents in all states, however, are allowed to remove their children from AIDS education programs.

During the mid-1990s, a new welfare reform law was passed to ensure that sex educators place greater emphasis on abstinence until marriage. Approximately $88 million was spent on education programs.

SEX AND CENSORSHIP

Until as recently as the late 1950s, the law severely restricted the freedom to publish or broadcast material with a sexual content in most parts of the U.S. Virtually all material with a sexual theme was censored.

U.S. law covering "obscene" material tended to follow an 1868 English legal precedent that held that material is considered obscene if it tends to "deprave and corrupt those whose minds are open to such immoral influences." Such a broad and subjective definition gave legislators a free hand to ban any material that might affect a single member of the public.

The Federal Anti-Obscenity Act of 1873 (known as the Comstock Law) prohibited the mailing of any printed matter that was considered to be "lewd," "filthy," "indecent" or "obscene," and individual states had total autonomy with regard to censoring books, art exhibitions, films and theatrical productions.

Texts that are now considered to be of great literary value were once outlawed because of their perceived potential to cause offense. Chaucer's *Canterbury Tales*, Daniel Defoe's *Moll Flanders* and the 5th-century B.C. Greek comedy *Lysistrata*, by Aristophanes, were all banned on the grounds of obscenity under the Comstock Law. Laws relating to obscenity even allowed states to censor school textbooks by removing images of nudity and anatomical diagrams. The state of Maryland went to the extent of banning the 1957 film *The Moon Is Blue*, on the grounds that the use of the words "pregnant" and "virginity" were "lewd" and "lascivious." Twelve years later, the Police Board of Censorship in Chicago regarded as "obscene" a Walt Disney documentary that showed a buffalo giving birth in a snowstorm.

Chief Justice Earl Warren, interviewed in 1969, said that the U.S. Supreme Court's most difficult area of adjudication was

A NEW ERA OF SEXUAL OPENNESS

The most radical changes concerning the censorship of sexual material occurred between the mid-1950s and early 1970s. In a series of landmark cases, the U.S. Supreme Court redefined the law to provide a much tighter definition of obscenity. To be classified as obscene, material had to portray sexual conduct in a "patently offensive way" and be devoid of serious "literary, artistic, political or scientific value" (this second criterion was known as the "LAPS value test").

The LAPS value test brought an end to the role of state and federal legislators as moral censors and opened the floodgates to a spate of sexually explicit books, films, magazines and theatrical productions. Among these groundbreaking early shows was the musical *Hair*, which featured full-frontal nudity for the first time on a mainstream American stage. In contrast, the more recent photo exhibit by Robert Mapplethorpe met with widespread censure.

The controversy surrounding Hair
This 1960s rock musical was the first to show nudity on stage. At its release, many people judged its content offensive or obscene. In St. Paul, Minnesota, a frustrated clergyman released 18 white mice into the theater lobby in an attempt to scare away the audience.

defining obscenity, because what one person might see as "obscene, lascivious and lewd" another might regard as "realistic, colorful and instructive."

PORNOGRAPHY

Opinions are fiercely divided on the effects of pornography (see page 73). Some people argue that it degrades the user and objectifies women. They claim, too, that pornography has a desensitizing effect, causing the user to seek progressively more explicit material to achieve the same state of sexual arousal.

Moral campaign groups support their belief that pornography incites sex crimes with the claim that offenders are often found with sexually explicit material in their possession.

Opponents of this viewpoint claim that Scandinavian countries that have adopted liberal laws on pornography have lower rates of sex offenses than countries such as the U.K., where pornography laws are more strictly enforced.

Denmark abolished all legal sanctions against sexually explicit material for adults following a 1969 report by the Danish Com-

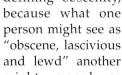

The Language of Sex

The words "pornography" and "obscenity" are often used interchangeably in general conversation, but there are important differences between them. "Pornography," which comes from the Greek, literally means "writing of harlots" and refers to words or images that depict erotic acts intended to be sexually arousing. The dictionary definition of "obscene" is "abhorrent to morality or virtue, designed to incite lust or depravity."

mission on Criminal Law. Members were persuaded by psychologists and sociologists that there was no provable connection between pornography and moral corruption. Some experts believe that pornography provides a sexual release and reduces the risk of individuals carrying out aggressive sexual acts. Supporters of pornography also say that it can help people to overcome sexual difficulties and enable couples to reach new heights of sexual expression.

To find a definitive answer to this contentious issue, President Lyndon Johnson set up the 1968 Federal Commission on Obscenity and Pornography. After two years the commission could find no evidence of a link between "erotic materials" and "sex crime or sex delinquency among youth or adults." Commission members recommended an end to the censorship of pornography for consenting adults, the addition of good-quality sex education to all school curriculae and ongoing research into the effects of pornography. The commission's verdict was not unanimous, however. A minority disagreed with these findings. At the same time, moral pressure groups stepped up their campaigns, and the Senate rejected the commission's findings.

A subsequent Presidential Commission, set up by President Ronald Reagan in the 1980s, took an opposing view, stating that all pornography is harmful and likely to lead to sexual violence. As a result, a nationwide crackdown was strongly advocated. The commission's report has not so far resulted in any significant toughening of the laws covering pornography.

DIVORCE

The act of marriage creates a legally binding contract between a man and a woman. In the past, in order to break the marriage contract, the unhappy spouse had to claim that

Should divorcing couples be "at fault"? Today divorces are frequently granted to couples simply because their marriages have broken down. In the past, and still in some U.S. states, couples have to find fault with their spouses in order to get divorced.

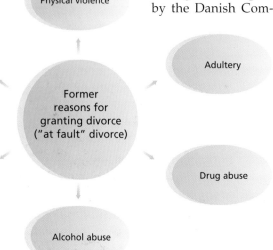

his or her partner had done something in breach of that contract. In other words, either the wife or the husband had to be at fault. The legal grounds for divorce included the following:

~ Adultery (one of the parties was engaged in extramarital sexual relations, thus breaching the fidelity pledged as part of the marital contract).
~ Chemical dependence (one of the parties was addicted to drugs, alcohol or both and as a result was not able to meet his or her marital obligations).
~ Physical and/or emotional abuse (one of the parties broke the commitment to love, honor and cherish).
~ Abandonment (one of the parties broke the contractual agreement to be present to fulfill one's marital duties).

During the 1970s, a time of sexual metamorphosis, the basis for divorce began to shift as society's perspective on marriage changed. More states adopted the concept of "irretrievable breakdown" or "irreconcilable differences" as sufficient grounds for divorce. By the early 1990s, all states had abolished wrongdoing, or "fault," as necessary for divorce, although a minority still use fault as a basis for determining the division of assets and liabilities of a marriage. No-fault divorce is again under debate now.

In certain circumstances, such as when one partner lacks physical and/or mental capacity or is under the age of consent, a marriage can be annulled. In other situations, the law deems marriage impossible. For example, marriages between homosexuals (except in Hawaii), marriages entered into before a prior marriage has ended and marriages between family members (in most states this includes adopted family members) are all declared null and void.

In states that retain the principle of fault as a possible grounds for divorce, adultery is most often the basis for a claim that the aggrieved party should be compensated with equal division of assets. Proof of adultery must be provided if the accused spouse denies the charge.

BIGAMY

Bigamy is a criminal offense in which a married person enters into one or more additional marriage contracts while the first

marriage remains undissolved. Many people find bigamy more offensive than adultery because it involves an emotional and long-term commitment to the adulterous relationship. In the case of the adulterer, many people perceive the offending partner as straying—an act apparently easier to forgive than the intentional commitment involved in a bigamous marriage.

For bigamy to be prosecuted as a crime, the offender must have entered the marriage knowingly and willfully. No crime has been committed if a person commits him- or herself to a bigamous marriage innocently, for example, believing that the former spouse was dead or that a former marriage had been legally dissolved.

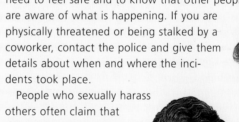

Can We Talk About It?

SEXUAL HARASSMENT AT WORK

Sexual harassment can be subtle—you may sometimes be unsure whether what has happened to you constitutes harassment—or it can be blatant. Trust your own judgment about what behavior you find acceptable, or ask someone you trust how they would feel in a similar situation and what they might do. If you decide that the incident was offensive and unacceptable, or if you feel frightened or at risk, then you should certainly seek help.

Individuals sometimes find a sympathetic or serious hearing difficult to get. If you experience harassment at work, find out whether your employer has any policies to protect you. Many companies and institutions have equal opportunity policies and employ a personnel officer responsible for staff care. If this is not the case, check out your rights by contacting either a citizen's advice agency or a legal center. You need to feel safe and to know that other people are aware of what is happening. If you are physically threatened or being stalked by a coworker, contact the police and give them details about when and where the incidents took place.

People who sexually harass others often claim that their victims provoked them by their appearance or behavior. Whatever you do, you cannot be held responsible for the harassment or for anyone else's inappropriate sexual behavior—it is simply unacceptable.

ADULTERY

The term "adultery" refers to voluntary sexual intercourse between a married individual and a person, whether married or single, who is not the individual's husband or wife. In some states this is a crime, but it is a common crime and one that is rarely prosecuted.

A person can legally have only one spouse. The wife or husband of someone who is already married is described as a "putative spouse." Once a putative spouse learns that his or her marriage is bigamous, spousal status and any legal rights associated with it come to an end.

Because a bigamous marriage is legally void, no divorce or annulment is necessary to terminate the relationship. If a couple want to validate a bigamous marriage, the prior legal marriage must be dissolved, and a legal marriage ceremony must take place.

PATERNITY

The word "paternity" refers to the issue of who is the biological father of a child (*pater* is Latin for "father"). In the U.S., when a child is born during a marriage, the husband is generally presumed to be the father. The presumed father can dispute this presumption, however, if he can establish that he had no access to the mother during the time period when the child would have been conceived—for example, a man who travels as part of his job could prove that he was out of the country.

Even if paternity can be refuted, most courts are reluctant to issue an order depriving a child of paternity. Many states set a time limit on contesting paternity. This creates a dilemma for a man who learns that he is not the biological father only after this time period has elapsed. The courts in these states argue that a form of adoption has occurred and that, regardless of what this man and/or the mother may now feel about his paternity, his rights of fatherhood have been irrefutably established under the law. The child is entitled to financial support from the "father."

Proving paternity when a couple are not married requires blood tests to establish a genetic link. Umbilical blood taken at birth, or blood taken from a child when he or she is several months old, is compared with blood from the mother and the alleged father. If further evidence is required, *DNA* testing is sometimes used to establish paternity conclusively.

Once a man's paternity is established, he is legally obligated to give financial support to his child until the child reaches age 18 or until graduation from high school, whichever occurs later, but in no event beyond age 20.

ASSISTED CONCEPTION

While assisted conception, in one form or another, is not a new procedure, recent societal changes, together with modern technological innovations in fertility treatment, have occurred so rapidly that the law has often been left behind. The oldest and most established form of assisted conception is *ARTIFICIAL INSEMINATION*, using a syringe or other form of applicator. The sperm may be provided by the husband or partner of the woman, or by an anonymous donor.

In either case, the legal situation is normally straightforward. When the husband or partner provides the sperm, he has the same parental rights as if conception had taken place through sexual intercourse. Men who donate sperm must do so on the understanding that they have no parental rights to any children arising from the procedure. The identity of the sperm donor is kept secret from the couple, just as the couple's identity is kept secret from the donor.

ESTABLISHING PATERNITY

Debates about the identity of a child's father can sometimes be resolved with blood tests or put to rest with DNA tests.

BLOOD TEST

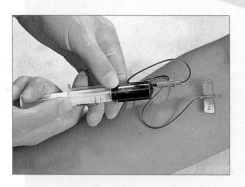

A doctor can take a sample of a man's blood from a vein in the arm. His blood type is then compared with the blood type of the baby he claims to have fathered.

Blood typing tests are limited, however, in that they can only establish that a man could not have been the father of a particular child. If there is any ambiguity, a DNA test can be performed.

DNA TEST

Doctors can now accurately map individual's chromosomes. The DNA map shown here can provide conclusive evidence about whether or not a particular man fathered a specific child.

The husband of a woman who has received donated sperm is held to be the legal father of any resulting offspring.

An exception to the confidentiality rule may apply if a baby produced from donor sperm is discovered to have a gene disorder. Sperm donors are legally obliged to declare a family history of genetic illness. If such a medical problem exists and a donor knowingly fails to acknowledge it, he may be held legally responsible for a baby's subsequent genetic condition. The parents can then request the donor's identity so that they can seek a claim through the courts.

Legal issues surrounding artificial insemination have become controversial in cases where a husband or partner who has had sperm placed in storage has died before the material could be used to inseminate the woman. In cases on both sides of the Atlantic, the right of the woman to obtain the sperm for insemination has been challenged when it was alleged that the man did not intend to father a child after death.

Modern medical procedures now make it possible for women to donate eggs to enable infertile women to give birth—for example, through in vitro fertilization (see page 156). Just as in sperm donation, the recipient and her husband or cohabiting partner are considered to be the legal parents, and the egg donor has no parental claim on any resulting child.

SURROGACY

In recent years, the issue of surrogate motherhood, in which a woman gives birth to a child on behalf of another—usually infertile—woman, has proved to be a difficult issue for the law to resolve.

A surrogate mother gives birth to a baby conceived either from her own ovum or from an ovum implanted in her from another woman. The father's sperm is usually administered by artificial insemination or mixed with the ovum in a container such as a test tube. In some cases, the surrogate mother is impregnated through sexual intercourse with the man.

Before the surrogate mother actually becomes pregnant, she must enter into a binding agreement that she will hand over the baby as soon as it is born. Legal disputes arise only if the surrogate mother fails to honor the contract she has made and chooses to keep the baby.

The majority of states still have no stringent laws to deal with surrogacy, although in a few states, surrogacy is tightly regulated or covered by some legal constraints. In Arkansas, for example, a baby born through artificial insemination as part of a surrogacy contract is deemed to be the child of both the biological father and his wife, if married. If unmarried, only the father is considered to be the legal parent.

So far, only in Arizona is it considered an offense to "arrange, procure or otherwise assist" a surrogate parentage contract. In drafting the laws on surrogacy, the state was attempting to prohibit "baby brokers," but the U.S. Supreme Court has declared Arizona's rulings on surrogacy unconstitutional, which may render the laws unenforceable in the courts.

Surrogacy is generally treated in the courts as a case of stepparent adoption. The man who provides the sperm is regarded as the biological and legal parent, and his wife must then obtain consent from the "host" mother and the biological father to adopt the child.

ABORTION

An abortion is a procedure that terminates the development of an embryo or fetus before the age of viability (the stage at which the fetus becomes capable of independent life). Tiny babies of just 24 weeks can survive with the aid of intensive care. The term "abortion" is usually applied to induced terminations (those that are brought about by artificial means), but it can also mean one that occurs naturally—known more conventionally as a miscarriage or a spontaneous abortion.

Surrogacy court cases When a surrogate mother reneges on her decision to hand over the baby she has been carrying, the resulting court cases can be fraught with emotion. Here the "commissioning" mother argues her case with an attorney.

Termination of pregnancy is a frequently performed surgical procedure in the U.S. According to the Centers for Disease Control and Prevention, over 1.5 million abortions were performed in 1992, but estimates suggest that this figure had dropped to 1.4 million by 1994. Worldwide, it is thought that approximately 50 million abortions are performed each year.

The vast majority of abortions in the U.S. are performed within the first 12 weeks of pregnancy, with just 1 percent performed for nonmedical reasons after 20 weeks. According to 1992 figures, only 320 abortions were performed after 26 weeks. Questions regarding whether abortion should be allowed by law and, if so, at what stage and by what method are some of the most controversial of all social issues, involving extremely difficult legal, moral and religious considerations.

Those with the strongest views on the subject have tended to form into opposing factions: "pro life," who believe that all abortion is wrong because it denies the fetus the right to life, and "pro choice," who believe the decision to abort a fetus is the mother's to make, rather than the court's.

Until 1967, abortion was treated as a criminal act in most states, except in the case of therapeutic abortion when the mother's life was at risk. These exceptional cases mostly involved complications of pregnancy such as eclampsia (a condition characterized by convulsions) or pernicious vomiting. Legal abortions in other circumstances were available only in a very few states, such as New York, Hawaii and Alaska.

Women from varying backgrounds have sought abortions for a wide range of reasons. Young, unmarried women might seek

an abortion to avoid the social stigma of having an illegitimate child; married women might seek an abortion because they have become pregnant as a result of an extramarital affair. One of the most common reasons that women from the poorer socioeconomic groups might seek an abortion is that they cannot deal with the financial hardship that would arise from having an extra child to feed, clothe and raise.

Many people have felt that the law as it stood tended to discriminate against poor women, who, unlike those from wealthy backgrounds, were less able to travel to states where abortion was available or to find sympathetic doctors prepared to sanction an abortion on therapeutic grounds.

Criminal abortions were widespread and usually performed by unqualified people or the pregnant woman herself, often under very unsterile conditions and with no anesthetic or postoperative care. Death through infection or excessive bleeding was common.

Factors such as these led to moves to change the abortion laws. Between 1967 and 1973, 17 states reformed or repealed their abortion laws, and most others started to liberalize their rules to a degree. A 1971 U.S. Supreme Court ruling helped to accelerate this process by establishing that a physician, when choosing whether or not to perform an abortion, could take into account psychological factors, as well as a woman's physical health.

In 1973, in two landmark rulings relating to the state of Texas, the U.S. Supreme Court removed the power to ban abortions from the hands of the state legislatures. The Court ruled that during the first trimester (three-month period), a woman has the right, under the Constitution and in consultation with her physician, to terminate her pregnancy without state interference. In regard to the second trimester, the state can make laws designed to protect the health of the mother but cannot forbid an abortion. In

fact or fiction?

Surrogate motherhood is a new phenomenon.

Fiction. It even appears in the Old Testament. In Genesis, Chapter 16, Sarah, the barren wife of Abraham, enlists her handmaiden, Hagar, to bear her husband's child. In Genesis, Chapter 30, Bilbah, maid of Isaac's infertile wife Rachel, acts as surrogate mother for the couple.

12-week-old fetus
At 12 weeks (the time limit for a vacuum aspiration abortion), a fetus weighs approximately 0.75 ounce (18 grams). Doctors can determine gender, and facial features are visible.

the third trimester, particularly after the fetus has reached the age of viability, the state may forbid an abortion, except when it is deemed necessary for the preservation of the life or health of the mother.

In the decade following the U.S. Supreme Court's rulings, many unsuccessful attempts were made to overturn this decision through an amendment to the Constitution. However, in recent years many state legislatures have reduced the scope of the abortion legislation by demanding that minors get the consent of at least one parent before seeking an abortion, banning the use of public services for abortion and preventing state medical aid (Medicaid) from being used to pay for the abortions of the poor. Other attempts to amend abortion legislation have so far been unsuccessful.

In 1996 the American Medical Association reaffirmed its long-standing policy that abortion remain a matter for medical, not political, decision making. Abortion rates among teenagers in the U.S. have declined steadily since 1980. Fewer teenagers are becoming pregnant and, of these, fewer are choosing to have abortions.

RAPE

The crime of forcing a person to have sexual intercourse against their will is known as rape. In all states it is a felony, which means that it is punishable by a heavy fine and imprisonment in a state prison. In some states, rape includes nonconsenting fellatio (oral sex) and sodomy (anal sex).

A woman is considered to be a victim of rape in all circumstances in which sex occurred against her will, whether because threats or violence were used, or because she was asleep or was unconscious due to alcohol or drug use.

Sex with a mentally retarded woman who is considered by the courts to be incapable of giving consent is also rape. Statutory rape, which involves intercourse with a woman who is below the age of consent, differs from other forms of rape in that the woman concerned may be a willing participant in the sex act (see page 252).

A wife cannot allege rape against her husband in many states, even if he forced her to have intercourse. The exception to this is legal separation at the time of the offense. The rationale for this law is that marriage is taken to imply tacit consent to sex. A woman is legally able, however, to charge her husband with assault and battery.

The number of rapes reported each year is believed to be only a small percentage of the actual number of offenses committed— some estimates put the number at 4 to 10 times the official figure.

Ordeal of rape trials

Many rape victims are anxious about or afraid of reporting rape because they cannot face the embarrassment and humiliation of police questioning and hostile cross-examination in court. The worst ordeal of the

◀ *Women on trial?* *Court trials involving rape cases have been criticized in the past for putting pressure on women to prove their sexual integrity. This may stem from the many myths about rape. For example, "women provoke rape by their dress or behavior," or "women secretly want to be raped."*

Self-defense Some women take action to protect themselves against violent crimes such as rape.

STATUTORY RAPE

People tend to be more concerned about the offense of statutory rape than mutually consenting underage sex. Statutory rape—in which an adult has intercourse with a female under the age of consent—is a crime in all states, but the penalty varies according to the state in which the offense occurred, the age of the participants and, most important, the age gap between them. In Alabama, for example, it is a capital offense for a male aged 16 or over to have intercourse with a girl under 12 years old.

Until recently, statutory rape was rarely enforced, except in extreme cases. However, two factors have caused the federal government to encourage a change: concern about the link between statutory rape and teenage pregnancy (a 1995 study by the Alan Guttmacher Institute showed that more than 50 percent of babies born to under-age females were fathered by adults) and the concern that young women are vulnerable to abuse and exploitation by older men.

Since the mid-1990s, federal welfare law has required that states enforce statutory rape legislation and develop an educational program for law enforcement officials, counselors and educators that focuses on the problem of statutory rape. The attorney general has been urged to study the link between statutory rape and teenage pregnancy and, in particular, to concentrate on the problem of "predatory older men."

The issue of consent
Even if a young girl has voluntary sex with an adult man, she is judged to have been the victim of statutory rape.

WHAT TO DO AFTER RAPE

Although the greatest psychological and emotional need of a rape victim is to imme-diately shower and change, this will oblit-erate all kinds of evi-dence that will be vital for a conviction. The rape should be report-ed as soon as possible, and the place where it occurred should be left undisturbed.

judicial process for many rape victims is that details of their previous sexual history may be presented to the court as evidence that the victim has low moral standards and therefore, by implication, must have tacitly or overtly encouraged the rapist or consent-ed to have sexual intercourse.

In an attempt to address these concerns, many cities and college campuses have set up rape crisis centers where victims can go to receive sympathetic treatment, profes-sional counseling, and legal and medical advice. Some states have also prohibited the presentation to the court of a woman's pre-vious sexual history, and there are moves to change the law to give more weight to the victim's testimony.

Even with these changes, the onus of proof is still with the victim, who must establish that sexual intercourse took place and that it was unambiguously without her consent. In rape cases, there are very rarely any independent eyewitnesses, so the evi-dence usually centers around semen and DNA tests and physical injury to the woman. Without any of these being present, many courts opt for acquittal.

Profile of rapists

The majority of convicted rapists are single men aged 18 to 24, although a large minori-ty are older married men, often with fami-lies. According to a study that was conduct-ed by Kinsey's Institute for Sex Research, convicted rapists can be grouped into sever-al broad categories.

Around 30 percent of rapists fit the typical profile of "sex maniac." Psychologists say that these men show a deep-seated sense of hostility toward women and derive sexual satisfaction as much from threats and phys-ical violence as from the actual act of forced sexual intercourse.

Another 30 percent of rapists are men with a hidden personality flaw that reveals itself under the influence of drink or drugs when they behave in an aberrant way, or in sudden, explosive and seemingly uncharac-teristic acts of sexual aggression.

The remainder are men who believe that women exist primarily to satisfy their sexu-al needs. Many of the men in this category apply a double standard where women are concerned. They consider that some women, notably their wives or female relatives, deserve respect and should never be sexually ill-treated, while they view all other women as "fair game."

Many rapists seek to perpetuate the myth that women secretly wish to be forced to have sexual intercourse and do not mean "no" when they attempt to resist. All studies have shown this assumption to be completely false. In fact, all rape victims report finding the experience degrading and humiliating, and many women feel emotionally damaged for the rest of their lives.

Forced sex

According to *The Social Organization of Sexuality* (1994), a survey into human sexuality conducted by Edward Laumann and others, only one woman in a thousand aged 18 to 44 found anything attractive about the idea of being forced to have sex, while no older women surveyed thought forced sex was appealing.

The researchers used the term "forced sex" in preference to "rape" because of the stigma that has become attached to the latter word. What constitutes rape is also open to various interpretations; some women perceive it differently from the way the courts might view it.

The Laumann report discovered a very clear difference between the way that men and women view the subject of forced sex. Nearly a quarter of the women (22 percent) said they had been made to perform a sexual act against their will, either because they were threatened or because they felt they had no other choice. Of these, the majority of cases involved the women's husbands, men with whom the women were in love or men who were well known to them (77 percent). Only a minority of the men who forced sex were acquaintances (19 percent) or strangers (4 percent).

Three percent of the men sampled said they were attracted by the thought of forcing a woman to have sex, and the same percentage (but not necessarily the same men) admitted to actually having acted upon their desires and fantasies.

Date rape

Date rape is a particular category of rape. It occurs when there has been some social, sexual or romantic contact between a man and a woman in the form of a date. Laumann and his colleagues say that there

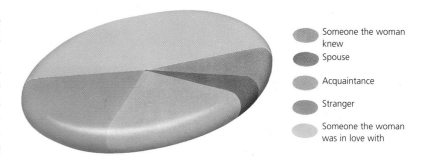

- Someone the woman knew
- Spouse
- Acquaintance
- Stranger
- Someone the woman was in love with

may be a difference in the way that men and women perceive the issue of consent while on a date. They suggested that many men look at certain intimate situations—such as being alone in a car with a woman in a secluded area or being invited into her apartment—as tacit consent to have sexual intercourse. Similarly, actions by the woman, such as sitting close, being attentive and touching his hand or arm, may be seen as a "come-on."

As far as the women were concerned, far from being signals indicating agreement to have sex, their actions were simply an attempt to get to know the man better and to show that they felt initial attraction and therefore saw a basis for future meetings.

To the men concerned, the woman's negative reaction was simply initial reluctance that would quickly disappear—in effect, the men were persuading the women to have sex. To the women, their rejection of sex was

Relationships of women to men who force sex A man who forces a woman to perform a sexual act is likely to be known to the woman. Only 4 percent of forced sex cases involve a man who is a complete stranger to the woman.

TYPES OF RAPE

TYPE	CHARACTERISTICS
Date rape	A man on a date takes advantage and forces sexual intercourse. Date rape usually involves the male's need for power and control.
Acquaintance rape	The woman is raped by a person who is familiar or recognizable to her, but not necessarily someone whom she knows personally or has ever been intimate with.
Social rape	This usually occurs with a teenage girl because sexual boundaries have not been clearly defined. The social rapist may feel that the woman "owes" him intercourse.
Stranger rape	Rape by someone the woman has never encountered before is the least common, the most publicized and the most dangerous type of rape. Stranger rape may be accompanied by violence, torture or even murder.

HOLLYWOOD SCANDALS

Known worldwide as the Hollywood Madam, Heidi Fleiss is the central figure in one of the biggest Hollywood scandals of the 1990s. She was arrested for running a $5 million-per-year international prostitution ring, with well-known business and celebrity clients paying up to $40,000 for sex sessions. Fleiss's story was top news during the months surrounding her arrest, confirming suspicions of a Hollywood that is infested with pimps who prey on impressionable young women. Fleiss's story has now been made into a major movie titled *Hollywood Madam*.

Heidi Fleiss
In her late twenties, Fleiss gained worldwide notoriety for her call-girl empire for the rich and famous.

MALE SEXUAL HARASSMENT

Harassment of men by other men, particularly in the workplace, has recently become something of a hot issue in the U.S. Technically it is illegal for any employer "to discriminate against any individual because of such individual's race, color, religion, sex or national origin." In practice, however, few judges feel able to rule on harassment cases involving male defendants, especially when one heterosexual man is sexually harassing another. The number of such cases reaching the courts has risen sharply in recent years, from 490 cases in 1990 to 1,534 cases in 1996. Also, as the role of women in the workplace has changed, with more women being appointed to managerial jobs and directorships, there has been an increase in the amount of sexual harassment between female bosses and male employees. This is another gray area in which prosecutions are infrequent.

How cases of man-to-man harassment have been treated has varied greatly from one state to another. In New Jersey, a male mechanic whose male boss directed lewd comments at him and slapped him suggestively was awarded $4.2 million by the courts. In contrast, a sexually harassed oil-rig worker was told by the U.S. Fifth Circuit Court of Appeals, comprising the states of Texas, Mississippi and Louisiana, that no law had been violated because sexual harassment by a person of the same sex does not exist. The oil-worker had been sexually assaulted while in the shower and threatened with anal rape by two heterosexual colleagues.

Due to the rise in the number of cases of male sexual harassment by other men, the Supreme Court is likely to reach a decision about how to proceed with such matters.

PROSTITUTION

The act of being paid for sex is known as prostitution. Prostitution is often called the "oldest profession" because throughout history certain women have gained wealth, and sometimes political influence, by providing sexual services. Today, it is the one sex crime for which many more women than men are convicted.

The image of a prostitute that most people hold is that of the "streetwalker"—a woman dressed in sexually provocative clothing who has her own set location on a street cor-

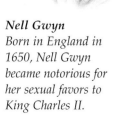

Nell Gwyn
Born in England in 1650, Nell Gwyn became notorious for her sexual favors to King Charles II.

clear and should have been accepted. Instead, they were forced into having sex. Sometimes a woman may begin to have foreplay with a man, allow herself to become intimate with him but nevertheless draw the line at having full sexual intercourse.

These problems of communication and misinterpretation between the sexes have been tackled by many institutions; for example, Antioch College in Ohio issues guidelines to its students telling them to seek permission at every stage of a sexual encounter to ensure that there is no risk of ambiguity or misunderstanding. Whether the man wants to kiss the woman, remove her blouse, touch her breasts or go further than that, he has to ask for her explicit consent at every stage and not go ahead unless it is given. Obviously, no practical way exists for these sorts of guidelines to be enforced.

Sexual activity should stop when either participant requests this. There can be no question of a man's misreading a woman's signals and thinking she means "yes" when she says "no."

ner from which she encourages passing men to pay for a variety of sexual acts. While this is still the working pattern for many "sex workers," there is evidence that this applies to a minority of prostitutes. A special investigation into prostitution set up by the San Francisco Board of Supervisors over an 18-month period beginning in March 1994 found that street prostitution constituted no more than 10 to 20 percent of the sex industry in the city.

The investigative team, called the San Francisco Task Force on Prostitution, found that the majority of prostitutes were employed in escort agencies, massage parlors and brothels, or operated from private premises. In addition, the task force found that many women who worked as prostitutes were also closely involved in related industries, such as pornographic films, magazines and live theater.

Most states have laws against prostitution or activities associated with it. Procuring or pimping—providing prostitutes to others—is prohibited, as are madams and others who operate brothels or bordellos, or knowingly act as landlords of such properties.

Massage parlors and escort agencies can often operate outside the prostitution laws because the services they provide—therapeutic massage and companionship, respec-

tively—are held to be nonsexual. Unlike brothels, they can advertise openly. They must be licensed to operate, however, and can have their licenses revoked if they are found to be operating "a disorderly house," an establishment in which prostitution regularly takes place. In practice, this is very rarely enforced; the proprietors of such businesses can easily make the claim that the individual employee, if found to be acting as a prostitute, was doing so without their knowledge.

American Gigolo

Most prostitutes are female. Men who advertise sexual services for women are known as gigolos. The movie American Gigolo *presents a highly glamorized portrayal of male prostitution—the reality is often quite different.*

fact or fiction?

Blonde hair is historically associated with prostitution.

Fact. In the days of ancient Rome all prostitutes had to have their hair dyed blonde so that they could be clearly identified by potential clients. This was particularly relevant during Roman orgies, when it was important that other women, such as the house slaves, were not mistaken for expensive and trained prostitutes. For a host who wanted his or her party to be a success, a complement of "fun-loving" blondes was indispensable. According to many historians, this custom may have led to the unsubstantiated notion, still widely held today in the West, that blondes are sexier, friendlier and more approachable than other women.

Although streetwalkers are in the minority in the sex-for-sale industry, they are the most visible and for this reason they are by far the most likely to be prosecuted. Most prostitutes who are brought before the courts are charged with the offense of solicitation—this is the act of enticing a member of the public to receive sexual favors in return for payment.

In order to obtain a conviction, police officers often use what are known as entrapment procedures. This means that they pose as prospective clients and try to get potential suspects to solicit them.

Those men who use the services of prostitutes—known as "johns" or "tricks" in the vernacular—are rarely arrested or charged with any offense, although some police forces have taken to publishing the names of men found with prostitutes as a deterrent to other men.

Sex Research

Until the middle of the 20th century, sex research was fairly limited. Then came large-scale sex surveys in which individuals and couples were asked detailed questions about their sexual habits and preferences.

Direct observation
There are two basic methods of finding out about sex: asking people questions about their habits and experiences—as Kinsey did— or actually observing people make love—as Masters and Johnson did. Monitoring and observing couples during sexual intercourse provides conclusive information about physiological responses.

In the sex manuals and pamphlets of the first half of the 20th century, masturbation was usually strongly discouraged, and premarital sex, extramarital sex and homosexuality were considered distasteful and immoral activities confined to a tiny minority of the adult population.

These attitudes were widely supported, but they were based on ideas about how people ought to behave rather than how people actually did behave. When Alfred C. Kinsey published a report in 1948 suggesting that, in reality, most American males masturbated, most had indulged in premarital sex, 40 percent of married men had had extramarital affairs and 37 percent had experienced homosexual activity to orgasm, there was an immediate public outcry.

Kinsey was widely criticized by politicians, religious leaders and the media, all of whom attacked the methods he used, questioned his conclusions, and accused him of ignoring morality and reducing sex to a mere animal function.

Kinsey based his work on the theory that the frequency of a particular sexual activity, such as masturbation, among a sample of the population would indicate its frequency among the population as a whole. This theory has since been used in countless sex surveys, but it can produce reliable results only if the sample population is truly representative of the whole population and if the people taking part in the survey give completely truthful answers about the intimate details of their sexual activities.

The best-run sex surveys, such as that produced by a team based at the University of Chicago and summarized in *The Social Organization of Sexuality* (1994; see page 230), take great pains to ensure that their sample populations are as representative as possible. They also word their questions carefully to encourage truthful answers. In contrast, popular surveys, such as those conducted by commercial magazines, are so badly designed and conducted that their results are almost meaningless.

Despite the storm of criticism unleashed by *Sexual Behavior in the Human Male*, Kinsey continued his research and in 1953 published *Sexual Behavior in the Human Female*. This detailed survey of the sexual habits of women caused even more controversy than his earlier report, mainly because it showed that women were as capable as men of enjoying sex. Kinsey's work opened up the discussion of sex and

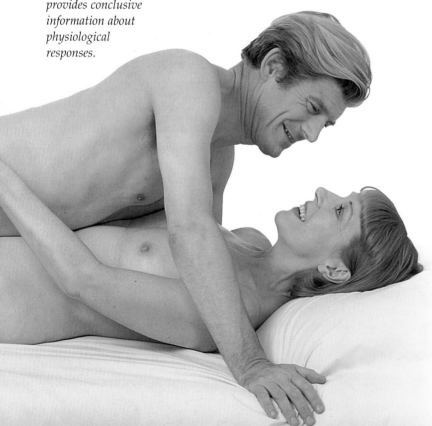

Famous Sexologists

The first large-scale attempt to collect statistics about sexual behavior was Kinsey's report *Sexual Behavior in the Human Male*, in 1948. Kinsey based the report on interviews with more than 11,000 men conducted over a period of 10 years. It constituted an important step in the evolution of sexology—the scientific study of sexual activity.

Sexology was then a relatively new field of scientific investigation, having first appeared in the late 19th and early 20th centuries and documented in the work of researchers such as Richard von Krafft-Ebing, Iwan Bloch, Magnus Hirshfeld and Sigmund Freud (in Germany and Austria), and Henry Havelock Ellis (in England). These early sexologists pioneered the gathering and collating of information about human sexual activity. They were the first to draw broad conclusions from the study of real-life case histories, a method that forms the basis of most modern sexological research.

Today, people are accustomed to reading sex surveys and reports in books and magazines, but just a few decades ago, attempts at sex research were treated as suspicious or immoral. Sex researchers Masters and Johnson caused a great deal of controversy with their direct observation techniques and, in particular, with their use of an artificial coital machine—a hollow, transparent plastic penis, driven by a motor and fitted with lights and a movie camera. It was used to observe and record the physiological changes within the vagina during simulated intercourse.

People working in the biological sciences have often been motivated to conduct research into sex because, through their work, they become aware of the dearth of information on such an important human and animal activity. Kinsey, for example, was inspired to produce his reports when, as a professor, he was asked to teach his students about sex and could find no accurate data.

HENRY HAVELOCK ELLIS

Havelock Ellis, a British psychologist, was one of the first people to set about studying sex in a scientific way. Between 1897 and 1928, he produced a seven-volume study entitled Studies in the Psychology of Sex.

ALFRED CHARLES KINSEY

Kinsey was a professor of zoology at Indiana University in Indiana when, in 1938, the university asked him to teach human sexuality as part of an interdisciplinary course on marriage. He produced two groundbreaking reports.

SAMUEL & CYNTHIA JANUS

When The Janus Report *was published in 1993, it had been many years since a scientific sex study had been conducted. Samuel Janus, a sex counselor, and Cynthia Janus, a doctor specializing in gynecology, analyzed nearly 3,000 questionnaires.*

WILLIAM MASTERS & VIRGINIA JOHNSON

This husband-and-wife team produced the first comprehensive reports about the physiology of sex based on direct observations of couples having sexual intercourse or masturbating. Masters was trained as a gynecologist and Johnson as a psychologist. Their names are probably the most readily associated with sexology in the 20th century.

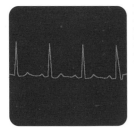

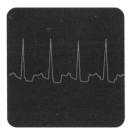

Monitoring heart rates Masters and Johnson monitored people's ECGs (electrocardiograms) during sex. The slow, regular heart rate in the top ECG was taken prior to sex; the faster heart rate in the lower ECG was taken during foreplay.

Sex manuals The wide range of sex books on the market has helped men and women to understand their sexual responses.

helped to liberalize public attitudes toward the subject. It also led to a rapid growth in sexological research and the publication of a great many sex surveys in the U.S. and elsewhere around the world. Most of these surveys were concerned with sexual behavior, but two researchers, William H. Masters and Virginia E. Johnson, took a unique approach and studied the physiological aspects of sex. In 1966 Masters and Johnson published *Human Sexual Response*, a detailed description of the human body's physical responses to sexual stimulation. As with Kinsey's reports, this work was greeted with much condemnation, partly because of its content and conclusions, but mainly because of the research methods that had been used. To study the mechanisms of arousal and orgasm, Masters and Johnson paid men and women to masturbate and have intercourse while under observation in a laboratory.

The publishers of *Human Sexual Response* initially printed just 10,000 copies and targeted the book to doctors and specialists; but the public's appetite for reliable information about sex was such that over a quarter of a million copies were sold in a few months in the U.S. alone. In 1970 Masters and Johnson published *Human Sexual Inadequacy*, which applied the principles of sex therapy to sexual problems such as premature ejaculation and ANORGASMIA.

FAMOUS SEX STUDIES

Studies of sexual behavior range from sensationalist magazine features to serious, detailed surveys employing the best avail-

able techniques of opinion research and statistical analysis. Most are soon forgotten, but some, like those of Alfred Kinsey and Masters and Johnson, have had an enduring influence on sexology and public attitudes.

The Kinsey Reports
Kinsey began by questioning his students about their sex lives and later expanded his research to include other social groups. His work attracted financial support from the Rockefeller Foundation in 1942, and by 1952 Kinsey and his principal associates had interviewed nearly 18,000 people.

The large number of people interviewed did not, however, make the results of Kinsey's studies an accurate reflection of the sexual behavior of most adults. This is partly because Kinsey and his associates settled for convenient groups of interviewees (such as members of student groups and other social organizations) rather than attempting to interview a true cross section of the adult population. The studies also relied heavily on volunteer interviewees, and people who volunteer to reveal details of their sex lives tend to be more sexually experienced and adventurous than those who choose not to.

Despite these flaws, the two Kinsey Reports—*Sexual Behavior in the Human Male* (1948) and *Sexual Behavior in the Human Female* (1953)—gave a more realistic picture of the sex lives of the American populace than anything that had previously been published. The controversy that followed the publication of *Sexual Behavior in the Human Male* resulted in the Rockefeller Foundation's withdrawal of its support in 1952. But Kinsey continued his work, and prior to his death in 1956, he had begun investigating the physical aspects of sex by studying and filming people masturbating and making love, an area of research that was to be taken up by Masters and Johnson.

Masters and Johnson
Over a period of 11 years, William H. Masters and Virginia E. Johnson studied the sexual responses of 694 people—382 women, whose ages ranged from 18 to 78, and 312 men aged 21 to 89. These paid volunteers were inter-

viewed about their medical and social histories and their sexual behavior. Their sexual responses were studied in the laboratory where they masturbated to orgasm or had intercourse. Masters and Johnson filmed and monitored the volunteers using equipment that measured heart rate, breathing and blood pressure. They estimate that they monitored at least 7,500 female orgasms and 2,500 male orgasms during this research program. People reached these orgasms through masturbation, stimulation of the breasts, intercourse or by using an "artificial coital machine."

Masters and Johnson documented that stimulation of the clitoris is the key to female orgasm, as Kinsey had argued, and noted that their female study subjects reported that orgasms achieved through masturbation were usually more intense than those reached during intercourse. The implication of this—that clitoral stimulation gives a woman more physical pleasure than vaginal penetration—was a theme taken up by feminist writers such as Shere Hite.

The Hite Reports

Shere Hite graduated from the University of Florida with a degree in history and went on to study for a PhD in social history at Columbia University, New York. She left Columbia without completing the degree and worked as a fashion model for a while, before becoming involved in feminism.

In 1972 she began the research for her first sex survey by sending out questionnaires to women on the mailing lists of groups such as the U.S. National Organization for Women. Her analysis of the completed questionnaires, plus quotes from the replies, were published as *The Hite Report on Female Sexuality* in 1976. This included the statistics that 29 percent of the women surveyed never achieved orgasm from intercourse, but 95 percent were able to reach orgasm through masturbation.

The report was widely criticized, partly on the grounds that Hite's sample population did not represent the female population as a whole (fewer than 2,000 questionnaires were analyzed) and partly because of the strongly feminist conclusions that she drew from the survey results.

Since the publication of *The Hite Report on Female Sexuality*, Hite has produced two further reports, both based on extensive ques-

tionnaires. These are *The Hite Report on Men and Male Sexuality* (1981) and *Women and Love: A Cultural Revolution in Progress (The Hite Report on Love, Passion, and Emotional Violence;* 1987), which explored the emotional side of female sexuality.

The Laumann Report

In 1987 the U.S. National Institutes of Health acknowledged that efforts to find an effective strategy to combat the spread of AIDS were being hampered by a lack of reliable, up-to-date knowledge about sexual behavior. As a result, a team from the University of Chicago, led by Edward Laumann, was awarded a contract to design

ALEX COMFORT AND *THE JOY OF SEX*

Sex manuals, in one form or another, have been around for centuries, and they remain an important source of information and advice about sex. One of the most successful modern examples is *The Joy of Sex*, a frank, informal, witty but comprehensive guide to lovemaking that covers everything from sexual anatomy to making love on horseback. Written by Alex Comfort—a British doctor and associate member of the American Psychiatric Association—*The Joy of Sex* was first published in 1972 and has sold over eight million copies worldwide.

Alex Comfort—poet, physician, gerontologist, novelist and philosopher During his life Alex Comfort has written approximately 50 books, including novels, textbooks, poetry and plays. The Joy of Sex *remains his most famous work.*

a national sex survey that would be carried out with U.S. government funding.

Political opposition to the project, led by Senator Jesse Helms of North Carolina, resulted in the withdrawal of government support in 1991. The team continued its work, however, with financial backing from private organizations, and the survey was conducted during 1992. From February to September of that year, a team of 220 interviewers, supervised by the U.S. National Opinion Research Center, completed 3,432 interviews of carefully selected men and women between the ages of 18 and 59.

Sex and Technology

The late 20th century has seen a phenomenal advancement in the use of digital technology applied to all aspects of life—including sex. CD-ROMs, computer games and the Internet give people the ability to interact sexually at a distance.

Interactive sex games, easy-to-access pornography, "cybersex" and the opportunity to meet new partners or to flirt with strangers across the world using e-mail are all recent innovations, undreamed of by most people even a decade ago. These have given rise to a vision of sex in the future in which people interact entirely at a distance or with an image on a screen. Having "virtual sex" without ever coming into contact with another person obviously eliminates certain complications: there is zero risk of contracting a sexually transmitted disease and, some people say, no risk of sexual jealousy, betrayal or emotional pain. Others insist that the disembodiment of the sexual experience can have only a negative impact.

Virtual reality technology Headsets such as these enable people to engage in sophisticated computer simulations, but virtual reality sex remains a far-off possibility.

Most people, however, feel that advances in technology will not necessarily force people into seeking remote or virtual sexual pleasure. As Lisa Palac, producer of the erotic virtual audio series *Cyborgasm*, writes: "There have always been those who prefer books to people. (Alienation existed long before the computer.) So there will be a marginal percentage who prefer telesex over face-to-face sex. Others will eschew everything cyber and return to the handwritten love letter. But I believe most people will incorporate new technologies as a way of expanding their erot-

ic repertoire." Palac defines cybersex as "an erotic encounter that involves a computer . . . any time a piece of digital technology comes between you and your orgasm."

THE IMPACT ON WOMEN

Feminists say that the digital revolution has profound implications for women. Traditionally, women have been excluded from such conventional forms of erotica as pornographic magazines and videos, and the depiction of women in these media has often been degrading. Interacting with "sexual partners" and accessing erotic stories and images on the Internet may become popular with women because it is a private pursuit that can be done at home; it does not involve entering a traditionally male-dominated environment; and there is no danger associated with it. Interactive computer technology, such as CD-ROM, will allow women to exert greater choice and control over the sexual scenarios and fantasies they play out.

For the moment, however, most users of both the Internet and interactive multimedia continue to be men. For this reason, erotica in these media is nearly always male-fantasy driven. Until the female audience increases, this is unlikely to change.

SEX ON THE INTERNET

The growing use of computers in households and offices alongside a telecommunications revolution has led to an explosion of popularity for the Internet—a worldwide system of linked computers. Now music, sound, pictures and even video images can be passed effortlessly along a phone line. By the year 2000, it is estimated that more than one billion people will have access to the

Internet. Seventy percent of this total will be men.

The range of sex-related material that can be accessed on the Internet is vast. Information is available on every subject from contraception, infertility and sexually transmitted diseases to fetishes and sex laws. People can view hard and soft pornographic images and have conversations of a sexual nature with people all over the world in various live "chat rooms."

Some people say that they find interacting sexually on the Internet appealing because they can maintain complete anonymity. People can even reinvent themselves, creating an Internet identity portraying themselves as older or younger or even of a different gender than in reality.

PORNOGRAPHY

It is not known how much pornography already exists on the Internet. Conservative estimates say that between 30 and 45 percent of all digitized images on the Internet are pornographic. Just under half of the information passed around daily is of a sexually explicit nature. Commercial pornography sites claim to receive in the region of 150,000 visits a day. Popular "search engines"—directories of the Internet that look for specific words or subjects the user wishes to find information on—report that the most popular search word (used over 2 million times a month) is "sex."

The expansion of the Internet has led to a hitherto unforeseen increase in the spread of pornography—both soft- and hard-core. Pictures of centerfolds and topless models are often grouped in the same areas as illegal hard-core images, often fetishistic or violent in nature. The potential exists for sexually explicit or violent pornography to be received by anyone, no matter where or who they are. Young children could easily access explicit images. Material that in the past circulated only in underground circles—pedophile rings, for example—may now be freely available.

To counter this, energy has gathered behind a movement, largely from government bodies, to create a system that will try to police what goes onto the Internet and who is able to access it, perhaps through a regulatory body of some kind. Unfortunately, owing to the size of the Internet and the speed at which it is expanding, such a group is at present unrealistic. The number of pages of information that are available on the Internet has increased by 3,000 percent a year—over 1 percent a day. Already it would take a single individual 450 years to read every single page.

Supporters of content control on the Internet have applied some pressure for service providers—who sell accounts for Internet access—to limit or block access to well-known sex forums. While this is technically possible in certain areas of the Internet, new pages or secret sites are being created every minute. Logistics aside, provider companies tend to shy away from this kind of activity because it smacks of censorship, a concept that violates the current "freedom of speech" ethos of the Internet community.

Sex sites on the Internet Sex features heavily on the World Wide Web. Many web sites feature soft- or hard-core pornography, while others are informative or educational. There has also been an explosion in the number of personal contact or dating sites.

CYBERSEX IN THE MOVIES

In futuristic portrayals of sex in such films as *The Demolition Man* and *The Lawnmower Man*, cybersex has become a reality. Movie characters wear headsets that allow them to enter a virtual reality environment in which they can perform sexual acts with a computer-generated image of a person of their choice. In some movies, the sexual partner does not even have to appear human.

Current technology is not yet sophisticated enough to permit this kind of virtual reality sex. The images are not convincingly lifelike, and body suits and electronic genital sheaths, which would relay pressure to the sex organs at the appropriate time, have not been developed (although gloves with a tactile feedback mechanism have).

The Lawnmower Man

The virtual reality sex scenes in The Lawnmower Man *were much hyped back in 1992 when the film was released. The plot centers around a mentally challenged gardener let loose into a virtual reality environment.*

The Internet is still in its infancy, however, and controversy surrounding availability of material may yet be resolved by the development of new technology or the drafting of new legislation. In the meantime, the Internet has made some attempts to police itself. Age-verification systems seek to ensure that only those who can prove their age with passport or credit card information may enter adult sites, and most browser software now comes with a variety of parental controls.

In the U.S., a nonprofit organization called the Recreational Software Advisory Council on the Internet has produced a ratings system for Internet material: a rating of "0" means no sex except innocent kissing or romance, while the highest rating of "4" means explicit sexual acts or sexual crimes. The problem with these ratings is that they do not take into account the context of words and pictures. For example, a pornographic photograph of a woman would be rated in the same way as Botticelli's painting *Birth of Venus*.

Experts encourage parents to embrace technology and learn about the Internet themselves so that, armed with information and know-how, they can take primary responsibility for exactly where and when their children are on-line.

CD-ROMs and sex
The technology involved in CD-ROMs allows people to play interactive sex games and watch sex simulations on computer.

CD-ROMs

The technology for virtual sex in its idealized form may still be a distant possibility (some experts predict the middle of the 21st century), but certain packages in the form of CD-ROMs enable people to play interactive sexual games. The goal of such games is typically to gain access to a character's bedroom or to arouse or seduce a character. Tools made of computer graphics (in traditional computer games these would be weapons) include vibrators, dildos and other phallus-shaped objects. Other CD-ROMs allow the user to view what is effectively a pornographic video, but instead of watching passively, the viewer can select different options to control what happens during the video.

The most significant aspect of virtual sex is that people no longer merely watch and fantasize but are encouraged to participate in and act out their fantasies. The proliferation of interactive games that are violent, misogynistic or fetishistic has caused concern. The games industry is usually only a few steps behind Hollywood in terms of visual sophistication. As computer-generated imagery and higher-quality photorealistic cinematics become commonplace in video games, the line between violent fantasies within a computer-generated world and real life may become blurred.

PRACTICAL
ADVICE FOR
PARENTS &
TEENS

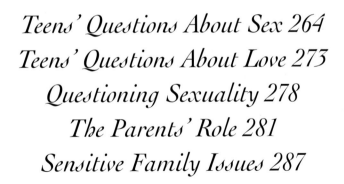

Teens' Questions About Sex

The time between childhood and adulthood, called adolescence, is a time of massive physical and emotional change. Over a period of several years, your body becomes sexually mature and you become capable of having children of your own.

As you approach your teen years, you need to be fully prepared for the changes that are about to happen to your body. You may have picked up some information about sexual body changes from friends, magazines and school health classes, but it is important to feel that you have an understanding person whom you can ask to fill in any gaps in your knowledge. Often the same-sex parent is a good person to talk to. A straightforward question about periods from girls or shaving from boys can pave the way to an open discussion about sex and puberty.

Q What is puberty?

A Puberty is a time when chemical messengers called hormones trigger a series of dramatic developments in your body, changing it from that of a child to that of an adult. This does not happen overnight, and it may take most of your teenage years for all the changes to occur.

Q When does puberty take place?

A The rate of development varies from person to person, and girls tend to mature before boys. Girls may start puberty as early as age 9 or 10, or as late as 15 or 16. On average, boys start puberty at around 14, although this can vary by a couple of years in either direction. By 18 most teenagers are at a similar level of development. They are sexually mature and fertile, and they have reached their full bone growth and adult height.

Q What happens to girls at puberty?

A At puberty your body begins to make female sex hormones, which have a variety of effects on the body: pubic hair starts to grow, your body begins to look more curvy, and your breasts and nipples grow larger and fuller, so you may want to start wearing a bra.

How breasts develop
There are five stages of breast development. The final shape and size of your breasts depends on your genetic make-up and body weight. There is no biological advantage to having either small or large breasts.

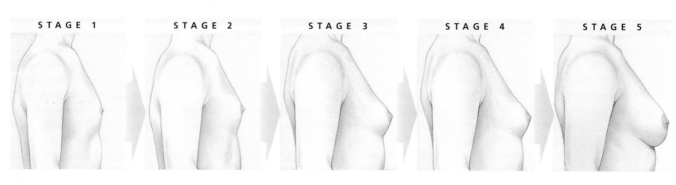

STAGE 1	STAGE 2	STAGE 3	STAGE 4	STAGE 5
When you are a child, your breasts are completely flat, apart from a small raised part in the center called the nipple.	Most girls begin to develop breast buds between the ages of 9 and 14. A small mound of fat tissue develops underneath the nipple.	The breasts begin to fill out and become noticeable beneath your clothes. The nipples and the areolae become larger.	The breasts are nearly fully formed. By this stage you might start to wear a bra that supports your developing breasts.	Adult breasts are full and round. When you are not wearing a bra, they may droop slightly, although everyone's breasts differ.

The size and shape of their breasts is often a source of concern among girls. If you have small breasts, you may be worried that you are not developing normally or that you do not look feminine or attractive enough. If you have large breasts or you are an early developer, you may feel embarrassed and self-conscious, especially around boys. It is very common for one breast or one nipple to be slightly bigger than the other, or a slightly different shape. This is nothing to feel worried about, since there is no "correct" or "normal" size for breasts; they come in all shapes and sizes.

Q What about periods?

A Puberty is the time that girls begin to menstruate. Every month from now until menstruation ceases, usually in a woman's forties or fifties, a small amount of blood-stained fluid flows from the vaginal opening. This is called a menstrual period, or simply a period, and each occurrence lasts for a few days, usually between three and seven. The blood that flows out of the vagina comes from the womb, or uterus, which is the place where a baby would develop if you became pregnant. In fact, periods normally occur every month that you do not become pregnant, because the uterus needs to shed its lining each month.

Most women use sanitary napkins or tampons (see page 175) to absorb the blood that is lost during a period. Sanitary napkins are placed inside your panties and tampons are inserted into the vagina. Because periods can take up to two years to settle into a regular pattern, it is wise to carry tampons or minipads around with you, in case bleeding starts unexpectedly. It is common to feel cramps and some discomfort for the first couple of days of a period.

Q How do you know when your periods are about to start?

A For a few months before you have your first period, you may notice a sticky whitish yellow stain on your panties. This increased discharge is a sign that you have started producing female hormones. If the discharge is an unusual color or smells strongly, you may have an infection and should consult a doctor.

REMOVING BODY HAIR

Body hair starts to grow at puberty. Boys will notice that the hair on the face becomes coarse and darkens, and both girls and boys will develop pubic and underarm hair. The fine, downy hair on the legs and arms also becomes darker and more noticeable in both sexes. When boys have an obvious growth of facial hair, they may decide to start shaving. Whether girls decide to remove body hair is a matter of individual choice too.

Wet shaving
Boys remove facial hair by wet shaving or with an electric razor. Wet shaving, using soap or shaving foam, produces a closer shave.

Depilatory creams
Creams containing hair-dissolving chemicals can be applied to the skin, where they dissolve hairs at the root.

Once you have started your periods, you may notice various signs each month that tell you that a period is about to start. These signs include tender or swollen breasts, tiredness, and mood changes. The name for these and other related signs is premenstrual syndrome (PMS). PMS symptoms are mild in most women.

Q Do girls get body hair at puberty?

A Pubic, genital and underarm hair starts to grow at puberty, and the fine, downy hair on the arms and legs may become thicker and coarser.

Attitudes toward body hair vary among different cultures, and you should not feel that the amount you have is unacceptable because of what your friends or images in the media tell you. Body hair is not necessarily unattractive; nor is it unhygienic if it is kept clean. Some women remove the hair from their legs, underarms and bikini line, but many others do not. If you wish to remove it, there are a number of options.

Shaving is cheap and can be done in your own bathroom. The main disadvantages of shaving are that the hair may grow back quickly and it is possible to cut yourself. Shaving is best reserved for areas such as the legs and under the arms.

Depilatory creams contain chemicals that dissolve hair. They remove hair for a longer time period than shaving, but they are more expensive and can be messy. In a minority of people, they can irritate the skin. If you use a depilatory cream, be careful not to leave it on for too long. Do not use one at all if you have a skin condition such as eczema.

Waxing can be done at home with special adhesive strips or wax that melts in a bowl of hot water. Professional waxing in a salon may produce better results, but it can often be expensive. Waxing removes hair for weeks rather than days because the hairs are pulled out at the roots. Many women find that this process is painful and, if you choose to wax at home, it can also be very messy.

Bleaching, which involves lightening small areas of hair, such as facial hair, can be done at home or in a professional salon. Products are available specifically for this purpose.

My friends are taller than I am You may feel concerned that you are not maturing as fast as your friends, but as you can see from these two boys, both age 13, different developmental stages are completely natural. The boy on the right may end up taller than the boy on the left.

fact or fiction?

Boys who develop breasts are turning into girls.

Fiction. It is actually quite common for boys to experience lumps, bumps and swelling in one or both breasts. Sometimes the swelling is accompanied by tenderness. This is a normal and natural change that will disappear in its own time. It definitely does not mean that you are turning into a girl.

Q *What happens to boys at puberty?*

A At puberty your body begins to make the male sex hormone testosterone, which causes your body to grow and change in various ways. Your testicles grow larger and fuller; your penis grows larger and longer and the color darkens; your scrotum (the bag containing the testicles) expands, hangs lower, turns a darker color and becomes more wrinkly; pubic hair grows around the penis; and sperm (the male sex cells needed to make a baby) start to be produced in the testicles. You will also notice that your shoulders and chest grow bigger and broader, your muscles develop, your voice deepens in pitch, and your Adam's apple may become more noticeable.

At puberty you also produce more perspiration, and it may have a distinct odor. Your body grows and gains weight, and the bones in your face develop so that it looks more mature. Hair grows under your arms and around your genitals, and the hair on your arms and legs becomes more prominent. Acne is also common.

Q *When do I need to start shaving?*

A Some boys start shaving around puberty, although facial hair may be sparse until young adulthood. How often you need to shave is an individual matter— some boys and men need to shave every day, while others shave twice a week. It depends on your rate of facial hair growth and how you feel about your appearance.

Q *What if my friends develop at a different rate from me?*

A You may worry that you are developing too fast or too slowly and feel inadequate compared with a friend who has more body hair, more muscles and a larger body frame. Everyone's body develops at its own rate, and many people feel uncomfortable with their new body during adolescence. Remember that everyone has at least one feature that they feel awkward about. Eventually, everybody reaches their natural adult body size. In the meantime, try not to compare yourself negatively.

Q *Why do I keep getting erections?*

A An erection is when the penis enlarges and becomes hard. Erections are usually induced by sexual arousal, but during puberty they occur for no apparent reason. This can be embarrassing if it happens in a public place, but it is completely normal, and spontaneous erections are typically short-lived. As you get older, spontaneous erections will occur much less often. Loose clothing usually hides these erections.

Q *What is ejaculation?*

A Ejaculation is when a fluid called semen is expelled from the head of the penis. On average, around one teaspoonful of semen comes out of the penis with each ejaculation, and this small amount contains millions of sperm. Ejaculation happens when you are sexually excited and you touch or rub your penis during masturbation, but it can also occur during a wet dream (also known as a nocturnal emission). Semen is ejaculated while you are asleep. It can be a shock to wake up for the first time with wet or sticky pajamas or sheets, but wet dreams are completely normal. Like spontaneous erections, they become less frequent as you grow older.

Q *How should girls and boys look after themselves during puberty?*

A Your body changes during adolescence and you need to take care of yourself and your health in a new way. Both sexes need to pay attention to personal hygiene, especially the underarms, genitals and feet, which all begin to secrete a different type of sweat. You may want to start using an underarm deodorant or antiperspirant. Uncircumcised boys need to wash regularly beneath the foreskin. Girls usually begin getting Pap smears six months after first sexual intercourse. Girls should begin to check their breasts for lumps. Boys should check their testes for lumps or any changes in texture, firmness and size.

Q *What can I do about skin blemishes?*

A Your skin and hair become oilier at puberty, and this can cause pimples or acne. These can be distressing at a time when you may already be self-conscious about your appearance, but you are not alone; almost everyone suffers from pimples at some time. If you have severe acne, visit your doctor, who may prescribe antibiotics to help clear your skin. In addition, there are skin washes and acne lotions available from pharmacists. Seek advice about what is best for your individual skin type before you buy one of these products.

Eating excessive amounts of chocolate or greasy food is not good for your general health, but there is controversy about its effect on the skin. Some nutritionists say that diet has little effect on acne, which tends to be caused by hormonal changes rather than what you eat. Others say that highly sugared foods can affect the body's hormonal balance and encourage skin problems. The best idea is to eat a balanced, nutritious diet.

Q *Why am I so moody?*

A As your body goes through changes, so do your feelings, thoughts, ideas and attitudes. Adolescence can be a time of great passions, creativity and intimate friendships, and you may find that you experience more intense feelings than you have done before. Moods can change fast— you may feel irritable or moody one day and

Looking after your skin Skin problems are common in adolescence. Keep your skin clean and, if you have very oily skin, use an astringent lotion. Some people find that antibacterial skin products are helpful.

HOW DO YOU KISS SOMEONE?

A lot of peer pressure arises over kissing: what age you should have done it by, the right way to do it and how many people you have done it with. Your friends may tease you if you have not yet kissed someone, and this may make you feel unattractive or as though something is wrong with you. This is not the case—do not be pressured into anything. There is no such thing as a right time or method, and if you are rushed into your first kiss, it is more likely to be a disappointing experience.

Common worries about kissing include where to put your hands or whether to kiss with an open or closed mouth. The secret is to relax and enjoy someone's physical presence first. Getting close, or hugging or embracing someone, is a good preparation for a kiss. There are no rules about what makes a good kiss. Kissing is something that will come naturally to you when you do it.

Your first kiss
Almost everyone can remember their first kiss: whom it was with, where and how they felt. Most people feel nervous about kissing, but there are no right or wrong ways to do it.

IS SEX PAINFUL FOR WOMEN?

Many young people worry that sex will be painful for women because they imagine that the woman's vagina is quite small and delicate compared with the man's penis. In fact, this is not true. The vagina is a stretchy, elastic organ that expands greatly during sexual arousal. The vagina also produces slippery fluid during arousal, and this alleviates any uncomfortable friction during intercourse.

exhilarated the next. You may also find that growing independence from your parents creates conflict with them, especially if you want more privacy and time to spend with your friends. Rather than getting into arguments with your parents, try to discuss things openly. Talk with them, and try to negotiate solutions rather than simply fighting or even defying their wishes, which will almost certainly be based on genuine concern for you.

Q How does sex feel?

A Making love should be a pleasurable, intense and intimate experience for both partners. Most people say that the best sexual experiences happen when you are not just relaxed and aroused but also when you have very deep feelings for and a mutual commitment to your partner.

Foreplay can make a big difference between a good sexual experience and a disappointing one. This means arousing your partner by kissing, fondling, caressing and stroking the sensitive areas of his or her body. The brain then sends messages to the genitals to get ready for sexual intercourse: the man's penis becomes erect and hard; the

woman's vagina and vulva become wet and slippery, her clitoris enlarges, and her nipples become more sensitive.

During intercourse the man penetrates the woman's vagina with his penis and then thrusts rhythmically inside her. This in itself can be a highly pleasurable experience, and many couples like to prolong this stage of intercourse. It can last from a few minutes to over an hour, with changes of rhythm and rest periods.

Sexual intercourse usually ends when the man has an orgasm and ejaculates. After that his penis becomes soft and flaccid, and he will not be able to have an erection for a short while. The woman may also have an orgasm during intercourse. Intercourse can occasionally be uncomfortable if a woman is not sexually aroused and ready.

Q What is an orgasm?

A An orgasm is a series of pleasurable convulsions that are felt most strongly in the genitals but also throughout the rest of the body. People reach orgasm in many ways, including, but not only by, having sexual intercourse. Men can reach orgasm easily this way, but some women find achieving orgasm through intercourse difficult. Women are more likely to experience orgasm through stimulation of the clitoris. This can happen during the thrusting movements of intercourse, but sometimes stimulation of the clitoris by hand is needed.

It may be only a short time before young men are able to get another erection. Women may be able to have a number of orgasms in quick succession.

Q What is masturbation?

A Masturbation means touching your genitals for sexual pleasure. For boys this means stroking or rubbing the penis, usually until ejaculation occurs. Girls masturbate by stroking the clitoris, usually until they reach orgasm. Masturbation is a common practice, and many people get their first experience of sexual pleasure this way. It is perfectly normal, harmless and natural, although it is frowned on by certain cultures and religions.

By their late teens, most boys and girls will have masturbated, although some feel no need to do so, which is also perfectly normal. Contrary to old-fashioned opinion, masturbation is a way of learning about your body—it enables you to tell your future sexual partner what gives you sexual pleasure and satisfaction.

Q What is first-time sex like?

A It is difficult to generalize about what it is like to have sex for the first time—everyone is different—but many people feel a mixture of contradictory or confusing emotions that may include anxiety, excitement, relief, elation, disappointment, achievement and guilt.

People commonly worry that they will not know what to do during sex. Young men may worry that they will not achieve or keep an erection, that they will ejaculate too soon, or that they will not be able to find the vagina. Young women may worry that sex will be painful or that the penis will be too big to fit into the vagina. All these fears are very common. People most successfully overcome them by educating themselves about the facts of sex beforehand and trying to relax when the time comes.

If a young woman still has an intact hymen—this is a piece of skin that may partially cover the entrance to the vagina—she may feel discomfort when the penis enters the vagina for the first time, and there may also be a small loss of blood.

Can We Talk About It?

SHOULD I HAVE SEX WITH MY PARTNER?

Once you start having sexual intercourse, relationships become more complicated. Your feelings for someone intensify if you start having sex with them, with more scope for jealousy, possessiveness and insecurity. If you have unprotected sex, you also risk pregnancy and contracting a sexually transmitted disease.

For these reasons, and others, you should give yourself plenty of time to know who you are and what you want from a relationship before you commit yourself to having sex. Reasons to have sex do not include pressure from friends or a boyfriend or girlfriend, being under the influence of drugs or alcohol, or feeling as though sex is just one of those things you should have done by a certain age.

It is possible to have a good, caring and loving relationship with someone without sex. If you have strong moral, religious or cultural views on sex outside of marriage, state them clearly and stand by them. Also, to have sexual intercourse legally, you must have reached the age of consent—the age at which you are judged by law to be capable of deciding of your own free will that you want to have sex. The age of consent, which varies according to the state, is intended to protect you from sexual experiences that may be damaging to you. The hope is that you will wait until you are emotionally mature enough for a sexual relationship.

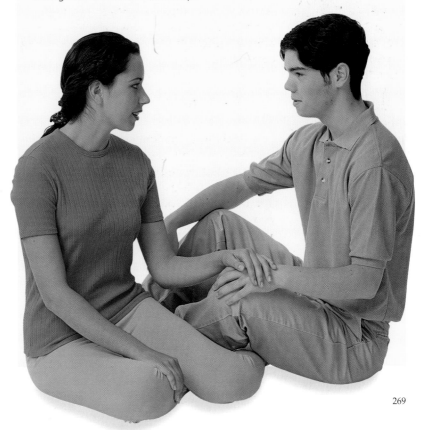

MYTHS ABOUT CONTRACEPTION

MYTH	REALITY
A girl cannot get pregnant the first time she has sex.	If you do not use contraception, it is possible to get pregnant the first time you have sexual intercourse. Fertility may be high in early adulthood, which increases the chance of conception.
A girl cannot get pregnant if a boy takes his penis out of her vagina before he ejaculates.	This is called the withdrawal method of contraception, and it is very unreliable. Before ejaculation a small amount of fluid leaks out of the penis. This fluid contains sperm, which can make you pregnant.
A girl cannot get pregnant if a boy does not penetrate her vagina.	It is possible to get pregnant even if penetration does not take place. If a boy ejaculates near the vagina, sperm can still find their way into the girl's body.
A girl cannot get pregnant if she has sex standing up.	She can get pregnant in whatever position she and her partner choose to make love—this includes standing.
A girl cannot get pregnant if she has sex during her period.	It is not completely safe to have unprotected sex while a girl is menstruating because a ripe egg could leave an ovary and be fertilized by a sperm. Sperm can live inside a woman's body for up to three days.
A girl cannot get pregnant if she does not have an orgasm.	It is not necessary for a girl to have an orgasm in order to conceive and become pregnant.
Washing out the vagina after sexual intercourse prevents pregnancy.	This is completely ineffective as a form of contraception. By the time you wash out the vagina after sex, the sperm will already be swimming into the uterus.

It is relatively unusual for women to have an orgasm the first time they have sexual intercourse. The reasons for this include anxiety, not receiving enough stimulation or the right sort of stimulation, and a simple lack of understanding of how their body functions sexually. Men may reach orgasm sooner than they want to (known as premature ejaculation; see page 213). This may be due to a combination of nervousness and being extremely sexually aroused. For both women and men, sexual enjoyment often increases as they become more experienced and more at ease with their own and their partner's body.

Q *Can I have a physical relationship without having intercourse?*

A There are plenty of ways to be physically intimate with someone without having sexual intercourse. The decision to lose your virginity is an extremely important one; exploring alternatives gives you greater power to make a wise decision about when and with whom you will have sexual intercourse.

The most obvious way to show affection to someone is to hug and embrace them. You can also kiss and cuddle and enjoy the proximity of someone else's body. Some people become sexually involved with their partner by deep kissing, mutual masturbation, massage and caresses. Some people also try oral sex, which means stimulating a partner's genitals with the lips, tongue and mouth. It is important that you do not feel pressured into any of these activities.

Q *I am sexually active. Can I have sex during my period?*

A If you have made the decision to become sexually active, you may want to have sex during menstruation. This is fine, as long as both you and your partner feel comfortable. You may wish to cover the bed with a large towel to prevent staining the sheets. You need to use a condom both to prevent pregnancy and to avoid contracting a sexually transmitted disease.

Q *Why can I reach orgasm by masturbating but not during sex?*

A Many women find that penetrative sex does not stimulate the right area of the genitals for long enough to make them reach orgasm. In contrast, during masturbation the clitoral area is stimulated by hand for as long as you wish and in the way in which you choose, so that reaching orgasm is likely to be easier. Women can explain to or show a partner what arouses them and makes them climax. If a woman does not reach orgasm during sex, she can climax before or after by letting her partner stimulate her clitoris with his hand.

Some women do not reach orgasm during sex because they feel nervous or anxious. If you feel self-conscious, it will be hard to concentrate on the sexual pleasure you need to reach orgasm. Try to remember that you are not expected to perform during sex, and it is not a test of your abilities. Simply relax and concentrate on the physical sensations you are experiencing. If you find that you never enjoy sex, perhaps you are not ready or you have chosen the wrong partner. It is fine to stop having sex.

Q *Why do I ejaculate so quickly when I have sex?*

A Premature ejaculation is very common when you are sexually inexperienced, so don't be surprised if you ejaculate very quickly the first few times you have intercourse—some men even ejaculate before they have intercourse. It just means that you are very excited and haven't yet learned how to control that excitement.

With time, practice and experience you will learn to control ejaculation so that you can climax when you want to. There are also some techniques that you can use to prevent premature ejaculation (see page 213).

Q *How can I have a conversation with my parents about sex?*

A You may feel unwilling to talk to your parents about any personal subject during adolescence. In fact, sex may be the last topic you feel comfortable about broaching, but bear in mind that parents can often provide practical, commonsense advice based on years of experience. They may also be very flattered that you trust and respect them enough to seek their advice.

You can either ask about very specific issues or initiate a general discussion about love and sex by asking such questions as "What did you do when you were my age?" or "When did you get your first girl-friend/boyfriend?"

Some parents find it difficult to talk to their children about sex. If your attempts at discussion fail, remember that your parents are probably embarrassed rather than being deliberately unhelpful. Try different tactics, such as talking to the same-sex parent when you are alone together, or being very informal or relaxed yourself.

Q *How important is contraception?*

A Contraceptives should be used from the first time you have sexual intercourse. Contraception is the responsibility of both partners, and you should discuss it fully. Contraception may mean that sex is not as spontaneous as you would like; but planned sex is preferable to an unplanned baby or a sexually transmitted disease.

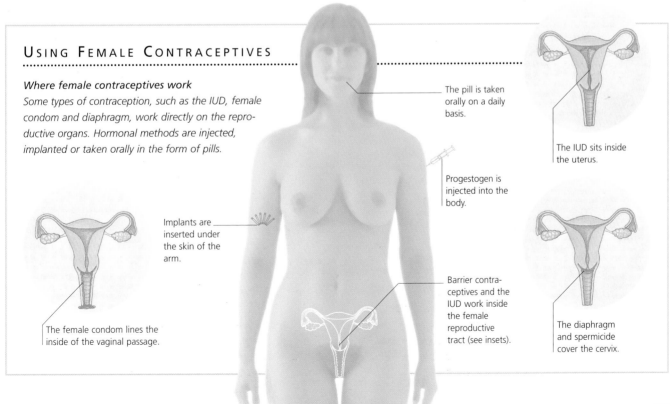

USING FEMALE CONTRACEPTIVES

Where female contraceptives work
Some types of contraception, such as the IUD, female condom and diaphragm, work directly on the reproductive organs. Hormonal methods are injected, implanted or taken orally in the form of pills.

The pill is taken orally on a daily basis.

The IUD sits inside the uterus.

Progestogen is injected into the body.

Implants are inserted under the skin of the arm.

Barrier contraceptives and the IUD work inside the female reproductive tract (see insets).

The female condom lines the inside of the vaginal passage.

The diaphragm and spermicide cover the cervix.

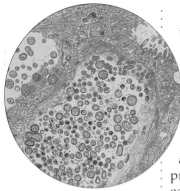

Chlamydia *This is the bacteria* Chlamydia trachomatis *magnified under a microscope. It causes one of the most common sexually transmitted diseases in North America. Chlamydia is dangerous because it may be symptomless in women but go on to cause complications that lead to infertility.*

A number of different forms of contraception are available to you. Among the most reliable are the contraceptive pill and the condom. The pill is popular among young women because it allows spontaneity and gives them control over contraception, thereby increasing their sexual freedom. Given that it is taken correctly, it provides good security against pregnancy. However, it does not protect against sexually transmitted diseases (STDs). You should consider this when deciding which contraceptive is best for you, especially if you or your partner has previously had sex with other people.

Male or female condoms provide protection against STDs as well as being a reliable way of preventing unwanted pregnancies. Male condoms are the most widely used and consist of a sheath of latex or plastic that fits on the erect penis before a couple have intercourse (or any sexual contact). Some men worry that they will not be able to enjoy sexual intercourse if they are wearing a condom, but condoms are very thin and should not reduce sensitivity. A reduction in sensitivity should not be accepted by either partner as a reason not to use them. Condoms may also be known as sheaths, rubbers, French letters or johnnies.

Other available contraceptives include intrauterine devices (IUDs), implants and injections, but these are long-term contraceptives. The IUD, in particular, has to be inserted into the uterus by a doctor, and many doctors feel that the IUD is suited to older women who have had their families.

The rhythm method of contraception involves calculating when an egg, or ovum, is released from a woman's ovary, since this is the time of the month when fertility peaks. The woman and her partner then avoid sex around this time. The rhythm method is not recommended for adolescents because a girl's periods may be irregular and ovulation is difficult to predict.

Q *What are sexually transmitted diseases?*

A Young men and women who are sexually active run a risk of picking up sexually transmitted diseases (STDs) unless they have safer sex (see page 178). The more partners someone has, the greater the risk, but using a condom reduces the dangers. There are many different STDs, and symptoms vary. Common signs of infection include pain or a burning sensation in the genitals; painful or frequent urination; an abnormally colored, unpleasant-smelling discharge from the vagina or penis; itching, lumps, sores or blisters; and abdominal pain or tenderness. If you experience any of these symptoms, you and your partner must consult a doctor. Some STDs are symptomless, and if someone you have had sex with starts to have symptoms, you must have a checkup, even if you seem healthy.

Q *How can I protect myself from HIV?*

A Abstaining from penetrative sex is one of the only ways to ensure full protection from sexually transmitted HIV, but using a condom offers substantial protection. HIV (human immunodeficiency virus; see page 180) is a virus that can cause AIDS (acquired immune deficiency syndrome). HIV can be contracted by having unprotected sex with an infected person, sharing infected needles or receiving infected blood from a blood transfusion. As yet there is no cure, so prevention is essential. If you are worried, ask your doctor about an HIV test.

SYMPTOM CHECKLIST FOR 5 COMMON STDS

NAME OF STD	MOST NOTICEABLE SYMPTOMS
Chlamydia	Women may have no symptoms or a vaginal discharge. Men may have pain when urinating and a penile discharge.
Herpes	After a feeling of tingling or itching in the genitals, both sexes develop painful recurrent blisters that burst to form sores that heal spontaneously.
Genital warts	Both sexes develop small hard lumps anywhere around the genitals. Warts can grow rapidly and become large. They increase the risk for cervical cancer.
Gonorrhea	Women may have no symptoms or a vaginal discharge. Men may have pain when urinating and a penile discharge.
Trichomoniasis	Women have a frothy green/yellow vaginal discharge. Men may have no symptoms or pain when urinating.

Teens' Questions About Love

Adolescence can be a difficult and confusing time. Your body is changing, and your emotions and moods are fluctuating. You may be physically ready for a sexual relationship but feel emotionally unprepared and unsure of what it involves.

Adolescence is often the time when new friendships and relationships are formed. Relationships—particularly those with the opposite sex—can seem very intense at this time in your life. It's natural that you will have lots of questions about yourself and the nature of your relationships. Try to share your feelings with your friends. Talk to your family members. Maybe you have an older sibling who can offer advice and answer the questions that are most important to you.

Q How do I meet a boyfriend or girlfriend?

A There is no simple way to meet a boyfriend or girlfriend. The best idea is to mix with a group of people of both sexes whom you like and trust. Whether you are 15 or 55, one of the most common ways to meet a partner is through friends. Friends usually have plenty in common: they are often the same age and share the same tastes and attitudes toward life. You will stand a better chance of meeting someone compatible with you among an extended group of friends than through a chance meeting with a stranger.

Through being with friends, you establish your own identity and become an individual. The close friendships that you have during adolescence are an important prelude to intimate relationships. They allow you to see things from other people's points of view and to adapt your behavior to encompass another person's needs.

Your friendship group or groups can develop in many different places. You will meet people at school, among neighbors and family, at summer camps, enjoying

hobbies, and at sports clubs, to give just a few examples. Once friendships are formed, others can be made through friends of friends, through brothers and sisters of friends, and by attending parties and social events. Try to think of meeting new people as an adventure and aim to make friends with people you like and are interested in, rather than single-mindedly setting out to find a boyfriend or girlfriend.

Q Is something wrong with me if I do not have a boyfriend or girlfriend?

A Everyone develops relationships at their own pace. You do not need to feel pressured into dating just because everyone else seems to be doing it. When you are a teenager, it is normal to want to fit in by doing exactly the same things as your

Feeling left out

There is enormous pressure to "belong" when you are a teenager. If you are not in a relationship or do not belong to a big group of friends, it's very easy to feel lonely and miserable at times. Try to be positive: discover activities that you enjoy, and cultivate just one or two friendships that are important to you.

HOW DO I LET SOMEONE KNOW THAT I LIKE THEM?

One way to express interest in someone is to tell them very simply that you enjoy their company and love spending time with them. If you don't feel confident enough to say this, you can show interest by being friendly, starting conversations, listening to what they say (and remembering it), telling the person things about yourself, and making them feel included and interesting.

Dating Learning to relax and interact naturally with members of the opposite sex is something that people may find difficult. Usually, going out in a crowd is easier than the formality of a one-to-one date.

friends. But rather than copying the behavior of other people, think carefully about your own needs and wishes.

If you are not ready for a relationship, particularly a sexual relationship, bide your time. Close friendships with members of your own and the opposite sex can be both intimate and fulfilling.

If you feel ready for a relationship but just do not seem able to find that special person, be patient and positive; do not assume that there is something wrong with you. It often takes a long time to meet someone with whom you really want to have a relationship. Stay socially active and try to extend your circle of friends by joining clubs. Accept as many invitations and opportunities that fit who you are as you can.

Think carefully about whether there is something else that is stopping you. Are you too particular in your idea of the perfect partner? If you lack self-confidence, are you obsessed with a certain feature of your own body that you cannot accept? Just because you feel this way about yourself doesn't mean that other people will. Before you can expect someone else to like you, you may have to learn to like yourself.

Q How do I overcome shyness?

A Shyness is a form of social anxiety that is very common in both teenage boys and girls. Some people are shy only in particular situations—such as going on a date, being interviewed or speaking in public— while others can feel shy in almost any social situation. Intense shyness may indi-

cate emotional insecurity, a lack of confidence, or feelings of uncertainty and anxiety about a particular person or place.

Feelings of shyness usually disappear with time. As your self-confidence grows, you will find that you can cope more easily with a range of social situations. A supportive network of people, such as parents or friends, can help you to do this and reassure you that you look great and are doing and saying the right things. If you know someone who suffers from shyness, a good way to increase their self-confidence is to encourage them to think positively about themselves and to reassure them that they are loved and lovable.

Shyness can sometimes cause you to send out the wrong signals to people. Inside, you feel scared or intimidated, but your body language can make you seem cool, reserved, withdrawn or aloof, which can make people think that you are bored or indifferent to them. This may drive them away, leaving you to feel even shier and more insecure than you did before.

There are some simple tactics that shy people can adopt. Small changes in body language can have immediate results. The key things are to smile, make direct eye contact with the person you are talking to, have an open posture (instead of folded arms and crossed legs), and lean forward and nod in response to what the person is saying.

Listen carefully to what people say: if you become interested in them and what they are talking about, you will forget your shyness. Most people enjoy being listened to and being asked questions—listening attentively is an underrated skill.

Q What if my boyfriend or girlfriend dumps me?

A When interest in a partner fades, either party may end the relationship. This means that the other person is as much at risk of being rejected as you are. If you are always anxious that your partner will leave you, you will probably not be free to relax and enjoy the relationship. Ask yourself why you feel anxious. Are your fears realistic or paranoid? Talk to your boyfriend or girlfriend and find out whether his or her feelings about the relationship are the same as yours. There is nothing wrong with asking for reassurance.

Relationships during adolescence give you a wonderful opportunity to get to know other people and yourself. Although first relationships can feel very intense, few people spend the rest of their lives with the first person they date. If your relationship is going wrong, it may be time to let go and move on, especially if you feel unhappy or dissatisfied most of the time. Try to look at a relationship that has ended as part of a learning process from which you have gained valuable insight.

Q *I have a crush on someone. Is this the same as being in love?*

A A crush is a form of hero worship and is common in adolescence. You may feel strongly attracted to a sports figure, a pop star or someone you know personally, such as an older student or a teacher. The person on whom you have a crush is someone you admire or idealize; they may be sophisticated, talented, enigmatic, powerful or simply very attractive to the opposite sex. Wanting to be close to them may partly be the desire to learn their secret.

Crushes are different from being in love since they involve admiring someone from afar, placing them on a pedestal and being in awe of them. The object of your crush may have no idea of your feelings—in fact, he or she may not even know that you exist. Being in love is more about knowing someone personally and well, and also about them knowing you: you share experiences with them and recognize their bad points as well as their good points.

Although clear differences exist between crushes and being in love, it is hard to tell the difference when you are in the throes of a crush. Your feelings may be very intense, but being in love requires a relationship and some degree of intimacy. In some ways crushes are a preparation for a mature adult relationship. You learn what it feels like to have intense feelings for another person,

but there is the advantage that you do not have to actually get involved with them or run the risk of being hurt.

Q *How do you know for sure that you are in love?*

A The best kind of loving relationship occurs when two people fulfill each other's needs for affection, support, praise and intimacy. Each partner is able to give and receive love equally. Love will increase your levels of self-esteem and make you feel stable and content.

Good communication is an important aspect of loving someone. By talking, partners discover each other's needs, and they can share their innermost feelings. They enjoy each other's company, care for each other, like doing the same things, and share or appreciate each other's goals. Romance also plays a part in love. The early stages of a relationship are often exciting and romantic, but in good relationships, couples try to sustain a sense of romance.

When you are a teenager, it can be hard to differentiate between love and infatuation. Infatuation is a short-lived attraction to someone based on what you think they are like rather than how they really are. Loving

Love or infatuation?
Having a crush on a pop star is an experience that many teenage girls share. Although crushes feel very intense, it is impossible to be truly in love with someone with whom you have never had direct contact.

fact or fiction?

First love is always the deepest.

Fiction. The first loving relationship you embark on may well feel like the most passionate, intense and romantic experience of your life. Some people, however, find that they are capable of deeper or longer-lasting loves later on in life, when they know themselves very well and know what qualities they seek in a partner.

Feeling jealous
Sometimes you may have good reason to feel jealous: someone you care deeply about is expressing interest in another person, and you feel powerless to do anything about it. On other occasions, your jealousy may be groundless and based on insecurity. Always examine your motives for jealousy carefully and try not to jump to conclusions.

Deciding whether to begin a relationship
Maybe you have just been asked out on a date for the first time; maybe you are thinking about starting your second or third relationship after some time on your own; or maybe you have recently split up with your boyfriend or girlfriend and are considering jumping into a new relationship. Whatever your situation, think about your reasons for being with someone before you take the plunge.

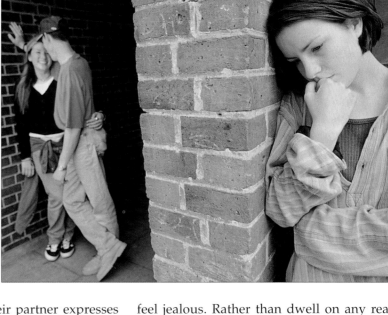

someone is about knowing them very well and developing a good insight into their character. Feelings that seem to change from one day or week to the next are more a sign of infatuation than of true love.

Q *Is it natural to feel jealous?*

A Some amount of jealousy is common in both sexes. Many people feel resentful when their partner expresses an interest in someone else of the opposite sex. Others, however, feel consumed with jealousy if their partner even looks at someone else. This type of excessive jealousy can do a lot of damage to a relationship.

Jealousy is less about love than self-pity. If one partner feels at a disadvantage compared to the other, he or she can succumb more easily to jealousy. For example, if one partner feels less attractive than the other, he or she may fear that the other partner is looking for a more beautiful mate.

A jealous girlfriend or boyfriend may have little confidence and see every other girl or boy as a threat. People who have plenty of self-confidence are less likely to

feel jealous. Rather than dwell on any real or imagined inadequacies, it is better to concentrate on your good points and remember that you are unique and special.

You may also feel jealous of people of the same sex who you think are prettier or handsomer than you, or more talented, creative, clever, rich or successful. Left to fester, jealousy can tear friendships apart. Resentment and hurt feelings can grow to the point that you end up hating someone who was once a good friend. Remember that everyone has their bad points and that there will be qualities special to you that other people will find enviable. True friendship is not about competition but about being yourself.

Jealousy does not always involve another person—you can be jealous about the amount of time your boyfriend or girlfriend spends on a hobby or studying. Friendship between two people grows and blossoms best when you let your friend have time and space apart, especially to do what is important to him or her.

Q *My partner and I are always arguing. Is this a bad sign?*

A No two people agree on everything. In fact, disagreements can be an interesting way of finding out about someone, as long as neither person is obsessed with proving that they are always in the right. Sometimes it is not a matter of rights or wrongs, just different perspectives. A loving, caring relationship can withstand dis-

Good reasons to enter a relationship

- Knowing someone well and liking them
- Feeling comfortable in someone's presence
- Sharing interests and attitudes and wanting to find out more about a person
- Having fun and sharing a sense of humor with someone

- Wanting to make someone else (such as an ex-partner) jealous
- Feeling that having a boyfriend or girl-friend is a status symbol
- Feeling lonely and believing that "any-one is better than no one"
- Being afraid of saying no because you don't want to offend someone

Bad reasons to enter a relationship

agreement on many issues, and a certain amount of argument is healthy. The amount you argue with your partner depends on the type of relationship you have, the way you are used to communicating and how secure you feel. When arguments become very frequent or hostile, or if they cause a bad atmosphere that lingers between you and your partner, there may be a problem that needs sorting out. Who starts your arguments? What are they usually about? Do you argue because you or your partner feels jealous, insecure or bored in the relationship? Arguments can seem to be about petty things when, in fact, more important issues lie beneath the surface.

Constant arguments reduce the tenderness in a relationship. The way to stop fights before they start is for one partner to say, "Let's sit down and talk about this." This gives the complainer the chance to get his or her grievances off their chest without interruption. After that, negotiations can start to sort things out. Couples who argue all the time use up all their emotional energy and have little left for anything else. If you and your boyfriend or girlfriend argue constantly, it may be worth reconsidering the relationship. If a couple disagree on many things, they may not be cut out for a long-term relationship with each other.

Q How do I leave my boyfriend or girlfriend?

A If you find that your feelings of attraction to someone have worn off, you need to find a way to tell that person that you do not want to see them anymore. Sometimes the decision to split up with a boyfriend or girlfriend is a joint one. Maybe both of you feel that you have outgrown each other, or that you have become bored with the relationship.

The problem with a breakup arises when one person wants to end the relationship and the other does not. For the person who does not want to break up, being left can be a very painful experience. If you decide to stop seeing your boyfriend or girlfriend, make an effort to explain your reasons to them. Talking in person is far better than simply avoiding them or not phoning. Never hang on to a relationship because you are afraid of upsetting someone. Try to be as honest, open and direct as you can.

This will help them come to terms with the breakup and may pave the way to a different sort of friendship later on.

Q How do I get over being left?

A However hurt you may be after the breakup of a relationship, try to allow yourself a mourning period. It is natural to feel upset and rejected for a while. Treat yourself kindly and talk about your feelings with people who care about you—your friends or your family, for example.

Although you may feel tempted to rush into a new relationship immediately after you have split up with someone, give yourself time to take stock and assess what happened first. If your confidence has been dented, rebuild your self-esteem by spending time with your friends and doing things that interest you.

If well-meaning friends try to set you up with somebody new, tell them that you would like to spend some time getting over your previous partner first. It may take you weeks or months before you feel ready for a new relationship or before someone you really like comes along. You can be certain that this will happen when the time is right. Think of yourself as more experienced and knowledgeable for the next time.

If you start dating someone new soon after a breakup, examine your motives. Are you trying to make your ex-partner jealous? Are you scared of being alone or lonely? Although relationships that begin soon after a breakup can succeed, the chance of that is greater, and you are less likely to hurt the new partner, if you think about your needs carefully.

Write it down Telling someone that you no longer want to be with them is very difficult to say and for them to hear. Expressing your feelings and doubts in a letter is one way of breaking the news. Letters enable you to express yourself clearly and honestly when you are alone and calm.

Questioning Sexuality

Homosexuality—sexual interest in, or relationships with, people of the same sex—is a subject full of myths and misconceptions. This may be due to the focus of sex education on heterosexual behavior or to beliefs that homosexuality is abnormal.

The teenage years are a time for exploring sexual feelings. It is common to wonder whether you are attracted to the same sex or to experience a "homosexual" crush or an infatuation. These kinds of feelings can be very confusing and difficult to make sense of. You may have many questions you want to ask about homosexuality but feel ashamed or embarrassed about asking them. A good way to embark on a discussion about homosexuality with your family is to begin with questions that are neutral or impersonal.

Q What are the factors that make someone homosexual?

A Nobody knows for sure what makes a man or woman homosexual, just as nobody knows what makes someone heterosexual. Some research suggests that a proportion of men are genetically predisposed to be homosexual, although it seems that not all gay men carry the so-called gay gene, and no lesbians are known to have it. Many gay people are concerned that the search for a cause for their sexuality might imply that a "cure" could or should be found. Others believe that proving a genetic cause for homosexuality will provide a crucial step in securing tolerance and civil rights for gay people.

Q Is homosexuality a disease that can be caught?

A Homosexuality is not a disease. It is an emotional response and a decision that some people make about their sexual behavior. Homosexuality cannot be caught any more than heterosexuality can. Most lesbians and gay men were brought up by heterosexual parents among heterosexual friends and siblings. If someone who is unhappy about his or her homosexual feelings is exposed to a group of happy, well-adjusted gay people, this might give the individual the support that he or she needs to "come out," that is, to let others know, and to act on his or her inclinations. Some people might perceive this as "catching" homosexuality, but such an attitude comes from ignorance.

Q Are homosexual feelings unnatural?

A Homosexual feelings are not unnatural. Individuals can have sexual feelings and fantasies about all kinds of people or situations, even though they may not want to act on the feelings or fantasies in reality. People who choose to have sex only with partners of the opposite sex or those who choose only partners of the same sex may still fantasize about homosexual and heterosexual lovers. These feelings may be surprising or unnerving, but they are both common and normal.

Q Does having homosexual feelings mean that you are gay?

A Some people have sex only with partners of the opposite sex, whereas some always choose partners of the same sex. Many people, however, explore homosexual or heterosexual feelings or activities before acting on a more or less permanent sexual orientation. They do this either to satisfy curiosity or to test their attraction to a particular person. Experimenting with

Physical affection
Some people are afraid that if they show physical affection to members of the same sex it is a sign that they are gay. These two boys are simply being friendly, and no sexual element is present. Taboos about touching same-sex friends are strong.

The Language of Sex

The prefix "homo" means "same," whereas the prefix "hetero" means "opposite." This is why "homosexual" is used to describe an attraction to the same sex and "heterosexual" is used to describe an attraction to the opposite sex.

sexuality may be important for individuals in doubt about their sexual orientation. This type of behavior does not necessarily determine future sexual identity.

Q Is a person attracted to one sex only?

A Most people eventually choose sexual partners from either one sex or the other, but there are people, who call themselves bisexual, who are equally attracted to men and women throughout their lives. Despite this, they can decide to stay with only one partner.

Q Should you show physical affection to friends of the same sex?

A People generally choose friends because they enjoy their company. Friendship means mutual affection, interest and trust—the same qualities that people value in sexual relationships. Regardless of sexuality, there is nothing wrong with showing affection toward friends if those feelings exist. The important issue is that people understand what you mean and intend by physical expression.

Q Can you be certain about being gay when you are a teenager?

A Some gay people claim that they knew they were gay from a very young age. Other people experiment with homosexuality as teenagers and then decide that they are heterosexual. Still others discover late in life that they have homosexual feelings. Young people who are certain about their sexual orientation and are confident enough

to tell others about it will often be told, "It's just a phase you're going through." For some it is just a phase; others, however, simply recognize their sexuality at an early age and will never change.

Q Should people experiment with both sexes to be sure?

A Sex seems designed to be pleasurable, and experimenting can be fun, but in all sexual activity, moral, psychological and health-related issues need to be taken into account. Experimenting with sexual partners is not like trying on shoes. If people treat themselves and their partners with respect and honesty, time and experience will reveal the kinds of sexual activity that are right for them.

Q What is homophobia?

A "Homophobia" means fear and hatred of homosexuality. Almost all gay men and lesbians encounter some kind of homophobia, ranging from verbal abuse to physical violence, at some time in their life. Some of the most homophobic people are those who are confused or distressed by their own sexuality. Others attempt to justify their hatred of lesbians and gay men by claiming

HOMOSEXUAL CRUSHES

From a young age, people emulate role models. Friends, teachers, and characters from television, films and books all provide examples of behavior to copy or to avoid. If a teenager has a crush on someone, they aspire to be like that person or to attract their attention. Close friendships often assume particular importance during adolescence. Girls and boys who share strong bonds of intimacy and companionship may wonder whether their feelings extend as far as sexual interest. This may lead them into sexual experimentation, but it does not necessarily make them gay.

Intimate friendships
Close friendships may provide a short-term focus for sexual feelings. Girls sometimes practice flirting with each other.

Confiding in a parent
Talking about any kind of homosexual feelings may be one of the most difficult conversations you will ever have with a parent. One starting point is to ask your mother or father about his or her own experiences and opinions.

INTRODUCING A GAY PARTNER TO YOUR FAMILY

Introducing loved ones to one another can be stressful, so a lesbian or gay child should choose an occasion without additional tension. For example, start with a simple meal in a restaurant or at home rather than a weeklong visit over Christmas. Pick a place where everyone feels comfortable and relaxed.

---

that their religion teaches against homosexuality; many religions do teach that homosexuality is wrong, but many also accept lesbian and gay people. Gay rights organizations are active in fighting homophobia—feeling confident about their sexual orientation helps many gay men and lesbians to confront homophobic attitudes.

Q How do parents feel about homosexuality?

A Parents whose son or daughter is gay or lesbian may be concerned that their child will never lead a happy, fulfilled life. It is important for them to realize, however, that their acceptance and love could be the most important element in ensuring that their child is happy. They can help to create a firm base of support from which their child can negotiate the difficulties presented by society's divergent attitudes toward homosexuality.

Parents may feel that they are in some way responsible for their children's sexuality. They may worry that they did something wrong in the way they raised their son or daughter and blame themselves. Alternatively, some parents blame the child in the mistaken belief that sexuality is something that can be "chosen." In fact, nobody knows exactly why some people are gay or lesbian, but parents who accept that homosexuality is no one's "fault" are taking the first step toward accepting their child's sexuality.

The most important things that parents can give their children are love and support. They may find it difficult to understand or accept their child's sexuality, but if the channels of communication are open, they will have a much better opportunity to offer guidance and advice.

It is important for parents to make their child's partner feel welcome in their family. If their own marriage has been a happy one, their example will be useful to their children, regardless of sexuality. In addition, establishing a friendly rapport with their gay child's partner may bring them closer to their own child.

Q What if parents refuse to accept homosexuality?

A Sometimes, no matter how happy and well-adjusted their son or daughter is, parents cannot or will not accept that their child is living an active gay or lesbian life. Depending on how important family relationships are to the child, he or she may keep trying to build understanding with parents; alternatively, the lesbian or gay man may turn to friends to provide the love and support that other people get from their biological families.

In some cases the child can put the parents in touch with a support group for those with gay children. If parents' objections are based on religious grounds, the child may want to ask a representative of the parents' religion who is supportive of homosexual people to talk to them.

Q What about other family members?

A When their child comes out as gay or lesbian, parents may be faced with questions about the child's lifestyle from inquisitive friends or other family members. Parents should respect their child's choices and attempt to answer the questions as honestly as they can.

Parents who feel that they simply cannot admit that their child is homosexual should avoid embarking on a discussion, because lies and half-truths usually lead to confusion, mistrust and resentment. There are a number of support groups for parents of lesbians and gay men that can be contacted for advice and information.

The Parents' Role

Parents play an important role in helping their children to learn about love and sex. By talking about the facts of life and setting the example of a loving, open relationship, they can show their children the value of affection and honesty.

Educating children about love and sex is something that many parents find difficult. They may not know what information is appropriate at a given stage in their child's life. They may feel embarrassed about discussing intimate subjects. They may be unsure about how much knowledge a child has already picked up. They may not know whether they have the right language or information to educate a child. Alternatively, some parents are open about sex from the time their children are young, so that conversations during adolescence simply require more practical and detailed information than before.

Although many sources of information about sex exist for children and teenagers, there are also many sources of misinformation. Parents can give their children an overview of love and sex, fill in the gaps in their knowledge, and correct any misconceptions that their children have picked up. Parents can also set sex in the context of a loving relationship—something that information gleaned from peers is unlikely to do.

The notion of parents sitting down with their child to talk about the "birds and the bees" in one session is long out of date. It is far better to establish an open, frank relationship so that sex education can be incorporated into the family's daily life over a period of many years.

TALKING TO YOUNG CHILDREN

The earlier you begin talking to your children about sex, the easier it will be. In general, young children just want simple facts to satisfy their curiosity. Answer their questions in the same way that you would answer questions about any subject. Try to match the information to your child's stage of development and do not worry about providing too much information. There is little risk of children knowing too much too soon—what they don't understand now, they will shrug off until later, and if you have been open with them, they will feel able to ask you when that time comes. It is better to say things too early than to wait until it is too late.

Experts agree that parents should start telling children about sex as soon as they begin to ask questions. This often happens between two and five years when children become aware of gender differences.

From 5–8 years, children become increasingly curious about their own and other people's bodies.

Talking about pregnancy The arrival of a new brother or sister is a good opportunity to explain to a young child how babies are made. Picture books with large, candid illustrations can make this easier.

The menstrual ▶
life cycle Explain to your children that the menarche marks the beginning of a woman's fertility and that a woman will continue to menstruate for her entire reproductive cycle. At about age 50 menstruation stops and a woman is no longer fertile. This is called menopause.

Preparing your daughter for menstruation *You need to explain to your daughter exactly what will happen when she starts menstruating. You should also consider practicalities: if she is leaving home for any length of time, give her some sanitary napkins to keep in her bag.*

Boys and girls often explore one another's bodies, particularly the sex organs, in games like "doctors and nurses." Parents may worry about these types of games, but they are normal and common.

Once you have started discussing sex, you can continue a dialogue with your children over many years whenever questions or issues arise. As a child grows older, you can place more and more emphasis on the emotional aspects of sex and its role in love.

There are a number of common questions that young children ask:

〜 Where do babies come from?
〜 Can I have a baby?
〜 How are boys and girls different?
〜 What is that (pointing to a body part)?
〜 How does a baby get in?
〜 How does a baby get out?
〜 Why don't girls have a penis?
〜 Why can't men have a baby?
〜 When do you and dad make babies?

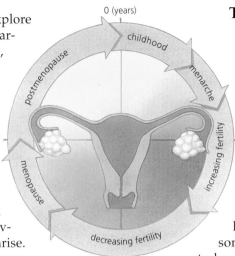

TALKING TO OLDER CHILDREN

If you have already fostered an open atmosphere about love and sex with your children, communication during their adolescence will be fairly easy. This is because you already know how much information your child has received; you have some idea of his or her attitudes toward sex and relationships; and your family will be accustomed to talking about intimate subjects.

If you are starting to talk to your child about sex for the first time, try to encourage a mood of open discussion. Rather than giving your child a lecture, talk informally and encourage him or her to share any knowledge he or she already possesses. Try to make your child feel that he or she has the freedom to ask you any question, however small, silly, rude or inappropriate he or she may feel it to be.

Bear in mind that teenagers need reliable information about subjects such as menstruation, breast development and sperm production before they experience these bodily changes. Girls need to be prepared for menstruation and boys need to understand why erections and ejaculation happen. Entering puberty can be a daunting or frightening experience if a child or teenager has no understanding of the biological causes that underpin such developments.

Also keep in mind that teenagers may appear to be more knowledgeable than they actually are. They may be reluctant or embarrassed to admit that there are subjects that they don't know about. For this reason it is important to talk about issues that, to you, seem basic or obvious.

Start a discussion informally at a time that seems appropriate. Maybe a question or a comment will arise from a television program. Perhaps young teenagers can be brought into a discussion about an older adolescent in the family. Life events that happen to other family members, such as pregnancy, marriage, or the beginning or ending of a relationship, can also provide good starting points for conversations.

Questions that teenagers often ask—although they may not address them to their parents—include:

~ What is an orgasm?
~ What is masturbation?
~ What is intercourse?
~ What happens during sex?
~ What is oral sex?
~ What does it mean to be gay or lesbian?
~ How do you French-kiss?

ANSWERING YOUR CHILD'S QUESTIONS

Try to be approachable and sympathetic to your child's questions by taking time to explain as much as you can. Children do not expect their parents to be experts on sex, but they do want to know as much as possible. If you hesitate, refuse to tell your child something or cut a conversation short, you may leave him or her feeling confused or under the impression that sex is bad.

Children are good at picking up nuances and hidden meanings in what their parents say to them, so try to use simple language and be relaxed. Ideally, both parents should be involved in the sexual education of their children, although girls and boys often prefer to ask questions of their mother or the same-sex parent.

If your child asks questions in a public place or at a bad time, suggest that you continue the conversation later at home. Don't forget to pursue the issues that your child brings up—if you do, he or she may feel ignored or chastized. It is almost always better to answer questions when they are asked. If you don't know the answer, say that you will find out and let your child know. There are plenty of good books on love, sex and relationships—keep one in the house so that you can read it together, explain the illustrations and discuss the words used. Children should also be free to look at books by themselves—this will help children who may be embarrassed to ask their parents about sex.

Teaching children about sex at home has several advantages. It gives you control of how much your child knows; you can make sure that he or she receives accurate information and that he or she is taught within the framework of a loving and committed relationship. Also, by learning intimate facts from people who are close, your child

will feel more confident about asking questions and discussing sex issues whenever questions arise. It also means that you can teach your child according to your own religious and moral values.

As well as conducting open discussions about sex, parents also teach by example, whether knowingly or unknowingly. If a couple are loving and affectionate with each other, their child will learn that love and sex are based on mutual respect. Psychologists claim that sometimes a child's sex education is not so much a matter of what parents say as what they do.

Although children must be told about the dangers of sex, it is important not to overemphasize the problems and create anxiety—sometimes strict messages about sex can lead to hang-ups later on in life. If adolescents grow up knowing only about unwanted pregnancies, sexual abuse and sexually transmitted diseases, they may come to regard sex as repugnant and dangerous and something to be avoided.

Is sexual openness always good?

Some parents worry that sexual openness will lead their children into underage sex and unwanted pregnancy. Research has found that the opposite tends to be true. Children whose parents talk to them frankly about sex often delay losing their virginity, and when they do have intercourse for the first time, they are more likely to exercise caution and use contraception. It seems that an open attitude toward sex can help children to say no to sex until they feel they are absolutely ready.

Positive role models
If you and your partner are mutually demonstrative and clearly love and respect each other, your child may adopt this as a template for his or her own future relationships.

PERSONAL QUESTIONS

Your children may ask you personal questions about your own sex life. If this makes you uncomfortable, say that it is private and something that you want to keep between you and your partner. Alternatively, give direct, positive answers that emphasize sex as something you and your partner do as part of a loving, committed relationship.

SEX EDUCATION IN SCHOOLS

The idea that early sex education helps teenagers to deal sensibly with sexual issues is one that has been adopted by many schools. Schools in the United States—which has the highest rate of teenage pregnancy in the industrialized world—now begin sex education at around age 11 in an attempt to combat this trend. A report based on 42 studies of teenage pregnancy in the U.S. and U.K. suggests that sex education in schools, including information about contraception, leads to a reduction in early sexual activity and teenage pregnancy. By contrast, abstinence programs—teaching children simply to say no to sex—have been shown to have little effect on behavior.

Sex education in schools has progressed in recent decades. Whereas children used to be taught about reproduction in the animal world and expected to apply this knowledge to human beings, adolescents are now taught directly about human sexual health, the practicalities of contraception, conception and pregnancy, and the emotional issues surrounding these subjects.

Sex education in schools is particularly valuable in the teenage years for boys and girls who have little or confused knowledge about sex or who feel awkward about approaching their parents. Much ignorance about sex among young adolescents can be offset by opening up to a caring, compassionate teacher. Subjects that may be troubling teenagers can be brought up in open discussion at school—it is often reassuring for boys and girls to realize that other children share their anxieties. Some schools use role-playing games to explore emotional issues to do with sex.

Physical comparisons *Your child will often form questions as a result of contact with other children. Playing naked with friends or siblings leads your child to compare him- or herself to other boys and girls. Be prepared for questions about genitals.*

FRIENDS AND SIBLINGS

From an early age, children share the experience of learning about sex with friends and siblings. For example, young children may look at one another's genitals and compare them with their own. This is perfectly normal and often gives rise to questions about sexual anatomy.

Older children swap stories, jokes and information that is often an unpredictable mixture of inaccuracy and fact. An anecdotal approach to sex education is cause for concern only if this is your child's sole source of information. As more parents realize the importance of their role in teaching their children about sex, and sex education becomes more prevalent in schools, this imbalance is less likely to occur.

Around the time of puberty, boys and girls may prefer to talk about sex with their close friends or elder siblings rather than their parents. Even if the facts are not completely accurate, this sharing of intimacies is an important part of growing up and should not be dismissed or trivialized.

TEEN MAGAZINES

Teenagers learn a great deal about love and sex from the media. Teen magazines with "real life" stories and advice columns can provide realistic sources of information that will help your child to realize how other people share their anxieties and problems. The drawback of teen magazines—and the media in general—is that they often imply to teenagers that sexual experience is a necessary path to acceptance by a peer group, without reference to respect, love or commitment. Teenagers may also see themselves as inadequate if they do not "look the part" or simply are not interested in sex.

The negative messages conveyed about sex by the media can usually be countered by information and reassurance from parents and sex education at school.

DOCTORS AND COUNSELORS

Although doctors and nurses are unlikely to be the main source of information about sexual issues for your child, medical experts can play a role in certain circumstances. Doctors may prescribe contraception to teenage girls (the pill is not always prescribed as a contraceptive—it can also treat some gynecological conditions). Pap smears are recommended for girls six months after they first have intercourse, and doctors can also advise about personal or sexual hygiene for teenagers who suffer from conditions such as cystitis, candidiasis and balanitis. Whether your teenage child involves you in matters such as these depends on the openness of your relationship.

Counselors can help to resolve the personal, emotional and sexual problems of teenagers. Problems can range from sexual trauma to emotional difficulties after the end of a first relationship, to excessive shyness and problems in forming relationships. Many schools offer counseling services, and professional counselors abound.

DEALING WITH ADOLESCENT CHANGES

Adolescence is a period of rapid growth and development that takes place between the ages of about 9 and 18, when children grow into young adults. The term "puberty" describes the hormonally stimulated physical changes that take place during this time. Puberty can be stressful for children; they tend to become self-conscious and preoccupied with their bodies and need frequent reassurance that they are normal. Puberty can be a testing time for adults, too—many parents feel upset by their adolescent children, taking sullen, moody, noncommunicative behavior as a personal rejection.

On some occasions your child may be fiercely independent and want to be treated as a grownup. At other times he or she will feel insecure with this new independence and want to be treated like a child. Patience and understanding are essential. As a parent, you must find a balance between giving your child freedom and independence and setting limits to his or her behavior. If you want to prohibit certain activities, give good reasons for doing so and prepare to be challenged.

The technical side of sex Schools often teach children about the physiology of sex and reproduction. This leaves parents free to emphasize the emotional and relational aspects of sex.

PUBERTY CHECKLIST
These are some of the things that girls and boys need to know about before they actually reach puberty.

Things to explain to a girl include the following:

Breasts will enlarge, and she may want to start wearing a bra.

Periods will start, and menstrual flow needs to be absorbed with sanitary napkins or tampons.

Body hair develops.

Things to explain to boys and girls include the following:

Mood swings are to be expected.

Sweat glands become active and antiperspirant or deodorant may be desirable.

Unprotected sex can lead to pregnancy or an STD.

Pubic hair will grow; the genitals will start to produce secretions; and more care needs to be taken with personal hygiene.

Things to explain to a boy include the following:

Erections of the penis are normal and often happen spontaneously.

Ejaculation occurs when semen is expelled from the penis during sexual arousal. It may happen during sleep.

Facial hair grows and can be shaved off.

Hanging out ▶
Teenage boys and girls may become more distant from their parents during adolescence, mixing instead with groups of friends. In fact, friends often fulfill needs that were once met solely by the family.

Father/daughter conflict Fathers are naturally protective about adolescent daughters. Teenage girls often misinterpret this as an attempt to impinge on their freedom and individuality. Conflict about wearing too much makeup and scanty clothes, and staying out late are all very common.

Changes in girls

Girls typically reach puberty earlier than boys, and parents often feel concerned about their daughters' sexual maturity because of the possibility of teenage pregnancy. Conflict may occur as a result of your daughter's desire to go out and test her newfound sexuality and your wish to restrain her activities and keep her safely at home.

Concerned parents can become strict about where their daughters go and what time they return home. Arguments often erupt over what clothes or makeup the daughter wears and the friends she sees.

Rather than being in open conflict with an adolescent daughter, try to understand and support her through a potentially difficult time. If your daughter feels that she receives only criticism from you, it may fuel her bid for independence. Try not to be too critical of her clothes and, if you genuinely think she looks good, pay her compliments.

Physical changes during puberty include breast development, pubic hair growth and the start of menstruation.

Daughters need to know about menstruation and what it involves well before they have their first period, ideally at the age of about eight or nine. The prospect of menstrual bleeding can be a frightening one for young girls. Try to give your daughter a sense of pride in her body. Explain that breast development and menstruation are important landmarks because they are positive signs of growing up and becoming a woman. Explain as well the different methods of sanitary protection to your daughter, and give her some sanitary napkins or small tampons that she can keep in her bedroom.

Changes in boys

Puberty is a time when your son will begin to focus on his peer group. Friends' opinions and attitudes become of paramount importance. Boys often want to conform to a group, adopting common views on fashion, hairstyles and music. Developing an identity based around clothes, music and friends is natural.

During adolescence boys often assert their independence and may become more emotionally distant from their mothers. This emotional distance is a natural process and part of a teenage boy's progress toward independence and individuality.

As they get older, boys are increasingly attracted to girls and the female body. They may buy pornographic magazines to fuel their fantasies and to satisfy their curiosity, although they are likely to do this in secret because they feel guilty.

Physical changes in boys include the appearance of body and facial hair, growth of the testes and the penis, and the urge to masturbate. This almost universal practice typically starts between the ages of 12 and 14. Boys may also engage in mutual genital display, comparison and masturbation. This is a completely normal phase. Boys masturbate to orgasm before they can ejaculate, and nocturnal emissions ("wet dreams") usually start between the ages of 13 and 15.

Sensitive Family Issues

The media often depict the family as a happy, self-contained unit that protects individuals against the harsher realities of the outside world. Yet sometimes problems originate within the family itself.

Managing internal problems presents one of a family's greatest challenges. On the one hand, one or both parents often feel a powerful drive to keep the family together. On the other hand, when problems or conflicts run deep, family members may think they are better off without each other. Family therapists say that even when only one member of the family is beset with problems—eating disorders or teenage pregnancy, for example—the dynamics of the whole family should be examined. Communication, they say, is the key to coming to terms with and resolving sensitive family issues.

EATING DISORDERS

The eating disorders anorexia nervosa and bulimia are psychological conditions in which individuals become excessively concerned with food and eating. The prevalence of bulimia is unknown, but it is thought that at least 1 percent of adolescents have anorexia. Both disorders are thought to be on the increase.

Eating disorders affect mostly young women aged 15 to 25, although girls as young as age 8 can suffer. Girls may be more prone to developing eating disorders than boys because more attention is given to the way they look and how other people perceive them.

In some cases, eating disorders function as avoidance mechanisms. By concentrating all their energies on food and eating—or not eating—some people manage to distract themselves from difficult or painful areas in their lives. For some people, eating disorders provide a way of coping with problems and conflicts that may go back over years. Sufferers may feel that their lives are

unmanageable; by controlling what they eat, they have the sensation that they at least have power over one aspect of life.

Several circumstances have been shown to make adolescents vulnerable to eating disorders: destructive relationships with their parents; a history of sexual abuse; perfectionist views on the female sex role; belief in the link between female beauty, thinness and status; early sexual development; and depression. People who suffer from eating disorders typically think of themselves as worthless and have low self-esteem and self-confidence.

Anorexia

Adolescents with anorexia refuse to eat and often drop to a very low body weight. They are afraid of getting fat, and because they have a very distorted image of the way they look, they are convinced that they are fat even when they are not. It appears that no amount of persuasion can make them realize the danger of being underweight. Anorexic girls also stop menstruating.

Driven by the desire to be thin—this is often influenced by media images of pencil-

Karen Carpenter
Former singer with The Carpenters, Karen Carpenter suffered from anorexia nervosa for many years before she died in 1983 as a result of the disease. She ate sparsely and trained herself to swallow up to 100 laxative pills at a time.

SOCIAL EFFECTS OF TEENAGE PREGNANCY

The social effects of a teenage girl having a baby can be enormous, adversely affecting the lives of both the mother and the child. Teenage girls who become pregnant are more likely to drop out of school, which harms their job prospects and lessens their earning power. Teenage mothers are more likely to be dependent on welfare and less likely to get married.

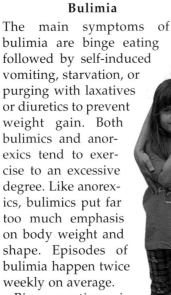
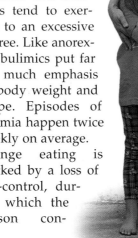

Generations of ▶ *young moms The woman in the middle of the photograph had her daughter (right) in her late teens. The daughter also became pregnant as a teenager and gave birth to a baby girl (left). Teenage pregnancy and motherhood is widely accepted in some families.*

thin models—anorexic girls may also feel conflict about becoming women. By starving themselves, they hang on to their prepubescent weight and body shape.

Although 90 percent of cases occur among young women, an increasing number of boys suffer from anorexia.

Anorexics typically go to great lengths to pretend to others that they are eating normally. They constantly think about what they will allow themselves to eat or not eat, and how much exercise will be necessary to burn off calories.

Anorexia is a very serious condition. It disrupts daily life and can have a devastating effect on families. In the worst cases, it can lead to complete emaciation of the body and death from starvation. In 10 percent of cases anorexia is fatal.

If you think that you recognize any of the signs of anorexia in your child, monitor him or her closely. Talk to your child about his or her attitudes toward body weight, appearance and sexuality. Discourage the attitude that "thin is beautiful." Bear in mind, also, that a reasonable amount of preoccupation with appearance and sexual attractiveness is quite normal during adolescence; you need to seek help only at a point when your child's behavior verges on obsessive. If you are in any doubt, consult a doctor.

Bulimia

The main symptoms of bulimia are binge eating followed by self-induced vomiting, starvation, or purging with laxatives or diuretics to prevent weight gain. Both bulimics and anorexics tend to exercise to an excessive degree. Like anorexics, bulimics put far too much emphasis on body weight and shape. Episodes of bulimia happen twice weekly on average.

Binge eating is marked by a loss of self-control, during which the person con-

sumes huge quantities of food. He or she will often choose high-carbohydrate foods, such as cookies, cakes or chips. Young people with bulimia typically go to great lengths to conduct their binging in secret.

If you suspect that your child may be bulimic, look out for the following telltale signs: visits to the bathroom after meals; using laxatives and diuretics frequently; swings of dieting and binging; and rotting teeth caused by the gastric acids that are present in vomit.

Treating eating disorders

The earlier that anorexia and bulimia are recognized and treated, the better the chances of recovery. The return to health is often a slow process, and only about 50 percent of those diagnosed with an eating disorder recover after a five-year period.

Therapy focuses on the underlying problems that have led to the disorders: teenagers' beliefs about themselves, their relationship with their parents, their eating behaviors and their need for control. Therapy is intended to help the adolescent to rethink the images and demands created by society, to examine expectations that are too high, and to recognize the risks involved in their behavior.

In severe cases, anorexics may need to be hospitalized and fed intravenously.

UNDERAGE SEX AND TEENAGE PREGNANCY

In the U.S., underage sex is rife, with the highest rate of teenage pregnancy in the Western world. Each year about 1 million teenagers become pregnant, and half of them are under the age of 18. Around 50 percent go through with the pregnancy and keep the baby, while most of the rest have abortions. Only a small percentage of teens give up babies for adoption.

Girls are reaching sexual maturity at an ever younger age. While they may be physically ready for sex, they are not psychologically and emotionally ready, especially because intercourse may result in pregnancy. Having casual sex during adolescence is tempting to many teens—it may be thought of as a status symbol or a passport to acceptance and popularity.

Adolescents engaging in sexual intercourse under the legal age of consent are said to be practicing underage sex. Although this is against the law, prosecutions are uncommon unless the man is much older than the girl. In a high-profile case, the film director Roman Polanski, who was in his 40s, was prosecuted for having sex with an underage teenage girl. Despite legislation against it, underage sex has been on the increase since the 1970s. Surveys conducted in North America show that adolescents are experiencing sexual intercourse at an earlier age and with a greater number of partners. A majority of North Americans become sexually active between 15 and 19 years of age.

Who gets pregnant and why?

Certain factors put girls at risk of teenage pregnancy: older boyfriends; academic failure at school; a history of emotional or sexual abuse; drug and alcohol abuse; a disadvantaged background; and friends and family members who are teenage mothers.

Some girls actively want to become pregnant in their teens. Like first-time sex, it can be seen as a rite of passage, proof of being sexually attractive to a man or part of the process of becoming an adult. Some girls don't mind getting pregnant or claim that their boyfriends wanted them to. Others may want someone to love who loves them back and therefore enter into motherhood for reasons of emotional need.

Teenage contraception

As few as a third of sexually active teens use contraception regularly. Experts say that there are many reasons for this, but that it is not usually due to a lack of knowledge or facilities. Some of the most common reasons are as follows:

∼ Fear of a contraceptive's side effects.
∼ Fear that parents will find out.
∼ Fear of having a physical examination.

Can We Talk About It?

USING CONTRACEPTION

If you are sexually active and you don't want to become pregnant, it is vital that you use contraception every time you have penetrative sex. Explain to your partner that pregnancy at this time in your lives would have enormous consequences for you both. Say that you do not feel ready to bring up children and that it is far simpler to plan ahead and take precautions. Explain that you will both feel more relaxed if you are not worrying about the possibility of pregnancy.

If you seek contraceptive advice from a clinic or doctor, don't be afraid of asking lots of questions. You need as much information as possible in order to choose the best contraceptive for you. Tell the doctor what kind of sexual relationship you are involved in and ask for his or her advice. If you are anxious about side effects of contraceptives, explain to the doctor that you are worried and need reassurance.

∼ Feelings of embarrassment or shyness.
∼ Not anticipating that sex was going to happen.
∼ Reluctance to accept or admit that they are in a sexual relationship.
∼ Fear of being interrogated or criticized by a nurse or doctor.
∼ The belief that "pregnancy won't happen to me."

Even when teenagers know about contraception, they may not use it because they lack the judgment to slow down in sexual situations and take consequences seriously. Of course, this is not universally true— some teenagers form steady relationships, in which case they may plan to have sex in advance, seek contraceptive advice and go on to use contraception consistently. Studies show that the use of contraception increases with age and the length of a relationship. Contraception is most likely to be used by middle-class adolescents.

If you think that your teenage child is sexually active, try to initiate a discussion about the entire relationship he or she is in, rather than singling out the issue of sex or contraception immediately. If your son or daughter senses criticism, whether implicit or explicit, he or she will probably withdraw or react defensively. Talk to your son or daughter as you would to an adult, pointing out the possible consequences of having casual or unprotected sex. Try to sound objective rather than judgmental.

DOMESTIC VIOLENCE

Today domestic violence is common and widely discussed. Around a quarter of couples report incidents of pushing, shoving, slapping or hitting within the previous year. Both men and women can be violent, but women are more likely to suffer severe physical injuries and depression as a result.

In some relationships violence is an occasional event that happens only under severe provocation. In others it becomes a regular pattern of behavior. Men who batter their partners have a powerful need to dominate. Their behavior may involve not only physical violence but also psychological and sexual abuse.

Men who commit violent offenses against their partners often also have a drug or alcohol problem, or both. Although violence is confined mainly to immediate family members, some violent men also display criminal tendencies.

Women who are victims of violence need to seek help. In an emergency they can call the police. There are several organizations that help women find a safe place and give practical advice and support. Many communities have shelters or advocacy groups for battered women. Phone numbers for these can be found by contacting the local police or a mental health agency. If you find yourself stuck in a regular pattern of giving or receiving abuse from your partner, tell him or her that you urgently need his or her support in seeking professional help. If this support is not forthcoming, you should seek help alone.

MARITAL DISCORD

Today couples who marry have an almost one in two chance of getting divorced, and many couples who stay together say that they are unhappy in their relationships. Conflict is an inevitable part of marriage, but it is the style in which couples handle these conflicts and disagreements that makes the difference between a happy marriage and an unhappy one.

Marital discord causes great anguish to both partners and their children. It is one of the most common causes of depression, and it can also badly affect physical health. An atmosphere of open warfare in the home between parents is thought to be one of the main causes of disturbed behavior in children. When there is violence between a couple, children struggle with conflicts of loyalty. They can feel hurt, destabilized and used as bartering tools.

Marital discord assumes many forms. Small arguments can escalate into ugly fights, or there may be repeated negative interaction between partners. Couples may criticize each other, call each other names, bring up old hurts, and denigrate each other's opinions, feelings, desires, competence or looks. Such behavior obviously makes people feel unloved and unvalued. Partners stop sharing their true feelings, communication breaks down, and trust and intimacy are slowly destroyed. Once this sort of damage is done, it may be very hard to undo—getting back to a tender relationship may take counseling and several months or even years.

If you and your partner are locked into a discordant relationship, one of you needs to back down, even temporarily, in order to have an honest conversation about the nature of your partnership. You may be accustomed to expressing your thoughts abusively or critically, but try to convey to your partner your sense of sadness about the way your relationship has deteriorated.

Marital breakdown
Couples can become stuck in a negative cycle of verbal abuse that becomes their accepted mode of communication. Eventually couples stop shielding children from their arguments—this is damaging because it threatens a child's sense of stability and creates divided loyalties.

If you never manage to communicate in a balanced way, counseling may be the only way to set your relationship back on track.

Affairs

Affairs rarely just "happen." There is usually a cause that lies at the core of the compromised relationship. Common reasons for affairs include constant quarrels at home; boredom; emotional rejection by one's partner; lost interest in sex; and fear of intimacy in a committed relationship. An affair does not solve any of these problems.

When affairs are confessed or discovered, a crisis occurs in the marriage that marks the end of the relationship as it has been. This brings strong feelings to the surface—shock, followed by pain, grief, misery, anger and jealousy.

Even a clandestine affair affects a marriage because one partner is keeping a secret from the other. Lying will bring about a loss of intimacy and close communication.

Today an affair does not automatically mean the end of a marriage. In fact, many couples stay together after the discovery of an affair. The most valuable and positive step that a couple can take is to uncover the reasons for the affair and work together to resolve their problems. They need to discover whether they have the commitment, love, passion or intimacy to rebuild a stable and lasting relationship. They will have to make their relationship a primary focus of their lives, which may require the help of a professional counselor.

DIVORCE AND CHILDREN

Almost half of marriages do not last, and as a result, thousands of children experience the separation and divorce of their parents before they leave school. Although children can experience grief, confusion, insecurity and disruption when their parents break up, they are less likely to suffer if both parents see them frequently and make a point of openly demonstrating their love.

Some children think that their parents' separation and divorce is a rejection of them. They may also feel that the breakup is their fault, and this can lead to feelings of intense guilt. Separating parents need to reassure their child that he or she is deeply important to them and that their separation or divorce is due solely to things that have happened between them. If parents think that their child is mature enough to understand, they should explain some of the reasons for separating.

Children often experience anger toward parents for separating. They may blame one or both parents for the breakup and feel hostile because their own interests have not been put first. Children do not possess the experience to understand the unhappiness that results from being in a bad marriage. They tend to want their parents to stay together regardless. Children may not be able to comprehend that their parents no longer love each other, or that one of them has fallen in love with someone else. In any case, they may not see this as a good reason for their parents to split.

A time lag may exist between separation and divorce—it can take two to three years before all the issues are sorted out. Separation—the point at which a parent becomes physically absent—hits children hard, and they may have an acute reaction that subsides only with time.

In very young children, this acute reaction may manifest itself as crying fits, fearfulness, and clinging, demanding behavior. Children may revert to a previous developmental stage. For example, a toilet-trained child may start bed-wetting, or a child who has given up thumb-sucking may regress to this comfort behavior. Children may become terrified of abandonment. Some children become aggressive, picking fights with their siblings, for example.

Older children can have feelings of inner hurt and anger that they may try to conceal. Teens may distract themselves with sports, schoolwork or going out with friends while feeling profoundly depressed over the breakup of their parents' marriage.

Children of divorced and separated parents can suffer long-term problems as well as acute reactions, particularly when one

◄ Celebrity marriages The media often portray an idyllically romantic image of celebrity relationships. Yet marital discord characterizes the life of many stars, such as actress Elizabeth Taylor. Her marriage, divorce and subsequent remarriage to actor Richard Burton made them the most notorious couple in Hollywood.

PARENT V. PARTNER

When partners break up there may be a fair amount of animosity, but try not to denigrate each other in front of your children. Your partner or ex-lover may have failed in his or her relationship with you, but being a parent is a very different role from that of partner. There is no reason why your ex-partner should not fulfill his or her role as a parent—remember this and try to present him or her in a positive light to your children.

parent has custody and the other parent has limited or no access. Such problems include low self-esteem, depression, problems maintaining stable relationships, problems in parenting and a greater chance of their own marriages ending in divorce.

Although children can and do suffer as a result of separation and divorce, bad marriages that continue to exist solely "for the sake of the children" can be equally damaging. Parents who remain in a hostile, cold, unhappy, unloving relationship make poor role models for their children, who may well grow up with a distorted image of what marital relationships can offer.

Drawing families ▶

This picture was drawn by a child from a stable family. (The parents are at the top and the child and siblings along the bottom.) Child psychologists may use children's drawings to try to understand family relationships. Children whose parents have divorced may draw one parent very small or omit the parent completely.

Many experts believe that it is better for the parents to split and establish healthy, happy relationships apart than to remain together. Children tend to thrive in households where there is an atmosphere of calm rather than one of conflict. Despite the inevitable trauma, many children of divorced parents can and do grow up to enjoy normal adulthoods and happy marriages themselves.

Children are less likely to suffer long-term psychological damage from the breakup of their parents' marriage if they know what is happening. They benefit from having both male and female role models and from continuing to see both parents.

Even if this proves to be impossible, it helps if a child has a good relationship with just one parent. Children brought up in happy and loving single-parent households can certainly be emotionally and psychologically healthy.

STEPFAMILIES AND NEW FAMILY RELATIONSHIPS

Many divorced people remarry, and stepfamilies and new family relationships are becoming increasingly common. Stepfamilies, or "blended families," can be complex; one or both partners may have children, or if parents have been married and divorced more than once before, there may already be stepchildren on one or both sides. Remarrying and taking on someone else's children can pose emotional and practical problems—the situation needs to be handled with care in order to minimize the psychological impact on children. Children typically worry that their mother or father will give the new partner and children all their love and attention, and they will be left out. They can feel abandoned, jealous and angry if a parent is totally wrapped up in a new romantic relationship.

If you are entering a new family, try to see things from your child's point of view. Spend time with your child, explaining all the changes that are going to take place, reassuring him or her, and being loving and demonstrative so that he or she will not start to feel rejected.

Entering or combining families requires sensitivity, tact and compromise so that everyone's feelings are taken into consideration. This may mean that no one is completely happy with what happens. A child may have to move out of a home he or she loves into a new place; a new couple cannot focus on each other all the time because children also need their love and attention. Children have an innate sense of what is fair and will feel badly treated if the needs of the new spouse are put before their own.

The logistics of domestic arrangements between divorced parents can be complicated—for example, the planning of who has which child when. When both parents have equal access to their children, the children must become accustomed to living in two homes. This can involve much coming and going, as well as the expense of providing essential possessions in both places.

Children who live with a stepparent may be faced with several dilemmas: How should they relate to the stepmother or father? Should they call them "Mom" or "Dad" or use their first name? If they call them "Mom" or "Dad" and show them affection, how will their biological mom or dad feel about it? Issues of loyalty and betrayal may be on your child's mind as much as they are on yours.

Stepparents face the corresponding problem of how to relate to a child who is not theirs. How should they allow the child to address them? Do they have the right to discipline the child? Telling a stepchild what to do can cause great conflict within stepfamilies if not handled carefully.

Children may also react negatively to sexual or loving gestures between partners. If your child has not seen you behave intimately with a partner before, this can come as a shock, particularly to preadolescent children; adolescent children can ask awkward questions that may be very personal.

Making a cohesive family unit can take time and hard work. Emphasize the importance of honest communication between all family members. If there is one particular issue that crops up repeatedly and never gets resolved, it may be helpful to see a family therapist (see page 297).

CHILD SEX ABUSE

The term "child sex abuse" refers to any exploitation of a child for the sexual gratification of an adult. Sometimes it means actually having intercourse with a child, but sexual abuse also includes fondling, making obscene telephone calls, "flashing" genitals at a child, taking obscene photographs or videos, or making a child watch sexual acts.

Both girls and boys are at risk of being sexually abused. Sometimes the abuse is committed by strangers, but most abuse occurs with a person the child knows and believes they can trust. This can be a family friend or someone in a position of responsibility who has easy access to the child. Most tragically, it can be a child's own parent.

Adults who are sexually attracted to children are called pedophiles. Any kind of sexual abuse is against the law, and offenders face punishment if convicted. Some neighborhoods and schools have a "safe house" scheme, providing a place children can go if they are being followed or molested.

If you suspect that a child close to you is being abused, sensitive management of the situation is essential. Avoid asking explicit or leading questions of children, since children will often reply in a way that they think will please an adult. Instead, encourage the child to feel comfortable in your presence and free to talk openly. A question such as "You don't look very happy today—is there anything I can do to help?" is more specific, open-ended and clearer than "Is something bothering you at home?" or "Is there anything you're not telling me?" The two latter questions may confuse or induce a feeling of guilt in the child.

Above all, remember that accusations of child abuse are extremely serious, and highly trained counselors are best equipped to question a child about such a sensitive subject. If you think your fears of abuse are well founded or shared by other adults whom you believe to be objective and impartial, contact a professional.

PHYSICAL ABUSE AND NEGLECT

Sadly, physical abuse and neglect of children are significant problems in North America. According to a report compiled by

Stranger
Family member
Trusted friend

Who abuses children? Most child abusers are already known to the child. Only 25 percent are strangers.

Don't talk to strangers Tell your child that he or she must not speak to strangers, however friendly or innocent their requests may seem. Getting into a stranger's car should be absolutely forbidden.

the U.S. Advisory Board on Child Abuse and Neglect, every year 2,000 American infants and young children die from abuse and neglect, 18,000 suffer serious disabilities, and 140,000 sustain serious injuries.

Children are most likely to suffer physical abuse and neglect from their parents or stepparents. Police statistics from Canada show that about one in five violent incidents occurs at the hands of a family member. It can happen when parents are undergoing stressful events; are depressed; are very young or immature; are in poor physical or mental health; or are trapped in unhappy relationships.

Abusive parents may have deep underlying feelings of resentment toward a child. The child may have been unwanted, the birth may have been painful or distressing, or the presence of a child may have had a disruptive effect on a couple's lifestyle or career. Sometimes, abusive parents even blame children for financial problems. If you feel that you or your partner is in danger of abusing your child, you should seek help from a professional therapist.

INCEST

Incest is the act of having sexual intercourse with someone in your family. It can occur between parent and child or between siblings. Wider family members, such as uncles, aunts and grandparents, may also commit incest.

One in a million individuals is a reported incest offender, although the practice is more widespread than the figures suggest. A more common development in troubled family situations involves intimate touching that does not go as far as intercourse.

Strongly held sexual taboos and values exist in society against incest. It is considered a sexual perversion and a deviant behavior to have sex with a close blood relative.

fact or fiction?

Those who abuse children are likely to have been abused themselves.

Fact. Physical abuse and neglect can continue from one generation to the next, so that abused children grow into abusing parents. They may have grown up in a household where violence was considered acceptable and continue the pattern.

Young models at a child beauty pageant
Children entered into beauty pageants are often dressed and made up to meet adult perceptions of feminine beauty.

THE SEXUALIZATION OF CHILDREN

The causes of child abuse are complex, but psychologists warn that making children into sexual objects is a particularly unhealthy trend. One accepted way in which children are sexualized at a young age is in child beauty pageants. Very young girls—and in some cases, babies—model in front of a panel of judges and are assessed on their clothes, hair, performance and overall appearance. But rather than presenting children in an age-appropriate way, beauty pageants often reward children who resemble miniature versions of adult women. Elaborate facial makeup, hair dye, hair extensions, tanning products and child-sized ball gowns are used. Girls aged three or four receive private training in modeling, deportment and elocution.

Supporters of child beauty pageants argue that the events are fun and enjoyable and instill a sense of self-worth in children. Critics argue that it is dangerous to make children so conscious of their appearance at a young age. Such preoccupations with beauty can lead to such later problems as anorexia. There is also concern that the depiction of toddlers as "mini-women" encourages child sex abusers to see them as legitimate targets.

The most universally abhorred is incest that takes place between a parent and child.

Victims of incest tend to suffer psychosexual problems for life. Incest will affect the development of a child's personality, confuse the child and result in severe disruption to the child/parent relationship.

A father who has sex with his daughter almost invariably has a strong need to dominate. Father/daughter incest appears to occur most frequently among fathers who are badly educated, unemployed and living in poor housing. The father may suffer from mental instability, alcoholism, or a disordered or aggressive personality. A father may find it easier to have sex with his daughter than with his wife. If his wife is denying him sex, he may inappropriately seek it with his child.

A daughter whose father has sexual intercourse with her is faced with an extremely damaging sense of conflict. She knows she is doing something wrong but feels she has to do what is asked of her. Perversely, incestuous behavior may make her feel loved and wanted in an otherwise cold and distant family. In extreme cases, the daughter may be psychologically disturbed and initiate sex with her father.

Incest between father and daughter can set up intense rivalry between mother and daughter, the mother competing with her own daughter for her husband's affection and attention, creating confusion about sex roles within the entire family. The daughter will suffer the greatest confusion because she does not know whether to behave as a daughter or a sex partner.

A traumatic result of a father/daughter sexual relationship is pregnancy. The repercussions of this can be devastating, and a recessive gene disorder may be passed on to the baby.

When brothers and sisters have sexual intercourse together, they sometimes behave as though the other is an eligible romantic partner and go through a kind of courtship. When a mother has a sexual relationship with her son, the son takes on the role of his mother's lover and even father to his brothers and sisters. Such a deviation from conventional family roles will be intensely confusing and disturbing for the entire family.

Incest is usually kept secret, and the adult involved is likely to use threats to keep the relationship clandestine. This leads the child to feel guilty and ashamed. If incest becomes known, major conflicts within a family invariably result.

If, for example, the wife decides to report her husband to the authorities for having sex with their daughter, he then risks a prison sentence. This can lead to further suffering—the child loses a father (becoming a "double victim"), the wife loses a husband and sometimes a breadwinner, and the whole family may be broken up by divorce.

Even though revelations of incest inevitably have serious repercussions, it is important for children who are involved in incest to tell someone they can trust. It is a great relief to them to bring it out into the open and to receive specialist therapy. Supportive care and counseling is available at mental health centers.

◀ *Support for victims Telephone counseling services exist to support children who are victims of incest or other psychological traumas. Sometimes children talk more easily to an anonymous counselor than to relatives whom they no longer know whether to trust.*

TYPES OF THERAPY

THERAPY	MAIN TENETS
Cognitive behavior therapy	Problematic thoughts are challenged and transformed to produce more positive patterns of behavior.
Counseling	By talking through problems the client gains personal insight, enabling him or her to explore appropriate solutions.
Psychoanalysis	A therapist analyzes and interprets a client's problems. The client and therapist work together to find solutions.
Family therapy	The dynamics of family relationships are evaluated by a therapist. Family members are encouraged to accept responsibility for what may have been seen as the problem of one individual.

Styles of interaction
Family therapists look closely at how family members interact. The initial impression that this family gives is a positive one. Body language is open and friendly, and the person speaking is being listened to—some families talk over each other so that no one's opinion is heard.

Carl Rogers This U.S. psychologist pioneered client-centered counseling in which the client determines the course of treatment.

ADOLESCENT THERAPIES

Puberty and adolescence are critical stages in an individual's personality development. Adolescence is typically a turbulent time—teens often have problems relating to their parents, and arguments about discipline are common. Although these years can involve a certain amount of upheaval, most people emerge emotionally unscathed. A minority of people do not, however—hostile or violent family relationships, poverty, racial conflicts, bullying, or sexual abuse can make the normal experience of growing up even more difficult and can result in problems such as depression, anorexia (see page 287), truancy or chronic anxiety. Some adolescents may benefit from therapy for such relatively "ordinary" problems as exam stress, loneliness or the ending of a first relationship.

When an adolescent child has emotional and behavioral problems, parents and other family members often need to receive counseling, individual psychotherapy or family therapy as well.

Various types of therapy may be suitable for adolescents. These include counseling, psychotherapy, family therapy and cognitive behavior therapy.

Psychotherapy

"Psychotherapy" is an umbrella term for all "talking therapies"—therapies in which a client and a therapist talk about the client's problems and explore solutions through discussion. Some psychotherapists are trained in a particular psychological discipline, the theories of Freud or Jung, for example. Broadly speaking, psychotherapists place more emphasis on analyzing and interpreting a client's speech than counselors, who listen and then simply try to reflect the client's feelings (the latter is particularly true of Rogerian counseling).

Adolescent psychotherapy is tailored to the particular age and needs of the teenager. The therapist will encourage the adolescent to speak about his or her problems (this is known as disclosure work) and will then try to encourage insight into how these problems could have come about. This may mean examining childhood relationships with peers and parents, or it may focus on present feelings. For some adolescents, speaking to a psychotherapist provides a unique opportunity to describe their feelings without fear of judgment or criticism. This in itself can be therapeutic.

Whether an adolescent is suffering from exam stress or psychological trauma resulting from abuse, the aims of psychotherapy are the same. The therapist will encourage the adolescent to become more autonomous, self-aware and self-accepting. For example, if an adolescent girl's only means of control lies in manipulating the amount of food she eats (as in anorexia), a psychotherapist will help her to find more positive ways of exerting power.

Psychotherapy can be short-, middle- or long-term, depending on the nature of the problem. Deep-rooted family problems are best treated by middle- or long-term psy-chotherapy. The aim in such a case is to achieve better communication between the adolescent and his or her parents. Subjects for discussion will include the young person's individuality within the family and how to deal with parents' expectations.

Family therapy

Family therapy is a form of group therapy especially suited to dealing with problems in children, adolescents or young adults. Because young people are still part of a family unit, their behavior almost always needs to be addressed in the context of other family members.

Family therapy is built on the premise that problems affecting one member of the family have resulted from faulty interactions among the whole family. They are not seen as solely affecting one family member. The family is seen as a "system."

Family therapists treat a wide range of problems—broadly speaking, anything that causes disruption or breakdown within the family. Problems can include depression, eating disorders, domestic violence, alcoholism, drug abuse, child abuse or incest.

The way family members interact may follow a repetitive pattern that is unproductive. Behavior patterns that are deeply entrenched may be difficult or impossible to break away from without outside help. Family members may not even be aware that they interact in a destructive way—sometimes it is necessary for a therapist to point out that the way individuals speak to each other is aggressive, critical or blaming.

One of the goals of family therapy is to help each individual develop a solid sense of identity that is independent of the family. Sometimes family members become dependent on one another in a negative way—for example, the partner and children of an alcoholic parent may be practiced at accommodating his or her drinking binges and mood swings. Rather than seeking change, they develop a tolerance to the parent's behavior and can become falsely comfortable in their respective roles.

The therapist joins with the family and uses his or her position to transform how the family members see one another. The therapist will observe how family members communicate—people tend to interact with one another in the therapy room in the same manner that they do at home. The therapist will work to improve communication and to break down negative alliances and coalitions in the family.

Therapy works best if all members of a family attend sessions together. Unfortunately, in many cases the patient's parents and siblings believe that the problem is not "their fault" and may refuse to participate. Although family therapy works best with all members present, it can be effective if only part of the family is there.

Cognitive behavior therapy

Cognitive behavior therapy starts from the assumption that humans can be both rational and irrational. When they are rational, they are effective, happy and competent. By contrast, irrational thinking results in emotional and psychological disturbance.

A cognitive therapist deals with negative, self-defeating thoughts, such as "I'm a failure," or "things always go wrong for me," by helping the patient to reorganize his or her perceptions. This may involve challenging irrational beliefs, such as "I will never be able to talk to people."

Therapists try to stop people from blaming themselves, other people, their past and the world in general. Once a client sees how thinking patterns have the ability to affect happiness and self-esteem, he or she can adopt positive strategies in order to take control.

Thought therapy
This simplified sequence of events shows the way in which a shift in a person's thought processes can help to lift them out of depression and make them more resilient to life events.

Self-esteem, mood and coping resources improve.

Trained to replace negative thoughts with positive ones.

Person is treated with rational behavior therapy.

Expresses mainly negative thoughts ("I am worthless").

Person suffers from depression.

Glossary

A

ABORTION
The termination of a pregnancy by any means before the fetus has developed sufficiently to survive outside the uterus. An abortion may be spontaneous (miscarriage); therapeutic (when the mother's health is at risk); or elective (done at the mother's request). Elective abortion may be induced with drugs or performed surgically. It is rarely performed after the 26th week.

ACQUIRED IMMUNODEFICIENCY SYNDROME (AIDS)
An infection with either human immunodeficiency virus (HIV) I or HIV II causing a deficiency of the immune system.

ACROSOME
A small area on the head of the sperm containing enzymes essential for fertilization.

ADRENAL GLANDS
A pair of small glands located on top of the kidneys. They produce many hormones, some of which influence sexual characteristics such as body shape and hair.

ADULTERY
Voluntary sexual intercourse between a married partner and someone other than their lawful spouse.

AMENORRHEA
The absence of menstrual periods.

AMINO ACIDS
A group of chemical compounds that form the building blocks of proteins.

AMNIOTIC FLUID
The clear fluid that surrounds the fetus throughout pregnancy.

ANAL SEX
The penetration of the man's penis into his partner's anus and rectum.

ANAPHRODISIAC
A substance, usually a food or drink, that inhibits sexual arousal.

ANDROGENS
The general term for male sex hormones. They are produced by the testes and adrenal glands and in very small amounts by the ovaries.

ANEMIA
A condition in which the blood cells contain abnormally low hemoglobin, the chemical responsible for carrying oxygen around the body.

ANOREXIA NERVOSA
A medical condition characterized by lack of appetite and inadequate nutritional intake. The person usually has a very distorted body image, believing they are fat. Some people die from self-starvation. The condition is seen most often in adolescent girls.

ANORGASMIA
The absence of or inability to achieve orgasm.

ANOVULATION
The condition in which the ovaries fail to produce mature ova, or eggs.

ANTIBODIES
Proteins produced by certain white blood cells. They neutralize invading microorganisms. Also known as immunoglobulins.

ANUS
The opening at the end of the digestive tract through which feces are expelled.

APHRODISIAC
A substance, usually a food or drink, thought to be able to induce an increased state of sexual arousal.

APOCRINE GLANDS
Sweat glands located in the armpits and genital region that do not become active until puberty.

AREOLA
A circular area of darker skin surrounding the nipple.

AROUSAL (SEXUAL)
A mental and physical state of awareness and stimulation; the stage in the sexual response cycle in which the body prepares itself for intercourse.

ARTIFICIAL INSEMINATION
The introduction of semen into the vagina or uterus by means other than sexual intercourse for the purpose of achieving pregnancy.

ASSISTED CONCEPTION
A term covering various methods by which a couple who are having difficulty conceiving naturally may be helped to have a child. This includes artificial insemination and IVF.

ATROPHY
The wasting away of a tissue or organ.

AZOOSPERMIA
An absence of sperm in the semen that results in male infertility.

B

BACTERIAL VAGINOSIS
An infection in the vagina caused by an overgrowth of bacterial organisms normally found there and resulting in an offensive, fishy-smelling discharge.

BALANITIS
An inflammation and irritation of the glans and foreskin of the penis, caused by bacteria, fungi or viruses; a tight foreskin; poor hygiene; or an allergy. Balanitis may be sexually transmitted.

BARTHOLINITIS
An inflammation of the Bartholin's glands causing intercourse to become very painful.

BARTHOLIN'S GLANDS
Small glands situated on either side of the vaginal opening that secrete lubricating fluid during sexual arousal. Also called vestibular glands.

BENIGN PROSTATIC HYPERPLASIA (BPH)
A nonmalignant enlargement of the prostate gland. The condition is normal in men over 50 years old.

BIRTH CONTROL
Natural or artificial methods of totally preventing or lessening the frequency of pregnancy.

BLADDER (URINARY)
A hollow organ for storing urine. It is situated near the sexual organs.

BLASTOCYST
The rapidly subdividing mass of cells resulting from the fertilization of the ovum by the sperm.

BONDAGE SEX
Sexual activity that involves being tied up.

BULBOURETHRAL GLANDS
Glands that secrete clear fluid during sexual arousal in men. They are situated below the prostate gland. Also known as Cowper's glands.

C

CANDIDIASIS
An infection of the sexual-genital system, rectum or mouth with a yeastlike fungus. Also known as "thrush."

CANTHARIDES
A very potent aphrodisiac that can prove fatal. It is made from the crushed bodies of a beetle.

CAP (OR CERVICAL CAP)
A barrier contraceptive made from plastic or rubber and placed over the entrance to the uterus, thus preventing sperm from entering.

CAPACITATION
The process involving changes to the enzymes in the sperm acrosome making it possible for the sperm to penetrate and fertilize the ovum. This process starts as the sperm comes into contact with secretions in the vagina and uterus.

CAPILLARY
A vessel that carries blood between the smallest arteries and the smallest veins.

CASTRATION
The removal of the testes or ovaries; usually performed due to disease or as a treatment for prostate or breast cancer.

CELIBACY
Complete voluntary abstinence from sexual relationships, often because of religious or moral beliefs.

CELLS OF LEYDIG
Cells within the testes that are almost exclusively responsible for the production of testosterone.

CERVICAL CANCER
Malignant growth affecting the cervix.

CERVICAL INCOMPETENCE
A weakness of the cervix that prevents full-term pregnancy of nine months. As the fetus increases in weight, pressure on the weak cervix causes it to open prematurely. Treatment involves temporarily closing the cervix with a stitch.

CERVICAL (OR UTERINE) POLYPS
Benign growths on the cervix (or uterus).

CERVIX
The medical term for the neck of an organ. Usually refers to the neck of the uterus, separating the uterus from the vagina and making a passageway for menstrual blood flow and sperm. The cervix dilates during labor, allowing the baby to enter the vagina.

CHAKRAS
According to the doctrine of Tantra, the seven major nerve centers through which sexual energy is mediated.

CHANCROID
An STD, common in tropical countries, that is characterized by genital ulcers and swollen lymph nodes in the groin.

CHEMOTHERAPY
Treatment of cancer or infection using drugs that act selectively on cells responsible for the disorder.

CHLAMYDIA
A bacterial infection that is the most common cause of the STD nonspecific urethritis (NSU). It may affect fertility.

CHROMOSOMES
Threadlike structures made up of DNA carrying inherited genetic information that influences physical and mental characteristics.

CILIA
Hairlike projections found in many organs of the body, including the fallopian tubes, where they transport the ova to the uterus by moving rhythmically.

CIRCUMCISION, MALE
Removal of the foreskin of the penis.

CIRCUMCISION, FEMALE
Removal of all or parts of the clitoris and labia.

CLITORIS
Part of the female genitalia; a small external, erectile organ located just below the pubic bone. It is the focal organ of female sexual arousal.

CLOMIPHENE
A drug used to treat infertility in women. It stimulates ovulation and may lead to multiple births.

COHABITATION
Living together as a sexually active heterosexual or homosexual couple.

COITUS INTERRUPTUS
The withdrawal of the penis from the vagina before ejaculation. It is unreliable as a method of contraception.

COLOSTRUM
The thin, yellowish fluid produced by the breasts just before and after childbirth. The proteins and antibodies in colostrum help the immune system of the newborn.

COLPOSCOPY
A visual examination of the vagina and cervix, usually using illuminated magnification.

CONCEPTION
The fertilization of an ovum by a sperm, followed by implantation of the resulting zygote in the wall of the uterus.

CONDOM
A barrier method of contraception, usually made of latex. The male condom is in the form of a sheath that is placed over the erect penis before intercourse. The female condom is inserted into the vagina and the penis enters inside the condom. Also used as protection from STDs.

CONTRACEPTION
The process of preventing conception by preventing ovulation, fertilization or implantation of the fertilized ovum.

CONTRACEPTIVE PILL
A method of female contraception in which hormones are taken in pill form to prevent ovulation, change the consistency of cervical mucus to hinder the passage of sperm and make the uterine lining inhospitable to implantation.

CORONAL SULCUS
The ridge where the glans joins the shaft of the penis, to which the foreskin is attached during infancy.

CORPUS CAVERNOSA
Columns of spongy tissue in the shaft of the penis that give it its erectile ability. The two corpus cavernosa run parallel along the length of the penis.

CORPUS LUTEUM
The remains of the Graafian follicle after ovulation. Secretory cells grow in this empty follicle and produce progesterone and estrogen in early pregnancy until the placenta takes over. If conception does not occur, then the corpus luteum stops hormone production, regresses and is overgrown by scar tissue.

CORPUS SPONGIOSUM
The smallest column of tissue in the shaft of the penis, surrounding and protecting the urethra and expanding at the tip of the penis to form the glans.

CUNNILINGUS
Sexual stimulation of the vulva area with the tongue by a partner.

CYSTITIS
An inflammation of the inner lining of the bladder caused by infection, injury or irritation.

D

DNA (DEOXYRIBONUCLEIC ACID)
The principal carrier of genetic information in almost all organisms.

DETUMESCENCE
The process by which the penis becomes flaccid after orgasm when blood flows away from the genitals.

DIABETES
A condition in which the pancreas cannot produce sufficient insulin. Sufferers take pills or inject insulin in order to process glucose. Sufferers may experience sexual problems.

DIAPHRAGM
The most commonly used female barrier contraceptive. Made of plastic and rubber and available in different sizes, it fits inside the vagina to cover the cervix and prevent sperm from entering. Used with a spermicide.

DIETHYLSTILBESTROL (DES)
A synthetic hormone currently used as a "morning-after pill." It was previously given to women to prevent miscarriage but was found to raise the incidence of genital cancers in the female children of these pregnancies.

DILATATION AND CURETTAGE (D&C)
Widening of the cervical opening to enable scraping of the uterine lining. Used for termination of pregnancy, to prevent infection after miscarriage, to diagnose uterine problems or to remove uterine tumors.

DOUCHE
A cleansing liquid introduced into the vagina for hygienic or therapeutic reasons. Now believed to increase the chances of infection. Ineffective as a method of contraception.

DYSMENORRHEA
Pain or discomfort during or just before a menstrual period.

DYSPAREUNIA
Painful sexual intercourse.

E

ECTOPIC PREGNANCY
A life-threatening condition in which an embryo develops outside the uterus, most commonly in the fallopian tubes.

EJACULATION
The expulsion of semen from the penis, usually at orgasm—a reflex action that occurs when the penis is physically stimulated during intercourse or masturbation. May occur spontaneously during sleep.

ELECTRA COMPLEX
The psychological state in the Freudian model of psychoanalysis in which a girl "falls in love" with her father and emotionally rejects her mother.

EMBRYO
The term for the fetus between the second and eighth week after conception.

ENDOMETRIAL CANCER
Cancer of the uterine lining.

ENDOMETRIOSIS
A painful condition in which parts of the uterine lining attach to other parts of the body, perhaps inside the fallopian tubes, on the ovaries or on the outer surface of the bladder. The fragments of tissue are subject to hormonal control and bleed in response to the menstrual cycle, causing pain.

ENDOMETRITIS
An inflammation of the lining of the uterus due to infection, incomplete abortion, irritation from an IUD or fibroids. May also be part of menopausal changes.

ENDOMETRIUM
The inner lining of the uterus.

ENDORPHINS
A group of chemicals produced by the pituitary gland. Similar in structure to morphine, they help to control pain and are involved in orgasm.

ENZYMES
Proteins that catalyze chemical reactions in the body.

EPIDIDYMIS
A tiny tube about 18 feet long coiled inside the testes; the place where sperm are transported, are stored and mature.

EPIDIDYMITIS
An inflammation of the epididymis due to an infection, cyst, spermatocele or tumor.

EPISIOTOMY
A surgical cut made from the edge of the vagina toward the anus to prevent tearing during delivery of a baby. Performed during a breech birth, a forceps-assisted birth or when the baby is large.

ERECTILE INSUFFICIENCY (DYSFUNCTION)
The inability to achieve or maintain an erection adequately for intercourse.

ERECTION
The enlargement and stiffening of the penis or clitoris during sexual arousal due to the tissues filling with blood. The penis elevates during erection.

EROGENOUS AREAS
Parts of the body that lead to some degree of sexual arousal when touched.

EROTIC
Anything associated with or causing feelings of sexual arousal.

EROTICA
Material of a sexual nature that portrays sexual activity in a more sensitive and often less graphic manner than pornography. The term can also refer to anything that triggers or increases sexual desire, such as erotic clothing, aphrodisiacs, sexual fantasies or sex toys.

ESTRADIOL, ESTRIOL AND ESTRONE
Types of estrogen.

ESTROGEN
A group of hormones produced in the ovaries and placenta, in the adrenal glands in both sexes, and in the testes. The most common forms are estradiol, estriol and estrone. They control female sexual development and the functioning of the reproductive system. Their function in men is to inhibit male secondary sexual traits.

ESTROGEN DRUGS
A group of drugs that synthetically replicate the estrogen hormones found naturally in the body. They are used in conjunction with progesterone drugs in the contraceptive pill; to treat infertility caused by underdeveloped ovaries; and in the treatment of menopausal disorders, prostate and breast cancer, and abnormal vaginal bleeding.

F

FALLOPIAN TUBES
A pair of tubes in which fertilization takes place. Cilia in these tubes transport the ovum to the uterus.

FAMILY PLANNING
Limitation of family size and regulation of the period of time between pregnancies by the use of contraception or abortion.

FELLATIO
Oral sex performed on a man's penis by a partner.

FEMININITY
Gender characteristics and performance associated with the female sex; the quality of femaleness.

FERTILITY
The ability to reproduce.

FERTILIZATION
The moment when a sperm penetrates a mature ovum in the fallopian tube. This is usually after sexual intercourse but may also be the result of artificial insemination or take place outside the body (see *In vitro fertilization*).

FETAL MASCULINIZATION
A rare condition that occurs in female fetuses with overactive adrenal glands. The hormones produced by the adrenal glands have an effect similar to that of male hormones, and baby girls may be born with a penis and scrotum. Corrective surgery and hormone treatment ensure normal female sexual development.

FIBROID (OR MYOMA)
A benign tumor developing in the wall of the uterus, whose growth depends on estrogen stimulation.

FIMBRIAE
The fingerlike projections that line the end of the fallopian tubes and meet the ovaries. At ovulation, the fimbriae wave in unison to sweep the ovum into the tube.

FLACCID
The relaxed state of the penis when it is not erect. Intercourse is impossible when the penis is flaccid.

FOLLICLE-STIMULATING HORMONE (FSH)
A hormone produced by the pituitary glands of both sexes that stimulates the gonads to produce sperm and ova.

FOREPLAY
The period of sexual play (touching and kissing) preceding intercourse in which both partners become aroused.

FORESKIN
The loose piece of skin that covers the glans of the penis in uncircumcised men.

FRENULUM
A small, triangular fold of highly sensitive skin on the underside of the penis where the foreskin is attached to the glans.

G

GAMETE
A male or female sex cell—sperm or ovum. Gametes contain half the normal number of chromosomes.

GENDER
A person's social or legal role as a sexual person, as opposed to their genital anatomy.

GENES
Units of hereditary information contained within chromosomes; they pass on an inherited developmental blueprint and determine the physical and mental differences between people. Half come from the mother and half from the father via the union of the ovum and sperm.

GENITALS
The male and female external reproductive organs.

GENITAL TUBERCLE
The fetal structure that goes on to develop into either the glans or the clitoris.

GENITAL WARTS
Warts that grow around the vagina, anus or penis. They can be sexually transmitted and increase the risk of cervical cancer.

GESTATION
The length of pregnancy—from conception to birth—in which the developing fetus is carried in the uterus. In humans this is nine months.

GLANS
The head of the penis.

GONADOTROPIN
Any hormone that influences the functioning of the ovaries or testes. Two are produced by the pituitary in males and females (follicle-stimulating hormone and luteinizing hormone), and a third (human chorionic gonadotropin) by the placenta in early pregnancy.

GONADOTROPIN-RELEASING HORMONE (GRH)
The hormone produced in the hypothalamus that controls the release of male and female sex hormones from the pituitary gland.

GONADS
Reproductive organs—testes in men that produce sperm, and ovaries in women that produce ova.

GONORRHEA
A sexually transmitted disease caused by bacterial infection. If left untreated, it can have far-reaching effects and complications on various parts of the body and may lead to infertility in both men and women. The disease may also be passed to the newborn baby during delivery.

GRAAFIAN FOLLICLE
The fluid-filled structure in the ovary that releases the ovum into the pelvic cavity at ovulation.

G-SPOT
Theoretically, a highly erogenous area located on the front wall of the vagina, between the back of the pubic bone and the front of the cervix.

GYNECOLOGIST
A doctor who specializes in diagnosing and treating problems related to the female reproductive system.

GYNECOMASTIA
An enlargement of one or both breasts in men due to the presence of excessive amounts of the female hormone estrogen. Slight gynecomastia is quite common at puberty.

H

HEMATOCELE
A swelling due to collection of blood in the scrotum, usually secondary to an injury. Similar to a bruise.

HEMOPHILIA
A hereditary blood disorder that almost exclusively affects men. The blood lacks clotting factor VIII. Hemophiliacs may suffer recurrent external and internal bleeding.

HEMOPHILIAC
A person suffering from hemophilia.

HEPATITIS (VIRAL)
An inflammation of the liver caused by one of many viruses. Hepatitis A is spread by contact with food or water contaminated with infected feces. Hepatitis B and C are spread mainly through sexual contact or infected blood.

HERMAPHRODITISM
An extremely rare congenital disorder in which both male and female

gonads are present and the external genitalia are not clearly male or female. Sufferers are infertile.

HERPES SIMPLEX

A family of two viruses responsible for "cold sores" around the lips, mouth and genitals. Both viruses can infect either area and are sexually transmissable through direct contact with sores. The main symptom of herpes is small, itchy fluid-filled blisters that burst and form scabs.

HOMOSEXUALITY, FEMALE

Sexual attraction between women; also known as lesbianism.

HOMOSEXUALITY, MALE

Sexual attraction between men.

HORMONES

Chemicals produced by various organs that affect physical and emotional changes in the body.

HORMONE REPLACEMENT THERAPY (HRT)

The use of any synthetic or natural hormone to treat a condition caused by deficiency in a particular hormone; usually refers to the use of estrogen hormones taken with progestogen to treat menopausal symptoms.

HOT FLASHES

A symptom of menopause that causes a rush of heat to the upper body and head, accompanied by sweating and sometimes dizziness.

HUMAN CHORIONIC GONADOTROPIN (HCG)

A hormone produced by the placenta during pregnancy. It maintains the corpus luteum and its production of estrogen and progesterone. Its detection in urine is the basis of most pregnancy tests.

HIV (HUMAN IMMUNODEFICIENCY VIRUS)

The virus that is the cause of AIDS and AIDS-related complex. Transmitted via blood transfusions, other blood-to-blood contact, the sharing of nonsterile needles and sexual intercourse. A fetus may also contract the virus from its mother. HIV attacks the T-lymphocytes, which are a part of the immune system, and may destroy their normal functioning.

HUMAN PAPILLOMAVIRUS (HPV)

A virus that causes genital warts. Infection with some forms of HPV increases the risk for cervical cancer.

HYDROCELE

A painless swelling of the scrotum, common in middle-aged men, that is caused by a buildup of excess fluid. It may be attributable to a number of causes, including infection, injury to the testes or a tumor.

HYMEN

A thin membrane that partially covers or occasionally surrounds the entrance to the vagina; usually broken during physical exercise or initial sexual intercourse.

HYPOGONADISM

Underactivity of the gonads caused by disorders of the pituitary gland, ovaries or testes that results in deficient production of gonadotropin hormones.

HYPOTHALAMUS

A region of the brain that controls much of the nervous system and hormonal functions. It is involved in regulating sexual response and activity, most of which takes place via the pituitary gland, to which it is connected.

HYSTERECTOMY

A surgical procedure to remove the uterus, usually performed for gynecological reasons. Sometimes surgery involves removal of the ovaries too.

I

IATROGENIC DISEASE

A disease that is induced by a drug or other medical treatment.

IMPERFORATE HYMEN

A congenital condition in which the hymen has no perforation through which menstrual blood can pass. The condition is generally not discovered until the onset of menstruation, when the buildup of blood behind the hymen causes severe abdominal pain. The condition can be remedied by a simple operation.

IMPLANT

Any material inserted into the body to replace a diseased structure, to deliver hormones or drugs at a steady rate, or for cosmetic reasons (for example, silicone implants to increase the size of the breasts).

IMPOTENCE

The inability to achieve or maintain an erection. This may be caused by a variety of psychological or physical prob-

lems or by the use of certain drugs. It becomes more common with age.

INFANTICIDE

The intentional killing of a baby or infant. Sometimes practiced in cultures where male offspring are valued over female offspring.

INFERTILITY

The inability to conceive and carry a fetus to term and delivery.

INTERCOURSE (SEXUAL)

Sexual activity involving penetrative sex.

INTRAUTERINE DEVICE (IUD)

A contraceptive device, usually made of plastic (with or without copper), that is placed in the uterus to prevent implantation of the fertilized ovum. It remains in place constantly and is replaced every two to five years.

INVERTED NIPPLE

A nipple that is turned inward rather than protruding. The condition does not normally interfere with breast-feeding. In older women, it may be a sign of breast cancer.

IN VITRO FERTILIZATION (IVF)

A method of treating infertility in which ova are removed from the ovary and fertilized outside the body.

IN VIVO FERTILIZATION

The natural fertilization of an ovum in the reproductive tract by artificial insemination or sexual intercourse.

K

KAMA SUTRA

An ancient Hindu text, written by Vatsyayana, that celebrates sex as a means of harmony between men and women and gives advice about sex and lovemaking.

KAPOSI'S SARCOMA

A malignant growth of the capillaries and connective tissue, previously considered rare and slow-growing but now seen frequently in an aggressive form affecting the skin and gastrointestinal and respiratory tracts of those suffering from AIDS.

KLINEFELTER'S SYNDROME

A chromosomal abnormality in which male infants are born with an extra X chromosome. The presence of any abnormality may go unnoticed until external symptoms become evident at puberty, the most notable being enlarged breasts and failure of testes to grow. Affected males are infertile.

L

LABIA
The lips of the vulva that protect the entrance to the vagina and urethra. There are two sets of labia. The external pair, the labia majora, are fleshy, with pubic hair and sweat glands, and stretch from the perineum to the mons pubis. They cover the internal labia minora, which are smaller and hairless and meet to form the hood of the clitoris.

LABIOSCROTAL SWELLING
The fetal structure that goes on to form the scrotum in boys and the labia majora in girls.

LABOR
Childbirth, the process by which a child is delivered from the uterus into the outside world. It starts with the dilatation of the cervix and ends with the delivery of the placenta.

LAPAROSCOPY
The examination of the abdominal organs using a laparoscope, a viewing tube with a light attached, which is passed through a small incision in the abdomen. The abdominal cavity is filled with gas to separate the contents and make viewing easier. Useful to diagnose pelvic pain, infertility or other gynecological problems.

LESBIANISM
Female homosexuality.

LEUKOPLAKIA
Raised white patches on the mucous membranes of the mouth, vulva or glans of the penis. They are usually harmless but must be distinguished from similar premalignant changes in these areas.

LIBIDO
Sexual desire. Low libido can have psychological or physiological causes.

LUMPECTOMY
A surgical procedure to remove a benign or malignant lump from the breast. If this completely removes a cancer, the rest of the breast can be left intact.

LUTEINIZING HORMONE (LH)
A gonadotropin hormone produced by the pituitary gland.

M

MAMMOGRAPHY
A special X-ray examination sometimes using injected dye to detect abnormal growths in the breast. It cannot always distinguish between benign and malignant growths.

MANUAL STIMULATION
Rubbing or applying pressure to the penis or clitoris with the hands to produce arousal or orgasm.

MASCULINITY
Gender characteristics and performance associated with the male sex; the quality of maleness.

MASTECTOMY
A surgical procedure to remove all or part of the breast as a treatment for breast cancer. The amount of breast tissue that is removed depends on the progression of the cancer and the age and health of the woman.

MASTURBATION
Sexual self-stimulation usually by massaging the penis or clitoris with the hand to achieve arousal or orgasm.

MENARCHE
The onset of menstruation. This usually occurs in girls 2 to 3 years after the onset of puberty but may start anytime between the ages of 9 and 17.

MENOPAUSE
The point at which hormonal changes cause the cessation of menstruation. It typically occurs between ages 45 and 60 and is associated with various physical and psychological symptoms. Also called "the change of life."

MENORRHAGIA
An excessive loss of blood during menstruation due to benign or malignant growth in the uterus, blood disorders, or occasionally an IUD or hormonal imbalance.

MENSTRUAL CYCLE
The complex chain of hormonal reactions that trigger ovulation and menstruation. The average menstrual cycle is 28 days long.

MENSTRUATION
The periodic shedding of the uterine lining that occurs at the end of the menstrual cycle in ovulating women who are not pregnant. Menstrual blood flow lasts from three to eight days in each cycle.

MISCARRIAGE
The spontaneous loss of a fetus before it is able to survive outside the woman's body without artificial support. Ten to 15 percent of all pregnancies end in miscarriage.

MISSIONARY POSITION
A face-to-face sexual position in which the woman lies on her back and the man lies on top of her.

MITOCHONDRIA
The energy-generating units of most cells in the body. Mitochondria in sperm convert the nutrients found in semen to energy used to swim toward the ovum.

MITTELSCHMERZ
Lower abdominal pain, occurring on one side, suffered by some women during ovulation. Pain is not usually severe and lasts only a few hours.

MOLLUSCUM CONTAGIOSUM
A harmless viral infection affecting both children and, less commonly, adults. Symptoms are small, shiny, white lumps that release a cheesy substance if squeezed. They appear on the genitals, the inside of the thighs and the face, in groups or alone. The infection is transmitted by direct skin contact or sexually.

MONOGAMY
Marriage or cohabitation with only one person at a time, usually involving a sexual relationship.

MONONUCLEOSIS
A viral infection that causes a high temperature, sore throat, and swollen lymph glands and tonsils. Occasionally mild liver damage may occur. The disease usually occurs in adolescence, when the immune system is most likely to respond to contact with the virus.

MORNING-AFTER PILL
A form of postcoital contraception consisting of a high-dosage, combined pill that must be taken within 72 hours of unprotected sexual intercourse. The initial dose is repeated 12 hours later.

MORULA
The stage in the development of the embryo that occurs after the zygote has been through a process of three or four cell divisions and has become a solid cluster of cells. The morula continues to divide until it forms what is known as the blastocyst.

MOTILE

A term referring to the ability to move. For example, a sperm must have good motility in order to reach the ovum and fertilize it.

MULLERIAN DUCT

A paired set of ducts that is present in both male and female fetuses but goes on to develop into fimbriae, fallopian tubes and uterus in the female fetus.

MULTIPLE ORGASMS

The potential of some women to have several orgasms in quick succession if sexual stimulation is continued. Men are able to have multiple orgasms if they can learn to reach orgasm without ejaculating.

MUTUAL MASTURBATION

Masturbation engaged in with a partner before or as a part of sexual intercourse. Both partners stimulate each other simultaneously, possibly to orgasm.

MYOMAS (FIBROIDS)

Noncancerous muscle tumors, most commonly found in the intestine, uterus and stomach.

MYOMETRIUM

The layer of muscle in the uterus that lies beneath the mucous membrane of the endometrium. It is this muscle that contracts to expel the baby during childbirth.

N

NIPPLE

The small prominence at the tip of each breast that, in women, contains the openings from which the milk ducts emerge. Muscle tissue in the nipple allows it to become erect, which helps during breast-feeding.

NOCTURNAL EMISSION

Commonly referred to as a "wet dream"; ejaculation that occurs during sleep. It is normal in adolescent boys, and may occur in older men who are not sexually active.

NONOXYNOL-9

An active ingredient in some spermicides (some condoms are impregnated with nonoxynol-9). Also provides increased protection against certain sexually transmitted diseases and has been shown to kill the HIV I virus—impregnated condoms form part of a safer-sex routine.

NONPENETRATIVE SEX

Making love without the penis entering the vagina. For example, mutual masturbation or oral sex.

NYMPHOMANIA

A term used in the past to refer to women who were judged to have an abnormal sexual appetite. Nowadays used only in cases of sexual obsession arising as a result of mental illness.

O

OBESITY

A condition in which excess body fat exceeds by more than 20 percent the recommended amount for a person's height and age.

OEDIPUS COMPLEX

The psychological state proposed by Freud in which a boy is thought to "fall in love" with his mother and emotionally reject his father.

OLIGOSPERMIA

A sperm count below the level considered necessary for fertility; currently set at 20 million sperm per milliliter of semen. Low sperm count may be temporary.

OOPHORITIS

An inflammation of the ovaries that may be caused by infection with the virus that causes mumps or by a sexually transmitted disease.

ORAL STIMULATION

The action by which a man or woman brings their sexual partner to arousal or orgasm by stimulating the genitals with the mouth.

ORCHITIS

An inflammation of the testis commonly caused by an infection such as the virus that causes mumps. It causes swelling, severe pain and fever. This may result in a shrunken testis after the infection has subsided and can cause fertility problems.

ORGASM

Intense physical sensations caused by muscular spasms that occur at the peak of sexual arousal. In men, contractions of the inner pelvic muscles cause ejaculation of semen. Female orgasm is associated with contractions of the walls of the vagina and uterus. Orgasm can last up to a minute, although a duration of between 3 and 10 seconds is more usual.

ORGY

Group sex, often associated with the feasting of Roman times, that for many people carries connotations of debauchery.

OSTEOPOROSIS

A condition, commonly called "brittle bones," caused by a decrease in bone density. It is most common in post-menopausal women, whose ovaries have ceased producing estrogen, which helps maintain bone mass.

OVA

Female sex cells, or eggs. Women are born with a full complement of ova that mature and are released after puberty, usually at a rate of one per menstrual cycle.

OVARIAN CYSTS

Abnormal fluid-filled swellings of the ovary. Only rarely is a cyst caused by cancer of the ovary.

OVARIES

The paired female reproductive organs, situated at either side of the uterus, close to the opening of the fallopian tubes. The ovaries contain follicles in which ova are produced. The ovaries also produce the female sex hormones estrogen and progesterone.

OVULATION

The maturation and release of an ovum from a follicle within the ovary. It occurs midway through the menstrual cycle and is regulated by follicle-stimulating hormone. If a woman is not ovulating, she cannot conceive.

OXYTOCIN

A hormone produced by the pituitary gland that causes the contractions of the uterus during labor and stimulates the flow of milk in nursing women. Synthetic forms of the chemical are used to induce labor, to empty the uterus after an incomplete miscarriage or death of the fetus, and sometimes to stimulate the flow of milk.

P

PARAMETRIUM

The outer layer of the uterus that consists of tough fibrous tissue.

PELVIC CAVITY

The area in the lower part of the body trunk containing the genitourinary systems in both sexes, including the reproductive organs.

PELVIC INFLAMMATORY DISEASE (PID)

An infection affecting the internal female reproductive organs. PID often occurs as a result of a sexually transmitted disease such as chlamydia. It occurs mostly among young, sexually active women or those using IUDs. It may cause infertility or increase the risk of ectopic pregnancy due to the scarring of the fallopian tubes.

PENETRATIVE SEX

A sexual act involving the penetration of the vagina or the anus by the penis.

PENILE RINGS

Rubber rings that are placed around the shaft of the penis to allow an erection to be maintained; used to treat erectile insufficiency. Some penile rings are designed as sex toys to stimulate the woman's clitoris during intercourse.

PENIS

The male sex organ, through which urine and semen pass.

PERIMENOPAUSE

From the Greek "peri," meaning "around," the years and months leading up to and immediately following menopause.

PERINEUM

The area between the thighs in both sexes that lies behind the genitals and in front of the anus.

PESSARY

A device placed in the vagina to correct the position of a prolapsed uterus.

PHALLUS

Any pointed or upright object that resembles or symbolizes the erect penis.

PHEROMONES

Chemical substances, related to hormones, that are secreted by the body possibly to send signals of sexual readiness. The smell of these substances may trigger an instinctive sexual response in potential mates.

PHIMOSIS

Tightness of the foreskin that prevents it from being drawn back over the glans of the penis. Phimosis is normal in babies up to six months but is problematic if it persists.

PITUITARY GLAND

An important gland located at the base of the brain beneath the optic nerves and the hypothalamus. The pituitary gland produces a number of hormones affecting vital functions of the body, including growth, sexual activity and reproduction.

PLACEBO EFFECT

A psychological phenomenon in which a substance taken to achieve a certain physical or mental state is effective not because of any actual properties it possesses but because the user believes in its effectiveness. For example, most aphrodisiacs.

PLACENTA

The organ that develops during pregnancy to allow fetal respiration, feeding and excretion via the mother. The placenta also produces hormones that alter the woman's body and help maintain the pregnancy.

PLATEAU STAGE

A stage in the sexual response cycle that follows excitement. The culmination of the plateau stage may be orgasm or a slow resolution.

PNEUMOCYSTIC PNEUMONIA

An infection of the lungs caused by a microorganism that is dangerous only to individuals with an impaired immune system. It is a major cause of death in people suffering from AIDS.

POLYCYSTIC OVARY

Also known as Stein-Leventhal syndrome, a condition in which there is development of multiple cysts in the ovaries triggered by increased levels of testosterone. The condition results in a lack of menstruation, excessive body hair and infertility.

PORNOGRAPHY

Sexually arousing material, such as literature, films or magazines, that is usually simpler and more explicit than erotica. Pornography often has less artistic pretension than erotica.

POSTCOITAL

A term referring to the period after sexual intercourse and orgasm.

POSTCOITAL FATIGUE

A relaxed and drowsy feeling following sexual intercourse and orgasm.

POSTMENOPAUSAL

A term used to describe a woman who has been through menopause, ceased to ovulate and so come to the end of her reproductive life.

PREGNANCY

The time during which a new individual develops in the uterus, starting with conception and continuing until delivery of the baby. In humans, pregnancy lasts an average of 266 days from conception.

PREMARITAL SEX

Sexual intercourse or activity engaged in before marriage.

PREMATURE EJACULATION

Ejaculation that occurs before penetration or very rapidly afterward. It is a problem that is especially common in adolescent boys.

PREMENSTRUAL SYNDROME (PMS)

A condition affecting 90 percent of ovulating women at some time in their lives, characterized by a combination of emotional and physical symptoms, including irritability, depressed mood, fatigue, breast tenderness, head- and backache, and abdominal pain.

PREPUCE

The foreskin of the penis.

PRIMORDIAL FOLLICLES

Groups of cells in the ovaries that contain potential ova. Primordial follicles develop in the ovaries of a developing fetus 4 to 5 months after conception. They are activated at puberty by follicle-stimulating hormone, when some of them mature to release mature ova.

PROGESTERONE

The sex hormone secreted by the ovaries and by the placenta during pregnancy. It is essential for the normal function of the female reproductive system.

PROGESTERONE DRUGS

A group of drugs replicating the hormone progesterone that are used in birth control pills, either on their own or in conjunction with estrogen. They are also used with estrogen to treat menstrual problems and in HRT (reducing the risk of uterine cancer).

PROLACTIN

The pituitary gland hormone that stimulates breast enlargement during pregnancy and initiates milk production after delivery.

PROLAPSE

The displacement of part or all of an organ from its normal position. A structure that commonly prolapses is the uterus, which drops down into the vagina.

PROSTAGLANDIN

A fatty acid that acts in similar ways to a hormone. Prostaglandins occur in various body tissues and are found in semen. They have several functions, including stimulating contractions during labor. Overproduction of prostaglandin causes abdominal pain and may contribute to PMS.

PROSTATE GLAND
A walnut-sized glandular structure surrounding the neck of the bladder and the urethra in men. It secretes substances into the semen as the fluid passes through ducts leading from the seminal vesicles into the urethra. Enlargement and cancer of the prostate gland become more common in men over 50.

PROSTATITIS
An inflammation of the prostate gland that normally affects men between the ages of 30 and 50 and is usually caused by a bacterial infection, which may be sexually transmitted.

PROSTATODYNIA
A relatively common male problem characterized by the presence of prostatitis symptoms but the absence of any infection.

PSEUDOHERMAPHRODITISM
A condition in which the individual possesses male testes and female genitalia or female ovaries and male genitalia. See also *Hermaphroditism.*

PSYCHOANALYSIS
Treatment for mental illness or psychological problems based on psychoanalytic theory, delving deeply into the patient's past. Psychoanalysis can help neurosis and personality disorders and has also been used to treat psychosis.

PSYCHOSEXUAL
A term that refers to a sexual problem or condition that, although the effects may be physical, has a psychological basis. For example, vaginismus resulting from the psychological impact of a previous traumatic sexual experience.

PUBERTY
The period, usually in the early teens, when an individual approaches sexual maturity and develops secondary sexual characteristics, such as pubic hair, breasts (in girls) and facial hair (in boys). The sex organs mature, making reproduction possible. Puberty usually occurs between ages 10 and 15 in both sexes, although it tends to occur earlier in girls.

PUBIC HAIR
Hair that grows around the genitals in males and females and that appears at the onset of puberty.

PUBIC LICE ("CRABS")
Small insects that can attach themselves with crablike claws to the pubic hair. They can be sexually transmitted or caught from infested bed linen and towels.

PUBOCOCCYGEAL (PC) MUSCLES
Muscles of the pelvic floor that support the internal sex organs.

R

RADIATION THERAPY (RADIOTHERAPY)
The use of a source of radiation, such as X rays, to treat certain kinds of cancer, including cervical and uterine cancer. It is also used to destroy remaining tumor cells after surgery in the treatment of breast cancer.

RECTUM
A short muscular tube forming the last section of the large intestine and continuing to the anus. Feces collect here, causing it to distend, creating the urge to defecate.

REFRACTORY PERIOD
A period of sexual unresponsiveness after male orgasm in which the body recovers. The man may become sleepy, and further sexual stimulation will fail to produce an erection. The length of the refractory period can be minutes or hours and depends on age.

RESOLUTION STAGE
A period after orgasm in which the body returns to its prearoused state. The breasts and genitals decrease in size, muscles all over the body relax, and blood flows away from the pelvic region so that the penis becomes flaccid. The heart rate and breathing return to normal.

RETROGRADE EJACULATION
A disorder in which the semen is forced back into the bladder (due to the valve at its base failing to close) during ejaculation. This may be due to disease or the result of invasive surgery in the pelvic region. Having intercourse while the bladder is full may sometimes lead to normal ejaculation, but there is no permanent cure.

RETROVERTED UTERUS
Sometimes called "tipped uterus," a condition in which the uterus is inclined backward toward the intestine instead of forward. Retroversion is a harmless variation from the norm and should not cause gynecological problems.

RHYTHM METHOD
A type of contraception using periodic abstinence from sexual intercourse during times when the woman is fertile and able to conceive. It works by attempting to predict ovulation. The method is unreliable and has a high failure rate.

RUBELLA
Also known as German measles, a viral infection that causes minor illness in children and usually only slightly more problematic illness in adults. If contracted by a woman in the early months of her pregnancy, however, it can lead to a number of severe birth defects. Rubella vaccination of infants and of women approaching childbearing age has significantly reduced the incidence of congenital rubella.

S

SAFER SEX
A term used to describe preventive measures taken to reduce the risk of acquiring or passing on an STD, including HIV.

SANITARY NAPKIN
A disposable pad of material designed to absorb menstrual flow while attached to a special belt or to underwear.

SCABIES
A highly contagious skin infestation caused by a mite that burrows into the skin and lays eggs. Scabies is passed on by close physical contact such as sexual intercourse or even holding hands. The condition causes severe itching, especially at night, and scratching results in scabs and sores.

SCROTUM
The pouch that hangs below the penis and contains the testes, epididymis and parts of the spermatic cords. The scrotum has an outer layer of thin, wrinkled skin with scattered hairs and oil-secreting glands on its surface.

SEBACEOUS GLANDS
Small glands in the skin that open

either into hair follicles or directly onto the surface of the skin, releasing an oily, lubricating substance called sebum. They are abundant on the scalp, labia minora and penile glands.

SEBUM
A secretion of the sebaceous glands that is composed of fats and waxes; it lubricates the skin, keeps it supple, makes it waterproof and protects it from cracking when exposed to a dry atmosphere. It also provides some protection from bacterial and fungal infections. Oversecretion causes overly greasy skin and may lead to acne or dermatitis.

SECONDARY SEXUAL CHARACTERISTICS
Sexually defining features that develop after the onset of puberty. In males they include facial and body hair, a heavier musculature, and deeper voice; in females they include breast development, broadening of the hips and thighs, pubic hair, and a generally more curved body shape.

SEMEN
The sperm-containing fluid produced by the man on ejaculation.

SEMINAL VESICLES
A pair of small glandular sacs that secrete most of the nutrient fluid in which sperm is transported in semen.

SEMINIFEROUS TUBULES
Tiny tubes inside the testes, in which the sperm are produced.

SENSATE FOCUS
A technique used in sex therapy, involving reawakening sensual responses using specific touch and massage exercises.

SEROCONVERSION
The production of antibodies after infection with HIV. It usually takes between 6 and 10 weeks for the body to produce enough antibodies for an HIV test to be accurate.

SERTOLI CELLS
Cells supporting the developing sperm, situated in the coils of the seminiferous tubules.

SEX ADDICTION
An uncommon condition, affecting both men and women, that is defined as a compulsive dependence on frequent, ritualized sexual activity. Such activity may be a substitute for an intimate relationship, which the sufferer is incapable of.

SEX SURROGACY
A branch of sex therapy, first adopted in the 1970s, in which the therapist attempts to treat a patient for sexual problems by having intercourse or being sexually intimate with him or her. A procedure that was always controversial and that carries great risks to emotional and physical health, it is now largely discredited.

SEXUAL AIDS
Also called "sex toys," a number of products available that are designed to increase sexual excitement and arousal, with or without a partner. Some of the most common are vibrators and dildos.

SEXUAL INTERCOURSE
The act of making love. The term is usually used to refer to penetrative sex, although it is sometimes used to describe other forms of sexual activity, such as oral sex, intimate touching or mutual masturbation.

SEXUAL POSITIONS
The positions adopted by a couple engaged in sexual intercourse. These range from man- or woman-on-top positions to side-by-side positions and rear-entry positions.

SEXUALLY TRANSMITTED DISEASES (STDS)
Infections transmitted primarily by sexual contact. Also known as venereal diseases.

SHALLOW THRUSTING
A technique used to help a man delay ejaculation. As he feels himself coming close to orgasm, the man resists the instinct to thrust deeper and instead slows down and makes his thrust more shallow. This helps to prolong intercourse.

SIXTY-NINE POSITION
Also called "soixante-neuf," a sexual position that allows a man and a woman to give oral sex to each other simultaneously. The position gets its name from the fact that the couple, one kneeling on top of the other, may be likened to the numerals 6 and 9 in close proximity.

SKENE'S GLANDS
Thought to be equivalent to the male prostate gland, female glands that are thought by some to be involved in female ejaculation following stimulation of the G-spot.

SMEGMA
An accumulation of sebaceous gland secretions beneath the foreskin of the penis, usually due to poor personal hygiene.

SOFT-ENTRY SEX
A technique that allows intercourse to continue if a man partially loses his erection during sex or if a couple wish to continue having sex after the man has had an orgasm. The man uses his fingers to gently guide the end of his penis into his partner's vagina.

SOMATOTROPIN
Also known as "growth hormone," a hormone secreted by the pituitary gland to stimulate tissue and bone growth.

SPERM
The male sex cell that fertilizes the female ovum. Sperm are produced within the testes in a process dependent on the production of testosterone and gonadotropin hormones commencing at puberty. Each sperm consists of a head that contains the genetic material and a tail that propels the sperm to the ovum.

SPERMARCHE
The onset of the male's ability to produce sperm in early adolescence.

SPERMATIDS
Cells in the last stage in the development of the sperm before they break free of the Sertoli cells, in which the final process of cell division and specialization takes place.

SPERMATOCELE
A cyst containing fluid and sperm that occurs in the epididymis.

SPERMATOCYTES
Cells in the second stage of the development of the sperm cells, which divide in such a way as to contain only half of the chromosomes contained in a normal human cell. The potential sperm are by this stage becoming increasingly specialized.

SPERMATOGENESIS
The process of sperm production that takes place in the seminiferous tubules of the testes.

SPERMATOGONIA
The first stage in the development of the mature sperm cell; simple germ cells are capable of becoming highly specialized spermatocytes and ultimately sperm.

SPERMICIDE

A contraceptive substance that kills sperm, normally used in conjunction with barrier method devices to increase effectiveness. Some spermicides may also help protect against STDs.

SPHINCTER

A ring of muscle around an orifice or internal passage that regulates inflow and outflow. For example, the sphincters that form the anus.

SPONGE, CONTRACEPTIVE

A method of contraception consisting of a disposable circular piece of polyurethane foam injected with spermicide. The sponge is moistened with water to activate the spermicide and is inserted in the vagina before sex.

STEIN-LEVENTHAL SYNDROME

See *Polycystic ovary*.

STERILIZATION

A procedure that renders a person infertile. In women, sterilization involves cutting, clipping, tying or otherwise obstructing the fallopian tubes. Male sterilization, known as vasectomy, is a surgical procedure in which the vas deferens are cut or tied.

STEROID HORMONES

A group of hormones that includes the male and female sex hormones: androgens, estrogens and progesterone as well as hormones from the adrenal glands. All steroid hormones are synthesized in the body from cholesterol.

SUBFERTILITY

A condition affecting a couple who are having difficulty conceiving. It may be due to physical causes such as low sperm count or mental causes such as high stress levels.

SURROGACY

A contractual agreement entered into for a woman to become pregnant and give birth for another woman (sometimes using the ovum of the latter woman with the sperm of her partner), with the understanding that the birth mother will surrender the child, after birth, to the contractual parents.

SYPHILIS

A sexually transmitted or, less commonly, congenital bacterial disease that if untreated passes through a number of distinct stages, usually over several years. The primary and secondary stages are characterized by a primary genital sore or chancre, and a rash and lymph node enlargement. The disease is highly infectious and may be contracted by kissing and other sexual contact.

T

TAMPON

Sanitary protection consisting of a "plug" of absorbent material, usually cotton, that is inserted into the vagina to absorb menstrual blood and is removed by an attached string.

TANTRIC AND TAOIST SEX

Two techniques for prolonging sexual intercourse. Tantra is an ancient Indian doctrine based on the Hindu ideas of balance and unity. Its principle is that sexual energy can unite male and female to achieve spiritual enlightenment. Taoism is an older, Chinese doctrine that teaches, among other things, that longevity and tranquillity can be achieved by sexual harmony in which the male uses self-control to ensure female sexual satisfaction.

TENTING

A feature of the plateau stage of the sexual response cycle in which the uterus rises from the pelvic cavity into the abdominal cavity. This results in the expansion of the vaginal cavity, creating an area where semen can pool after the man has ejaculated into the vagina.

TERATOGEN

An external agent, such as a disease, drug or environmental factor, that causes the development of physical abnormalities in the embryo or fetus.

TESTICLES (TESTES)

The paired male reproductive organs that produce sperm and the male sex hormone testosterone. They are located within the scrotum and connected to the penis via the spermatic cords.

TESTOSTERONE

The most important of the male sex hormones; it stimulates sexual development and controls reproductive functions. It is produced by the testes in men, and in lesser amounts by the female ovaries.

T-HELPER CELL

Also called T-lymphocyte, a type of white blood cell that is an essential part of the immune system, the normal function of which is affected by infection with HIV.

THROMBOSIS

The formation of a blood clot within any blood vessel. When in an artery it can block the blood supply and is a common cause of heart attack or stroke (a form of brain damage). The risk of thrombosis is increased in women taking the contraceptive pill who smoke.

THRUSH

See *Candidiasis*.

THYROID HORMONES

Hormones that regulate metabolism and in children are also essential in normal physical growth and mental development. They are produced in the thyroid gland, and their secretion is regulated by the hypothalamus and pituitary gland.

TORSION OF THE TESTICLES

Twisting of a spermatic cord that causes severe pain and swelling of the testes and if untreated leads to permanent damage. If performed in time, a simple operation can save the fertility of the testicle.

TOXIC SHOCK SYNDROME

A rare condition caused by an overgrowth of a toxin-producing bacterium in the vagina that may be triggered by the use of tampons. Symptoms occur suddenly and include high fever, vomiting, diarrhea, dizziness and muscular aches. This is followed by a rash and a sudden drop in blood pressure that causes shock.

TRICHOMONIASIS

A common infection of the vagina, often producing no symptoms. It is caused by a microorganism and is usually sexually transmitted. The infection may also be passed to men, in whom it affects the urethra. It may cause an offensive vaginal discharge.

TRIMESTER

A period making up one-third of a specified length of time. Pregnancy is divided into three trimesters, characterized by different developmental stages, both of the mother and of the fetus. The first trimester corresponds to weeks 1 through 13, the second to weeks 14 through 27 and the third to weeks 28 through 40.

TUMOR
A mass of tissue that forms when cells in a specific area reproduce at an abnormally increased rate. Tumors may be benign or malignant. All malignant tumors are classified under the general term "cancer."

TURNER'S SYNDROME
A rare chromosomal abnormality, affecting only females, in which one of the X chromosomes is absent or damaged. The syndrome causes a variety of physical and mental abnormalities, retarded development of secondary sexual characteristics, and infertility.

U

ULTRASOUND
Scanning with high-frequency sound waves to produce images of internal cavities without performing invasive procedures. It is commonly used to check on the development of the unborn child.

URETHRA
The tube by which urine is excreted from the bladder.

URETHRAL BULB
The portion of the urethra that expands like a balloon to hold semen just before ejaculation.

UROGENITAL FOLDS
The fetal structure that closes up to form part of the penile shaft in males and stays separate to form the inner labia minora in females.

UROGENITAL TRACT
The urinary, genital and reproductive organs in both sexes.

UTERINE CAVITY
The hollow inside the uterus that is lined by the endometrium and where the fetus develops during pregnancy.

UTERINE PROLAPSE
Displacement of the uterus from its normal position down into the vagina. This may be slight or, in the most severe cases, can result in a condition in which the uterus protrudes outside the vagina.

UTERUS
The hollow muscular organ of the female reproductive system, situated behind the bladder and in front of the bowel. At the narrow, lower end, it opens into the vagina via the cervix; the upper part opens into the fallopian tubes. During pregnancy the uterus expands to accommodate the growing fetus.

V

VACUUM ASPIRATION
A common method of surgically aborting a fetus.

VACUUM PUMP DEVICE
A piece of equipment that can be used by men suffering from impotence in order to achieve an erection.

VAGINA
The muscular passage that links the cervix to the external genitalia. The vagina has three functions: as a receptacle for the penis during intercourse, as an exit channel for menstrual fluid and as a birth canal.

VAGINAL TRAINERS
Devices used in the treatment for vaginismus. Increasingly larger, penis-shaped trainers are inserted into the vagina to gradually relax the muscles there and ultimately allow intercourse.

VAGINISMUS
Painful, involuntary spasms occurring when intercourse is attempted, making penetration impossible. The condition may be the result of a past traumatic sexual experience.

VAGINITIS
General medical term for vaginal inflammation and infection. Vaginitis may be due to bacteria, yeasts or a virus. It is sometimes called vaginosis.

VARICOCELE
A varicose enlargement of the veins surrounding the testes. The condition is common and is usually painless, requiring no treatment, although it is a possible cause of low sperm count.

VAS DEFERENS
Ducts that carry sperm from the testes to the seminal vesicles, where they are stored until ejaculation.

VASECTOMY
See *Sterilization.*

VASOCONGESTION
An increase in the amount of blood in body tissues, especially the penis, clitoris and labia during sexual arousal.

VENEREAL DISEASES
See *Sexually transmitted diseases.*

VESTIBULAR GLANDS
See *Bartholin's glands.*

VESTIBULE
The space at the opening of a tube or canal. The vulva is a vestibule receiving the urethral and vaginal openings.

VESTIBULITIS
An inflammation of the vestibular glands on either side of the vaginal entrance, causing severe pain during sexual intercourse.

VIBRATOR
An electrically powered device that when held against the genitals brings about arousal or orgasm through its vibrating action.

VIRGINITY
The physical state of not having experienced sexual intercourse.

VULCANIZATION
A process in the manufacture of rubber that made possible the production of condoms.

VULVA
The external female genitalia. The vulva includes the clitoris, labia majora and labia minora.

W

WITHDRAWAL METHOD
See *Coitus interruptus.*

WOLFFIAN DUCTS
The paired set of ducts found in both male and female fetuses that go on to develop into the epididymis, vas deferens, seminal vesicles and prostate gland in the male fetus.

Y

YOHIMBINE
An aphrodisiac made from the bark of a central African tree. It causes erections in men and arousal in women but causes a dangerous drop in blood pressure.

Z

ZYGOTE
The cell produced when a sperm fertilizes an ovum. It contains all the genetic material necessary to produce a new individual—half from the father's sperm and half from the mother's ovum.

Useful Addresses

**American Anorexia/Bulimia
Association (AABA)**
165 West 46th Street, Suite 1108
New York, NY 10036
Telephone: (212) 575-6200
Internet: members.aol.com/amanbu
⌐ Provides information and referrals.

**American Association for Marriage
and Family Therapy (AAMFT)**
1133 15th Street, Suite 300
Washington, DC 20005
Telephone: (202) 452-0109
Internet: www.aamft.org
⌐ Can be contacted for referrals to
therapists or clinics.

**American Association of Sex Educators,
Counselors and Therapists (AASECT)**
P.O. Box 238
Mount Vernon, IA 52314
Telephone: (319) 895-8407
Internet: www.aasect.org
⌐ Can be contacted for referrals to
therapists or clinics.

**American Society for
Reproductive Medicine**
1209 Montgomery Highway
Birmingham, AL 35216-2809
Telephone: (205) 978-5000
Internet: www.asrm.com
⌐ Provides patient education brochures
and other public forums.

Centers for Disease Control STD Hotline
Telephone: (800) 227-8922
Internet: www.cdc.gov
⌐ Provides referrals and information
about STDs and their symptoms.

**Centers for Disease Control National
AIDS Clearinghouse**
P.O. Box 6003
Rockville, MD 20849-6003
Telephone: (800) 342-2437 (Hotline)
(800) 342-AIDS (Hotline)
Internet: www.cdcnac.org
⌐ Provides information on HIV/AIDS,
24 hours a day, 7 days a week.

**The Kinsey Institute for Research
in Sex, Gender and Reproduction**
Indiana University
Morrison Hall, third floor
Bloomington, IN 47405
Telephone: (812) 855-7686
Internet: www.indiana.edu/~kinsey/
⌐ Provides information on all aspects
of sexuality.

**National Coalition Against
Domestic Violence**
P.O.Box 18749
Denver, CO 80218
Telephone: (303) 839-1852
Internet: www.webmerchants.com/ncadv
⌐ Provides information, referrals and a
variety of publications on violence against
women and children.

National Council on Family Relations
3989 Central Avenue NE, Suite 550
Minneapolis, MN 55421
Telephone: (612) 781-9331
Internet: www.ncfr.com
⌐ Provides information on all aspects
of family relationships for professionals.

**National Organization on Adolescent
Pregnancy, Parenting and Prevention**
1319 F Street, NW, Suite 400
Washington, DC 20004
Telephone: (202) 783-5770
Internet: www.noapp.org
⌐ Provides a variety of publications.

National Women's Health Network
514 10th Street NW, Suite 400
Washington, DC 20004
Telephone: (202) 347-1140
⌐ Offers information and materials on
topics, including hysterectomy, abortion,
yeast infections and menopause.

**SIECUS (Sexuality Information and
Education Council of the U.S.)**
130 West 42nd Street, Suite 2500
New York, NY 10036
Telephone: (212) 819–9770
Internet: www.siecus.org
⌐ Provides information on all aspects
of sexuality.

Canadian Breast Cancer Network
207 Bank Street, Suite 102
Ottawa, Ontario, K2P 2N2
Telephone: (613) 788-3311
⌐ A support organization for people
affected by breast cancer.

Canadian Mental Health Association
550 Sherbrooke Street West, Suite 310
Montreal, Quebec, H3A 1B9
Telephone: (514) 849-3291
⌐ Can be contacted for referrals to
therapists, clinics or counseling services. A
variety of pamphlets are available.

**Canadian Public Health Association
National AIDS Clearinghouse**
400-1565 Carling Avenue
Ottawa, Ontario, K1Z 8R1
Telephone: (613) 725-3769
Internet: www.cpha.ca
⌐ Offers information on HIV/AIDS
and also provides referrals to clinics.

**Laboratory Center for Disease Control
Health Canada**
Tunney's Pasture
Ottawa, Ontario, K1A OL2
Internet: www.hwc.ca/hpb/lcdc/bah
⌐ National center for the identification,
investigation, and prevention of human
disease; provides information on STDs,
HIV/AIDS and reproductive health.

Planned Parenthood Federation of Canada
1 Nicholas Street, Unit 430
Ottawa, Ontario, K1N 7B7
Telephone: (613) 241-4474
⌐ Provides Canadians with information
on birth control, human reproduction and
sexuality. In Ontario, call 1-800-INFO-SEX.

**Sex Information & Education
Council of Canada (SIECCAN)**
850 Coxwell Avenue
East York, Ontario, M4C 5R1
Telephone: (416) 466-5304
⌐ Offers educational material on
sexuality, primarily to educators and
researchers.

Index

menstrual cycle and 140,
141-142
multiple births and 149
pain at 145
predicting 144-146
rhythm method and 168
sterilization and 171
Oxytocin 43
after birth 88, 104

P

Pap tests 198
adolescents and 267
cervical cancer 126, 196, 198
genital warts and 187
Parametrium 127
Parental attitudes
toward homosexuality 99,
280
toward masturbation 91, 286
toward sex education
281-286
toward teenage pregnancy
98
Parenthood
marital changes 103-104
skills 33
Partnerships *see* Relationships
Paternity, legal 248
PC muscles *see* Pubococcygeal
muscles
PEA (phenylethylamine) 43
Pelvic inflammatory disease
(PID) 194-195
chlamydia and 186
combined pill protection
and 164
complications of 195
dysmenorrhea and 191
gonorrhea and 185
infertility and 195
symptoms of 195
treatment of 195
Penis 119-120
cancer 203
detumescence 138
foreskin 120-121
glans 120, 201-202
phimosis 202
puberty 92-93
sexual intercourse 135-138
shaft 119-121
see also Ejaculation; Erections
Perimenopause 106-107
Perineum 86
Periods *see* Amenorrhea;
Dysmenorrhea;

Menorrhagia; Menstruation
Personal hygiene 68, 174-176
Personality disorders 14
Petrissage 72
Peyronie's disease 119
Phenylethylamine *see* PEA
Pheromones 41, 44-45, 75-76
Phimosis 202
Physical abuse 293-294
Physiology of attraction 43-45
PID *see* Pelvic inflammatory
disease
Pill *see* Oral contraceptive pill
Pituitary gland 93, 123, 129,
PMS *see* Premenstrual
syndrome
Polyandry 224
Polycystic ovaries 194
infertility and 151
Polygamy 21, 224
see also Polyandry;
Polygyny
Polygyny 224-225
Islam and 238
Mormons and 236
POP *see* Progesterone-only pill
Pornography 64-65, 73-74
availability of 232-233
laws 246
in other countries 246
Positions, sexual 78-81
Postcoital pill 169
Postmenopause 111
Postoperative sexual
intercourse 114
Preconception 143-144
Pregnancy
assisted 154-159, 248-249
body changes during 103
confirming 147
ectopic 149
emotional changes during
103
fear of 215
fibroids and 193
glow of 103
hormones and 147
libido and 103
mother/child bond and 88
multiple 149
and premenstrual syndrome
147
progesterone and 129
sex after 103
teenage 97-99, 288-289
testing 129, 147
unplanned 97-99

Premarital sex 22-23, 64
Premature ejaculation 67, 71,
101, 271
treating 213-214
Premenstrual syndrome (PMS)
190-191, 265
pregnancy and 147
treatment for 129, 190
Primary amenorrhea 94
Primary testicular failure
154-155
Pro-choice groups 250
Pro-life groups 250
Progesterone 127, 129, 141
blood hormone test and 151
intrauterine device and 129,
167-168
oral contraceptive pill and
129, 163-165
Progesterone-only pill (POP)
164
Progestogen 108, 116
endometrial cancer
prevention and 108
Prolapse 111, 195-196
Proliferation phase, menstrual
cycle 141
Promiscuity 19, 64, 96, 208, 230
Prostaglandins 99, 122, 142,
191
Prostate gland 121, 199
anal sex 86
benign prostatic hyperplasia
199-200
cancer of 202
chlamydia and 186
development 118
enlarged 199-200
examination of 199
gonorrhea and 185
prostatitis and 200
puberty 93
Prostatitis 200
Prostitution 254-255
HIV/AIDS and 179
laws 254-255
Protestantism 235-236
Psychoanalysis 295
Psychological problems, and
libido 207-208
Psychology of love 12-13
Puberty 92-94
age of 92
bone and muscle growth
at 92
boys and 92-94, 264, 266-267,
286
girls and 92, 94, 264-266,

285-286
rituals 30
see also Adolescence;
Adolescent; Menarche;
Spermarche; Teenage
Pubic hair
female 94, 116
male 93, 116
Pubic lice 188
Pubococcygeal (PC) muscles
83, 196

R

Rape 251-254
Rear-entry sexual positions 67,
79-80
Rectum 86, 177, 186
Reflex arousal 117
Refractory periods 68, 82, 100-
101, 138
Reiter's syndrome 186
Relationship counseling 60,
222
divorce and 60
infidelity and 103
marriage and 101-102
menopause and 109
sustaining love and 27
Relationships
arguing 276-277
boredom in 25
breaking up 274-275, 277
commitment in 20
communication 55-58, 60
crises in 20, 23
emotional demands of 21
emotional dishonesty in
55-56
ending 27, 58-59
father/daughter 15
father/son 15
forbidden 20
independence in 22
mother and baby 14, 15
mother/daughter 15
mother/son 15
multiple 19
one-sided 58
platonic 23, 32-33
psychological problems in
207-208
roles 21
separation 19
sex in 22-23, 270
sexual therapy in 219-222
unsatisfying 21
see also Adolescent;

Acknowledgments

Additional editorial assistance
Nigel Cawthorne, Richard Dawes, Stephanie Driver, Richard Emerson, Madeleine Jennings, Joel Levy, David McCandless, Linda A. Olup, Laura Price, Jo Stanford, Deirdre Wilkins, Ian Wood
Illustrators Jane Cradock-Watson, John Geary, Tony Graham, Pond & Giles, John Temperton, Halli Verrinder, Paul Williams
Picture researcher Sandra Schneider
Makeup artists Bettina Graham, Kym Menzies
Proofreader Clare Hacking
Indexer Derek Copson
Clothing and equipment suppliers
Berlex Laboratories, Inc., Boots the Chemists Ltd., Hoechst Marion Roussel, Owen Mumford Ltd. Medical Division, Solvay Pharmaceuticals, Inc., The Upjohn Company, Wyeth Laboratories
Photograph sources American Board of Sexology 261
Archive Photos 233 (*bottom*: Reuters/Eric Gaillard)
AKG London 49 (*top*: Lessing), 257 (*second from top*)
Angela Hampton Family Life Pictures 16 (*bottom*), 263, 265 (*top*), 268, 280
Bert Torchia 257 (*third from top*)
Biophoto Associates 120 (*top*), 120 (*bottom*), 127 (*right*), 130 (*all images*)
Bridgman Art Library, London 14 (Maternity by Maurice Asselin/Galerie L'Ergastere, Paris), 70 (Johnson Album no.17 item 6, Ahmad Khan Bangash/British Library, London), 73 (prince and lady/private collection), 75 (*top*: The Orgy by Paul Cezanne/private collection), 83 (*bottom*: dancing Shiva/Oriental Museum, Durham University), 229 (*top*: Lovers from the Poem of the Pillow by Kitagawa Utamaro/British Library, London; also page 7), 244 (portrait of Oscar Wilde/Stapleton Collection)
Bruce Coleman 180 (*bottom*: Werner Layer)
Computerized Matchmaking Online 261
Corbis-Bettmann/UPI 243 (*top*), 257 (*bottom*), 291, 296 (*bottom*)
David Murray 30 (*top*)
Digital Playground 261
Dr. R. Given-Wilson, Consultant Radiologist, St. George's Hospital NHS Trust 131 (*left*)
Eye Ubiquitous 42 (*top*)
Frank Spooner 157, 162 (*top*: Jacques Prayer), 251 (Hemssey/Liaison), 294

(Bernstein/Spooner)
Gaze 49 (*bottom*: Sunil Gupta)
Giles Duley 110
Hutchison Library 225 (*bottom*: Sarah Errington)
Image Bank 44 (*top*: Werner Bokelburg), 59 (*bottom*: David Delossy), 77 (*top*: David Delossy), 106 (Jay Freis), 109 (Real Life), 236 (Maria Taglienti), 243 (*bottom*: Marc Romanelli), 249 (Jeff Cadge)
Images Colour Library 30 (*bottom, center*), 228 (*right*)
Images of Africa 227 (David Keith Jones)
Mary Evans Picture Library 11, 13 (*bottom*), 18 (*bottom*), 31 (*right*; also page 6), 78 (*top*), 91 (*left*), 160, 162 (*bottom*), 225 (*top*), 254 (*bottom*)
Michael Marsland, Yale University 26
Mitchell Beazley 259 (James Merrell)
Mirror Syndication 260
National Cancer Institute 50 (*top*)
Niall McInerney 35 (*far right*), 35 (*third from right*), 39 (*all except main pic*), 65 (*right*)
Oxford Scientific Films 45 (*bottom right*: Gerd Pennel/Okapia)
Pictorial Press 35 (*main pic*), 39 (*main pic*), 95 (*main pic*), 95 (*third from right*)
Rex Features 13 (*top*), 17, 30 (*bottom right*), 41 (*bottom, right*), 48 (*bottom*), 54 (*top*), 57 (*bottom*), 65 (*left*), 65 (*center*), 159, 219, 223, 234, 237 (*top*), 239 (*all pics*), 245, 254 (*top*), 275, 284, 286 (*top*), 287
Science Museum/Science and Society Picture Library 161 (sponge, douche and sheep-gut condom)
Science Photo Library 43 (*top*: Alfred Pasieka), 44 (*bottom*: David Parker), 85 (Eye of Science), 93 (*right*: Prof. P. Motta/Dept. of Anatomy/University "La Sapienza," Rome), 114 (Princess Margaret Rose Orthopaedic Hospital), 119 (*top*: CNRI), 119 (*bottom*: Alain Dex, Publiphoto Diffusion), 120 (*center*: Astrid & Hans-Frieder Michler), 122 (*top*: Petit Format/CSI), 122 (*bottom*: John Walsh; also page 6 and 115), 123 (Sidney Moulds), 124 (BSIP VEM), 125 (*top*: Prof. P. Motta & E. Vizza), 125 (*center and bottom*: Astrid & Hans-Frieder), 126, 127 (*left*: Petit Format/Nestle), 127 (*bottom*: Manfred Kage), 128 (Neil Bromhall), 131 (*center and right*: King's College School of Medicine), 146 (*both images*: Biophoto Associates), 148 (*left*: Francis Leroy, Biocosmos), 148 (*right*: CNRI), 149 (J. Croyle/Custom Medical Stock Photo), 152 (*top and bottom*: James King-Holmes), 153

(*top*: Dr. Tony Brain), 155 (John Meyer/Custom Medical Stock Photo), 156 (*top left, center left and bottom*: Hank Morgan), 156 (*top right*: James King-Holmes), 156 (*center right*: D. Phillips), 158 (*left*: Richard Rawlins/Custom Medical Stock Photo), 158 (*right*: Hank Morgan), 163 (*top*: Sidney Moulds), 163 (*bottom left*: Alfred Pasieka), 177 (*top*: Hank Morgan), 180 (*top*: Vanessa Vick), 181 (*third from left*: Alex Bartel), 182 (NIBSC), 184 (*top*: Alfred Pasieka), 184 (*bottom left*: CNRI), 184 (*bottom right*: Jean-Loup Charmet), 187 (*bottom left*: Biology Media), 188 (E. Gray), 189 (*bottom left*: Astrid & Hans-Frieder Michler), 194 (*bottom*: Z. Binor/Custom Medical Stock Photo), 198 (*top and bottom right*), 199 (*right*), 201 (*top and bottom*), 248 (*top*: Saturn Stills), 250 (Keith/Custom Medical Stock Photo), 272 (Dr. R. Dourmashkin)
Simon & Schuster 16 (*top*: reprinted with the permission of Simon & Schuster from THE MOUNTAIN PEOPLE by Colin M. Turnbull. Copyright © 1972 by Colin M. Turnbull)
Tate Gallery, London 59 (*top*)
Telegraph Colour Library 279
The Cameron Life Collection 95 (*far right*)
The Kobal Collection 12, 57 (*top*), 233 (*top*), 255, 262 (*top*)
The Royal College of Physicians of London 257 (*top*)
The Stockmarket 3 (*right*), 15, 33, 45 (*center*), 50 (*bottom*), 91 (*bottom right*), 95 (*second from right*), 102, 211, 223, 226, 229 (*all pics surrounding main pic except penis sheath*), 231, 237 (*bottom*), 278, 290
The Wellcome Institute Library, London 161 (tortoiseshell condoms)
Thomas L. Kelly 30 (*bottom left*), 53, 176, 224
Toni & Guy Artistic Team 35 (*second from right*), 35 (*bottom*)
Tony Stone Images 3 (*left*), 32, 46, 47, 48 (*top*), 54 (*bottom*), 113, 153 (*bottom*), 169 (*bottom*), 181 (*second from left*), 215 (*top*), 229 (*bottom main pic*), 242, 248 (*bottom*), 273, 274 (also page 8), 276 (*top*), 283, 295, 296 (*top*)
Trip 24 (H. Rogers), 228 (*left*: H. Rogers), 229 (*third from right*: J. Sweeney), 238 (Dinodia), 240 (J. Stanley), 288 (B. Turner)
Tropix 20 (D. Jenkin), 29 (*bottom*: I. Sheldrick), 43 (*bottom, left*: Craig Duncan)
Werner Forman Archive (Private Collection) 29 (*top*)